Self-Directed Behavior

SELF-MODIFICATION FOR PERSONAL ADJUSTMENT

4th Edition

Self-Directed Behavior

SELF-MODIFICATION
FOR PERSONAL ADJUSTMENT

4th Edition

David L. Watson
Roland G. Tharp
University of Hawaii

Brooks/Cole Publishing Company
Monterey, California

Brooks/Cole Publishing Company
A Division of Wadsworth, Inc.

Printed in the United States of America

10 9 8 7 6 5 4 3 2 1

Library of Congress Cataloging in Publication Data

Watson, David L., 1934–
    Self-directed behavior.

    Bibliography: p.
    Includes index.
    1. Behavior modification.   2. Success.   I. Tharp,
Roland G., 1930–   .   II. Title.
BF637.B4W38   1985   158'.1   84-21442
ISBN 0-534-04776-9

Sponsoring Editor: *Claire Verduin*
Editorial Assistant: *Pat Carnahan*
Production Editor: *Fiorella Ljunggren*
Manuscript Editor: *Margaret C. Tropp*
Permissions Editor: *Carline Haga*
Interior and Cover Design: *Vernon T. Boes*
Cover Illustration: *Andrew Myer*
Art Coordinator: *Judith Macdonald*
Interior Illustrations: *Andrew Myer*
Technical Illustrations: *Lori Heckelman*
Typesetting: *Graphic Typesetting Service, Los Angeles, California*
Cover Printing: *The Lehigh Press Co., Pennsauken, New Jersey*
Printing and Binding: *R. R. Donnelley & Sons Co., Crawfordsville, Indiana*

For our parents,
Faye and Manly Watson
Berma and Oswald Tharp

PREFACE

This book is designed to acquaint you with a general theory of behavior, to guide you through exercises for developing skills in self-analysis, and to provide you with concrete information on how to achieve the goals you hold for yourself. The most important goal of this volume is to help you, the reader, achieve more self-determination, more "willpower," more control over your own life.

The book can serve as a textbook in psychology courses but does not depend on a formal course structure. Any reader can use it for self-instruction; no "prerequisites" are necessary. Clients of therapists or counselors can use it as an adjunct in planning their own self-change.

You should be warned about one possible side effect: you may become interested in the science of behavior. A number of people do find themselves delving deeper into the subject as a result of studying this material and in response to the experiential learning that can result from the self-change process.

The vehicle for learning will be your own self-analysis, your own program for implementing your values. Throughout, you are urged to accompany your reading with your own self-improvement project. In a sense, your daily life will become the laboratory in which you will study and develop your own behavior.

Foreword to the Professional

This book's fourth edition maintains the authors' same intentions: to provide scientifically based instruction in the principles and practices of self-applied psychology. In the proliferation of self-help manuals, we have defined our niche as the one that offers an opportunity for students to learn principles of scientific psychology in the laboratory that is most important to them—the laboratory of their own life problems. Simultaneously, they will learn verified coping skills for personal problem solving.

To achieve these goals, we have set certain standards: to maintain an up-to-date review of all important literature, including both empirical and theoretical publications relevant to self-managed behavior; to maintain accuracy of summary and interpretation, so that instructors can be confident in assigning this text; to be conservative in making recommendations that arise only from a secure data base; and, finally, to advance integrative interpretations that offer some coherence to a vigorous and expanding field. We have also striven to maintain the readability that has characterized our previous editions.

The field of self-directed behavior began as self–behavior modification, but it has expanded in a vortex that has swept in vicarious and observational learning, cognitive behaviorism and verbal self-control, imagery and information science. This fourth edition has incorporated a wealth of new theoretical and empirical concepts that are currently influencing the field: skills analysis, delay of gratification, learned resourcefulness, control theory, relapse prevention, neo-Vygotskian developmental theory, self-efficacy, commitment theory, decision making, and attribution theory. In our reading of the field, this enrichment has provided key conceptual links that have made self-direction more coherent, more understandable, and more integrated. More depth and variety of work than has ever before been available has been included in this edition.

Since the previous editions, there has been considerable discussion of the ethical principles involved in the promulgation of self-help information. We are gratified that empirical field testing of this text has been uniformly positive: students using this text have achieved their goals for self-change in percentages varying from 66% to 84% (Hamilton, 1980; Clements & Beidleman, 1981; deBortali-Tregerthan, 1984; Rakos & Grodek, in press).

Some changes in the organization of the book are designed to make it even more useful for the student. For example, this edition contains a set of learning objectives at the beginning of each chapter. Key terms are highlighted in boldface, and a special rule identifies the successive steps of the self-direction project throughout the book. The "Tips for Typical Topics" (at the end of most chapters) have been expanded to allow for a more rapid formulation of a self-modification plan, and a topic index allows the student to retrieve all information relevant to a particular behavior.

Acknowledgments

For this edition, we are particularly indebted for the excellent critical analyses provided by Patricia Baasel of Ohio University, Harriet Kathryn Brown of the University of Hawaii, Elaine Heiby of the University of Hawaii, Donald K. Pumroy of the University of Maryland, and John Ward of Carroll College. Special thanks go to Richard Suinn, Jerry Deffenbacher, and Steven Richards for their useful advice and correspondence. Joyce Frank provided expert bibliographic work, editing, and manuscript preparation. Peggy Tropp was a sensitive and accurate manuscript editor for Brooks/Cole.

Our greatest debt of gratitude is to all our students at the University of Hawaii at Manoa. Their self-change projects have taught us much and made this edition, like the previous ones, possible. We would like to cite especially

Harriet Kathryn Brown and Gail deBortali-Tregerthan, who—former students themselves—have now provided us with reports from their own students. The list of all these student names has grown too long to cite. We have always disguised their identities in the case reports that illustrate the book; we hope that in this anonymity each of them will accept a tribute to the Unknown Student.

David L. Watson
Roland G. Tharp

CONTENTS

CHAPTER FOUR
THE PRINCIPLES OF SELF-REGULATION   87

CHAPTER FIVE
ANTECEDENTS   111

CHAPTER SIX
BEHAVIORS   139

Self-Directed Behavior

SELF-MODIFICATION FOR PERSONAL ADJUSTMENT

4th Edition

CHAPTER ONE

Adjustment and the Skills of Self-Direction

OUTLINE

- Self-Direction and Willpower
- The Skills of Self-Direction
- Self-Direction as a Skill
- Behavior and the Environment
- The Process of Self-Modification
- Does Self-Modification Really Work?
- Chapter Summary
- Your Own Self-Direction Project: Step One

LEARNING OBJECTIVES

Each chapter begins with a set of learning objectives, in which all the major points in the chapter are listed. The learning objectives are phrased as questions. When you can answer all these questions, you will have mastered the chapter. The learning objectives are divided into sections corresponding to the sections in the chapter.

Self-Direction and Willpower/The Skills of Self-Direction

1. How is adjustment defined?
2. What is the best way to study this book?
3. What are the various approaches one can take to adjustment, and what are their implications for self-direction?
   a. What is the medical model?
   b. What are the problems with the idea of willpower?
   c. What are the implications of thinking of self-direction as a skill?
   d. How are self-regulation, self-control, and self-modification defined?

Behavior and the Environment

4. What are antecedents, behaviors, and consequences?
5. How does learning affect them and their relationship to each other?

The Process of Self-Modification

6. What are the steps in most self-change programs?

Does Self-Modification Really Work?

7. Are people able to change themselves when they have a relatively serious problem with their behavior?
8. What does the research show about the success of students who use this book?
9. When a self-modification plan doesn't work, what are the likely causes?

To arrange, to harmonize, to come to terms; to arrange the parts suitably among themselves and in relationship to something else—that is the definition of adjustment. Adjustment can mean harmony among parts of the self—harmony of thoughts, actions, and feelings. The person who is torn by internal contradictions, the person who wants love but hates people, is not balanced or happy. We might say that such a person is badly adjusted, or disturbed. Significantly, we say that a person who is mentally ill is "unbalanced."

Adjustment can also mean harmony between the self and the environment. When people are out of phase with the world around them, we say that they are out of touch, gone, way out—words implying that they are not in harmony with the environment.

When we say that someone is "badly adjusted," we are making a value judgment. To the total conformist, any individualist seems badly adjusted, out of line with the group. To the individualist, total conformity seems bad adjustment, out of harmony. It is sometimes difficult to know if one should conform or rebel. When we say that someone is badly adjusted, we make a value judgment that the person should not be doing something, or should be doing something else.

We make value judgments about our own behavior, too. You may feel that you eat too much and weigh too much, and you'd like to be slimmer. You feel that your life would be improved if you weighed less. You'd be more attractive, feel more energetic. You might make new friends, or be more captivating to old ones. If that is your own value judgment about your weight, you would probably like to change your eating habits.

But can you? Do you have the skills to change? If you don't, people who can make a decision to change themselves and then do so probably seem a marvel to you. A slim friend says, "Yes, I decided I was about five pounds overweight, so I just took it off." You listen with mouth agape—you who have been trying unsuccessfully for years to do the same thing.

All of us have certain goals we cannot reach "just like that." Most of us have skills for certain situations but not for others. You might easily increase studying, while your slim friend needs to do the same thing but lacks the skill. When we have the ability to change ourselves, we have the skills that make up good adjustment.

Adjustment is better understood as a *skill* than a *condition*. Self-direction means that your own behavior is under your control—that when it is necessary to change, you can. Events change our environment, and as we devise new goals, we need to change our responses. We want to be able to control our behavior so that we change in the desired way—to increase study time, to develop better social skills, to stop overindulging in food or drugs.

Self-direction means recognizing the changes you want and being able to actualize your own values. The skills of self-direction include choosing goals and designing strategies to meet them, evaluating outcomes, changing tactics when needed, and solidifying new gains. Self-direction is the combination of skills by which goals are achieved.

The purpose of this book is to present these skills of personal adjustment. As you will see, there is a strategy for achieving change. The same principles can be employed for becoming less shy, for giving up smoking, for losing weight, or for increasing your studying. The same principles are involved in gaining skills at tennis, in taking examinations, or in reducing anxiety. We will deal with specific topic areas, but our goal is to teach you the basic skills for maintaining good adjustment.

As in all teaching, our success depends on you, the learner. All skills begin at simple levels and rise to more complex ones. Understanding requires effort and study; perfection requires practice. Specific exercises are suggested at the end of each chapter. It is important that you carry out these practice assignments. Like someone who is learning to ride a bicycle, you must actually ride, be willing to wobble a bit, even take a fall. The only way you can learn to ride "just like that" is through practice.

SELF-DIRECTION AND WILLPOWER

Is it really possible to learn self-direction? The answer is *yes*. You can increase the control you exercise over your own behavior and your own life. Obviously you can't control all the events in your life. We are all limited by lack of talent, energy, or plain bad luck. But within broad limits you can direct yourself toward your chosen goals, and change when you want to.

Some people are excellent managers of their lives. They aren't shy, they can study when they need to, they are in charge. By analyzing the ways these good managers achieve their goals, we discover principles and techniques we can all use. Research on methods of teaching these techniques has led to the discovery of principles that can be applied to self-direction, resulting in a body of knowledge that describes how self-direction occurs and how it can be increased.

Some people say, "I can't give up my old habits. I have no willpower." They speak as though "willpower" involved standing in the face of temptation, fists clenched, jaws tight, refusing to do what one shouldn't do, even though one wants to do it. After several decades of practicing chastity, Mahatma Gandhi sometimes slept with attractive young followers in his camp to demonstrate his ability to abstain from sex. Most people with effective willpower avoid that kind of situation in the first place. It is far easier to remain chaste while sleeping alone. People use foresight, self-analysis, and planning to avoid temptations. This point can be found in many ethical and religious systems. St. Paul, St. Augustine, and St. Thomas Aquinas, for example, taught that to avoid sin one should avoid the occasion for sin.

For each of us there are powerful temptations. That is, there are situations in which we make the choice for immediate pleasure even though it goes against our long-range goals. If you, like Gandhi, can resist temptation, then you don't need the techniques in this book. But for most of us there are situations in which we choose for the short run over the long run, even though we regret it later.

How can we make ourselves do things we find so difficult? This has been a topic of concern from time immemorial. Our own mythology shows, for example, how one wily man scored a victory over temptation. In Homer's *Odyssey*, written about 800 B.C., Odysseus and his crew sailed through straits where the Sirens sang a song so alluring that it drew sailors to their death on the rocks. Odysseus wanted to hear their wonderful music, but he wanted to avoid sailing too close. A shrewd man, he used a clever strategy to achieve both goals. He ordered his men to lash him to the mast and, no matter how much he begged to be set free, to keep him there until they had passed through the straits. Then he plugged their ears with wax so they could carry out his orders and row safely through without hearing the music (Ainslee, 1975).

BOX 1-1

HOW TO STUDY THIS BOOK

At the beginning of each chapter is an outline of the chapter and a set of learning objectives that are phrased as questions. The learning objectives cover all the major points in the chapter. If you can answer them, you will have mastered the text material. Your task while studying is to find the answers to those questions and then learn them well.

1. Break up your reading so that you do just one or two sections of the chapter at a time. The learning objectives and chapter summary are divided into sections that correspond to the sections of the chapter.
2. First read the outline for the whole chapter. Then read the learning objectives and the part of the chapter summary that corresponds to the section you are working on.
3. Now read the material itself.
4. Then reread the summary material.
5. Finally, close the book to see if you can answer the learning objective questions for that section.
6. Repeat this process for each section.

When you are studying for a course examination, give yourself a pretest by answering the learning objectives. Check your answers against the text. Reread the whole chapter summary, and reread those parts of the chapter necessary to answer the learning objective questions.

This method may sound cumbersome compared to your present way of studying. However, research has shown that it is the best way to learn the material in a text (Robinson, 1970; McKeachie, 1978). As you practice this method, it will become easier and easier for you. Our advice is this: *Try it and then evaluate it.* You can always go back to your old way of studying if this doesn't work better for you.

The same strategy—acting in advance to prevent a behavior we do not want—is used by many of us every night when we set an alarm clock. The crucial element is to make the desired choice when we are more likely to choose correctly. We choose before the Sirens sing, not while they are singing; before we are sleepy, not in the drowsy morning hours (Rachlin, 1974). Self-direction is "a skill involving anticipation and cleverness, so that immediate and tempting rewards do not impede progress toward a long-range goal" (Fisher, Levenkron, Lowe, Loro, & Green, 1982, p. 174).

THE SKILLS OF SELF-DIRECTION

How should we think about problems in adjustment, or in self-direction? When a person has such a problem—take, for example, Janet, who can't seem to get herself to study even though she is flunking—we feel that there is something wrong. But what? How Janet thinks about the problem has a strong impact on what she thinks should be done about it. There are different ways to think about a problem in self-direction, and each has a different implication for Janet's response.

We could say that Janet is possessed by a demon. If we believed this, there would be certain implications: we should try to exorcise the demon, and thereby restore her to the right path. Today, few people think of demons as the source of problems in self-direction, but there was a period in history when this was common. Often a woman who was guilty of deviance was thought to be possessed (Wine, 1981). Today we hold what we believe to be more enlightened views.

The Medical Model

Physicians have looked at problems of adjustment and considered these problems similar to those in physical health—that is, similar to diseases. This view is the **medical model** of adjustment. It is certainly an improvement over the demon model, as it is more humane and scientific. However, the medical model has become so entrenched in our thinking that we sometimes use it without considering alternatives.

The basic characteristics of the medical model are the concepts of inner cause and outer symptom. In the medical model, inner problems cause outer symptoms, and the proper course of treatment is to eliminate the inner problems. Suppose that you have a fever of 102 degrees. The doctor sees that fever as a symptom, or signal, that something is wrong inside you. Eliminating the fever would only take care of the symptom, leaving the inner illness untreated, so the doctor tries to discover and eliminate the inner problem. Presumably if the inner problem can be eliminated, the outer symptom—the fever—will disappear. Of course, doctors also give treatment that provides symptomatic relief, but whenever possible they seek to eliminate the basic problem.

What are the implications of this model for Janet? What is the analog of the symptom—the fever? She is unable to concentrate while studying, and now she is avoiding her textbooks altogether. Looked at from the viewpoint of the medical model, Janet's lack of concentration is a symptom of some inner tension or conflict. The implication is that she must discover and cure that inner problem.

The nature of the supposed inner problem has been seen differently by different theorists. Sigmund Freud, the father of psychoanalysis, viewed behavior problems as symptoms of inner sexual or hostile conflicts and frustrations. Later theorists agreed that the inner problem was conflict, but denied that it was necessarily sexual. They argued that any unresolved inner problem can lead to outer problems in behavior.

A major advantage of the medical model is that physicians have successfully searched for the medical reasons for certain behavioral problems—for example, some forms of mental retardation or diseases of the nervous system. Further, physicians have discovered symptomatic treatments, such as drugs to reduce hallucinations, that are effective in alleviating the suffering that so often accompanies major psychological disturbance.

But the medical model has its limitations. First, the importance of a person's inner characteristics can be overemphasized, with too little attention paid to the external situation. For example, should the fact that a child raised in a slum becomes a juvenile delinquent be interpreted as a symptom of some inner malfunctioning? Second, the medical model doesn't help you understand your own striving toward goals. For example, if you are making no progress toward some major goal, such as selecting a career, does that mean that you have some psychological disease? No, and there is no research that supports that explanation. Was Odysseus psychologically "healthier" than average, or was he more skilled at self-control? Is Janet sick, or does she lack some crucial skills? Is Janet a passive victim of her illness, or can she actively learn new and effective ways of coping?

Willpower as a Trait

You may not feel that your problems of adjustment are due to malfunctions of inner, personal traits, but you may still feel that your problem is a lack of willpower. This is a common way of thinking about our problems in self-direction. "I want to quit smoking, but I don't seem to have any willpower."

What do we gain by thinking about problems of self-direction in terms of willpower? The word *willpower* implies some entity, something in your psychological makeup, something that allows you to do hard jobs, overcome temptations, stick to your goals. But what is it—an electric current, some form of energy? It's just a word, a label we use when we want to describe how people deal with problems in self-direction. "She could do it because she has lots of willpower. He couldn't do it because he doesn't have much willpower." As a label, the word has certain problems.

It overlooks the fact that you may be able to stick to your goals in some situations, but not in others. Most of us find that in certain situations we have plenty of "willpower," but in others not enough. If you observe yourself, you may find that there are certain things you can do—for example, resist smoking although you used to smoke, or get your assignments done on time—and certain things you can't do—for example, relax on a date or quit biting your fingernails. You might say, "Well, I have *some* willpower, but I could use *more*."

A better way of thinking about these strengths and weaknesses is to realize that they are tied to certain situations. When faced with the situation I-have-to-do-my-assignment, you are able to do what has to be done, but when in the situation I-should-relax-on-this-date, you don't do what has to be done. The word *willpower* overlooks important variations in our behavior from one situation to another.

A second problem with the idea of willpower is that it is not clear what you can do to get more of it. What do people do who seem to have lots of willpower? How can we be more like them? If Janet decides that she lacks willpower, what does she do next?

How you think about a problem you have in self-direction has important implications for your success or failure in dealing with that problem. Thinking of problems in self-direction as stemming from inner malfunctions doesn't help. Thinking of them as due to a lack of willpower ignores the fact that problems are tied to specific situations. Neither of these ways of thinking suggests what we might do to be more successful at self-direction.

How did Odysseus' behavior differ from the behavior of the men who were lured to their death by the Sirens? He planned ahead and exercised skill in guarding against temptation. Is successful self-direction a skill?

What Is a Skill?

A skill is the ability to do something well. It is developed through knowledge and practice. We believe that we have an aptitude for certain skills when we are able to learn them easily, but in all cases we acknowledge that skills have to be learned. If one person practices certain behaviors while another does not, we expect that the person who practices will become more skilled at those behaviors. It does not surprise us to learn that our friend who has been practicing the piano six hours a day has become a skilled musician. Nor are we surprised to learn that many great musicians come from families in which music is an important part of daily life. The example set in the family and the opportunity to develop skill are important precursors of the development of skill at music.

The idea of skill implies behavior that is adapted to a particular event or situation. We do not expect a skilled pianist to be skilled at languages. The idea of skill, then, implies *specific* skills. We do not learn general skills that apply across a wide range of situations, but rather specific ones that apply to specific tasks. Contrast this idea of skill with that of willpower. Skill seems the more subtle idea, allowing for variation from one situation to another and implying the necessity of learning.

Skill implies the ability to deal with variations in the task. Being skilled at something means that action is adapted to the event (Fischer, 1980). Every time an action is carried out, it is done a little differently. Exactly how the pianist plays B-sharp depends on just where her hands were on the previous chord, how rapidly she is playing, the condition of the piano, any distractions from her surroundings, and so on. Being skilled implies that one can perform some action in spite of the fact that the task varies. A soccer player who could kick a goal only from one precise spot on the field would not be considered skilled. It is the ability to kick from any position, through opposing players, having received the ball from various other positions on the field and at different speeds, that makes a player skilled.

SELF-DIRECTION AS A SKILL

If self-direction is a skill, we must think about both the behavior we need to perform and the situations in which we will perform it. Our goals for self-direction are defined in terms of particular behaviors in particular situations. If you can only kick a goal from one spot on the field but your position on the field keeps changing, then you need to practice kicking from a variety of spots.

Sometimes your goal is to stop behaving in a particular way. For example, you may become nervous when you take tests, and this anxiety may interfere with how well you perform. If you were calm, you could remember more, think more clearly, and generally perform at a higher level. Your goal, then, is to stop being nervous when you take tests.

Sometimes your goal is to start behaving in a certain way. You may not be studying enough, and as a result you may be doing poorly in school. Your goal then is to increase the behavior of studying in those situations in which you should be studying—for example, in the library, or in your room at certain times.

In either case—increasing or decreasing a behavior—it is the relationship of the behavior to its situation that you must analyze and then control. The skills of self-direction involve analyzing tasks and our reactions to them and providing for behaviors that are appropriate to the tasks.

Self-Regulation, Self-Control, and Self-Modification

Often we adapt our behavior to variations in a task without thinking about it. If you are talking with a friend, for example, and notice that your friend is frowning, apparently because of something you said, you will probably change your behavior. You might ask what's wrong, or smile and change the subject, but in either case you have exercised skill at regulating your behavior to adapt to the changed situation.

Even as simple a skill as changing your behavior when you are irritating your friend has to be learned. A baby or young child—and, unfortunately, sometimes older people as well—won't notice that the friend is upset, or won't realize that his or her own behavior is the problem, or won't know what to do to rectify the situation. People who have difficulty getting along with others lack the skills they need to get along.

All of us are somewhat skilled at a variety of behaviors and constantly regulate our behavior to adapt to changes in the environment—to changes in the task before us. Often we do this without thinking about it, as if we were on automatic pilot. If we think about it and make a conscious effort to change our behavior, it is called **self-regulation.** When your friend frowns and you say to yourself "I better change the topic" and then do so, you are self-regulating.

In specific situations, some people are more skilled at self-regulation than others. For example, when a person is in a stressful situation, it is not simply how much stress the person experiences but how the person copes with stress that makes the difference (Roskies & Lazarus, 1980). Consider the experience of being seasick. Even sailors get seasick, and when they have to carry out their duties while experiencing this stress, you would expect that their performance would suffer. It's been shown, however, that not all sailors show the same degree of impaired performance. Even when sailors are matched in terms of their degree of seasickness, some are able to carry on much better than others (Rosenbaum & Rolnick, 1983). Those sailors who perform adequately even when seasick use more self-regulation skills than those who perform less well.

This suggests that it is possible to teach people who do not cope well with certain stressors how to cope better with them, and in fact this has been shown. Learning an active skill to use when faced with anxiety-provoking tasks actually prevents the anxiety (Barrios & Shigetomi, 1980). Students may begin to feel nervous while taking a test, realize that the anxiety will make their performance worse, and deliberately take a couple of minutes out to calm down. They can tell themselves to be calm, think calming thoughts, avoid thoughts that lead to the anxiety, and consciously relax. The person who does not do this lacks the skill that calmer students have (Rosenbaum, 1983).

As we grow up, we learn self-regulation skills that help us deal with temptations. If you are tempted to take a second helping of chocolate cake but don't take it because you don't want to gain weight, you have exercised self-regulation. Resisting a tempting situation is often called **self-control.** In a series of studies, Walter Mischel (1981) has shown how children learn self-control by increasing the skill with which they deal with tempting situations. Not surprisingly, it was found that very young children have greater difficulty in coping with temptations than do older children. What do older children do that younger ones don't do? Children who successfully resist temptations tend to think about the tempting object—for example, a marshmallow—using "cool" cognitions. "The marshmallows are puffy like clouds." Children who are less successful tend to think about the tempting object with "hot" cognitions. "The marshmallows taste yummy and chewy." "Hot" thoughts make it harder to resist temptation because one is imagining what it would be like to consume the tempting object. Children who successfully resist temptations also distract themselves from "hot" thoughts. They avoid thinking about the tempting object altogether, or think about other, irrelevant "hot" objects not currently present.

Thus, *the ability to resist temptation appears to be a learned skill.* Certain kinds of thoughts and self-distractions allow a person to exercise greater self-control. Many children, of course, learn these skills without being aware of it. They know only that they want to avoid a particular temptation—perhaps because they will gain a larger reward if they wait. This suggests that we can study what skills are necessary to resist certain temptations—for example, what should the chronic overeater learn to do and think?—and then set out to learn these skills.

There are times for all of us when our usual self-regulation or self-control skills fail us. Our usual behavior won't let us reach our goals. In this situation, we begin to self-regulate in a more self-conscious fashion (Rosenbaum, in press). A planned, continuing effort to change behavior to cope with a task we cannot presently master is called **self-modification.**

Task/Skill Mismatches

There are times when one's skills at self-regulation or self-control are not up to the task at hand (McFall & Dodge, 1982). Whatever skills one has, there are always tasks that call for more than one can muster, whether it be the fairly good tennis player matched against the state champion or the person unskilled in resisting good food faced with a table full of tempting morsels. If self-control and self-regulation are skills, then one would expect that certain tasks would call for more skill than a person possesses. Since people differ in their level of skill, what is an easy task for one person may be impossible for another. Our slim friend takes off five pounds "just like that," while we cannot. Some tasks call for skills that we have not yet learned. *Our goal in this book is to teach ways to improve your skills in situations where the task has been difficult for you.* This requires a planned effort at self-modification, enlarging your self-regulation and self-control skills. We will do this by teaching new actions, coping skills, problem-solving skills, and knowledge to use in generating adequate matches between your skills and the tasks you face.

BEHAVIOR AND THE ENVIRONMENT

If you are shy, just seeing a roomful of strangers at a party is enough to make you feel uncomfortable. Nothing bad has actually happened, but you feel nervous. You think "I don't know anybody here!" Feelings and thoughts of discomfort have been cued by the sight of a roomful of strangers. This party isn't for you, you think. Suppose you flee. Immediately your nervousness begins to fade. You feel relaxed, and your thoughts turn to where you will go next. Fleeing has consequences: you feel better. Having learned the benefits of flight, you are more likely to do something similar the next time you are in that situation.

You have begun to learn a skill for dealing with that kind of situation—fleeing—but you can see that in the long run this kind of skill may create other problems.

Your behavior and thoughts are always embedded in a context—the situation. Situations can be divided arbitrarily into two elements: the events that come before a behavior and those that come after it. In psychology these are called **antecedents** and **consequences**. Antecedents are the setting events for your behavior. They cue you or stimulate you to act in certain ways. They can be physical events, thoughts, emotions, or inner speech. Consequences affect whether you repeat certain acts or not. They reinforce behavior or fail to do so. And they affect how you feel. Consequences, too, can be physical events, thoughts, emotions, or inner speech. The antecedent for the behavior of the shy person is seeing the roomful of strangers and thinking "Get out of here!" The behavior is turning around and walking out of the room. The consequence of fleeing is feeling better, and that is reinforcing. A simple way to remember this idea is to remember A-B-C: Antecedents-Behavior-Consequences.

The effects of situations—antecedents, behavior, consequences—are influenced by the learning experiences a person has had in similar situations. Entering a room full of strangers, one person—who has learned to be nervous in this situation—flees. Another—who has no experience of fear in a roomful of strangers—thinks "Terrific! A party!" Different learning experiences produce different behaviors even when we are dealing with the same antecedent or consequence. One of our students, John, was the night manager of a small grocery store. He had many male friends, found time for some weekend basketball, and played the piano. But he had one goal that remained unachieved: he was lonely for female companionship and felt pessimistic about his future love life. John analyzed his behavior in terms of situations. When he talked to women in class or at the store, he felt relaxed and spoke fairly easily, but when the talking occurred in a social context, such as a party or a date, he became ill at ease and acted very awkward. In these situations he would initiate a series of abstract conversations, looking away from the woman and speaking in a vaguely philosophical way that he himself admitted was impossible for anyone to understand. He gave the impression of being aloof, although he was, in fact, nervous and shy. At the beginning of a conversation, then, the woman might be interested in John, but after several minutes of what appeared to her to be uninterested, aloof, unintelligible talk from John, she was no longer interested. John's behavior in the social situation changed the nature of the situation, and as the woman became uninterested in him, John acted more aloof. Thus his behavior produced a new situation, one that made him unhappy, but one that he seemed unable to remedy.

John later undertook a self-modification project. He told us that he had profited from observing the behavior of a friend who was not at all nervous or aloof when dealing with women in social situations. John was struck by the great difference between his own behavior and that of his friend. John's learning history had been very different from that of his friend. Consequently each young man felt and behaved differently, even though the situation was the same.

The fact that behavior has to be learned does not imply that once you are an adult all you do is produce behaviors that you learned as you were growing up. We change, grow, and develop throughout the life span. New or changed situations may produce new behaviors. For example, a young woman who has become a mother finds herself in a novel situation. She has a real, breathing baby to cope with, and she will learn ways of behaving as she deals with the novel situation. Some of her behavior, however, will have been learned in the past. She didn't come to motherhood completely naive about caring for a baby. She has learned certain attitudes, ideas, and specific ways of dealing with babies. For example, she may have had practice in caring for someone else's baby, she may have observed others caring for babies, or she may have taken classes or read books about child care.

The effect of the environment, then, is to evoke behaviors already learned and to teach new behaviors. The implication is that adjustment reflects learned behaviors in specific situations. You deal with your problems in adjustment by dealing with what you have learned—or not learned—to do in a particular situation. Thus, in the process of self-modification you set out to produce new learning for yourself in specific situations. To modify your own behavior—to bring it under control or determine its course—you will have to learn new skills for particular situations.

To change yourself, you need to develop the ability to change the antecedents and consequences that affect your behavior. This means that you must first notice them and then devise a way to change them.

THE PROCESS OF SELF-MODIFICATION

Successful self-modification always contains certain essential elements: self-knowledge, planning, information gathering, and modification of plans in the light of new information. There is a definite sequence in deliberate self-modification. Most self-change programs involve these steps:

1. Select a goal and specify the behaviors you need to change in order to reach the goal. These behaviors are called **target behaviors.**
2. Make observations about the target behaviors. You may keep a kind of diary describing those behaviors or count how often you engage in them. Try to discover the events that stimulate your acts and the things that reward them.
3. Work out a plan for change, applying basic psychological knowledge. Your plan might call for changing a pattern of thought that leads to unwanted behavior. You might gradually replace an unwanted behavior with a desirable one. You might reward yourself for a desired action. These options are outlined in Figure 1-1 as the A-B-Cs of self-change.
4. Readjust your plans as you learn more about yourself. As you practice analyzing your behavior, you will be able to make more sophisticated and effective plans for change.

Antecedents (A)	Behavior (B)	Consequences (C)
You can change the triggering events for a behavior by building in antecedents that lead to wanted behavior and by removing antecedents that lead to unwanted behavior.	You can change actions, thoughts, feelings, or behaviors themselves by practicing desirable acts or substituting desirable alternatives for unwanted acts.	You can change the events that follow your behavior by reinforcing desired actions and not reinforcing unwanted behavior.

Figure 1-1.   The A-B-Cs of self-change

Carrying Out a Self-Change Project

Here is the report of one of our students who carried out a self-change project in our class. His name is Dean, and he is 20 years old. Dean's experience with his self-modification plan is presented largely in his own words, along with our comments.

"I started off with this feeling that I don't make the right impression on people. I got that feeling a lot. I tried to notice when it was happening and made notes in my diary. It usually happens when I don't express myself very well. When I can't think of the right words, what do I do? I swear. I swear a lot. My foul language has gotten to be a habit. It turns people off and makes me feel stupid. I think that if I could stop swearing I'd become more articulate. So that's my goal."

Dean has taken the first step in self-modification: he has translated a vague sense of dissatisfaction into a concrete goal. He has expressed his personal values in terms of a specific behavior.

"I used a 3 × 5 card to count how often I swore. I found that I swore approximately 135 times per week. I'm sure I missed some, but I don't think I missed many. The card was in my wallet, which I take everywhere with me. I noticed that just making the count cut down how much I swore. Every time I had to make a mark on that card, I felt guilty. So I was more careful in trying not to swear. The figure of 135 per week is an approximate figure. It would be higher if I hadn't counted it."

Dean has taken the second step in self-modification: making observations. He started with a few diary entries, then moved to a specific count of his problem behavior. He was wise to get this record before attempting to change. To begin an improvement program before getting careful information usually results in failure. Dean wouldn't have known enough to successfully change unless he had first observed himself. Also, his counting record made it possible to measure the success or failure of his self-modification program.

"After counting my swearing for a week, I narrowed my behavior down to a specific situation. The situation in which my swearing occurred the most was when I was with the guys at work. I am a food runner at a restaurant. I replenish the food on the buffet line. All of us in the kitchen swear all the time. There, swearing is like another language."

Often self-observation results in the realization that the target behavior occurs, or fails to occur, because of specific circumstances. This makes changing easier because you can change the circumstances. And that is what Dean did, as we will see in a moment. Notice that you have to make the self-observations in order to discover the circumstances.

"I really enjoy using my car radio when I'm driving. You don't know how difficult it is for me to drive without music! I fixed a plan so that I had to earn the right to listen to the car radio by cutting down on my swearing."

Dean has taken the third step in self-modification: he has made a plan for change. Unfortunately his plan calls for self-punishment. Dean says that if he swears too much, he will take away one of his favorite activities—listening to the radio. We recommend *against* self-punishment because, as you will see, it doesn't work. But self-modification skills include being able to detect and correct errors in one's plan.

"I needed something to bridge the time between my performing the desired act and the time when I could listen to the car radio. So I worked out a point system. For every hour that I didn't swear, I would get one point. I work six hours each night. I decided that I had to get all six points if I wanted to listen to the car radio while I was driving home. If I got only four points, then I couldn't use the car radio until the next morning on my way to school. Less than four points, no car radio till the next afternoon.

"But I wasn't making the points. Too much swearing still. So I decided to avoid going into the restaurant kitchen whenever possible. Since we can't swear when we are out on the dining room floor, I would avoid the situation that led to a lot of swearing. When I had to go back to the kitchen to get more food, I'd tell myself 'Remember, don't swear.' "

Dean's idea to use points was a good one, as the point system helped him bridge the gap until it was time to listen to the radio. He found that his point system didn't work, however, as he still swore. He might have quit at this point, but he thought again and decided to avoid the situation in which he was tempted to swear—an excellent idea. Later he will have to deal with that temptation directly, but in the early stages of his plan it was a wise technique.

Dean's project was a success. He learned to cope with the "tempting" situation of the kitchen, and two months later his swearing was near zero. At the semester's end he intended to begin a new plan, this time to increase accurate self-expressions of his opinions and feelings. He did, and now he continues to work toward his long-range goal of being more articulate.

Applying Principles

What makes a self-modification plan like Dean's different from any New Year's resolution? Is self-modification nothing more than a resolution to do better? Sometimes we just make up our minds to change and then do it. "I turned over a new leaf!" or "It was time to get my act together." But it is not always so easy. Often something more than just good intentions is needed.

That something more is a correct, conscious application of the principles of behavior change.

Self-modification is a set of techniques that must be learned. To see if you already know some of the major points, evaluate the following report, which is a first effort at a self-modification plan by one of our students. Is it a good plan? Does it make sense to you?

Bryan, a 21-year-old college junior, writes: "I'm a nail biter, but I wish I weren't. It's embarrassing, sometimes it's painful, and it seems childish to me—something that is OK when you are a kid, but not now.

"*Target behavior:* Reduce nail biting to zero.

"*Count:* I counted for three weeks. The frequency of nail biting ranged from one to eight times a day, with the average about four or five at first. During this last week it's down to two times per day. I think counting the biting makes me more aware of it, and sometimes I stop myself from doing it before I begin.

"The situations that seem to produce more biting are (1) watching TV, (2) being bored, almost anywhere, and (3) listening to lectures. I don't see any way I can change these situations, since I don't want to give up TV, I have to go to lectures, and how can anybody completely avoid being bored?

"*Plan for changing:* I have signed the following contract and put it up on the mirror where I see it every morning. 'I promise not to bite my nails at all each day. If I don't bite my nails all day, then (1) I get to eat dinner, and (2) I get to see my girlfriend that night. If I refrain from biting my nails all week, I get to go out Saturday night, which I usually do. Otherwise, I must stay home. Signed, Bryan W.' "

This plan has some good points and several bad ones. The good points are that Bryan has an accurate count of how often he bites his nails and that he knows the situations in which he is likely to bite them. Having a self-contract is also a good idea. One of the bad points—bad because it decreases Bryan's chances of success—is that if he bites his nails, he intends to do away with a major pleasure, being with his girlfriend. We suspect he won't stick to this intention. More generally, the plan is unrealistic. Is he really going to give up eating dinner every night and never see his girlfriend if he continues to bite his nails? Again, self-punishment usually doesn't work. Another weak point is that Bryan has no plan for developing a behavior to replace nail biting.

Think critically about the many cases that are included in this book. What about them will increase the chances of success, and what will decrease the chances?

Adjusting and Changing Plans

If Bryan is going to successfully change his nail-biting habit, he will have to change his plan as he learns more about the skill of self-modification. Often people start with what they think is a sound plan, but as they try it, they find that it needs adjusting. Plans must be changed as one finds parts that are not working. Sometimes an entire plan must be redesigned, as our third case illustrates.

Kate felt that she was not studying enough. "Like a lot of students, I only study just before a test or when some deadline is coming up. I decided to reward myself with some favorite activity—going out for pizza, watching *Entertainment Tonight,* playing with my parakeet—if I completed at least two full hours of studying each day. I planned to increase this later to three or four hours per day, since actually I think I would like to go to graduate school. If I didn't do the studying, I would get to play with the bird anyway— he needs the attention—but wouldn't go out for pizza or watch the TV program.

"My plan quickly ground to a halt. I didn't do any studying; I just didn't go out for pizza or watch the TV program. After about a week of that, I quit keeping records. So I was pretty much back where I started.

"Then you announced in class that we would have to make progress reports on our projects, so I got serious again about keeping records. I realized that my thoughts at the time I was supposed to study were probably keeping me from studying. I was thinking things like 'I don't want to do this now . . . I really don't have to do it now . . . It's so boring'—things like that. So I have decided to begin a new plan. I will schedule study times for myself and will figure out some rewards that are actually worth working for. But more important, I will watch myself for those kinds of thoughts that lead me to avoid studying. I really do want to study more, as I feel I'm not living up to my potential, and—let's face it—I won't have a chance to get into graduate school with my present grades. So when those thoughts occur, I will try to spot them and change them."

It often happens that once you begin a plan, you realize that you need to change some of the details, as Bryan did, or even that you have to reorient the goal of your plan entirely, as did Kate. Start with a simple plan that seems to meet your needs. Then *find out what interferes with success.* That was Kate's approach: she found that her thoughts at the moment she sat down to study were interfering with her studying. Whatever interferes with your success will tell you what the new, changed plan should be.

But will any plan work? Can you change yourself?

DOES SELF-MODIFICATION REALLY WORK?

When people have a moderately serious problem with their own behavior, are they able to change themselves? Of course. An estimated 29 million Americans quit smoking between 1965 and 1975, following the first surgeon general's report indicating that smoking causes cancer (Prochaska, 1983). Most of these did it without any sort of professional help. It has been estimated that 55% to 65% of smokers eventually quit (Schachter, 1982). Well over half the males and females who take up smoking not only quit but do it on their own, without benefit of clinics or professional help.

The people who go to clinics or seek professional help may be the ones who are least likely to quit—the hardcore cases who haven't been able to quit on their own. The statistics on the success rates of these people is lower (Schachter, 1982). But the fact remains that more than half the people who start smoking eventually do quit.

The success rate for such relatively serious problems may be higher than is usually thought. It has been noted, for example, that a surprisingly large number of veterans who returned from the Vietnam War as heroin addicts were able to stop their habit (Horn, 1972). Research estimates of the number of obese people who have returned to normal weight vary from 29% to 55% (Schachter, 1982; Jeffery & Wing, 1983). Whatever the frequency, a substantial number of people who have been fat no longer are.

So people do change problem behaviors by themselves—they engage in successful self-modification. But why are some successful, while others are not? Remember the study of seasick sailors who nevertheless continued their duties (Rosenbaum & Rolnick, 1983). Their resourcefulness is not some magical characteristic. It can be analyzed and learned. Studies of people who are competent at self-modification—who can quit smoking or lose excess weight—teach us principles we can all use to deal with our problem behaviors.

Published Cases of Successful Self-Modification

A number of successful cases of self-modification have been reported in the professional psychological research literature. People have been successful at:

> improving their study habits (Richards, 1976);
> controlling their weight (Mahoney, Moura, & Wade, 1973);
> handling anxiety in social situations (Rehm & Marston, 1968);
> coping with loneliness (Steenman & Watson, 1984);
> controlling nervous habits such as scratching, nail biting, and hair pulling (Watson, Tharp, & Krisberg, 1972; Perkins & Perkins, 1976);
> overcoming depression (Tharp, Watson, & Kaya, 1974; Hamilton & Waldman, 1983);
> eliminating teeth grinding (Pawlicki & Galotti, 1978);
> speaking up in class (Barrera & Glasgow, 1976);
> exercising (Sherman, Turner, Levine, & Walk, 1975; Kau & Fischer, 1974).

Certainly not every problem will yield to self-modification, and not every reader will master self-control. Our purpose is to detail the procedures that make mastery more likely. What is the likelihood of your own personal success? To answer this, more than case histories are needed. When entire college classes are examined, what is the success rate of the students in the class?

Research in Self-Modification Courses

Scott Hamilton at Colorado State University (1980) taught self-change techniques to 72 students using this text. He reported that 83% of the students met their goals for behavior change. He also found that having a successful experience with self-modification increased students' expectations of success in later projects.

Carl Clements and William Beidleman (1981) at the University of Alabama taught self-change to 161 students and found that 66% reported measurable success.

One of the most recent tests of the hypothesis that students can learn self-modification was carried out by Gail deBortali-Tregerthan (1984). She used high school students in New Zealand—students who had not volunteered to learn self-modification but were required to do so as part of a psychology class. She tested 100 students and found that 66% of those who learned self-modification were able to change their target behaviors, while only 26% of those who selected a behavior to change but did not learn the techniques were able to change.

"Participants in the class demonstrated improvement in their target behaviors and reported significant positive changes in dysfunctional attitudes, fear of negative evaluation, and general self-control skills. The absence of self-reported change . . . in controls suggests that the gains were a function of the specific class." These were the conclusions of a recent research study of university-level self-management instruction conducted by Richard Rakos and Mark Grodek (in press). The text in that course was the third edition of the book you are now reading.

Other systematic reports have been presented, with similar results (Barrera & Glasgow, 1976; Payne & Woudenberg, 1978; Menges & Dobroski, 1977). Two-thirds or more of students who use self-modification techniques are able to change successfully. The question "Can one teach self-modification to students?" has been answered with a resounding *yes*. But one must consider which techniques are best, for which students, for what kinds of problems, for how long, and with how much contact with the teacher (Peterson, 1983).

An interesting fact emerges: the students whose self-modification projects did *not* work did not fail because the *techniques* did not work. They often failed because *they did not use the techniques*. For example, in one study (Holden, O'Brien, Barlow, Stetson, & Infantino, 1983), a manual was developed for people who have a strong fear of open places (agoraphobia). The manual described the techniques that subjects could use to lessen their agoraphobia. The subjects in one group were simply given the manual and invited to change themselves. The manual was not effective because the subjects did not use the techniques suggested in the manual. Later, when the same people were led by a professional therapist in using the same techniques, the subjects were more successful.

Michael Perri and Steve Richards (1977) studied the differences between people who succeeded at self-change and those who did not. They found that successful self-modifiers used *more* techniques and for a *longer period of time*. The particular techniques you use will depend on the things you want to change, but the message is clear: to increase your chances of success, use as many techniques as you can, and be ready to use them long enough to have an effect.

The Uses of Self-Modification

Self-modification is used increasingly as an adjunct to therapy. For example, in therapy for couples with sexual problems, couples who receive minimal therapist contact plus a self-change manual improve as much as those with

---

BOX 1-2

SUCCESSFUL SELF-MODIFICATION OF DEPRESSION DURING A COURSE IN SELF-MODIFICATION

In the journal *Cognitive Therapy and Research,* Scott Hamilton and David Waldman (1983) report the case of Al, who successfully reduced his moderately severe depression. The case illustrates the process of self-modification.

Al was a 20-year-old student taking a course similar to the one you are taking, in which he was asked to carry out a self-modification project. He chose to attack his depression, which had lasted for four years. It was associated with severe family stress, the divorce of his parents, and continued criticism from his mother. Al often engaged in self-criticism—"I'm stupid and a total failure because my grades are bad"—and often had negative thoughts about his insufficient studying, poor grades, inadequate time scheduling, and lack of career goals. These negative thoughts sometimes lasted as long as four hours, leading to intense depression.

Al began by counting the number of negative thoughts he had each day—ignoring whether they were long or short—and also rated how depressed he felt each day on a scale from 0 for no depression to 6 for extreme depression. He made this count for 18 days. During this time he averaged 3.2 negative thoughts per day, and his average depression rating stayed at about 3 on his scale.

For the next 14 days Al tried to lift his depression by doing something about the topics that depressed him. He attempted to reward himself for getting information about various careers, meeting daily study goals, and following through with his appointments and deadlines. He continued to count his negative thoughts and to rate his moods.

During this period his average number of negative thoughts dropped to 2.8, a slight improvement over his earlier average, but his rated mood actually worsened—to an average of 4 on his scale.

Al now started a second attack, a new self-modification plan in which he worked directly on his negative thoughts. As soon as he began a negative thought, he required himself to record what had set it off, how depressed it made him feel, and a rational reevaluation of the situation. He also required himself every day to review written positive statements about himself while engaging in pleasant activities, and to imagine himself in a stressful situation but coolly working out the best possible solution to it. This period of working on his thoughts lasted 70 days.

Throughout the 70 days Al's number of negative thoughts per day dropped, and in the last 10 days of the period he had only one. His rated mood also improved, and in the last 10 days he felt no instances of depression. When asked to comment, Al's roommate rated him as much less depressed. Six months later Al again recorded negative thoughts for two weeks, during which time he had an average of less than one per day, and his mood stayed undepressed during that period. He had successfully changed himself.

more extensive therapist contact (Zeiss, 1978). A manual for problem drinkers has shown just as much positive effect—about 80% improved—as extensive therapist contact (Miller, 1982; Miller & Muñoz, 1982). There is a long list of specific behavior changes that can be achieved through the use of self-modification procedures with minimal therapist contact: control of chronic hair pulling (Bernard, Kratochwill, & Keefauver, 1983), control of obesity (Pezzot-Pearce, LeBow, & Pearce, 1982), improved parenting skills (Sanders & Glynn, 1981), compliance of diabetics with a prescribed diet (Rainwater, Ayllon, Frederiksen, Moore, & Bonar, 1982), improved social skills in delinquent boys (Brigham, Contreras, Handel, & Castillo, 1983), maintenance of treatment effects in assertion training for women (Schefft, 1982), control of nail biting (Frankel & Merbaum, 1982), and control of anxiety (Jannoun, Oppenheimer, & Gelder, 1982).

BOX 1-3

UNSUCCESSFUL SELF-MODIFICATION OF A CASE OF "WRITER'S BLOCK"[1]

It would be misleading to suggest that everyone who tries self-modification is successful. There are, however, very few published examples of unsuccessful cases. Here is one, in its entirety:

THE UNSUCCESSFUL SELF-TREATMENT
OF A CASE OF "WRITER'S BLOCK"

DENNIS UPPER
Veterans' Administration Hospital, Brockton, Massachusetts

REFERENCES

———————————

———————————

[1]Portions of this paper were not presented at the 81st Annual American Psychological Association Convention, Montreal, Canada, August 30, 1973.

From "Unsuccessful Self-Treatment of a Case of 'Writer's Block,' " by Dennis Upper, 1974, *Journal of Applied Behavior Analysis, 7.* Copyright 1974, Pergamon Press, Ltd. Reprinted by permission.

CHAPTER SUMMARY

Self-Direction and Willpower/The Skills of Self-Direction

Adjustment is better understood as a skill than a condition. One can think of problems in adjustment from several points of view: as symptoms of inner malfunctions, as a lack of willpower, or as a lack of the skills necessary to cope with certain situations. The skills of self-direction involve being able to stop behaving in ways you don't like and start behaving in ways you do like. When we consciously exercise self-regulation to resist temptations, we call it self-control; when we make a deliberate effort to change our behavior, we call it self-modification. These skills can be learned.

Behavior and the Environment

One's behavior, thoughts, and feelings are embedded in contexts—the things that go before them (antecedents) and the things that come after (consequences). A shorthand way of expressing this is A-B-C: Antecedents-Behavior-Consequences. The effects of situations (As and Cs) upon our behavior (Bs) are influenced by learning experiences that continue throughout our lives.

The Process of Self-Modification

In the process of self-modification, you produce new learning for yourself in specific situations. You select a target behavior, make observations, work out a plan for change using psychological principles, and readjust your plans as you learn more about yourself.

Does Self-Modification Really Work?

Millions of people have successfully changed their behavior to stop unwanted acts such as smoking or overeating, and there are many published case histories of successful self-modification. Research has shown that students using this book can learn the principles of self-change and carry out successful projects. You are more likely to be successful if you use a variety of techniques for a long period of time, and if you follow the exercises at the end of each chapter.

YOUR OWN SELF-DIRECTION PROJECT: STEP ONE

There's a big difference between knowing ideas well enough to pass a test on them and knowing them well enough to use them in your daily life. To reach this more advanced stage, you must practice self-change.

Make a list of at least five personal goals. These can be major, long-term goals or minor, short-term ones. They should be important to you. You won't learn much by trying to change something trivial about yourself. Think over your list for a day or two, perhaps adding some goals to it or changing some. Then select one goal for a learning project. Remain flexible in your choice. Some projects that seem simple turn out in practice to be complicated, and some seemingly complicated projects turn out to be simple. The main purpose is to learn the steps and techniques of self-management by practicing them. The best project for learning is one that is important enough to you to make it worth going through the steps in this book.

Should you select one of the really difficult tasks in your life, or should you choose something you feel will be easy to bring under control? There is no clear answer, but here are some considerations. If you are involved in a difficult problem—for example, a weight problem or drinking or drug abuse— you should know that although you may learn how to use self-modification, reaching your final goal and maintaining it may take longer than one semes-

---

BOX 1-4

CRITERIA FOR A GOOD PROJECT

Your instructor will probably tell you that success or failure in your self-change project is less important—even to your course grade—than your sophistication in carrying out the project. Sophistication (or complexity) refers to the number of different techniques you try and to the relationship between the techniques and your self-observation. If you observe yourself carefully, you will see ways to use more techniques. Sheer effort also makes a difference. If you want to take on a difficult project, be sure your instructor realizes that the project is a difficult one for you and agrees to grade you on sophistication and effort, not just on success.

Here are some tips that we give our students. Your instructor may have additional ones that will influence your grade.

Make careful observations. Learn about the actual A-B-C relationships in your behavior. Figure out the conditions that facilitate or compete with the target behavior. Keep good records throughout the project, even if you change plans.

Use a variety of techniques. These techniques for change are grouped under the A-B-C headings in the book. Try to use some techniques from each category.

Change your plans as you find out what works and what doesn't work. Tinker with your system. This is discussed throughout the book and summarized in Chapters Eight and Ten. Be creative in your use of the techniques. Experiment with them.

Be persistent. Keep trying to change, and redo your plans as you learn more about yourself and your A-B-C relationships.

Be well organized in your final report. Here is a possible outline for the report:

The goal you selected (Chapters One and Two).
Your observations about your behavior (Chapter Three).
Your first plan for change. Draw on ideas from Chapters Five, Six, and Seven. Use several techniques. Show your results (see Chapter Nine).
Your second plan for change. If the first plan is not successful, readjust, tinker with the system, or draw up a new system altogether (Chapters Eight and Nine). Show your results.
Your plans for the future—what you will do to maintain your gains (Chapters Ten and Eleven).
Final conclusions.

ter. If you are overweight, for example, you will have to change several different things about your pattern of overeating and underexercising. Selecting just a few aspects of the problem to work on may be a major project. If you try for a less ambitious project, on the other hand, you may achieve complete success. But if success comes too quickly, will you learn enough about the process? So there is an argument both for and against the very challenging and the very easy projects.

Here's one last thing to keep in mind if you decide to tackle a big project. It comes in the form of an anecdote:

A woman in her 40s had gone back to school to become a doctor. After a year she ran into a friend who asked her how her new career plans were shaping up. She said she was considering dropping out. The friend asked why, and she replied, "It will take me six more years before I will be in practice. By that time I'll be 50!"

"Oh?" the friend said. "And if you drop out, how old will you be in six years?"

CHAPTER TWO

Specifying the Goal, Overcoming Obstacles, and Building Commitment

OUTLINE

- Specifying Behaviors-in-Situations
- Overcoming Obstacles: Why You Might Self-Sabotage
- Building Commitment
- Chapter Summary
- Your Own Self-Direction Project: Step Two
- Tips for Typical Topics

LEARNING OBJECTIVES

Specifying Behaviors-in-Situations

1. What are the tactics for specifying behaviors-in-situations?
   a. What are three basic tactics?
   b. What tactic should you use when your goal is to eliminate some undesirable behavior?
   c. What three tactics should you use if you are not sure what to do? Explain brainstorming.
   d. What tactic should you use even if your goal is not some behavior?

Overcoming Obstacles: Why You Might Self-Sabotage

2. What are three reasons why you might not carry out a self-modification project?
3. What are self-efficacy beliefs? What are five steps you can take to increase your self-efficacy beliefs in regard to the behaviors you want to change?
4. Why is it a good idea to make a list of the long- and short-term advantages of changing? How do you make the list?

Building Commitment

5. What are six steps you can take to avoid being tempted to stop your self-change plans?
6. Explain the use of subgoals in working toward a long-term goal.
7. What are escape clauses?
8. What is a self-contract? Does it really help?

All of us use abstract words like *aggressive, dependent, strong,* and *ambitious* to describe personality traits or motives. Words of this kind pose two problems: they don't specify the situations in which the behaviors occur, and they don't specify particular behaviors. You might say "I'm an independent person." But this kind of language is misleading because you may act independent in one situation and dependent in another. For example, Derek might be emotionally quite dependent on his girlfriend but rather independent in his schoolwork and relationships with his professors. And what exactly does he do when he is "emotionally dependent"?

Think of your behavior in conjunction with the situation in which the behavior occurs. Even if your problem relates to inner feelings—a sense that "something is wrong inside"—you should think of it as an emotional-reaction-in-a-particular-situation. You might think, "I'm nervous and depressed. I'm becoming neurotic." But a better formulation—one that can help you change—would be "At work, after I finish a big task, I get depressed" or "At night in the dorm I feel nervous." You must be very specific, because you can change only specific things in specific situations.

Regardless of the type of problem or goal you are dealing with, you must have well-defined objectives that are specified in terms of particular behaviors in particular situations. Here are several tactics that will help you specify your goals clearly.

SPECIFYING BEHAVIORS-IN-SITUATIONS

Tactic one: Make a list of concrete examples.   Suppose you're dissatisfied with yourself. You think "I'm too self-centered." This self-statement doesn't tell you what to change, because it is too vague. Give a concrete example of the problem: "I talk about myself too much when I'm with my friends." This specifies both the behavior and the situation in which the behavior occurs.

"I eat too much" is also too vague. Do you eat too many carrots? Do you eat too much at every meal? A better statement might be "I can never resist my grandmother's desserts when I have dinner at her house, and I often have second helpings." Or "Whenever I go on a picnic, I eat too much." Or "I eat too much on special occasions such as Thanksgiving or Christmas." Sometimes thinking of examples of the problem in question will make you more aware of the kinds of situations in which the behavior occurs.

Sally started with the vague statement "I'm not assertive enough." But when she gave specific examples, she turned a vague idea into a clear statement about her behavior and the specific kinds of situations in which her problem occurred. "It's not that I am always unassertive. I can deal with people who try to push ahead in line, or with friends who ask too much of me. But when men my age ask me to do things related to dating, going out, or being together, then I am not as assertive as I want to be." Now she has labeled the kind of situation in which her problem occurs and can begin to change the way she reacts in those situations.

Tactic two: List the details of your problem.   To solve problems, you must attend to the details (D'Zurilla & Goldfried, 1971). Make a list of these details; then select those that seem critical to the solution of the problem. Often our thinking about a problem is unfocused, and listing the details helps us to see precisely what our target goal should be. Research in problem solving suggests that people who list details improve their problem-solving ability compared with those who do not (Nezu & D'Zurilla, 1981; Presbrey, 1979).

A woman originally entered psychotherapy asking for treatment for severe anxiety while taking tests. She had two university degrees, but lately was becoming so nervous while taking tests that her performance was in jeopardy. The first detail she listed concerning her problem was that she did not have enough time to study. Listing other details revealed that because of her newborn baby, she sometimes had difficulty getting to class and sometimes couldn't even get to exams on time. Instead of treating her test anxiety directly, her therapist suggested she focus on coping with the problems that were interfering with her schoolwork. After learning ways to cope with the *details* of her problem, she found that her test anxiety was reduced (Mayo & Norton, 1980). That is, she went from an original focus on the problem of test anxiety to a focus on the specific details that were leading to the test anxiety.

Don "couldn't get along" with his parents. He wanted to undertake a self-modificaton project to change those behaviors that were contributing to the problem. Don's list of the details went like this: "When we argue, we just start screaming at each other. We don't actually negotiate solutions to problems; we just yell and make recriminations. And there's a lot of name calling." This list of details gave Don a focus for specific change.

Tactic three: Become an observer of yourself. *A critical step in specifying the problem is to stop speculating about your behavior and start actually observing it.* Your thoughts about your problem will probably remain vague until you begin to actually watch yourself behaving in various situations.

Besides observing your behavior, you should keep notes of your observations. You might keep a narrative account of your daily life, or simply note instances of behavior that seem related to the problem. After you have recorded observations of your behavior in various situations, read over your notes and see if a pattern emerges. The best way to make these observations is to write down your behaviors and the situations in which they occur as soon as you think you have an instance of the problem.

In the case of Sally, mentioned earlier, she began to actually observe her behavior. When a man she didn't like asked her out on a date and she said yes, she asked herself, "Was that an example of my being unassertive?" She decided that it was. Thus she observed that her lack of assertion occurred when a man asked her out on a date. Later, a man who lived in her rooming house barged into her room, and she didn't say anything. Again she asked, "Was that an instance of my being unassertive?" Eventually she saw that her problem—her lack of assertiveness—was very specific. It occurred only in certain personal situations and almost always involved men.

When the Problem Is Nonperformance of Some Behavior

Sometimes your goal is to start doing something that at present you're not doing. For example, you may realize that you are failing in college because you're *not* studying. What can you do? The same general strategy of specifying the problem applies. You should specify the situation in which you *want* the behavior to occur:

My goal is _____ when _____ .
                  (what you want to do)   (situation)

Paul, a student who had such a problem, kept a journal to record these situations. It had entries like this: "*Wednesday*. Roommate went out. Room quiet. Got out my history text and turned to the assignment. Remembered a baseball game was on TV and started watching it. Tried to study between innings but gave up. Studied about five minutes the whole afternoon. *Thursday*. Went to the library to study. Saw Karen. Didn't study."

These observations specify two situations in which studying would have been desirable: "room quiet in the afternoon" and "went to the library." The journal also contains other valuable information: it tells Paul what he did instead of studying. Paul was not simply "not studying." He was actively performing behaviors that made studying impossible. In other words, as far as studying was concerned, he was performing the *wrong* behaviors. So his task of problem specification was not really different from those we have already discussed: specifying the *situation* in question (for example, "room quiet") and then specifying the *behavior* in question (for example, "watching TV instead of studying").

Remember to specify not only the situation and the fact that the desirable behavior is not occurring but also the behaviors that do occur instead of the ones you want. Thus, Paul should first specify the situation in which he wants the behavior to occur—when he is alone in his room or when he is at the library—and then observe what occurs *instead* of the desired behavior. He wants to increase studying, but to do so he must see what he does that interferes with studying.

When the Problem Is Getting Rid of Some Undesirable Behavior

Paul might express his goal in one of two ways: (1) "I want to quit goofing off and study more" or (2) "I want to increase studying in those situations in which I should study." The second way is better, because it expresses the goal in terms of some behaviors that need to be increased.

Tactic four: Your strategy should always be to increase some desirable behavior.   Even if the problem is that you are doing something you want to stop, you should specify your problem in terms of a desirable alternative behavior.

For Paul, specifying a desirable alternative was easy. By keeping records of his behavior, he saw that when he was alone in his room he watched TV and that when he went to the library he talked to Karen. For each of those two situations, he could name the desirable alternative behavior: he should have studied. His intervention plan would not be to *decrease* directly the undesirable behaviors of watching-TV-when-alone-in-room or talking-with-Karen-in-library but, instead, to *increase* the desirable behaviors of studying-when-alone-in-room and studying-when-in-library. He therefore set up a plan to *increase* studying in these two situations.

Laura complained that she was bothered by frequent feelings of depression. She had begun searching for possible causes of these upsetting feelings and found that many things seemed to produce depression. A friend would mildly criticize her, her cat would disappear, she would spill coffee on her new dress—many fairly minor events seemed sufficient to set off hours of deep sadness. Laura had the feeling that it would take her a lifetime just to specify all the situations leading to depression, much less do anything about them. When asked to specify a desirable alternative, she replied that feeling good was an alternative. We suggested that she search for events that made her feel good and keep in mind the goal of attempting to increase them.

Earl's original statement of his problem was "I think I am morbidly shy, and I want to get rid of my shyness." After observing himself and analyzing his problem, he decided "Actually I need to relax and learn how to make a good impression." Thus he replaced his goal of "getting rid of shyness" with "increasing relaxation" and "making a good impression." Later he was able to become even more specific: "I want to relax when I'm with women. I want to make eye contact, smile, use good body language, and be able to express an interest in the person." These later goals are easier to achieve, because they are more specific than "getting rid of shyness" and because they involve developing new behaviors.

Denise began by saying that she wanted to be more assertive. But what exactly did that mean? What would she do when she was more assertive? She kept records of instances in which she had not been assertive and later thought what she could have done in each situation that would have been properly assertive. This gave her ideas for the kinds of behavior she wanted to increase. Here is a portion of her records:

10 P.M.	Buddy called me for a date.
What I did	I started to lie. "I have to work, I'm so busy. . . ." He wanted me to come over to his apartment. I didn't know what to say. Finally, I told him I would see him. (Damn!)
What I should have done	I wish I had said, "No, Buddy, I don't feel comfortable around you. We just don't get along. So, no, thanks."
3 P.M. Riding the bus home	A guy sat next to me and put his bag right on my lap. I was in a state of shock.
What I did	I didn't know what to say. I pretended not to notice, looked out the window, but I was thinking "You s.o.b." He started a conversation and I irritably gave one-word answers.
What I should have done	Said, "Excuse me, can you get your bag off my lap?"

When You Aren't Sure What to Do

Suppose you're not reaching some goal and aren't sure how to do so. Joanne wanted to be a poet but complained that she never seemed to get around to writing poetry. We pointed out that writers usually set aside some time at which they sit at the typewriter, whether they feel inspired or not, and suggested that she choose a specific hour, every other day, to do nothing but write poetry. She agreed, but just as she was leaving, she turned back to say "Actually I tried something like that last week, but I couldn't keep the schedule." She went on to explain that she had begun to worry about how her poem would sound to other people before she had even written it. This fear prevented her from writing and made the act of trying to write very unpleasant.

Joanne was able to state precisely the full chain of actions that would produce her goal: keep a firm schedule for writing, develop a feeling of confidence, and concentrate on the poem itself rather than on future readers' reactions. She chose the last link of the chain as her self-modification project, and in time she developed good concentration and became more productive.

If you aren't sure what to do to reach a goal, there are additional tactics available. You've just seen an illustration of the first one.

Tactic five: Specify the chain of events that will produce your goal.   The things that happen to you are the result of a series of events. There is a chain of behaviors (behaviors of your own and of other people) that, once set in motion, lead inexorably to a conclusion. The case of Joanne and her poetry illustrates such a chain. Your task in designing a plan for self-modification will often involve specifying not only the simple, targeted behavior, but the chain of behaviors that would produce it.

Suppose that your goal is to avoid eating ice cream before you go to bed at night. What chain of events might enable you to reach this goal? One is simple: don't buy the ice cream. Then it won't be there at bedtime, calling out your name. This tactic is often used by successful dieters. Some compulsive overeaters break their unwanted chains by shopping only from a list, avoiding the items that would later place them in a tempting situation.

These examples illustrate the power of a careful chain-of-events analysis. Once you know what events need to take place in order for a desired behavior to occur, you can set them in motion. At the same time, you can avoid chains of events that lead to undesired behaviors.

Tactic six: Observe people who do well what you are trying to do, and then try it yourself.   Sometimes you just don't know what the chain of events is that would lead to your goal. Ken wanted to "be a nicer person socially, have more friends." What should he do to reach that goal? What chain of events should he try to set in motion? He decided to observe a friend of his, Mary, who was a really nice person. "You know what she does?" he asked us. "She listens to other people when they talk. She is the world's champion listener. When you're talking to her, she concentrates on you fully. She doesn't look around the room or interrupt or talk to other people or anything. She listens, hard. And that makes her seem terribly interested, very nice." Now he knows one event—listening—that will lead to his goal of being better liked, and he can build that into his social behavior.

Often it is better to observe other people performing the behavior you want to perform than to ask for advice. Most people are not expert at behavioral analysis and may give you bad or worthless advice. "Just quit eating so much" is not much help. Observing a slim person might be a lot more helpful. One of our overweight students told about watching his slim wife when she ate. "She never takes seconds. Not even at Thanksgiving. Not even when the food is fantastic. Never."

However, if you can't observe people performing the desired behavior, you may need to ask their advice. "Jan, you always get A's on your term papers. How do you go about writing and researching them?" Remember that you are asking for descriptions of particular behaviors and chains of events that lead to the goal. "I just try hard" is a useless response. "I schedule two library sessions, consult with the reference librarian about what materials are available, then write a draft and ask the professor to look it over and make comments" is extremely helpful, because it describes the chain of events that leads to producing a good term paper.

Tactic seven: Think of alternative solutions.   D'Zurilla and Goldfried (1971) suggest that you think of several alternative solutions to the problem and then select one or more to implement. Your first thoughts may not be the most creative. It's helpful here to use a technique called **brainstorming.** The technique has four simple rules: (1) Try for quantity—quality will follow. (2) Don't be critical, greeting every idea with a "Yes, but . . ." Criticism can come later; for now, blow it all out. (3) Be freewheeling. Some ideas may be unrealistic or even weird, but that's OK. (4) Try to improve ideas by combining them. The case described in Box 2-1 illustrates this approach.

When Your Goal Is Not a Behavioral One

There are times when your goal is not a particular *behavior* but rather a *result you want to achieve*—being up on your homework, being slim, having a stack of your own completed poems. To achieve some of these results, the behavior you have to change is obvious. For example, the stack of finished poems will grow if you increase the time you spend writing them. But for other results, what you need to change may not be so obvious. If you want to lose weight, what behavior should you change? Of course you need to diet, but unless you change the behaviors that led to your being overweight, you will regain the weight you lose on a diet.

Tactic eight: Even if your goal is not a specific behavior, reaching the goal will require changing certain behaviors.   To lose weight, you need to control snacking, cut out empty-calorie foods, stay away from leftovers, and eat smaller meals. To keep the weight off, you have to change your behaviors—for example, you have to exercise regularly. Here's a sample of behaviors engaged in by many overweight people: They keep a ready supply of fattening foods in the house; they eat to avoid waste; they pile too much food on their plates; they eat rapidly and while reading or watching TV; they eat when they are emotionally upset (instead of making some other, nonfattening response); and they eat many times each day (Stuart & Davis, 1972; LeBow, 1981). They rarely weigh themselves and don't exercise enough. Also, they often skip breakfast. They starve themselves and then overeat (Mayer, 1968). In the long run, these behaviors will have to be changed.

BOX 2-1

THE CASE OF THE WORN-OUT STUDENT

Ruth is 26, married, working, and also going to college. She first majored in elementary education, then added a second major—general science—to increase her chances of getting a teaching job. Her first attempt to state the problem was vague: "I'm losing my motivation for school. I've become too emotional. I argue with my husband too much. I can't really get into my science projects, even though I love the field." We asked Ruth to list all the details of her problem and search for a specific goal. She wrote:

I feel that the arguments with my husband are due to my being upset about my schoolwork.
My generally bad moods are also reactions to school.
I haven't been going to classes regularly.
I feel under a lot of pressure from the buildup of assignments.
My study habits are deteriorating.
Classes just don't seem as important to me as they used to.
I am spending more time playing tennis.
The pressure is strongest in the two graduate courses in education. I am having trouble with these two courses. I'm actually getting frightened. The most difficult is History of Education.

Ruth then brainstormed several possible solutions to her problem:

I could drop out of school.
I could change my major, go back to elementary ed.
I could drop the education courses and forget about graduate school.
I could find someone to help me with my studies.
I could sell my car, so I couldn't get to the tennis courts.
I could go to a hypnotist.

After thinking about various solutions, Ruth decided to drop the difficult History of Education course, a plan she had not even considered in the beginning. She reasoned that the time she gained would enable her to catch up and do well in her other courses. At the beginning she had difficulty specifying her problem, but by listing details and brainstorming several solutions, she was able to formulate a reasonable plan.

Suppose an overweight person asks "What would I be doing if I were slim?" The answer is implicit in the preceding paragraph: as a slim person, he or she would engage in behaviors opposite to those that contribute to the problem of overweight—eating smaller meals, exercising regularly, and so on. The goal of slimness is not a behavior, but to reach it the necessary behaviors must be developed.

In order to reach a nonbehavioral goal, *you must change certain behaviors.* You need to eliminate old behaviors that contribute to the problem and develop new ones that help you reach the goal.

Start observing yourself, and do it over a relatively long period of time. You will begin to see relationships between what you do (or don't do) and the goal you want to reach. You'll notice patterns. For example, you may observe that each time you get down in the dumps, you respond by eating. If you keep records of your behavior in social situations, you'll see things you do that put others off—such as not listening—and discover things that you can do that will make you more attractive. You become a scientist of yourself, seeking aspects of your behavior that prevent reaching the goal and finding new behaviors that will help you to reach it. Through self-analysis you will be able to answer two essential questions: "What acts do I perform, what thoughts do I have, that keep me from reaching my goal?" and "What behaviors do I need to develop in order to reach my goal?"

The Evolution of Goals

As you learn more about how your own thoughts or actions interfere with the goal you want to reach, you may go through a series of self-discoveries. A night-school student of ours named Michael was often depressed. He began a self-change project with only a vague idea of how to get rid of his depression. His first step was to record the situations that made him feel depressed. From his record, he learned that all such situations stemmed from daily frustrations. Michael then observed his reactions and realized that once he was frustrated, any additional disappointment made him depressed. He continued to observe himself, now asking "Why do frustrations make me feel so bad?" The answer was that he brooded over the frustrations. For example, if his child misbehaved, he'd spend hours thinking that he was a terrible father and that he was responsible for raising a spoiled child. He decided that brooding was self-defeating and unnecessary.

After several weeks of self-observation, recording, and analyzing his records, Michael made a breakthrough. "All along I've suspected that not *all* frustrations have the same effect on me. My kid isn't really at the root of the problem. It's my own self-esteem. Frustrations that call my self-esteem into question are the ones that I magnify." Michael analyzed what "frustrated self-esteem" meant in terms of behavior and realized that he often compared himself with people at the top. In his sales job, he knew what the top people were achieving, and he felt bad because he couldn't do as well.

He concluded that his standards were too high and that always comparing himself to the leaders made him unhappy. "I seem to think that if I'm not the very best, I'm no good at all." So he set out to change his reference group. He would learn to compare himself to people who were at his own level.

Before Michael embarked on a self-change project, all he knew was that he was unhappy and too easily upset by frustrations. Through self-observation and thinking about the meaning of his observations, he learned about how his own actions and thoughts contributed to his problems.

People who are successful at self-change go through a series of successive approximations, often changing the target of their self-change efforts several times. For example, people seeking permanent weight control might start off with the goal of learning the caloric value of foods, exercising a little, and trying to eat less. As they learn more about their personal eating habits, they set new targets for themselves—for example, eating more slowly and eating only low-calorie foods. Later, the target of not eating when depressed might be added, and so on. As you learn more about yourself and about the actions that support or hamper your progress, you add new target behaviors.

Living means adjusting. As we go through life, we take up new goals and discard old ones. This same process applies to conscious self-modification. Michael's first target was to learn about his reactions to frustration. As he worked at this target, he discovered that his problem was frustrated self-esteem. This discovery led to other discoveries about himself. He realized that frustrated self-esteem occurred when he evaluated himself negatively by comparing himself to people who were the very best in their jobs. In turn, this new awareness led Michael to a new goal: avoiding comparisons that frustrated his self-esteem.

As your understanding of yourself deepens with self-observation, so will your understanding of the appropriate techniques for change. The two questions you need to ask and reevaluate throughout the process of self-change are: "What is the target I should be working on?" and "What techniques should I use to reach that target?" Self-understanding and a knowledge of possible techniques will permit you to give more sophisticated answers to these questions.

For complex goals, where do you begin? Which of several possible behaviors should be your first target? The basic rule is to start by making self-observations. *Get data about yourself.* Second, work on specifying your goal clearly.

If developing more friends is your goal, start by observing yourself in situations in which you might work on that goal, and try to specify what behaviors you want to develop in order to reach the goal. How do you act when you are with other people? What behaviors might you develop? If weight control is your goal, your first steps are to observe your eating behavior and start specifying the behaviors and chains of events you want to change.

OVERCOMING OBSTACLES: WHY YOU MIGHT SELF-SABOTAGE

There are several reasons why you might not carry out any self-modification plan at all: you are hoping for a miracle; you don't believe you can change; or you don't really want to change or are ambivalent about changing. Dealing with these issues now will increase your chances of success.

Expect Mistakes

When old, unwanted behaviors have been automatic for a long time, one slips back into them at unguarded moments. This happens to everyone. *Expect that you will relapse into old, unwanted behaviors—that you will make mistakes.*

A good plan for change includes what to do when you slip—when you fall off the wagon (Marlatt, 1982). (See Chapter Ten.) A man who had been trying for nearly a year to quit drinking too much told us, "I was working very hard and had a difficult time sticking to my prescribed number of drinks. I really expected to get high because some days that seemed about the only reward I got. But I also knew that I wanted to stop drinking so much. So I made a plan: I would continue to keep a record of my drinking even when I was drinking too much. That got me through. I felt I was still somewhat in control and figured that when I got time I would deal with my problem." Such persistence pays.

You won't be persistent, however, if you don't believe you *can* perform the actions you need to perform in order to change.

Your Beliefs about Changing

Suppose your rich uncle, the one who likes practical jokes, opens a box and says to you, "Here's a 6-foot Burmese python. I'll give you $50 if you will take it out and hold it in your lap for five minutes." *Would* you do it? *Could* you do it? You would if you could, but you can't?

Many of us would not earn that $50. We would not believe ourselves capable of performing the behavior. Thus we wouldn't try. And so, of course, we would fail.

If the uncle had said "There's a 6-inch earthworm in this box, and I'll give you $50 to hold it in your lap for five minutes," we would be more likely to perform the behavior. We believe our level of skill is up to that task. Thus we would try it, find we could do it, and succeed.

Our beliefs about our ability to perform tasks affect whether we try the tasks or not, as well as how emotional we feel during the attempt (Bandura, 1977, 1982). Whether we believe we can do what needs to be done depends on two things: our estimation of the difficulty of the task, and our estimation of our own skill in dealing with the task. In psychology this is called a **self-efficacy belief**. Given the task before you, do you believe you have the skill to cope with it? It is not a general belief about yourself, but a specific belief that is tied to a particular task. It is not a yes/no belief, but probably a yes-maybe-no continuum—with varying amounts of "maybe."

Patti was asked to give a talk in her social science research methodology class. "I can't, I really can't. I could talk in front of a small class, but this one has 200 people in it." She is saying that faced with this level of task difficulty, she does not believe that she is capable of performing the behaviors needed to accomplish the task.

Patti's biggest problem is her belief that she cannot perform the necessary actions. Lots of people talk in front of 200-person classes every day. It's not an inherently impossible task. Perhaps Patti could talk in front of the class if we said "We'll pay you $5000 to give the talk" or "We'll cut the class size down to 20 people." But in the present situation, her belief that she can't do it has two effects: it leads to not trying, and thinking about doing it makes her feel very nervous.

Our beliefs create reality for us. Patti makes herself incapable of speaking in front of a large class. What we believe about our ability to change affects how hard we try to change, and that in turn affects our success. Several recent research studies have shown this to be true. In one study, 40 tennis players stated their beliefs about their ability to successfully perform various tennis moves, and their beliefs were found to be related to their actual ability to perform (Barling & Abel, 1983). In another study, smokers who were trying to quit stated their beliefs about their ability to resist temptation in certain tempting situations—for example, when someone offered a cigarette. It was found that the persons who felt they could resist temptation were, in fact, more likely to successfully resist (Candiotte & Lichtenstein, 1981). A third study has shown that people who successfully quit smoking have stronger self-efficacy beliefs about dealing with temptations than do those who relapse (DiClemente, 1981).

Do these beliefs help to create reality, or do they simply reflect it? One way of answering this question is to see whether it is possible to increase people's self-efficacy beliefs and thus affect their ability to perform necessary tasks. In one study, involving people who were extremely afraid of snakes, a real 6-foot Burmese python was used. The subjects were given a detailed series of training experiences—using the same kinds of techniques we will teach you in this book—and were gradually taught first to approach and finally to fondle the snake (Bandura, Reese, & Adams, 1982). As their self-efficacy beliefs about performing the various steps increased, so did their actual ability to perform the steps leading to touching the python.

Three hundred years ago the philosopher Spinoza said, "So long as a man imagines he cannot do something, so long as he is determined not to do it, then it is impossible for him to do it." Today at the movies, in the *Star Wars* saga, the Jedi master Yoda performs a seemingly impossible feat. Luke Skywalker exclaims "I . . . can't believe it!" Yoda responds, with a knowing smile, "*That* is why you fail." The belief that you can cope does not in itself eliminate all difficulties. But it makes you try harder when attempting to overcome difficulties. People who are trying to lose weight or quit smoking persist longer and have better success if they believe that their efforts will produce change (Chambliss & Murray, 1979a, 1979b).

Do you believe you can do the things you have to do in order to change yourself? You can become aware of some specific beliefs that will affect your behavior by answering these questions:

1. Will you be able to read carefully to the end of the book?
   Yes _____ No _____ Maybe _____
2. Will you be able to try the ideas in the book before you evaluate them?
   Yes _____ No _____ Maybe _____
3. Will you be able to carry out the exercise at the end of each chapter, in which you apply the ideas from that chapter to your own self-modification project?
   Yes _____ No _____ Maybe _____

How to Increase Your Self-Efficacy Beliefs

First, pick a project for which you can say yes to the questions above. Don't start with something you expect to fail at. As you develop skill at self-modification, you can undertake projects that previously would not have been possible.

Second, discriminate between your past performance and your present project (Goldfried & Robins, 1982). You may have learned from past failures that you cannot do certain things. But past failures are not necessarily a portent of future failure. You can gradually develop skills you never had before. All the people who successfully learned to handle the Burmese python had previously been extremely afraid of snakes. The researchers used techniques such as gradual approximations to a goal (see Chapter Six) to teach the subjects to approach the snake, and the subjects learned to perform the new behavior.

Third, keep good records (see Chapter Three). In order for people to change their self-efficacy beliefs, they must notice their successes. A person who sticks to a study schedule for four days and then fails to do so on the fifth should not think, "It's no use. I can't do it." This ignores the four days of success.

Fourth, pay close attention to your successes. If you expect failure, you are likely to look for signs of failure. If you force yourself to look for signs of success, it affects your beliefs and your behavior. George, who wanted to improve his social relations with women, said, "I think I always expected not to make a nice impression, so I was looking for that. If there was a pause in the conversation, I'd think 'Oh, she's bored' or 'I'm not making a good impression.' I taught myself to look for positive signs instead. Now if there's a pause in the conversation, I think 'She feels relaxed—good.' "

In carrying out a self-modification project, you will learn to do things under your own control that will bring about positive results. Increasing your skill will lead to greater self-efficacy (Sonne & Janoff, 1979) and will increase your chances of changing.

Fifth, make a list of the specific kinds of situations in which you expect to have the greatest difficulty. For example, Rosa, who wanted to become more assertive, made a list of "situations in which I have a hard time doing what I need to do."

easiest: dealing with strangers—for example, clerks
fairly easy: students at school
moderate: my two brothers, my mom
getting difficult: my boss
the most difficult: my dad

Once she had made this list, her strategy was clear: begin with the easier tasks and tackle the harder ones after she had experienced success—and built some skill—with the easier ones.

Rank-ordering the situations in which you anticipate difficulty allows you to put off dealing with the harder ones until you are better prepared and allows you to avoid discouraging failures early in your self-change plan. It also allows you to discount mistakes you make early in the plan. If Rosa finds herself in a situation in which she fails to be assertive with her father, she can say to herself, "Well, I knew I was going to have a lot of trouble being assertive with my dad." Then she can remind herself of successes in other, easier situations. This way she is less likely to abandon a potentially successful plan.

But do you really want to change?

The Pros and Cons of Changing

Teruko was bothered by her poor performance at college. She had been valedictorian of her high school class and was considered brilliant by everyone, but now she was making mostly C's. She started a self-change plan to increase her studying, but after a few days it fizzled. "You know," she said, "it's really comfortable this way. I don't have to work at all to make C's. And I don't have to find out what my upper limits are, something my dad is always urging me to do. I can just coast. For now, that's all I want." Teruko found her behavior rewarding and really didn't want to change.

Tim, who had a terrible temper, told us a similar story. "I started out thinking that everyone resented my outbursts, and that was true. But I also found that I often get my way because of my temper. People give in to me. So, in fact, I get something out of it." Tim had to decide whether the short-term advantages of getting his way outweighed the long-term advantages of not having people resent his behavior.

When you cannot readily change some problem behavior or reach some desired goal, it may be because the immediate payoff of the behavior is greater than you suspected. Any behavior that continues is offering some advantage, no matter how slight or temporary. People who bite their nails find comfort in their habit. People who use drugs like feeling high better than feeling anxious. People who don't exercise enjoy the pleasure of inactivity. People who accomplish little like the freedom of not working on a schedule. Ask yourself, *"What will I lose by changing?"* Many times we are unaware of the reasons for a problem behavior until we try to change it. When temptation knocks, we become particularly aware of the advantages of not changing. An overeater told us, "It wasn't until I tried to stop snacking that I realized how I use between-meal snacks to cheer myself up. Then I saw that I really get a lift from food. There are advantages to overeating." When you embark on a program of self-change, all the negative consequences of changing may not occur to you, but they will appear in the form of temptations.

People may be unaware of the cost of changing their behavior. They want better grades, and so they set a study schedule. But increased study time means decreased leisure time. Is it worth it? If the answer is no, then the plan will most likely fail.

Sometimes changing means that we lose certain desired outcomes right now, as when we give up TV to study. But changing can also lead to new situations that we are not prepared to deal with.

Faith had been about 50 pounds overweight, and in the previous year she had lost almost 40 pounds. She explained, "I didn't lose it equally all over, though, and I was, to be candid, pretty busty. Men liked this, but I didn't like it at all. I hated all the attention they paid to my body. So I just let myself go and regained 30 pounds. Now I'm fat and unbothered once more." Lizette Peterson (1983) has reported similar cases. She also mentions a young man who improved his study skills and saw his grades go up, only to find that his parents expected more of him than they had before. Sometimes changing ourselves leads to other issues that have to be coped with.

To sum up, there can be long- and short-term advantages and disadvantages to any self-change plan. You are much more likely to succeed in your plan if you examine these at the beginning of your self-modification plan. Make a list of the long- and short-term pros and cons of changing your behavior. People who make out this kind of list are more likely to be successful in their plans for change (Brehm & Smith, 1982; Brehm, 1976; Janis, 1982).

Box 2-2 gives an example of one student's list.

Why does making this list help? *First,* it helps you anticipate obstacles to changing, so you can take steps to overcome them. For example, if you know your spouse is going to be made uncomfortable by the new you, you can make the changes gradually or try to build protection into your plan. *Second,* it encourages you to be realistic—to face what you want and don't want, and what you are willing to do to get what you want. If you know you hate to sweat and feel tired but think you ought to increase your exercising, realizing this now may enable you to work out a plan to deal with these obstacles. Try swimming, for example. Swimmers don't get hot. *Third,* it allows you to plan ahead.

BUILDING COMMITMENT

Even with the most detailed and specific plan, certain problems are bound to arise during the process of self-modification. You will be tempted to go astray, and you may grow weary of the work involved in changing. An effective plan takes these future problems into consideration. This section discusses how you can build commitment to change and how you can anticipate and neutralize inevitable temptations. Commitment to change is not something you *have;* it is something you *do* (Coates & Thoresen, 1977). Commitment itself is a set of behaviors.

Variations in the Strength of the Pros and Cons of Changing

The advantages and disadvantages of a particular behavior will vary. Odysseus knew this, and that is why he had a plan to keep him from making a regrettable decision when his ship sailed close to the Sirens. There were strong advantages to not sailing too close, but Odysseus knew that the strength of those advantages would pale once he heard the Sirens' song and that he would sail too close to the rocks. You need to anticipate the times when the advantages of changing will no longer seem strong (and the disadvantages momentarily seem stronger) and make plans to cope with the tempting situations.

Expect to be tempted. If you have a plan for dealing with temptation, you are more likely to be successful in your self-modification project (Patterson

---

BOX 2-2

THE PROS AND CONS OF CHANGING

Instructions: Consider the short-term and long-term pros and cons of changing. Take into consideration the effects upon yourself and others, both tangible and intangible. Consider how you will feel about yourself, and how others will feel.

Teruko's case: Why should I try to improve my grades in college?

Short-term	
Pros	*Cons*
Would get my parents off my case.	Would be doing just what my parents
Would enjoy classes more.	want me to do.
Wouldn't feel so hassled.	Would be a lot more work—I would
Might learn something of value.	have to give up some of my time
Might enjoy it—I'm smart, and	spent goofing off.
would like to be well-educated.	Would have to work on a lot of junk.

Long-term	
Pros	*Cons*
Feel I was making something out of	Maybe I would become a workaholic.
myself.	More responsibilities.
Might get a better career.	I'd just become a conformist.
Might make more money from a bet-	My parents would be delighted.
ter career.	
Might make new friends.	
Would be well educated.	
My parents would be delighted.	

& Mischel, 1975; Shiffman, 1982). List the times when you might expect temptations to occur, and devise ways to cope with those situations. Put another way, think of the times when the short-term advantages will take on great strength and momentarily outweigh the long-term advantages of changing. If you want to remain faithful to your lover, for example, don't allow yourself to get into situations in which making love with someone else seems, at the moment, a good idea. Short-term and long-term advantages are very often opposed, and one cannot have both. If you bite your nails, you won't have nice-looking hands. If you don't study, you won't get into law school. The trick is to be prepared for the times when the short-term disadvantages of change outweigh the long-term advantages of sticking to your plan.

What can you do to be prepared?

Preparing for Temptations to Stop Self-Modification

"Self-regulation is carried out partly by managing the environment and partly by managing one's own attention, memory and thoughts" (Kelley, 1983, p. 304). Try to strengthen the things that allow you to make the changes you want and weaken those that are inconsistent with change.

Avoid situations you know will be tempting. Don't go to the places where you might be tempted; don't do the things that will tempt you too much (Kelley, 1983). Later, when your newly developed behavior has become somewhat automatic—"I'll have ginger ale, please"—you can go back to your friends' parties where beer drinking is heavy.

Minimize the tempting quality of the situation. For those who want to reduce drinking alcohol, it is useful to drink water before going out to a party so as not to arrive thirsty. The effect is to reduce the tempting quality of the drinks that are offered.

When you are in the tempting situation, distract yourself. Small children are able to deliberately distract themselves to get through tempting periods (Patterson & Mischel, 1975). We adults can do the same. Faced with a luscious and fattening sundae, think about the person sitting across from you at the dinner table, the chair you're sitting on, the Queen—anything. But don't think about the dessert. And if you cannot resist looking at it, use "cool" perceptions: it is pink, it is made of milk products, the bowl has a diameter of 4 inches.

Invest a lot in the project as early as possible (Kelley, 1983; Cooper & Axsom, 1982). Put as much effort into it as you can. Do all the exercises suggested in this chapter, and keep very careful records, beginning with Chapter Three. When you are ultimately tempted, the more you have invested, the less likely you will be to give in.

Once you have achieved some success in your self-change, remind yourself of your investment of time and effort when you are dealing with temptation. "I've come too far to give in now." The exerciser coming home after a hard day thinks, "I could skip today's run. I'm not in the mood. But I've put a lot of effort into this exercise program, and that's worth more than loafing today." Tie your most rational thinking to the project. "It would be a real mistake not to make this self-modification a success, because it's something I really want."

Another way to increase your investment in the project is to make a public commitment that you are going to change (Shelton & Levy, 1981). If you tell people you intend to change, the threat of an embarrassing public failure may keep you working on your project. Unwillingness to tell people may be a sign that you don't really intend to change, or that you don't believe you can change.

When you are tempted—when you do hear the Sirens singing—*remind yourself of your goal* (Lazarus, 1971; Graziano, 1975). Grace took up jogging to lose weight and be healthier. She realized that she jogged along thinking "This is stupid—and so boring—I'm going to quit." These thoughts were self-defeating, so instead she reminded herself, "I really want to look

BOOTH

"I'll run through it again. First, the exhilaration of a work completed, followed by the excitement of approaching pub date. Reviews pouring in from everywhere while the bidding for the paperback rights soars to insane figures. An appearance on Merv Griffin or Dick Cavett, sandwiched in between like Engelbert Humperdinck and Juliet Prowse. Finally, a flood of letters from people to whom your name, yesterday unknown, now has the shimmer of national renown. Hit those keys!"

Drawing by Booth; ©1972 The New Yorker Magazine, Inc.

better and be healthier, and the best way is to jog. It's worth it. I won't quit." John wanted to improve his grade-point average so he could have a better chance of getting a good job after college. But at times the temptation to do some other activity was great—for example, when his friends asked him to play basketball in the afternoon. When that happened, he reminded himself "No, I really *do* want to improve my grades, and that means I have to study now." Making statements about long-term goals can help you resist many momentary temptations. "As much as I would like to eat this chocolate cake, it will blow my diet for the whole day, and I really want to lose weight." "It would be a relief to tell him to go to hell, but I really do want to learn to deal with people in a friendlier way." "I'd like to give in and watch TV, but I watch too much TV, and I do want to cut down." "I'm tired, and it would be easy to say 'No, I don't want to make love tonight,' but I really do want to be more loving."

Prepare a written list of self-reminders you can use when temptation strikes. Include in your self-reminders all the advantages of reaching your goal: "I'll feel so great when I have caught up with my homework—free as a bird!" "I'm going to look terrific when I've lost ten pounds—slim and sexy!" "I'm going to enjoy having new friends, so it's worth overcoming my shyness and going to the party."

You can see that this kind of reminder works only if you really do care about reaching your goal. You will be tempted to think "Well, just this one time. . ." But life can become a string of just-this-one-times, and before you know it years have gone by without your being a step closer to your goal. Lots of smokers go to their (early) graves thinking "Someday I'm going to give up cigarettes." Prepare a special reminder for the just-this-one-time situation: "I'm always telling myself 'Just this one time.' But I really do want to . . . (reach that goal)."

Ask other people to remind you. Darrell has been trying to cut down on his drinking. Tonight he and his wife, Tina, are going to a party. Darrell says to Tina, "Do me a favor. I'm going to be tempted to drink too much tonight, and you know I want to stop that. So if you see me taking a second drink, would you please remind me that I really want to cut down?" Research by Richard Passman (1977) suggests that you can increase your chances of success if you prearrange with another person to remind you when you are faced with temptation. Groups such as Weight Watchers and Alcoholics Anonymous use this technique (Stuart, 1977).

You are not asking the other person to punish you. Darrell doesn't want Tina to tell him he's a lush and a bum because he has taken a second drink. He wants her to remind him of his *own* resolve not to drink too much. If the others misinterpret the task and begin to inflict punishment on you, remind them that you're asking for a *reminder of your own goal,* nothing more. At the same time, you need to beware of the tendency to punish the person who does the reminding: "I know it's my second drink! I'm not stupid!"

Sometimes people work out a code in order to avoid an embarrassing interaction. One of our students reported that she and her husband had agreed that he tended to put her down in conversations with others, and he agreed to stop. He still did it out of habit, though, and both agreed she should remind him when she felt he was doing it. But they soon discovered she couldn't say "You're putting me down" in front of others, as they both found that embarrassing. Now when she feels he's putting her down, she touches the corner of her mouth, and he gets the message but others do not.

Set Goals and Make Plans to Reach Them

One increases commitment by setting goals for a self-modification project and then planning how to reach the goals. For example, Leonard's goal was to have more friends, so he made plans to observe how popular people acted around their friends in order to learn what he could do in social situations. Sometimes we give ourselves commands, things to do, in order to reach our goal. Patricia's goal was to be more assertive with her lover. She gave herself instructions about how to act in a particular situation: "When Rick touches my body when I'm not expecting it, I'll say to him 'Rick, please don't do that when I don't know it's coming. It's not sexy, it just startles me, and I don't enjoy it at all.' "

Patricia's long-term goal was to place her relationship with Rick on a more egalitarian basis, which would include issues such as who did chores, who made decisions, who would be responsible for child care, and so on. But she had started with one subgoal, that of being more assertive in issues relating to their love life. Often we break long-term goals into subgoals and work on one subgoal at a time. People realize that specific goals—"I'm going to study at least 15 hours per week"—are better than vague goals—"I'm going to study more." However, goals can be *too* specific. When Carrie says "I'm going to study Friday night from 6:30 to 8:30," she runs a risk: if that specific goal is not met, she may stop trying self-control, assuming that she is not capable of it. When Fred says "I will never eat chocolate cake again" and then backslides, he may draw the faulty conclusion that self-modification is not possible.

Short-range goals are more motivating than long-range goals. "I am going to study from 6:30 to 8:30 tonight" is more motivating than "I'm going to study on Tuesday of next week." But again, overemphasis on short-range goals can lead to a failed self-modification project. If you tell yourself you're going to study tonight at precisely a certain hour and then you don't do it, you may conclude that you are not capable of changing your study habits and stop the project altogether.

What you are really interested in is your long-range goal—to have better grades, more friends, less anxiety and depression. Setting intermediate goals with moderate degrees of specificity may be the best way to move toward your final goal (Kirschenbaum, Humphrey, & Malett, 1981). Your task is to keep moving—to continue in spite of the inevitable failures in reaching short-range goals. This will mean flexibility in short-term and intermediate goals. Keep the whole war in mind, and don't surrender because you lose a battle.

The general points are these: you need subgoals, and you need plans for how to reach them. In order to run a marathon, you must first learn how to run the first mile, and you must provide yourself with plans on how to do it. Some people fail at self-modification because they give up in disappointment when their goal is not quickly reached. Subgoals carry one along until the final goal is reached. A subgoal such as "I'm going to learn how to be a better listener" allows one to move toward the final goal of "having more friends" and can be reached sooner.

Too much emphasis on the here-and-now leads to discouragement, because you won't always reach your subgoals on time. One week you might not lose weight at all; one day you will eat a piece of chocolate cake. Intermediate-range goals and intermediate specificity of plans are often the best. These allow flexibility and encourage you to keep making the decision that your long-range goal is worthwhile. If your goal is to study so many hours per day, adjust to changes in certain days so that the average stays at or near your subgoal, even though individual days may not.

In order to maintain this kind of control over goal setting and goal seeking, you need correct information about your progress (see Chapter Three).

Escape Clauses (Good and Bad)

At the beginning of self-change projects, people may be vague about their intentions. "No more getting drunk (or stoned)!" Their real intentions, however, may include an unstated escape clause—"except at parties, when I really feel like it."

Some goals allow more escape than others. For example, you can increase your studying and still allow plenty of time for leisure. You can plan your time carefully and also include free, unscheduled periods. You can lose weight and still enjoy nice food. The danger with all escape clauses is that they may be so generous as to destroy the effects of a plan. On the other hand, the danger of not including *any* escape clause is that a plan may become hopelessly rigid and downright aversive.

Don reported that he had begun a time-management plan. He liked the sound of it—"time management"—because it made him think of efficiency and self-respect, as well as a change in his self-perception of laziness, drifting, and underachievement. He had always been more intelligent than his grades suggested, but during high school he hadn't needed to study and had never developed discipline in his daily routines. Time management offered him a vision of regular, efficient days, controlled energy, and a brighter future. The plan lasted eight days before he scrapped it. "I can't live like that. I'll do some other project, but that schedule stuff is crazy." He was right. The schedule was awful. He had blocked out every waking moment, from brushing his teeth in the morning to brushing his teeth at night. He waited at the bus stop 10 minutes, took 30 minutes for lunch, watched Monday night football and the 6 P.M. daily news on television. He scheduled the times he spent talking with his girlfriend on the telephone. Every moment was rigidly dictated by his time-management schedule.

We pointed out to Don that he hadn't included his favorite activity—being unscheduled. After years of doing whatever came up at the moment, it seemed likely that he really enjoyed a relaxed, casual approach to his days. He could have scheduled some unscheduled time—blocks in his schedule labeled FREE—during which he could do anything he wanted—including nothing.

Changing oneself is effortful, and it feels nice to have times when you don't have to work so hard. Escape clauses are those times. If you can bring these under your own explicit control, you are developing control.

Make escape clauses explicit, and set limits for the behaviors you want to control. A plan should clearly state all intended escapes, whether or not they are wise. If you really intend to overeat every Sunday when you are with your parents, say so. If this escape clause causes havoc with your diet, you can then make an intelligent choice as to which is more important—Mom's cake or faster weight loss. An unexamined escape clause may ultimately destroy your plan altogether.

Here is an example of a good, clear statement written by a young woman who had a tendency toward frivolous, impulsive spending. It has a reasonable escape clause built in.

Goal: Sticking to the budget	
Included	*Not included*
1. Make a new budget every month.	Don't have to write down what
2. Write down every expenditure in notebook. Don't forget the drugstore.	I spend out of the $20 a month that I put in my bag's zipper pocket. *Need some fun!*
3. Transfer expenditures from notebook to ledger, and add everything up. It's no good if I don't add them up. See how it matches the budget. *Every month!* On the 1st.	

There are, of course, certain problems for which it is usually better to eliminate escape clauses—drinking too much, smoking, and other addictions. Some people are successful in decreasing their smoking or drinking, but many find that total abstinence is the only way to avoid relapsing into overuse. In these cases, assume that you are going to have to quit altogether. In the process of quitting, you probably will experience lapses—reappearances of the old, automatic behavior. But the goal of total abstinence can eventually be achieved. These issues are discussed in detail in Chapter Ten.

The Self-Contract

As you build commitment to your goal for change, write out each element of your plan as a **self-contract**. The first paragraph of the contract is a statement of your intention. You will be able to add more details to your self-contract by the end of each chapter, from Chapters Three through Eight. For now, write your goal and intentions as clearly as possible. Then add, "I am willing to change my behaviors as necessary to reach the goal I have chosen and will carry out the steps suggested in the text. Specifically, I am willing to do the work suggested in this chapter and in Chapter Three." Then sign your name.

Does this really help? Griffin and Watson (1978) carried out an experiment in self-contracts in a college course in which the students had to take a large number of tests. Experience had shown that as the semester progressed, a larger number of the students were not taking the quizzes or were taking them unprepared. The researchers had half the students, randomly selected, write a self-contract in which they promised themselves that they would prepare for the tests and take them. The other half had no self-contract. Those students who made the self-contract took a larger proportion of the tests and were, in fact, better prepared. Similar results were obtained in an experiment on learning better study skills (Seidner, 1973, reported in Kanfer, 1977). By itself, a self-contract won't keep you from temptation, but it is one more effective technique to use in building your commitment to do the work of self-change.

CHAPTER SUMMARY

Specifying Behaviors-in-Situations

You need well-defined objectives that are specified in terms of particular behaviors in particular situations. The aim is to be able to complete this sentence:

My goal is to change _____ when _____ .
                  (thought, action, feeling)   (situation)

To specify behaviors-in-situations, try these tactics:

1. Make a list of concrete examples.
2. List the details of your problem.
3. Become an observer of yourself.

Even if your goal is to eliminate some unwanted action,

4. Always try to increase some desirable behavior.

If you aren't sure what to do,

5. Specify the chain of events that will produce your goal.
6. Observe other people who do well what you are trying to learn to do.
7. Think of alternative solutions.

And even if your goal is not some behavior,

8. Reaching it will require changing certain behaviors.

With complex problems, you are likely to move through a series of approximations to your goal as your self-understanding deepens. Start by making self-observations and specifying your goal clearly.

Overcoming Obstacles: Why You Might Self-Sabotage

Reasons for not carrying out a self-modification plan are that you may be hoping for a miracle, may not want to change, or may be of two minds about changing.

You should expect that you will make mistakes, sometimes relapsing into old, unwanted acts.

You may not believe that you are capable of performing the acts you need to perform in order to change. This is a type of self-efficacy belief, and it is specific to behaviors in particular situations. We act in accord with our beliefs, so if we believe we cannot change, we don't try. It is, however, possible to change your self-efficacy beliefs.

To increase self-efficacy beliefs, pick a project that will allow you to say yes to the questions on page 38. Discriminate between your past performance and your present project. Keep good records. Pay attention to your successes. Identify subgoals that have a good chance of attainment. And make a list of the specific kinds of situations in which you expect to have difficulty carrying out the necessary behaviors. Then use this list to guide your early experiences.

Building Commitment

Commitment is not something you *have*, it is something you *do*.

The relative strengths of the advantages and disadvantages of changing will vary from time to time. Plan for temptation—for times when it will seem better not to change than to do so.

What can you do to be prepared? Avoid situations in which you know you will be tempted. Minimize the tempting quality of the situation. When you are being tempted, distract yourself. Invest a lot in the project as early as possible. When tempted, remind yourself of your goal. Prepare a list of self-reminders to use when you are tempted. Ask other people to remind you, but be sure you are not punished, and that you do not punish them. Make a public commitment that you are going to change.

Work out subgoals, and make plans for how to reach them. If your ultimate goal is a long way off, aim to reach subgoals. Relatively specific plans on how to reach a goal are better than vague plans. But your subgoals should not be too short-range, and your plans should not be overly specific. Intermediate goals with moderate degrees of specificity of behavior to be performed may be best, because they allow some flexibility and do not discourage you if you fail on just one occasion.

Decide whether or not escape clauses should be included in your plans. If you do build escape clauses into your self-change plans, make them explicit.

Write a self-contract detailing the work you have to do in order to achieve self-change, and sign it if you intend to do the work.

YOUR OWN SELF-DIRECTION PROJECT: STEP TWO

Before going on to Chapter Three, do the exercises suggested here for specifying the problem and building commitment.

Part One: Specifying the Goal

Specify your goal as some behavior-in-a-situation that you wish to either decrease or increase. Even if you want to decrease some undesirable behavior, you should be able to state as your goal an *increase* of some other behavior that is incompatible with the undesired one. If at this point you cannot state your problem as a behavior-in-a-situation, go through each of the procedures in this chapter, step by step, for your chosen goal.

My goal is to increase _____ when _____ .
                                  (behavior)   (situation)

Part Two: Overcoming Obstacles

Make plans for what to do when you slip back into your old, unwanted behaviors. What will you do to be sure you don't quit your self-modification efforts?

Answer the questions on page 38 about your self-efficacy beliefs. Make a list of the situations in which you expect to have difficulty performing the desired actions, and rank the actions according to difficulty.

Make a list of the pros and cons of changing. What will you gain? What will you lose? What are the short-range and the long-range pros and cons of changing?

Part Three: Building Commitment

What are the situations in which the short-term advantages will take on great strength, momentarily outweighing the long-term advantages of changing? Make plans for how to deal with these tempting situations.

Answer these questions: How can I avoid tempting situations? How can I get as much invested in the project as early as possible? How can I minimize the temptation, or distract myself from it? To whom will I make the public commitment that I am going to change? List these people.

Make a list of reminders to give yourself when you are tempted. Also make a list of the people you are going to ask to remind you.

Establish subgoals leading to your final goal, and make plans for reaching them. Make a list of the subgoals.

Write down your escape clauses.

Now write a self-contract. First specify your goal, and then include this statement: "I am willing to change my behaviors as necessary to reach the goal I have chosen and will carry out the steps suggested in the text." Sign the contract.

This series of acts doesn't mean that you are permanently committed to your first goal. You may decide to change as you progress. The point of this self-promise is that you start with a goal that is important enough for you to actually perform the steps in self-modification.

When you have completed all three parts of Step Two, go on to Chapter Three.

TIPS FOR TYPICAL TOPICS

Most chapters end with a section called "Tips for Typical Topics," in which we point out how you can apply the ideas discussed in the chapter to the most common kinds of self-modification projects. Here is a list of common topics in our classes in self-modification:

anxieties
assertion
depression
family, friends, lovers, and coworkers
overeating
smoking, drinking, and drug use
studying and time management
the other sex

For each topic, the Tips section will call specific things to your attention, but it cannot be substituted for reading and thinking about the ideas offered in the whole chapter. The specific ideas should be integrated into your plan for self-change.

At the end of the book is a Topic Index, which lists all discussions of each topic throughout the book. For example, everything said about assertion is listed together for ready reference. Thus, you can check the Topic Index and read all the information about your particular topic for self-modification now, if you like.

CHAPTER THREE

Self-Knowledge: Observation and Recording

OUTLINE

- Structured Diaries
- Recording Frequency and Duration
- Rating Scales
- The Reactive Effects of Self-Observation
- Dealing with Problems in Getting Records
- Planning for Change
- Chapter Summary
- Your Own Self-Direction Project: Step Three
- Tips for Typical Topics

LEARNING OBJECTIVES

Structured Diaries

1. What do you record in a structured diary?
   a. What can you record under Antecedents?
   b. What can you record under Behaviors?
   c. What can you record under Consequences?
2. What is the point of a structured diary?

Recording Frequency and Duration

3. Give an example of recording the amount of time you spend doing something, and the number of times you do it.
4. Why is it important to record positive events as well as negative ones?
5. What are the four rules of self-observation?

Rating Scales

6. Give an example of a rating scale. In what situations are they most useful?

The Reactive Effects of Self-Observation

7. What does it mean to say that self-observation is reactive?
8. How can you use this reactivity to your advantage?

Dealing With Problems in Getting Records

9. What is negative practice, and in what kind of situation is it most useful?
10. How do you record behaviors you perform absentmindedly? How do you record behaviors that occur while many other things are going on?

Planning for Change

11. What is the baseline period?
12. For how long should you record in the baseline period?
13. What is reliability? What can you do to increase it?
14. Should you ever omit the baseline period?

Self-knowledge is the key to self-modification. Your actions—behaviors, thoughts, and feelings—are embedded in situations, and each of these elements must be carefully observed. Self-observation is the first step on the road to self-directed behavior—and it is the step most often omitted in our daily lives. Most of us assume that we understand ourselves, and we rarely feel that we need to employ any systematic self-observation techniques. But real surprises may be in store for the person who begins careful self-observation. Genuine discoveries are made.

Casual opinions about ourselves are often inaccurate (Nisbett & Ross, 1980). A group of people who wanted to lose weight were asked by an experimenter how much they ate. Many assured themselves and the researcher that they "really didn't eat very much." Then they were asked to remember and write down everything they had eaten in the preceding two days. Their lists were checked, and it appeared that the people were *not* overeating. The researcher then put them all on a diet consisting of the foods they had reported eating. Every one of them began to lose weight (Stunkard, 1958).

In order to change yourself, you have to know what you're doing. The purpose of this chapter is to present a set of techniques for gaining knowledge about your behaviors, thoughts, and feelings, and about their relationships to specific situations.

STRUCTURED DIARIES

In Chapters One and Two, you formulated your goals and values in terms of specific acts performed in specific situations. Before you begin to change things, you need to understand your current performance and discover the situations that are affecting your target behaviors. Then you can take steps to bring them under control. To achieve the first goal—better self-understanding—many people use a structured diary.

A **structured diary** is a record you keep of your behaviors and also of the antecedents and consequences of those behaviors. This is not the kind of diary in which you write down random thoughts or musings about the day. The diary entries are made in connection with your goal for change. Keeping this kind of diary will allow you to see what kinds of situations have an effect on your target behavior. Think of your behavior as embedded in a situation, with the antecedents before the behavior and the consequences after it. Don't wait until the end of the day to write your entries. As soon as you realize that a relevant behavior has occurred, note the behavior, as well as what happened before and after it.

This diagram gives you an idea of how to go about keeping your diary and the kinds of questions you must answer in writing your entries (Hay & Hay, 1975; Thoresen, 1975).

Antecedents (A)	Behaviors (B)	Consequences (C)
When did it happen? Whom were you with? What were you doing? Where were you? What were you saying to yourself?	Actions, thoughts, feelings.	What happened as a result? pleasant or unpleasant?

Under *Behaviors*, list the action, thought, or feeling that is your special focus—because it is your current problem, or because it is an example of the eventual goal. Then enter the antecedents that preceded it and the consequences that followed. Remember that thoughts and feelings, as well as overt events, may be entered in any of the columns, depending on their relationship to the problem event.

Les kept a record of the antecedents and consequences of biting his nails. Here are some entries from his diary:

Antecedents (A)	Behaviors (B)	Consequences (C)
Waiting for the bus	Nail biting	Embarrassed that others might see
Sitting in class listening	Nail biting	Same
Lying in bed thinking	Nail biting	Just wish I would quit
Reading	Nail biting	Same
Stressed	Nail biting	Gives me something to do

He wrote, "I knew I bit my nails when I was stressed, but I was surprised to find that I did it in other situations, too. It happens when my mind is occupied but my fingers are not." Knowing this, Les is in a position to make a plan to eliminate nail biting in those specific situations.

Tim began keeping a record of his sulking behavior. Here are two entries from his diary:

Antecedents (A)	Behaviors (B)	Consequences (C)
Sunday morning Was in a bad mood.	Sulking (not talking, feeling sorry for myself).	Judy [his wife] paid a lot of attention to me.
Tuesday afternoon Feeling frustrated about my work.	Sulking.	Judy gave me a backrub and we talked.

The diary showed the same kind of pattern for several days. Notice that Tim's sulking gets him love and attention from his wife. What effect might that have?

Evelyn, a young college student, felt that she needed to be more assertive, but she wasn't sure when and in what situations. She recorded in her diary the times when she thought she *could* have been assertive but was not, and the times when she *was* assertive.

Antecedents (A)	Behaviors (B)	Consequences (C)
11:30 P.M. I am about to fall asleep. Ed telephones. He starts to ramble.	I'm angry, it's late, and he is boring, but I don't say anything.	He talks about 20 minutes.
Noon the next day. Walking to work, I see Ed, try to avoid talking to him. He calls me. I keep on going. He grabs my arm. He asks me to lunch.	I look away, say "I don't know . . . (pause) okay."	We have lunch. He asks me out again.
Polly wants me to see a movie I swore I would not see. She complains that I haven't been to a movie with her in a long time.	I say, "I really shouldn't. I need to get some rest." But I give in and go.	The movie was gross.
1:00 P.M. Went to meet Jill. We were supposed to go jogging, but she wants to do it later in the day.	I tell her I can't go later. I have to work.	
6 P.M. My sister comes over to ask me to babysit.	I tell her I can't. I have other plans. A bunch of us are going out.	

Several days of this kind of observation revealed a pattern: When other people asked Evelyn to go places with them and she had nothing else specifically scheduled, she usually went, even if she didn't want to. If they asked but she had something specifically scheduled, she didn't. "But," she wrote, "why should I have to have something scheduled before I feel I can say no? Isn't the need to go to sleep enough? I need to be able to refuse even when I have no specific activity planned but just don't want to do it. Something better would have come up—like getting enough rest."

The Mechanics of Diary Making

As soon as you realize that you have performed some undesired target behavior or failed to perform some desired one, make an entry in your structured diary. Describe the physical setting, the social situation, your thoughts, and the behavior of other people. Journalism students learn that to write a good story they must answer five questions: *Who? What? Where? When? Why?* In order to keep a good structured diary, you must answer these same questions.

Be sure to make the diary entries as soon as the target behavior occurs or fails to occur. Don't wait. It's easy to overlook important details when you're reconstructing a past event. For example, if Tim had waited until evening to write down what happened when he sulked, he might not have remembered that his wife was acting especially attentive after he began sulking.

Here is a selection from the structured diary of Mike, a father whose goal was to stop spanking his children and start using nonphysical punishment. As soon as he had disciplined the children, he made an entry in his diary:

Antecedents (A)	Behaviors (B)	Consequences (C)
April 3. Sat. morning at breakfast. Kids bickered a lot.	I spanked both of them.	Made them even more cross.
April 6. Came home from work feeling tired. My boy talked back to me.	Started to spank him but stopped. Grounded him for an hour instead.	Felt pretty good about that. Was glad I didn't hit him. He calmed down while he was grounded.
April 10. Had an argument with Dora [his wife]. Then in the car the kids started quarreling.	Spanked them— actually, slapped them.	It spoiled our whole outing. I felt guilty. They felt rotten.

Mike is likely to see from his diary that he feels better when he doesn't spank. He may also note that it's not simply the behavior of the children that determines whether he spanks them or not. An argument with his wife or a hard day at work influences his behavior, too.

Recording Thoughts and Feelings

People's self-modification projects often involve changing their actions (or nonactions). But people also select as their targets for change their thoughts and feelings. Sarah reported, "I often put myself down in my thoughts. I'll do something rather well, and then I hear myself saying in my mind 'Pretty good for a basically mediocre person.' This makes me feel bad and seems unnecessary." So she began to record these self-putdowns, together with the situations that preceded and followed them. A clear pattern emerged: small successes were followed by negative thoughts and then came a feeling of dissatisfaction.

Thoughts can also precede—be the antecedent of—some problem behavior. For example, a shy man thinks "She's not going to like me" and makes a fumbling approach to a potential new friend. The softball player visualizes striking out and, as a result, clutches up. Martha wants to speak up in class but fantasizes everyone snickering at her question—and so she remains silent.

When you keep a structured diary, the relationship between your thoughts and problem behavior becomes clear. Try recording your thoughts in the B column, like this:

A	B	C
	Told myself I was really only average at best.	

and then look for the antecedents and consequences of this target behavior.

Or you may record your thoughts in the A column as antecedents, like this:

A	B	C
Saw an attractive woman and said to myself "Nobody that attractive is ever going to like me."	Didn't introduce myself.	Felt disgusted with myself.

Thoughts can be visual as well as verbal. Many people have short, visual fantasies, like film clips projected in their imaginations. For example:

A	B	C
Saw this attractive woman, then had a fantasy that I smiled at her but she completely ignored me.	Didn't introduce myself.	Felt disgusted.

Professor Bagwell in the history department had begun writing children's history books instead of research articles. He said that often while writing he had the following fantasy: A distinguished historian and senior professor in his department would come into his office, look at the manuscript on his desk, and remark, "*Children's stories? You're out of your mind!*" This fantasy, with many variations, was often played out in our friend's imagination. The antecedent to this fantasy was the fact that Professor Bagwell was working on children's books. The consequences were that he became nervous and stopped writing. He realized that the fantasy was probably a reflection of his ambivalence about writing children's history books, because sometimes he felt he should have been doing scholarly work instead. Keeping a record of the fantasies allowed him to face up to his ambivalence and ask himself if he really believed that children's history books were less valuable than more traditional research articles.

Record your thoughts or fantasies as soon as they occur. If you delay in making entries in your structured diary it is difficult to remember all the important details—and you will need to have those details in order to see what effect the thoughts and fantasies have on your actions and feelings.

What the Diary Tells You

People working on indulgent behaviors—such as overeating, drinking, or smoking—find that many situations that they expect to be unrelated to the problem are in fact closely connected to it. For example, a smoker who kept a structured diary centered around the question "Why do I light a cigarette?" found that all of the following situations stimulated smoking: any social gathering; a cup of coffee; being bored, angry, depressed, or excited; certain times of day; and after every meal.

Overeaters find that they eat in response to particular situations rather than in response to an internal feeling of hunger. If you don't believe that a situation can control your behavior, watch people who are trying to stop smoking when they are in certain settings—for example, during a morning coffee break when others are smoking.

The point of keeping a structured diary is to find out which situations are affecting your behavior. Discovering the pattern of your behavior may take time and patience, and you may need to make many entries. For some people, this may become a long-term project. We suggest that overeaters begin to keep track of all the food they eat and do so for several months. In this way, they can learn the various situations that seem to cue their eating. Here are excerpts from the eating records of Hal:

A	B	C
Invited to Bill's for supper. Thought "Great, all that free food."	Had second helpings of everything.	Tasted so good! But I felt stuffed, gained two pounds.
Three weeks later: Thanksgiving at the family's. Time for stuffing.	Ate immense amounts of turkey, dressing, cranberry sauce, potatoes, pie, coffee.	Literally got sick, but gained three pounds.
Office party at Christmas.	Ate all afternoon.	Stuffed again. Gained one pound.

Most of the time Hal ate only slightly too much, but at certain times—when invited out, at festive occasions—he grossly overate, and each time put on weight that he never lost. Record keeping over several months revealed this pattern.

The process of long-term diary keeping like this can be most helpful in showing you what it is that you need to change. The analysis may shift your focus of interest from the original behavior of concern to some feature that seems to influence it. Here is an example of this process.

An elementary school teacher, Jill, observed her patterns of depressed feelings. She wrote, "I was in my yard gardening, which usually makes me feel very happy. But I began to feel uncomfortable and stopped to think why. It felt like depression, but there was nothing to be depressed about. So I wondered about what I had been thinking just before I felt depressed. And then I remembered that, a minute before, I had imagined this scene: I'm in my classroom, at the beginning of next year, and I'm teaching fifth grade (just as I will be) instead of my usual third. The class is a shambles. The kids aren't understanding anything, they are misbehaving, and I can hear the principal coming down the hallway. She comes in the door, stands, and glowers at me. . . .

"I imagine things like this often. I even have a name for them—my incompetence fantasies. And I believe they do depress me. So I'm going to record instances of fantasies about incompetence, find out what sets them off, and try to get rid of them." She then moved "incompetence fantasies" to the center column of her diary and recorded antecedents and consequences of her fantasies.

In our earlier example, Sarah, the young woman who recorded self-putdowns, said that at first she didn't think of them as putdowns. "I just felt I was being properly modest or was being realistic in my self-evaluations. But after a while I saw that what I was really doing was putting myself down. It went beyond modesty or reality, and it was making me unhappy." You learn to make this kind of differentiation by keeping records of your thoughts or behaviors and thinking about the patterns that emerge.

RECORDING FREQUENCY AND DURATION

Some psychologists suggest that self-direction is a process of "personal science" (Mahoney, 1974). Keeping that definition in mind, you can see that the structured diary is a source of promising hypotheses about your behavior. The next step in that process of personal science is to collect systematic observations in order to prove or disprove your hypotheses. The two most common forms of records are for *frequency* and *duration*.

Simple Counting

The easiest kind of record keeping is a simple count of how often you do something. Allan wanted to know how often he practiced his music, so he kept a chart in the same drawer where he kept his recorder and music sheet. The sheet looked like this:

	Recorder playing			
	Week 1	Week 2	Week 3	Week 4
Monday	✓	✓	✓	
Tuesday				
Wednesday	✓		✓	
Thursday		✓	✓	
Friday	✓	✓	✓	
Saturday				
Sunday				

Whenever Allan took out his recorder to practice, he made a mark on the sheet. He could quickly see how many times a week he practiced and ask himself whether it was enough. Also, if he later decided that he wanted to increase his practicing, he knew exactly the level he was starting from. But the chart yields even more pieces of information. Just by glancing at it, Allan would notice that he never seemed to practice on Tuesdays, Saturdays, or Sundays. This observation would lead him to ask "Why don't I practice on those three days?" Then he could determine what it was that interfered with his practicing on those days.

Patrick kept a record of the times that he put down his friends in conversation, saying something negative to them. This is his record:

Date	Number of putdowns
October 8	ℍ ℍ ℍ
October 9	ℍ ℍ III
October 10	ℍ II
October 11	ℍ ℍ
October 12	ℍ I
October 13	IIII
October 14	IIII

Maureen decided to record the number of minutes she actually spent studying and the number of minutes she was "ready to study." The latter category included long sessions deciding which course to study for, and sitting at her desk talking to her roommate, thinking about other things, or reading a novel that was not assigned. Her chart looked like this:

	Mon	Tues	Wed	Thurs	Fri
Ready to study	45	30	35	50	0
Actually studying	15	10	20	30	0

Maintaining a strict count like this helps you understand the difference between engaging in the actual target behavior and engaging in other, related behaviors. You might come to realize, as in this example, that you spend a large amount of time doing things that are not your target behavior. Being "ready to study" is not studying. By keeping a strict count of the amount of time you actually engage in the target behavior, you can learn what you are doing instead of the desired behavior and how that interferes with the desired behavior.

Maureen recorded the *duration* of her behavior. This is desirable whenever length of time is an issue. Allan might have recorded not only how many times a week he practiced, and when, but also how long he practiced each time. There are other behaviors, of course, for which a simple count of the frequency is appropriate—the number of putdowns, for example, or cigarettes smoked.

Debbie wanted to increase her vocabulary. When she encountered a word she didn't know, she wrote it down in her notebook. Later she looked up its meaning in the dictionary. Inside the dictionary she kept a chart like this:

Number of words looked up					
Mon	√	Mon	√	Mon	√√
Tues	√√	Tues	___	Tues	√
Wed	√	Wed	___	Wed	___
Thurs	√√√	Thurs	√√	Thurs	√
Fri	√	Fri	√	Fri	√√√

Steven Richards (in press) of the University of Missouri has worked out model recording forms for people who want to keep track of behaviors connected with getting a job and with studying. These are shown in Boxes 3-1 and 3-2.

One purpose of the information stored in Box 3-1 is to keep the job seeker trying. The record lists concrete goals and includes behaviors the person wants to increase, such as mailing out résumés each week, and behaviors to be decreased, such as making mistakes in interviews. Similarly, the information collected in Box 3-2 allows students to see how they are spending their study time.

If you keep a record of the number of instances of a certain behavior in each of various situations, use code marks for the situations. For example, Nancy wanted to quit smoking, and she counted the cigarettes she smoked each day. She also noted the situations in which her smoking occurred, using this coding system:

E   (for eating) during or after a meal
S   when nervous in a social situation
D   when driving her car
O   other times

On the first day, Nancy's 3 x 5 card looked like this:

Smoking record—Monday, December 7		
Morning	*Afternoon*	*Evening*
E E D O S S S E	O S S D S E E E	E O

Her records for several days were very consistent, and she was able to plan a realistic antismoking program that concentrated on eating and social situations.

People undertaking self-change projects count many different behaviors. For example:

An office worker records the number of self-critical thoughts she has when dealing with rejection by others.

A woman counts the number of hours per day that she watches TV.

A father counts how much time he spends with his children.

A writer makes a note of the exact time she begins her daily writing, carefully notes each time she takes a break, and at the end of her scheduled writing period marks down the total time spent writing.

A jogger keeps track of how many miles he runs each week. Another jogger keeps track of the number of hours she runs per week. A third records the number of times he runs each week.

A woman working on her budget keeps track of all her daily purchases.

A man records all instances of impulse buying.

An overweight man counts daily instances of "eating errors," when he eats something he knows he shouldn't.

A dieter records all the food eaten each day.

A knuckle cracker counts the number of cracks per day.

BOX 3-1

SAMPLE SELF-MONITORING FORM FOR A JOB SEEKER

Name: _____ Date of first Monday: _____

Goals: 10 résumés and cover letters mailed per week; 10 follow-up phone calls per week; 2 interviews per week; 2 postinterview thank-you notes and phone calls per week; fewer mistakes per interview each week; 1 job offer per month (.25 per week).

Monday Date	Résumés	Calls	Interviews	Notes	Mistakes	Offers
10/11/83	7	5	0	0	0	0
10/18/83	8	6	1	1	5	0
10/25/83	10	7	0	0	0	0
11/1/83	11	9	2	2	4	0
11/8/83	10	8	3	2	4	1
11/15/83	12	9	2	2	3	0
11/22/83	8	7	1	0	2	0
11/29/83	12	9	3	3	1	1
12/6/83	12	10	4	4	1	0
12/13/83	10	10	4	4	0	1*
Weekly average	10	8	2	1.8	2	.3

*This job offer was accepted.

From "Work and Study Problems," by C. S. Richards, in press, in M. Hersen and A. S. Bellack (Eds.), *Handbook of Clinical Behavior Therapy with Adults*, New York: Plenum Press. Reprinted by permission.

A skin scratcher records the number of hours she goes without scratching.

A student keeps track of the number of times per week that he says something nice to his parents.

Avoiding Discouragement

Don't just record instances of *unwanted* behavior. Whenever possible, record positive things as well. This allows you to see when you make progress and when you don't. For example, dieters should keep records of the times they avoid the temptation to eat too much, as well as the times they give in to temptation. A mother should record the times she avoids spanking her kids and thinks of some more positive response, as well as the times she hits them. If you stick to your diet for six days and then overeat, you should feel good about the six days even if you regret the seventh. Too often, dieters notice only the times when they fail to stick to their diet (Ferguson, 1975). Depressed people suffer a similar distortion of perception, failing to notice the pleasant events of life. As a result, they see their whole lives as disappointing. Recording positive events will help in this situation, too (Rehm, 1982). One of the current treatments for low self-esteem and depression is to teach clients to notice the good things that happen to them and not to focus on the bad things (Layden, 1982).

BOX 3-2

SAMPLE SELF-MONITORING FORM FOR STUDYING

Name: _____   Date of Monday: _____

Goal for total hours studied per week: ____32*____

Day	Hours studied in hardest course*	Hours studied in easiest course*	Hours studied in all courses*
Monday	2	0	3
Tuesday	0	1	4
Wednesday	1	0	3
Thursday	2	1	5
Friday	1	0	2
Saturday	3	0	4
Sunday	1	1	6
Total	10	3	27

*Does not include lectures.

From "Work and Study Problems," by C. S. Richards, in press, in M. Hersen and A. S. Bellack (Eds.), *Handbook of Clinical Behavior Therapy with Adults*, New York: Plenum Press. Reprinted by permission.

Self-recording can be discouraging, particularly when the information tells you that your progress is very slow. Dieters who weigh themselves too often experience these feelings (Mahoney, 1977). In the first two or three days of a diet, a person's weight may drop several pounds—a loss that offers plenty of encouragement to continue the diet. But after those first few days (when much of the weight loss is only water loss that will be replaced as soon as the dieter resumes normal eating), the amount of daily weight lost is small— often as little as one quarter of a pound. A bathroom scale won't even pick it up. Dieters who weigh every morning soon begin to feel that such small weight loss is hardly worth the sacrifice the diet requires. The solution is to weigh oneself less frequently, perhaps once a week, so that a real weight loss can be seen. On a daily basis, dieters need to record whether they actually follow the diet and how much food they eat.

Self-recording can also be discouraging if you record only the negative or unwanted things you do. A lengthy record of all the times you are depressed or have negative thoughts about yourself may lead you to think even more negatively about yourself. Keeping records of your successes, even if they are small compared to your final goal, will increase your confidence that you are making progress and enhance your feelings of self-efficacy—the belief that you are indeed capable of reaching your final goal.

Be Sure to Count

It is essential to record the behavior as soon as it occurs. Patrick, the student who put down his friends, carried a 3 x 5 card in his pocket. As soon as he had finished talking with a friend and the two of them had gone their separate ways, he stopped and entered checkmarks in the appropriate columns— *put down* and *did not put down*. If he had waited until the end of the day, he probably would have forgotten important details. When he succeeded in not insulting a friend, immediately recording that fact provided instant self-satisfaction.

You may find yourself thinking that you don't need to write something down. You're sure you'll remember how much time you spent doing the target behavior. But if you don't keep fairly strict written records, you'll end up not keeping any records at all. Don't wait until the end of the day and then try to remember how many times and for how long you engaged in the target behavior. At best, your count will not be accurate. As soon as the target behavior occurs, stop and record it (Epstein, Webster, & Miller, 1975; Epstein, Miller, & Webster, 1976).

Donald reported that whenever he was working successfully on his plan to stop using drugs, he faithfully kept a daily written record of how often he indulged. But then would come a big weekend—three parties in a row. Monday morning would dawn, and he knew that he had been high much of the weekend. To avoid the bad news, he didn't record on Monday. But not recording bad news can easily become a habit. Soon, keeping track of one's drug use stops altogether, and the old habit persists.

Many smokers report that they avoid keeping a record because they are disturbed when they realize how many cigarettes they smoke each day. Dieters hate to record overeating. Cases like these show us how critically important record keeping is to achieving the desired goal.

The recording device has to be portable and readily accessible. A smoker may keep a notecard inside the cigarette pack. Many people use a 3 x 5 card or some other piece of paper that will fit conveniently in a pocket, bag, or notebook.

Fit record keeping into the pattern of your usual habits. Devise your system so that it will remind you of itself. For example:

smoking—a card inside the cellophane wrapper;
too much TV watching—a chart beside the chair where you sit to watch;
going to bed too late—a chart beside the bed;
not studying—a record inside your notebook or at the place where you study;
eating too much—a card beside your place at the table;
between-meal snacks—a record sheet on the pantry or refrigerator door;
exercising—a chart by the closet where you keep your exercise gear;
socializing—a 3 x 5 card that is always in your bag or pocket.

Verna had a hard time dealing with one of her coworkers. She made a list of four things she wanted to remember to do when she was with him: listen to him without interrupting, ignore his slightly rude remarks, pause before replying to him, and stop trying to figure out his motives. She kept this list in her desk. When she was about to talk with the man, she would take the list out, glance over it, and then hold it while talking to him. Then, as soon as she finished talking, she would check off each item she had successfully performed.

In some cases, you can use a wrist counter (which is worn like a watch) or a golf counter. This helps when the target is something you do very often, such as some nervous or verbal habit. For example, Ed wanted to stop swearing and found that it happened about 200 times a day. Taking out a 3 x 5 card and marking it so often would have been tedious, so he used a golf counter. Use whatever sort of counter you find convenient. The easier it is to keep records, the more likely you are to keep them.

Anticipate recording problems you will have, and figure out ways to deal with them. One of our students wanted to keep track of certain thoughts he had while talking with other people. To make notes on a card while talking would have looked silly. On the other hand, he felt he would forget if he waited until the conversation ended. So, each time he had the thought he wanted to record, he moved a penny from his left to his right pocket. After he left the person, he would count the pennies in his right pocket to see how many times the thought had occurred in the course of the conversation. Then he recorded it on a note card.

A woman who wanted to increase the number of times she performed a particular behavior carried toothpicks in her purse and moved one into a special pocket of the purse after each occurrence. A cigarette smoker started out each day with a specific number of cigarettes (30) and counted how many he had left when he got home in the evening.

If you perform the behavior but discover that your counting device—a 3 x 5 card or whatever—is not there, improvise. For example, a knuckle cracker found a big leaf at the beach and tore a small hole in it each time he cracked his knuckles. Later he transferred this record to his regular chart. A smoker who left his scoring card at home kept the matches he used to light his cigarettes as a record of how many cigarettes he had smoked.

BOX 3-3

POOR RICHARD'S RECORDS

Benjamin Franklin—statesman, scientist, inventor, and author—knew the value of record keeping in changing one's behavior. He had in mind writing a book called *The Art of Virtue* on how to achieve goals such as not overeating or overdrinking ("temperance," to use his word), letting others talk, keeping things in order, meeting goals, avoiding waste, being clean, staying calm, and being industrious (Knapp & Shodahl, 1974). *The Art of Virtue* never did get written, but Franklin left records in his personal journal of his attempts at self-modification, using techniques of self-observation much like those in this book.

Franklin first made a list of the target behaviors, which he called *virtues*. He then kept records of his successes and failures for each of the targets. Here is a sample of one of his record sheets:

	Sun	Mon	Tues	Wed	Thurs	Fri	Sat
temperance							
letting others talk	x	x		x		x	
keeping things in order	xx	x	x		x	x	x
meeting goals			x			x	
avoiding waste		x		x			
being clean							
staying calm							
being industrious							

He worked on one set of behaviors at a time, writing an X each time he didn't meet his personal goals. Later he would move to another goal, then to another one, until he had reached all of them.

Was he successful? He says he was. "I was surprised to find myself so much fuller of faults than I had imagined, but I had the satisfaction of seeing them diminish."

Written Storage Records

When using 3 x 5 cards, wrist counters, or other devices for keeping records, you need to transfer the information to a more permanent storage record. This storage record may not be exactly the same as the daily (or occasional) record. A woman with the nervous habit of pulling off the skin on her feet and legs kept a single count like this:

Pulling off skin														
Day	1	2	3	4	5	6	7	8	9	10	11	12	13	14
Number of times per day	7	9	11	8	4	8	12	7	10	7	9	2	9	2

For her storage record, she made a graph that she posted on the wall of her room (see Chapter Nine).

Our smoker, Nancy, transferred her daily record (illustrated on page 63) to a storage record. Her record sheet for two weeks looked like this:

		M	T	W	T	F	S	S	M	T	W	T	F	S	S
E		7													
S		6														
D		2														
O		3														
Total		18														

A woman who wanted to be a professional writer kept a record of the number of hours she wrote each day and the number of pages she wrote. At the end of each week, she added up the daily totals and transferred this information to a permanent chart she kept posted on the wall next to her writing desk.

	Total hours writing per week	Number of pages written per week
Week 1	14	5
Week 2	17½	20
Week 3	17½	19
Week 4	15	22
Week 5	9½	9

From this record, she could see the relationship between how much she worked and how much she produced, and she could then examine why the relationship was low at certain times.

Sometimes you can combine your daily observations with the permanent record. For example, Allan kept his chart with his musical instrument. This way, the chart was always there when he needed it and could serve as both a daily record and a storage record. Record keeping and record storing must be adapted to each person's own behaviors and situations. If the various systems described here don't suit you, improvise one that does.

RATING SCALES

So far we have presented methods for recording the A-B-Cs of a situation and for recording the frequency or duration of an act. Another element of the target that you may need to record is the *intensity* of an event (Nelson, Hay, & Hay, 1975). The pain of a headache, the difficulty of falling asleep, feelings of depression or joy—these are aspects of events that neither frequency nor duration adequately describes. Each can be more or less intense, and it is the intensity itself that is important to your goal.

A rating scale can be used to measure intensity. One assigns each event a number according to a prearranged scale. For example, the goal of a young woman was to increase her feelings of happiness and make her depression less intense (Tharp, Watson, & Kaya, 1974). She invented a 9-point rating scale, in which the points had these meanings:

+4	superhappy
+3	happy
+2	good feeling
+1	some positive feeling
0	neutral
−1	some negative feeling
−2	bad feeling
−3	sad
−4	superdepressed

Her recording method included not only the rating of the feeling but also the situation in which the feeling occurred. She briefly described each unit of her day's activities and then evaluated the intensity of her feelings about it. Then she averaged each day's ratings and recorded the average on a graph. Here is a typical day's record:

talked to Jean	−2
in class	−1
took test	0
saw Dean	−2
had lunch with Jean and Judy	+1
talked to Bill	+3
went home on bus	−3
talked to Jean on phone	−3
studied	0

Rating scales are useful in recording emotions and feelings because intensity is the crucial issue. Fears, depression, sexual arousal, jealousy, pain, joy, happiness, self-satisfaction, love, and affection can all be recorded with rating scales. You can express your goals with regard to these emotions and feelings as increases or decreases on the scale.

When your goal is to change some emotional state, you won't go immediately from discomfort to total comfort. By rating your comfort, you will be able to see that you are making progress.

A young man was working on his feelings of jealousy toward his girlfriend. This is the rating scale he used to assess the degree of jealousy he felt in various situations:

1   no jealousy at all
2   slight jealousy and irritation
3   moderate jealousy and some real discomfort
4   strong jealousy and discomfort
5   overwhelming jealousy and discomfort

Using this system, he was able to see that he became particularly upset at parties, where his average rating approached 5.

How many points should your scale contain? Most of our students choose 5, 7, or 9. For example:

1   perfectly calm
2   a little tense
3   somewhat tense
4   very tense
5   panic

Too small a scale does not allow for the subtle differences you want to record. Too large a scale produces inaccurate records. Expand or contract your scale to allow for the distinctions that are important to your particular goal. For example, a man whose goal was to overcome nervousness about speaking in front of a group started with the scale above. After rating a few experiences, he noticed that he often wanted to assign a number in between two of the numbers on his original scale, so he expanded it to a 10-point scale. "In class giving a speech" was about 9; "having a speech assigned" was around 3; "preparing the speech" was 5; "waiting to give it" was 8.

Rating scales produce better self-understanding because they help put events into perspective. For example, the depressed woman whose rating scale we discussed above reported that after recording the intensity of her feelings for several weeks, she realized that "depression is a part of life" and that she had been overreacting to her depression. When she saw the large number of pleasant events that filled her routine days, she gained a new perspective on her life.

Don't let the use of rating scales lead you away from the behavioral goal of your self-change efforts. Although rating scales can tell you whether your emotions are shifting in the desired direction (do you feel more joy? are you less depressed?), actual behavioral changes are needed to achieve the goal. To have a complete picture of how your plan is working, try combining a rating scale with a count of observed behaviors.

For example, one of our students was trying to avoid depression by fighting off her tendency to dwell on thoughts that people didn't like her. To achieve this goal, she decided to replace her negative thoughts with memories of situations in which people had obviously liked her. She used a rating scale to keep track of her feelings, but also counted "the number of times each day that I successfully switch from thoughts that people don't like me to memories of times when people do like me."

THE REACTIVE EFFECTS OF SELF-OBSERVATION

When a behavior is being observed, it often changes. Think what it's like to have someone closely observe your behavior. When your track coach or dance teacher or lab instructor says "I'm going to watch you very carefully now," don't you perform in quite a different way than you do when no one is observing you? You feel self-conscious; you take greater care.

Perhaps the behavior will become less smooth or automatic. Or it may improve, just as an actor's performance can be enhanced by the presence of an audience. These effects are also produced when you are your own observer (Kazdin, 1974e). Behavior "reacts" to the observation, and the effect is known in psychology as **reactivity.**

Occasionally students will complain that they are unable to work out a plan. When asked why, they explain that their problem has gone away. "I started recording my baseline data regularly, but then I just quit the undesirable behavior I was counting." This, of course, is the happiest form of reactivity. And in self-modification, it is the most common. Undesirable behaviors tend to diminish, and desired behaviors tend to increase *because you are observing and recording them.*

Your values are the most important factor in reactivity. If you are recording some behavior about which you don't really care, your behavior won't be much affected (Fixen, Phillips, & Wolf, 1972; Ciminero, 1974). On the other hand, when a person cares about a behavior, self-recording often changes the behavior in the direction of one's values. This effect has been documented in a number of case studies and experimental investigations dealing with a wide variety of problems (Bornstein, Hamilton, & Bornstein, in press). Here is a partial list of the kinds of problems that have changed as a result of self-observation:

excessive drinking (Sobell & Sobell, 1973);
stuttering (LaCroix, 1973);
weight loss from counting calories (Romanczyk, 1974);
smoking, particularly if the smoker records amount of nicotine consumed (McFall, 1970; Abrams & Wilson, 1979);
teeth grinding (J. C. Rosen, 1981);
fear of closed spaces (Leitenberg, Agras, Thompson, & Wright, 1968);
fear of animals (Rutner, 1973);
fear of the open street (Emmelkamp, 1974);
speaking up in class (Komaki & Dore-Boyce, 1978);
attendance and performance at swim practice (McKenzie & Rushall, 1974);
work productivity (Zohn & Bornstein, 1980);
positive comments from a parent to a child (Bornstein & Hamilton, 1978);

academic performance (McLaughlin, Burgess, & Sackville-West, 1981); compulsive face picking (Paquin, 1982).

A second generation of research is now aimed at understanding the conditions under which change most often occurs. That observing one's own behavior often changes it is no longer in doubt. In fact, the effect is so reliable that clients may be assigned to observe themselves as a part of their therapy, a first step in changing problem behavior (Bornstein, Hamilton, & Bornstein, in press; Gross & Drabman, 1982). About 13 times per day, for an average of 15 minutes each, a client was bothered by obsessive thoughts about cancer of the breast or stomach. She was taught to keep track of several situations that led to the onset of these unwanted thoughts. After only one week, their frequency dropped to an average of 2 per day, and after a month they had disappeared altogether (Frederiksen, 1975). Simply recording the occurrences has also reduced the frequency of tics, such as squinting, arm jerking, and making odd noises with the nose (Thomas, Abrams, & Johnson, 1971; Billings, 1978).

Self-recording is not sufficient to change all behaviors, but we estimate that in more than 15% of self-change projects, the goal is achieved by the use of self-recording alone. However, if self-recording is the only thing you have done in your effort to change, stopping the recording may stop the improvement (Maletzky, 1974; Holman & Baer, 1979).

Using Reactivity to Your Advantage

The reactive effects of self-recording can be turned to advantage. A student reported: "For some time I felt guilty for not sharing kitchen chores with my wife. But I always seemed to have something else to do, and cooking and doing dishes were not exactly appealing, so I just continued to do nothing. Then I put a chart in the kitchen. Each time my wife cooked or cleaned up, she made an entry, and each time I cooked or cleaned up, I made an entry. It took only a week to get me moving. Now I check the chart each weekend to make sure I'm doing my share."

Another student wrote: "I enjoy reading, and for a long time I wished I did more of it. But I'd come home from work tired and mindlessly switch on the TV. Then I bought a little notebook and began to keep a list of all the books or articles I read. I got very interested in my growing list. I enjoyed finishing reading something and making an entry in my notebook. I'd get the list out and skim it to see how I was progressing. I'm sure I read more now than I did before, because keeping track of my reading is meaningful to me. It makes me feel good."

If you are a smoker, keep long-term records of how many cigarettes you smoke per day. If you are overweight, keep long-term records of your caloric intake. Reactivity alone will not be sufficient, but it will help.

Even though recording by itself is not enough, once you have changed, continued recording makes it easier to *maintain* the change. For example, a man who had to use a fairly complicated schedule of manipulating antecedents to problem drinking found that, once his drinking problem had lessened, he could keep himself on the straight and narrow by keeping records of his alcohol intake. Another man who had been drinking seven to eight cups of coffee each day cut down to only two to three cups per day and, once he had cut down, continued to keep records to be sure he didn't gradually move back up. A woman who had become a long-distance runner reported that she no longer needed to use self-reward but that she did need to keep records of her running to avoid slacking off.

You may be able to increase reactivity by the timing of recording (Rozensky, 1974). Specifically, you can use prerecording to control behavior for behaviors you want to reduce. People who are dieting can record food either *before* or *after* they eat. Does it make a difference? It turns out that it does. In an experiment, some subjects first ate and then recorded the calories, while others reversed the order. Those who recorded *before* eating ate less (Bellack, Rozensky, & Schwartz, 1974). During the initial stages of recording your problem behavior, you may want to record *after* you do the act, to provide a more realistic record. Then, when you are actively trying to change the desired behavior, record *before* you perform it. This is because recording early in a chain of behaviors may suppress the unwanted link (Kazdin, 1974f). Mike, who used to blow up at his children and spank them, began to record "anger" *before* rather than after he struck, and this had the desired effect. The recording itself broke the automatic chain of anger-striking, and the man was then able to discipline his children less severely. If your goal is to *increase* a behavior, then record *after* performing it (Paquin, 1982). For example, don't record jogging until after the run.

DEALING WITH PROBLEMS IN GETTING RECORDS

Behaviors Performed Absentmindedly

Certain target behaviors are difficult to record accurately because you don't pay close attention to them. For example, you might absentmindedly pick your face while watching TV or reading. Other behaviors such as talking too loudly or overeating may be so well practiced that you don't notice them any more. When you do not have accurate records, it is more difficult to work out a plan for change.

How can you make yourself pay attention? The first step is to deliberately practice performing the behavior while consciously attending to it. This technique is called **negative practice**. Take the same approach you would for any other behavior that is not occurring—practice it.

Garrett, who habitually cracked his knuckles, spent five minutes each morning and five minutes each evening deliberately cracking his knuckles while paying close attention to every aspect of the behavior. This helped him learn to pay attention to the target behavior.

A sophomore had developed the habit of scratching her arms while sleeping. The practice had become so bad that some mornings she woke up to find her arms bleeding. How could she pay attention while she slept? Each night when she went to bed, she deliberately scratched her arms for several minutes while paying close attention to what she was doing. Being awake, she was not in danger of scratching until she bled. But the situation was similar to actually being asleep—she was sleepy, and in bed. After a few nights' practice, the young woman was not scratching in her sleep any more (Watson, Tharp, & Krisberg, 1972). The case was followed up after 18 months and then again after 7 years. In the first 18 months, the woman had two relapses and used self-modification both times to correct the problem. After 7 years she had no more relapses and remained free of nighttime scratching.

Once you have learned to pay attention to the habitual target behavior, you can begin a plan to eliminate it. The woman above worked out a plan to replace scratching—first with rubbing her arms, then with patting them, and finally with just touching them.

Another way to deal with unconsciously performed behaviors is to ask your friends to point out instances of the target behavior. "If you see me picking my face, will you say something to me? I want to stop."

A student had developed the habit of talking much too loudly—not all the time, but whenever she was enthusiastic about a subject. She would start raising her voice and practically shout for several minutes before becoming aware of it. To get a count, she asked her friends to tell her when she was talking too loudly.

This situation is similar to asking other people to remind you of goals; here, too, be sure the reminder is not punishing. When Ed's wife said "Ed! You're overeating!" he was embarrassed and irritated. So she changed her reminder to "Ed, dear, aren't you . . . ?" after which she dropped the subject. This incomplete, tactful way of reminding him was more effective.

Behaviors That Occur While a Lot of Other Things Are Going On

Sometimes you are too busy doing something to record a problem behavior just when it occurs. Or perhaps other people are present, and you would be embarrassed to haul out your record notes and make an entry. A widowed man who was frankly looking for a wife found that he put off possible partners by rushing much too quickly into discussion of marriage. He wanted to learn to go more slowly, allowing the relationship to develop. His unwanted, rushing behavior occurred while he was socializing with a woman, and of course he didn't want to take out his note pad and record the event when it occurred. But he wanted to be sure to remember to record it afterward, so he could think of better ways of dealing with the situation. He carried a few dried peas in his pocket, and when the behavior occurred that he wanted to stop he would unobtrusively move a pea into his "target pocket" and say to himself mentally "Now remember this incident so you can record it later." The pea served as a reminder to him that something had occurred that he wanted to remember, and his self-instructions to remember helped him recall the specific event later.

A young woman who was lonely at college concluded that her negative opinions of people when she first met them were one of the main causes of her loneliness. "I judge them and find them wanting before I ever get to know them. It's a terrible habit, but I pounce on every little thing the person says and think things like 'What a dork.'" This habit did not endear her to others, and her loneliness was the result. To keep a record of these thoughts, she moved her pen from one part of her purse to another, to remind herself of the event later. Then, as soon as she could, she would make an entry about the event in her structured diary.

Don't save all your reminders up until the end of the day. If you must use a temporary reminder, make a full record of the incident as soon as possible.

Devising a Plan for Record Keeping

Suppose that the very act of making observations is punishing to you. You don't keep records because you can't stand the news. That's not an unusual situation, and if you're in it, you will be tempted to stop keeping records.

Self-recording can also be punishing if you have not yet learned the skills of recording. But you can use self-direction strategies to develop record keeping. Chapters Five, Six, and Seven discuss these strategies in detail in the broader context of setting up plans for change. Here are three techniques that you can use to deal with problems in keeping records.

First, develop record keeping one piece at a time. When keeping the records seems too hard, try adding just one item at a time (Nelson, Hay, & Hay, 1975). Remember Verna, who had difficulty getting along with one of her coworkers. She realized that she needed to keep track of four different aspects of her relationship with him, but this seemed impossibly complex. So she required herself to record only one aspect—that of ignoring his unfriendly remarks. After she had practiced this for a few days, she added a second record—keeping track of listening carefully to him. After several more days, she was able to record both. She then added the third, and then the fourth.

A *second* tactic is to reward yourself for keeping records (Stuart & Davis, 1972). A woman who had been overweight for several years realized that she needed to keep records of what food she ate if she was going to lose weight. At first this seemed a burden, so she rewarded herself with $5 a week to spend on her hobby if she kept records of her food intake. Once this became a habit, she switched to rewarding herself for exercising.

A *third* system is to ask someone else to check whether you are keeping records. You don't have to show the actual records to the other person; just indicate that you are keeping the records. For example, a young man who wanted to cut down on his drinking was upset when his records showed that he was drinking an average of nine beers a day. His first reaction was to stop keeping records. But he wanted to cut down, so he asked a friend to inquire each morning if he had kept records for the previous day.

Self-recording is a behavior, and it follows the same principles as other behaviors. If you are failing in this step, view your failure as an appropriate goal for self-improvement, and work out a system to increase that particular behavior. In other words, make accurate record keeping your first goal.

PLANNING FOR CHANGE

The most obvious reason for collecting self-recorded data is to produce better self-understanding. You may see patterns in your structured diary that alert you to certain recurring connections between your thoughts and behaviors in specific situations. Your frequency counts will enable you to assess your distance from your goal. The data serve as a standard against which you can judge your future progress. In Chapters Five, Six, Seven, and Eight, you will learn to use this information to design a plan for self-directed change. In order to select and design the best possible plan, you need careful records of your behavior and the specific situation in which it occurs.

You are now in a phase known technically as the **baseline period.** The baseline period is a time when you make self-observations but don't engage in other efforts to change. Your present records constitute a baseline against which future changes can be evaluated. The records you collect and analyze for a baseline period are very important to the success of your plan.

For many forms of self-observation, you'll want to know how your behavior changes from day to day or from week to week. A graph is a useful device for this purpose. Chapter Nine includes detailed instructions for constructing graphs. If you are unfamiliar with graphing, you may wish to read that section next.

Getting an Adequate Baseline Record

How long should you gather baseline data? That is, for how long should you just observe yourself before trying techniques for change? The baseline period should be continued *until it shows a clear pattern.* There will be daily fluctuations, of course, but when you see a basic trend underlying the variations, the baseline can be said to be stable.

Figure 3-1 gives an example of a fairly stable baseline. In the figure, you can see that this cigarette smoker showed some variation in the number of cigarettes smoked each day. In the first few days, the pattern was not clear. But by the end of the 11th day, it was apparent that his daily average was about 25. After a baseline period of 11 days, this smoker was ready to begin an intervention plan.

Figure 3-2 shows the number of hours a college student studied each night. At the end of the first week, she had only the roughest idea of her weekly study time because within that week her schedule varied so much. Thus, she needed to continue her baseline period for at least another week.

The general answer to the question "How long should you gather baseline data?" is: long enough to have a good estimate of how often the target behavior occurs. You end the baseline period when you have some confidence that you understand the actual pattern of your behavior.

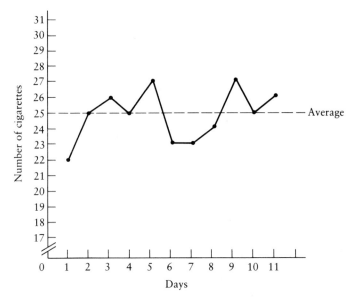

Figure 3-1. Cigarettes smoked daily.

You probably won't get a stable baseline in less than a week. Daily activities vary from day to day, and even for behaviors that occur quite frequently, it will take several days for a consistent pattern to emerge. The greater the variation from day to day, the longer it will take to get a stable estimate. If after three weeks you still have a lot of up-and-down swings on your graph, use a simple average.

Some behaviors do not show a stable baseline. Complaining, for example, or outbursts of anger may be quite variable, because they depend at least partly on how provoking other people's behavior happens to be.

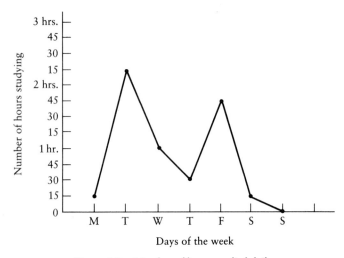

Figure 3-2. Number of hours studied daily.

Is the period of days or weeks during which you have been gathering baseline data representative of your usual life? If, for example, you are counting the number of hours spent studying and midterms were last week, then that week wouldn't be considered a typical week and shouldn't be used to make an estimate. If you smoke more at parties and in the last three days you went to three parties, you shouldn't use that period as a base for estimating how much you smoke on the average. Gather data for at least a week, and look for special occurrences that artificially inflate or deflate your estimate of the frequency of a target behavior.

Are the Baseline Data Reliable?

Reliability, in science, refers to a particular kind of accuracy of recording. Data are reliable when two or more observations of the same event result in the same recording. In the self-recording of behavior, ask yourself, "Am I really recording each occurrence? Am I recording the same events in the same way each time they occur?"

George was determined to improve his housekeeping behavior. Two sets of roommates had already thrown him out because he was so sloppy—left his clothes all over the place, never washed dishes, never cleaned the bathroom, and so on. He started keeping records of his behavior and established a category called "acts of good housekeeping." After two weeks, the baseline was very irregular. It turned out that his definition of "acts of good housekeeping" changed from day to day—and from case to case. Sometimes he earned a checkmark for good behavior when he put his empty beer glass in the sink, while on other days he would count only what he called "major acts"—for example, making his bed or taking out the garbage. The category definition was too vague, and as a result his records were hopelessly unreliable.

Here is a brief summary of the most common reasons why a person may not be making reliable observations.

1. You may not have defined your target behavior in terms of behavior-in-a-situation. In short, you are not being specific enough.
2. You may be performing the behavior without paying attention to it.
3. Engaging in the behavior may be so upsetting to you that you'd rather forget about it than record it.
4. Your record-keeping system may be too complicated, with the result that you are not keeping a record of all the instances of the target behavior.

Expect your self-observations to be slightly unreliable (Nelson, 1977). Be particularly careful to use techniques that maximize the chances of a high degree of accuracy. Here are steps to take to increase the accuracy of your self-observation:

1. Practice self-recording. You will get better at it with practice.
2. Have another person check your self-observational accuracy. Knowing that another person will check you will increase your accuracy, and the two of you can discuss any problems in observation.

3. Be aware that accuracy can be a problem. For example, if you are trying to change a verbal habit, such as saying "Ah" frequently, you will probably have difficulty being completely accurate (Willis & Nelson, 1982).
4. If necessary, formulate a plan to improve your accuracy. For example, you can reward yourself for accurate self-observations.

If you think that you tend to snack too much whenever you're at home, but in fact the problem behavior occurs mainly when you're watching TV, your plan for self-change is not likely to be successful. If you are unsure how many hours per week you really do study, then you may not notice a small but definite improvement in your study time and may abandon a self-change plan that in the long run would have worked. You must have relatively accurate records and self-observations in order to know how to begin to change and whether or not you are changing.

Omitting the Baseline Period

Is there ever a time when you can go directly to the stage of trying to change your behavior without going through a baseline period? You should never skip self-observation. But you can begin self-observation and start trying to change your behavior at the same time.

If a target behavior never occurs, there is no point in trying to record it. If you never study and your target is to develop studying, you already have a baseline count—zero. But even in this situation, there is value in self-observing in order to see what is the cause of your not studying. A short period of self-observation in which you ask "What are my opportunities to study?" or "What am I doing instead of studying?" is valuable in formulating a plan for change. If you want to take up exercise, it is a good idea to make a schedule of your daily activities to see when you might realistically schedule exercise sessions. If you don't do this, you are likely to start with an unrealistic plan for when to exercise.

In general, it is best to make some self-observations *before* trying to change. The advantages gained with more self-understanding outweigh the disadvantage of a short delay.

It is important to record observations in your structured diary when unwanted behaviors do occur. By doing so, you can detect the A-B-C patterns. Discovering the antecedents that lead to the unwanted behavior or the consequences that encourage it are essential in devising a successful plan for change.

CHAPTER SUMMARY

Structured Diaries

Situations can be divided into antecedents and consequences of behavior. To identify both, keep a structured diary in which you record the behavior and its antecedents and consequences:

Antecedents (A)	Behaviors (B)	Consequences (C)
When did it happen? Whom were you with? What were you doing? Where were you? What were you saying to yourself?	Actions, thoughts, feelings	What happened as a result? pleasant or unpleasant?

Entries should be made as soon as possible after the event. The diary will tell you what situations affect your actions, thoughts, and feelings. Use entries to figure out how to change your behavior by changing the situation.

Recording Frequency and Duration

Self-observation is the first element of self-direction. Recording your behavior provides the basis for self-observation. You can count either the amount of time you spend doing something or the number of times you do it. Record positive events as well as negative ones.

Make definite plans for how you will carry out your self-observations. Anticipate what problems may come up, and figure out how you will deal with them. *Four rules for self-observation* are:

1. Do the counting when the behavior occurs, not later.
2. Be accurate and strict in your counting. Try to include all instances of the behavior.
3. Keep written records.
4. Keep the recording system as simple as possible. Try to fit it into your usual habits.

Rating Scales

Rating scales allow you to gauge the intensity of an event. They are particularly useful for recording feelings and emotions. A good technique is to combine the use of rating scales with counts of actual behaviors.

The Reactive Effects of Self-Observation

Observing what you do may change what you do. Sometimes, the very act of recording your behavior is enough to produce change; more often, it helps. Use the reactivity of self-recording to your advantage.

Dealing with Problems in Getting Records

If you perform the problem behavior absentmindedly, practice performing it while paying close attention, so that your attention is switched on whenever the behavior occurs. Ask others to point out instances of the target behavior. For behaviors where it would be difficult for you to record immediately, find some way to make a mark and instruct yourself to remember and record the incident later. If you are failing to self-observe, your *first* plan for change should be to work out a system to increase accurate self-observation. Develop record keeping one step at a time. Reward yourself for keeping your records, and have others check on your record keeping.

Planning for Change

Data recorded before beginning a plan can serve as a baseline against which future progress is measured. This baseline should be continued until the pattern is stable. This almost always requires at least a week. The data should be as reliable as possible. Reliability is increased by specific definitions, careful attention, simple recording procedures, and practice. Other techniques for improving reliability may include the help of someone else and self-reward for good recording. As a general rule, a plan for self-change should not begin until after a stable, reliable baseline is achieved, because only then will you really know the extent of the problem and its exact nature.

YOUR OWN SELF-DIRECTION PROJECT: STEP THREE

You should now begin self-observation for the behavior-in-a-situation you have chosen in Step Two. For your self-observation, use a structured diary, a frequency count, or a rating scale.

Make record keeping easy, and build it into your daily schedule. Don't go directly into an attempt to change. First observe the target behavior as it is now occurring.

Collect baseline records for at least one week. As a rule, you won't need more than three weeks. Be as accurate as you can.

While you are gathering data, read the next five chapters, which deal with the principles of behavior and the techniques of change. When you have adequate self-observations, you will be ready to begin your plan for change.

TIPS FOR TYPICAL TOPICS

In some cases, you won't be sure of everything you should observe until you have read Chapters Five, Six, and Seven, because certain topics may require that you pay special attention to antecedents, behaviors, or consequences. If you have already identified antecedents, behaviors, and consequences of importance, begin observing them now.

Anxieties

By **anxiety**, we mean a condition of agitation, tension, and fear. Not all tensions are destructive; they may heighten performance when we are especially "anxious" to do well. In psychology, *anxieties* refer to agitation and fearfulness that are inappropriate, exaggerated, and self-defeating.

What are the specific situations that make you anxious? Is it a specific kind of situation such as test anxiety? Record the date, time, and situation, and then rate your feelings in the situation (Deffenbacher, 1981). Use a rating scale from 0 to 10, for example, where 0 is no tension and 10 is maximum tension. Keeping track of your rated anxiety may lower it (Hiebert & Fox, 1981). In studying the situation, note your own thoughts and reactions, as they may cue the anxiety. For example, people who get anxious on tests tend to think less about doing the test and more about their anxiety and/or the bad things that will happen to them if they don't do well on the test (Wine, 1980).

Assertion

Note specific kinds of situations in which you are not assertive. Record the situations in which you might have been assertive but were not. Also record what you did and *its* consequences. Later, make a note of what you might have done instead. What did you fear would happen if you were assertive? What did you do instead of being assertive? Look for some or all of the following obstacles: anxiety, thoughts about disasters that might happen, and actual reactions from others.

Depression

Every person experiences momentary feelings of sadness. But by **depression**, psychologists mean a more pervasive and longer-lasting condition of unhappy mood, lowered energy, and loss of interest in daily events.

In Chapter One we reported a case of self-modification of depression, and your general strategy should parallel that one. Keep track of both the positive and negative events in your life. People who are depressed tend to focus on the negatives—whether this is more the cause or the effect no one knows— but you can begin to lighten things by noting positive events in your daily life (Rehm, 1982).

Your depressed mood often follows certain thoughts or behaviors, so search for possible antecedents. Negative self-statements and negative self-evaluations are so common that some researchers find their subjects' moods are raised just by recording positive events and *not* engaging in negative self-evaluations (Gauthier, Pellerin, & Renaud, 1983; Layden, 1982). Note your self-putdowns that later lead to lowered feelings. What kinds of positive things could you be saying to yourself instead?

Rate your mood at least four times each day. Work out some sort of scale for this. You will probably find more fluctuation in mood than you thought. The day isn't all bad, after all (Rehm, 1982).

You may be depressed because of specific problems that are worrying you. For example, are you not getting along with important others (Biglan & Campbell, 1981)? Do continuous thoughts about these problems lead to lowered mood?

Family, Friends, Lovers, and Coworkers

Try to notice sequences: What do you do that leads to the irritating problem behavior? Do you sulk and want to go home early from a party? Do you say things that indicate why you are angry? What happens? Record these sequences fully. Be sure to include your behaviors as well as your thoughts.

Problems with other people often involve communication—not listening, not saying what one feels, being abusive, not communicating at all—and the way problems are solved—no solutions or poor solutions. Watch for these as you record the details of your target behavior.

Overeating

Successful weight loss requires observation of several kinds. Keep track of everything you eat, listing the time, physical place, and social situation (Campbell, Bender, Bennett, & Donnelly, 1981). Record the antecedents— your feelings, the locations, being with particular people or being alone. What were you saying to yourself just before you overate? Also record the consequences: what did you get out of it? You may eat to relax, to celebrate, or to get some reward from life. If you do, you want to find out, so that later you can consider seeking rewards or relaxation in other ways.

Remember that you don't have to eat less now, only record it. Recording the number of calories consumed is probably the best form of daily record. For your actual weight, a weekly record is sufficient. Also keep track of your exercise. This will become an important part of your eventual plan.

Smoking, Drinking, and Drug Use

Keep track of the time of day and the situation you are in, and make a rating of your emotional state when you indulge (Marlatt, 1982). Record the antecedents and consequences of your indulgence. When do you smoke or drink too much? What are you saying to yourself just before you indulge? What are the consequences: what do you get out of it? This will give you a daily count of the number indulged in and begin to show the reasons why you indulge. For example, certain situations or moods may always lead to indulging. When you have coffee, for example, you smoke. When you are nervous, you drink. In keeping a record, you are trying to find out why you indulge as well as how often. Later, you will be able to use that information to formulate a good plan for change (O'Connor & Stravynski, 1982). For example, if you find that you often indulge as a way of relaxing, you may start a plan to learn to relax in other ways and also try to cut down on your indulging.

Be sure to record urges to indulge that you resist. If you want to have a cigarette but resist the urge, then record it (O'Banion, Armstrong, & Ellis, 1980). You might also want to record how satisfying it is to give in to an urge (Gordon & Marlatt, 1981). Some cigarettes or some drinks, for example, are more satisfying than others. You can rate the satisfaction on a scale—for example, where 1 is no satisfaction and 7 is maximal satisfaction. This will remind you later which situations are the most tempting. You might then avoid these situations or require yourself to indulge only in less satisfying behaviors.

Studying and Time Management

Before establishing a full time-management schedule, you'll need to know how you currently use your time. Prepare a daily log, and mark the beginning and ending time for each change of activity. Buy a small daily appointment book for this purpose, or make your own daily sheets. Mark when an activity begins and when it ends. For example:

7:00 A.M.	Woke up and got ready to go to school.
7:42 A.M.	Watched television while I ate breakfast.
8:15 A.M.	Left the house.

For studying, record how much time you were in a position to study and how much time you actually spent studying. Prepare a recording sheet something like the model in Box 3-2. For times when you did not study, record what you did instead and the consequences.

Also record your actual studying behaviors. Do you read and underline? Do you make notes? Do you follow the suggestions in Box 1-1?

The Other Sex

Antecedents are vital in understanding shyness, because shy people often avoid social situations (Twentyman, Boland, & McFall, 1981). What are the antecedents that lead to your avoidance—physical situations, social situations, your own thoughts? For example, do you tell yourself you can't succeed or magnify your fears?

Being shy is similar to being unassertive in that you do one thing but wish you had done another. You can keep records similar to those of an unassertive person: write down what you did in the situation, and later write down what you might have done instead. This will help you see what behaviors you want to develop. Be sure to record positive instances of good social behavior as well as negative instances of fleeing.

What are the kinds of situations in which you feel shy? One of the biggest problem areas for both sexes is asking for dates (McFall & Dodge, 1982). Here's a list of other areas in a social relationship in which people have problems: starting a conversation, continuing it, being a good listener, asking for dates and dealing with refusals, going on the date, dealing with sex, expressing compliments and affection, expressing preferences to the partner, requesting feedback about the partner's preferences, handling criticism, apologizing for problems, maintaining or terminating relationships (Spence, 1983). Don't be daunted by the list; don't worry about the problems you don't have. Just concentrate on the one you're trying to improve. Which area should you pay special attention to?

Your problem behavior is going to occur while you are with other people, so make plans to record the details later.

CHAPTER FOUR

The Principles of Self-Regulation

OUTLINE

- Control Theory
- Regulation by Others and Regulation by Self
- Language Regulation
- Consequences
- Antecedents
- Respondent Behavior and Conditioning
- Modeling
- Chapter Summary
- Your Own Self-Direction Project: Step Four

LEARNING OBJECTIVES

Control Theory

1. According to control theory, what are the four basic elements in all self-controlling systems?
2. What are the limitations of control theory?

Regulation by Others and Regulation by Self

3. What are the developmental stages in learning new behaviors?
4. What is subvocal speech?
5. What is learned resourcefulness?

Language Regulation

6. Describe the process by which verbal control by others becomes self-control.
7. What does it mean to say that subvocal speech goes underground?

Consequences

8. What is operant behavior? What affects it?
9. What is a positive reinforcer?
10. What is a negative reinforcer?
11. Describe escape and avoidance learning. How do they differ?
12. What effect does punishment have on the frequency of behavior?
    a. What are the two types of punishment?
    b. What is the difference between negative reinforcement and punishment?
13. What is extinction?
    a. What is the effect of intermittent reinforcement on extinction?
    b. How can maladaptive behaviors sometimes be explained by the idea of intermittent reinforcement?

14. What are your beliefs on the issue of freedom and determinism? What is the text's position?

Antecedents

15. What is the role played by the cue, or antecedent, in operant behavior?
    a. When does an antecedent become a cue to behavior?
    b. What guides avoidance behavior? To what does the person respond?
    c. What is stimulus control?
    d. Why is avoidance behavior resistant to extinction?

Respondent Behavior and Conditioning

16. What is respondent behavior?
17. Explain respondent conditioning.
    a. What is higher-order conditioning?
    b. How does emotional conditioning occur?
    c. After a reaction has been conditioned, what effect does the stimulus—or antecedent—have?

Modeling

18. Describe learning through modeling.
19. List the principles presented in Box 4-2.

You have taken several steps toward self-change: selected a goal, identified the behaviors that need to be adjusted, and begun to keep records of your present behaviors. These steps are giant ones. Establishing goals and collecting self-observations are in many instances sufficient to bring about behavior change. This is often astonishing to people who find that they are somehow changing a problem behavior, after failing before, and the only apparent difference is keeping records. This has also been a puzzle to psychologists. But in the past 25 years, the mystery has begun to be solved. The power of setting goals and keeping records is now well explained by *control theory.*

CONTROL THEORY

Control theory, as developed by Carver and Scheier (for example, Carver & Scheier, 1982; see also Miller, Galanter, & Pribram, 1960), is an extension into psychology of the body of thought known as **cybernetics** (Wiener, 1948). Cybernetics, or self-regulation, has had a major impact on contemporary technology, producing all manner of self-regulating machines, from automatic pilots to the self-tuning radio. The thermostat of your home heating system is a simple example of the mechanisms discussed in control theory. The thermostat has very few parts and functions. It has a *standard* to be set, by which the desired temperature is indicated. It has a *sensor,* a thermometer, which responds to actual temperature. It has a *comparator,* a device that compares what the temperature is to what it should be. And, finally, it has an *activator* that—when the discrepancy between actual and desired is too great—closes the circuit and turns the heater on, or opens the circuit and turns it off. Thus, a reasonably good fit between actual and desired temperature is maintained. These few elements are at the core of all self-regulating machines, from self-guiding rockets to home robots.

Applied to the psychological and behavioral domains, control theory can be equally powerful. Most self-regulation of human behavior contains the same elements: we each have *standards* for our behavior; we have *sensors* to see what our behavior actually is; *comparisons* are made between the two; and when we perceive a discrepancy, we *activate* to change.

Not all of our behavior is effectively regulated, however. The reason for this—according to control theory—is that we lack standards, or we do not notice our own behavior, or we do not compare it to our standards, or we do not have available to us the actions that would bring behavior into line with our standards. Now you can see why your own first steps toward self-direction—setting standards and collecting observations—may bring about significant change. If you collect those observations and compare them to your standards, you may well activate for change. Simple *attending* to a problem area can clarify goals and standards and can energize us for careful observation and comparison (Carver & Scheier, 1982).

But activation for change does not always come about. In control theory, the argument seems to be that the human being is so constructed that sensing and comparing to standards "automatically" produces action. In effect, the argument is that human beings are "hard-wired" to behave that way, and no further explanation is needed on the psychological level. While there is much evidence to support this view of human nature, it cannot be seen as complete, for three reasons. First, psychological and behavioral systems are infinitely more complex than are mechanical systems. A thermostat activates by either going "open" or going "closed." When a person discovers a discrepancy between standards and actuality, he or she must choose among a thousand alternatives, and control theory does not guide us in understanding these choices. A second limitation is that the correct action may not be available. We may never have learned the appropriate action to bring our behavior closer to standard. The remainder of this chapter discusses the ways in which alternative behaviors are learned and kept at ready strength.

There is a third limitation to control theory that we will address immediately. *Not all human behavior is self-regulated.* This is particularly obvious in very young children, who are closely regulated by others, but it is also true for adults. Some behavior is under the regulation of the environment, not the self. Even for the most self-determining person, behavior is intimately connected to the setting in which it occurs. Much self-regulation is actually learning to control the environment that controls us.

Therefore, the next step in understanding the principles of self-regulation is to examine the relationship between regulation by others and regulation by self.

REGULATION BY OTHERS AND REGULATION BY SELF

All behavior, as it develops, passes through the following sequence: (1) control by others, (2) control by self, and (3) automatization. Thus, not all behaviors, much less all persons, are self-regulated. Self-regulation is a *stage* of development that lies between the point where assistance is required from other people and the point where it becomes automatic and no further regulation is needed. It is important to realize that we are discussing specific behaviors, not the person as a whole. That is, even for the most self-actualized adult, each new learned behavior passes through this same sequence (Tharp, Gallimore, & Calkins, in press).

Try to recall how it was when you were learning to drive an automobile. Your instructor is beside you. The traffic is moderately heavy as you approach an intersection, and you are concentrating on staying in your lane, at a safe distance from the car ahead. Twenty yards from the intersection, the traffic light snaps from green to amber. "Stop!" your instructor says. "There won't be enough time to get through." You stop slowly and safely.

The next intersection you watch the traffic light more closely. When it changes to amber, it is likely that you'll say to yourself "Stop!" and do so. You may actually speak to yourself aloud; more likely, it will be a "mental" message—*subvocal speech*. In either event, this is self-regulation—a self-instruction that assists you to come to a smooth and safe stop. In a short time, you need no regulation. Braking at the sight of the amber light is now so automatic that you need no instructor, and no self-instruction—you just stop.

Each new behavior that you develop through your self-modification project will go through that same sequence. In most instances, the regulation, assistance, or "control" by others will be provided by this text or by your instructor or other advisor. The second stage will be represented by your own acts of self-regulation: refining your standards, inventing observational methods, or self-instructing. In the last stage, your new behavior will become as automatic as driving your automobile, and you will need to think about it as little as you think about your own driving.

This sequence of behavior development is widely discussed in contemporary developmental psychology (Vygotsky, 1978; Tharp, Jordan, et al., in press; Tharp, Gallimore, & Calkins, in press; Wertsch, 1979; Rogoff, 1982). All the details of this theory do not concern us here. The main point is that each new competence added to your repertoire passes from regulation by some outside source to regulation by yourself. At the point that competence is fully developed, the behavior becomes *automatic*—consciously regulated neither by others nor by you.

Does automatic, fully developed behavior run free, entirely disentangled from the world around? Not at all. When behavior has become fully automatic, it has come under environmental control. But it is possible at any time to retrieve automatic behavior and bring it back under your own self-regulation if it does not meet your standards. Once self-regulation has produced the desirable balance between environment and behavior, the behavior will come under the control of new environmental stimuli—will become automatic again. This recurring cycle is typical of the self-directing, well-adjusted individual (Karoly & Kanfer, 1982).

Learned resourcefulness is the bundle of skills that allows us to retrieve our behaviors from an automatic, "mindless" state. Rosenbaum (in press) has discussed how learned resourcefulness is activated when "mindless" sequences are disrupted. The resourcefulness you will learn will allow you to self-consciously disrupt your unsatisfactory, mindless sequences and bring them under self-regulation.

In beginning to understand this recurrent cycle, it is important to understand the basic principles of regulation. Regulation of behavior, whether by others or by the self, takes place through the same basic mechanisms: language regulation, consequences, antecedents, respondent behavior and conditioning, and modeling. Each mechanism operates first by control from the outside and then through control by the self.

LANGUAGE REGULATION

The most common method of controlling behavior is through language. We give orders: "Platoon, halt!" or "Take out your driver's license, please!" We make requests: "Pass the salt, please." We give hints: "I suppose it's a good movie, but I'm so tired tonight . . . ." We coach: "Good, good; a little more to the right; that's better . . . ." Hundreds of examples occur in everyone's daily life. Of all forms of antecedents, the language of others (both spoken and written) may well have the strongest and most immediate effect on our behavior. Of course, we do not always comply. We may refuse, ignore, argue, resent, or laugh. But the effects are there. Language is a pervasive and inescapable influence on our reactions.

In charting chains of events, you will find that the language of other people represents the immediate antecedent of many of your behaviors, desirable as well as problematic. The human environment is in many ways a language environment, and the environment controls behavior largely through language.

"Talking to oneself," or self-directed speech, is often considered comical, if not aberrant. It conjures up a picture of an old man muttering to himself down a city street or even someone in a mental hospital. (Incidentally, the phenomenon is common enough on college campuses, where professors seem to walk across campus talking to themselves almost as an occupational hazard.) Actually, self-directed speech is common, useful, often highly adaptive, routine, and normal. For most adults, however, self-directed speech is subvocal. What is the relationship between talking to oneself aloud and talking to oneself subvocally (that is, silently, covertly, or "mentally"— thinking in words)? In fact, the effects of these two forms of self-speech antecedents are virtually identical.

As very young children develop, a first task of their parents is to bring them into the language community. Children learn to heed language and use it. Psychologists Luria (1961) and Vygotsky (1965, 1978) have studied this developmental process in detail and found a regular sequence that is roughly linked to the age of the child. Some aspects of this sequence are illustrated in this example.

"Don't kick over the wastebasket!" the father shouts to the 2- or 3-year-old. Too late; the trash is on the floor. The father rights it and says again, this time more gently, "Don't kick over the wastebasket now." Next day, the child approaches the basket, draws back the foot for a happy kick—and stops in midstride. "Don't kick over the basket!" the child says, and walks on by. The sight of the wastebasket may for some time cause the child to mutter the instruction aloud. For a while longer, the lips of the child may be seen moving in a silent self-instruction. Eventually, all traces of speech disappear, and the child merely walks by, leaving the basket unmolested. No external evidence of self-speech remains. In all likelihood, subvocal speech itself drops out, and the behavior becomes "automatic."

In the process of transferring from control by others to self-control, very young children imitate and incorporate adult speech. First the father says "Don't kick!" Then the child says the same thing, often imitating emphasis and inflection. Control of the child's behavior is passed from father to child. But notice this: the control by language instruction is maintained. Regardless of who says it, the antecedent "Don't kick!" affects the child's behavior. It is normal for young children to use imitated, spoken-aloud self-instructions for self-control (Vygotsky, 1965, 1978; Roberts, 1979).

At a certain point, around the age of 5, this self-controlling speech "goes underground," in Vygotsky's (1965) nice phrase. That is, the use of self-controlling language becomes subvocal—steadily more silent, rapid, and shorthand. Many psychologists would argue that this is when thinking begins, because so much thinking can be seen as subvocal speech. During earlier stages, before language "goes underground," self-instructing aloud helps children perform tasks more efficiently (Luria, 1961). And 5- to 8-year-olds, when doing schoolwork, say rules aloud to themselves to cope with difficult tasks (Roberts & Tharp, 1980; Roberts & Mullis, 1980).

Even in adulthood, the power of self-directed speech as an antecedent is not lost; it is merely not used as often. Donald Meichenbaum (1977) has demonstrated that verbal self-control can be reinstituted for older children and adults when new skills are being learned, when self-control deficiencies are present, or in problematic situations. Self-directed speech (vocal or subvocal) is a powerful controlling antecedent of behavior. It is particularly useful and natural in new or stressful situations.

It was useful and natural for you to say "Stop!" to yourself when you were learning to drive. You probably no longer do so. But the next time you are driving in a strange city, when the amber light stays on a much longer or shorter time than you are accustomed to, you may need to talk to yourself again. When the smooth flow of behaviors is somehow disrupted, conscious self-regulation comes into play (Kanfer & Karoly, 1972). Difficult situations make us more likely to use self-speech. This is one way in which we "rescue" automatic behavior when it no longer meets our standards.

Thus, you are probably talking to yourself in precisely those situations that you find most fearful, most depressing, or most difficult to cope with. This self-speech is likely to be "underground"—probably no more than a mutter, or only a quick "speech in the mind." Regardless of the form it takes, this self-speech antecedent has a powerful influence over your responses to difficulties. Have you ever said to yourself "This is probably one of those situations in which I make a fool of myself" and walked away, lonely and depressed? This kind of self-speech can perpetuate shy responses.

In your self-observation, observe yourself carefully as a problem situation begins to unfold. Try to detect the things you are saying to yourself. They act as instructions.

Principle 1: From early life to adulthood, regulation by others and the self (particularly verbal instructions) acts as a powerful guide to behavior.

CONSEQUENCES

The child walks up and kicks the wastebasket. Her mother scolds her and makes her replace the trash. This consequence makes it less likely that the child will upset the basket again.

Another child walks by the basket and does not kick it. "Good, Ginny!" her mother says. "What a good girl!" This rewarding consequence makes it more likely that Ginny will leave the basket unmolested in the future.

Two groups of workers in a furniture company decided to form "quality circles"—discussion groups that management consultants recommend as a way of increasing employee production and morale. One group's supervisor was resentful and accused the group of trying to "go union." The workers dropped the idea. The other supervisor encouraged his subordinates and praised them for their initiative. That group formed its quality circle and put real energy into it. Different consequences in the form of supervisors' reactions had strongly affected each group's behavior. Within the quality circle, when the discussions became difficult, the workers encouraged themselves with reminders that their initiative was valued by their supervisor. In this way, they transferred the positive consequences from the supervisor to themselves and moved into the stage of self-regulation.

Operant Behaviors

Behaviors that are affected by their consequences are called **operant** behaviors. The dictionary defines *to operate* as "to perform an act, to function, to produce an effect." An effect is a consequence. Through operant behaviors, we function, act, and produce effects on ourselves and on our environment. Through the effects—the consequences—the environment acts once again on us.

Much of our behavior falls into this category. Operant behavior includes all of the complex things we do as we weave the fabric of our daily lives. Our bad habits are operant behaviors we want to eliminate. The things we don't do but wish we did are operant behaviors we want to develop.

We develop operant behaviors—that is, we learn them—through the consequences of our actions. Operant behaviors are changed—learned or unlearned—as a result of their consequences.

Principle 2: Operant behavior is a function of its consequences. No matter what we are learning to do—kiss, type, speak, write, study, eat, or compose a string quartet—our behaviors will be strengthened or weakened by the events that follow them. A child learning to speak, for example, will become more verbal if praised than if scolded for talking. A composer will be more or less likely to write a second quartet depending on the events that follow the first attempt.

Consequences That Strengthen Behavior

The *strength* of behavior refers to the chances that a particular behavior will be performed. The best practical index for gauging the probability of behavior is its frequency. We usually infer the strength of a behavior from its frequency. That is, we count how often the behavior occurs. This is why the chapter on self-observation placed so much emphasis on counting behavior.

Reinforcers

If a consequence strengthens a behavior, it is called a **reinforcer**. How reinforcers strengthen behavior depends on the nature of the consequence.

Principle 3: A positive reinforcer is a consequence that maintains and strengthens behavior by its added presence. Positive reinforcers may be anything—kisses or food or money or praise or the chance to ride a motorcycle. What is a positive reinforcer for one person is not necessarily a positive reinforcer for another. The list is inexhaustible and highly individualized.

A little boy goes to his father and shows him a picture he has drawn. "That's lovely, son," the father praises him. "I really like it. Hey, what's this part?" he asks, giving the child attention. The father's praise and attention are probably positive reinforcers for the child. They increase the chance that in the future the child will continue to draw and will show his pictures to his father.

A positive reinforcer is anything that, when added to the situation, makes the behavior that preceded it more likely to recur. The composer is more likely to attempt a second quartet if the first composing behavior is positively reinforced. This positive reinforcement might consist of one or more consequences: applause from the audience, the pleasure of hearing the work performed, a sense of satisfaction in knowing that the work meets high standards.

It is important to note that praise, from critics or friends, has positive reinforcing effects. Thus, language acts as a reinforcing consequence, as well as an antecedent.

Principle 4: A negative reinforcer is an unpleasant consequence that strengthens behavior by being removed from the situation. If you are standing outside and it begins to rain hard, you might put up your umbrella to keep the rain from falling on your head. The act of putting up the umbrella is thus negatively reinforced by the removal of the unpleasant consequence of getting wet. The act that took away the unpleasant situation is reinforced—that is, made more likely to happen again.

Picture a person talking to a friend. The friend seems bored. The more the person talks on a particular topic, the more bored the friend seems to be. So the speaker changes to a new topic. Immediately the friend appears less bored. The act of changing topics is negatively reinforced by the fact that the friend is no longer bored. In other words, changing topics has removed the unpleasant consequence of the friend's boredom.

Just as with positive reinforcers, what is a negative reinforcer for one person is not necessarily so for another. The saying "One person's meat is another's poison" expresses this concept.

Escape and Avoidance

The principle of negative reinforcement explains how we learn to escape or avoid unpleasant consequences. Suppose a mother says to a child who is in a rebellious mood "Come here, please." The child does not come. The mother reaches over and swats the child. The child does not come. The mother raises her hand again. The child comes. The mother drops her hand. By complying, the child has escaped or avoided a second swat.

Technically, **escape learning** refers to behaviors that terminate the unpleasant consequence. The mother keeps spanking until the child submits and comes along. **Avoidance learning**, on the other hand, refers to behaviors that remove the possibility of an unpleasant consequence. The next time the mother says "Come here," the child obeys, thus avoiding a spanking like the one he got in the past. In escape learning the unpleasantness is actually delivered, but in avoidance learning it is avoided.

When you begin to analyze your own behavior, you may discover that you do things for which you get no apparent reward. People sometimes think of these behaviors as being "unmotivated," but they are often avoidance behaviors. For example, you may tend to go off by yourself rather than to places frequented by your friends, even though being by yourself is not reinforcing. You might ask "What am I responding to?" You may have learned an avoidance behavior. An important characteristic of well-learned avoidance behaviors is that often they are performed in an unemotional, even blasé, way. Such behaviors are not motivated by anxiety. Until it is called to your attention, you may be totally unaware that some of your behaviors are based on the avoidance of discomfort.

Reinforcing Consequences

You can see why an analysis of consequences is an important part of a plan for changing. You may find that you are *not* in fact positively reinforced for the behavior you want to perform. You may even find that you are being positively reinforced for some action that makes the desired behavior difficult or impossible. For example, one student wrote in a self-analysis: "I would like to be nicer to my roommate and be able to solve our little difficulties in a friendly way. But I usually fly off the handle and shout at him. The terrible thing is that I get reinforced for that: he gives in!"

By understanding how reinforcing consequences work—positive or negative—you can form better plans for changing your behavior. In self-change, sometimes you learn new behaviors—for example, an overeater learns to deal with tension in some new way instead of eating—and sometimes you arrange to be reinforced for acts you already know how to perform—for example, a nail biter is reinforced for not biting his nails.

Reinforcements are important for both learning and performance of actions. Theoretical psychologists argue whether, strictly speaking, reinforcement is necessary for learning or only for performance. But it is clear that your *performance* of behavior is affected by the reinforcement you get. You do what you are reinforced for doing.

Punishment

Principle 5: Behavior that is punished will occur less often. Psychologists distinguish two kinds of punishment. In the first kind, after a behavior has been performed, some unpleasant event occurs. For example, a child says a naughty word and is immediately reprimanded by her parents. An adult says something rude and immediately receives disapproval from friends. If these disapprovals are unpleasant enough, the naughtiness and rudeness are less likely to happen in the future. They have been punished.

In the second kind of punishment, after a behavior has been performed, something pleasant is taken away. For example, a child who is playing with her parents says a naughty word and is put in her room by herself. A man says something rude, and his friends go away. In both cases, it is the *loss* of something pleasant—playing with parents, being with friends—that punishes the behavior that preceded it.

What is the difference between punishment and negative reinforcement? In negative reinforcement, an act that allows the person to escape or avoid some event is reinforced by *removing* the unpleasant event. In punishment, behavior probabilities are reduced in one of two ways: (1) an unpleasant event follows a behavior, or (2) a pleasant event is withdrawn following a behavior.

This chart summarizes the difference between negative reinforcement and punishment:

Negative reinforcement
    Your behavior .... escapes or avoids a (usually unpleasant) consequence; this .... strengthens the behavior.

Punishment, type 1
    Your behavior .... leads to some unpleasant event; this .... makes the behavior less probable.

Punishment, type 2
    Your behavior .... leads to the loss of some-
                        thing pleasant; this .... makes the behavior less
                        probable.

Extinction

Suppose you first learn to do some act because you are reinforced for it, but then, on later performances, no reward follows. What was once reinforced no longer is. As a consequence, your act begins to lose some of its strength. This is called **extinction**.

Principle 6: An act that was reinforced but no longer is will begin to weaken. Two people have been going together happily for several months. But then a new pattern begins. He calls her up, but she's not home. He leaves a message, but she doesn't call back. Or she drops by to see him, and he doesn't seem very interested. Life, alas, changes, and acts that were once reinforced may no longer be. He will be less likely to call in the future. She will be less likely to drop by.

Extinction occurs all around us, continuously. It is the process by which we adjust our behavior to a changing world. If the woman never returned the man's calls, he wouldn't want to keep calling back forever. Nor would the woman want to keep on dropping by to see an uninterested man. Behaviors that are no longer productive are gradually dropped.

Extinction and punishment are not the same, incidentally. In extinction there is *no* consequence to an act. In our example, the calls are simply ignored. If the woman said, "Don't call me any more. I don't want to talk to you," that would *punish* the act of calling. If she simply didn't return calls—that is, she did nothing—that would *extinguish* the act of calling.

Do all acts extinguish equally? No.

Principle 7: Intermittent reinforcement increases resistance to extinction. Reinforcement that follows each instance of a behavior is said to be **continuous reinforcement.** This could be described as a 100% schedule of reinforcement. But most behaviors in the real world are not reinforced for each instance. Sometimes they are reinforced, and sometimes they are not. This is called **intermittent reinforcement.**

As you might expect, continuous reinforcement provides for rapid new learning. But intermittent reinforcement has a most interesting effect: *it makes behaviors more resistant to extinction.* The behaviors weaken more gradually. A behavior that has been reinforced randomly but on an average of every other time (a 50% schedule) will persist longer when reinforcement is withdrawn than if it had been reinforced continuously.

Let's go back to the example of the spurned lover. Suppose the woman has been careless about returning the man's calls and he has been reinforced about half the time for calling her. Finally, she loses interest in him entirely and no longer responds at all to his telephone messages. (These are called *extinction trials.*) The intermittent reinforcement schedule he was on before (when she returned about half his calls) means that it will take *longer* for his calling behavior to be extinguished than if he had been reinforced 100% of the time. If her nonreinforcement continues, of course, extinction will eventually occur. But the number of trials to extinction is affected by the previous reinforcement schedule.

This effect of intermittent reinforcement is significant for self-change because it helps explain the persistence of maladaptive behaviors. Why do you do things you are apparently not reinforced for or things you don't even want to do? You may not see the rare reinforcement—such as 1 in 50 or 100 times—that is keeping your behavior going. Or you may have been intermittently reinforced for maladaptive acts in the past, so that now they are very resistant to extinction. A casual observer might label such behavior "stubborn" or "foolish," not realizing the effect of intermittent reinforcement. Many maladjusted behaviors that you see in yourself or other people persist because they are reinforced on intermittent schedules.

Incidentally, changing from reinforcement to extinction often produces an initial increase in the behavior, before the gradual decline begins. At first,

---

BOX 4-1

FREEDOM AND DETERMINISM

Are we free to choose our own acts and destinies, or is the feeling of freedom an illusion of beings whose lives are determined by external forces? This issue has been debated since the beginning of time and is argued again and again in the mind of every thinking person: freedom versus determinism. What controls us? the gods, the world, the soul, the self?

Each religion, each philosopher, sooner or later has reached the same general conclusion, although the details vary: humankind is both free and determined. Only the degrees of freedom and determinism can be argued. Each person must live the drama of the conflict between submitting to deterministic forces and achieving available freedom. Religion teaches that we must submit to the will of God, but only by an act of free choice. Science—as exemplified by this book— argues that the environment determines behavior; yet it also argues that you can increase those aspects of your life that you yourself control.

Neither religion nor humanistic philosophy argues that humankind's basic freedom invalidates natural law. This chapter presents the principles of natural law that determine behavior. The balance of the book presents schemes for using those principles to increase your freedom. By assuming that your acts are determined and by finding what determines them, you can control the controlling forces, thus gaining freedom. So the old debate about freedom versus determinism is present in this book, too. Some readers of our earlier editions have written to say, "You speak of self-this and self-that; but if behavior is determined by the environment, how can a person be self-directed? You are self-contradictory." But it is not quite a matter of contradiction, for contradiction could arise only if either freedom or determinism alone governed our lives. Instead, our lives take their form in the space between these two abstractions.

when she does not return the calls, he calls more often; then the frequency of his telephoning gradually trails away, and is finally extinguished altogether.

ANTECEDENTS

We now turn to a general consideration of *antecedents* and how antecedent control of behavior develops. Regardless of the power of consequences, your behavior can never be stimulated by its consequences alone. Consequences, after all, occur after a behavior is completed. Antecedents, on the other hand, are the setting events for your behavior. As such, they control it, in the sense of calling it up, or stimulating it. When an antecedent calls up a behavior that is subsequently reinforced, the behavior and the environment are in good balance. When a behavior is firmly integrated with its antecedents and consequences, we experience a smooth flow. No thought or self-regulation intervenes, and the behavior has become "automatic."

Antecedents and Positive Reinforcement

Throughout our lives, most of our actions are controlled by **cues** (signals). For example, when the bell rings or the lecturer says "That's all for today," students get out of their seats and move toward the door. Each student knows perfectly well how to leave a classroom, but ordinarily no one does so until the cue is given.

Principle 8: Most operant behavior is eventually guided by antecedent stimuli or cues. The interesting question is "How do we learn the cues?" In any hour of our lives, thousands of cues are provided by the environment. The world is rich with stimuli—conversations, sounds, sights, events, smells—and our behaviors are orchestrated into this complexity.

Cues that evoke a particular action are called **discriminative stimuli**. This technical term is useful because it helps us understand how a cue works. A cue identifies the conditions in which an action will be reinforced or not reinforced. It is a cue that helps us *discriminate* conditions when the behavior will be followed by reinforcement from other conditions when the behavior will not be followed by reinforcement. In college you soon learn that when the lecturer says "That's all," you can leave in comfort. You also learn that in the absence of that cue, it would be wiser to stay in your seat.

An antecedent, or stimulus, becomes a cue to a behavior when the behavior is reinforced in the presence of that stimulus and not reinforced in the absence of the stimulus. When a stimulus and a behavior occur and the behavior is reinforced *only* when stimulus and behavior occur together, the stimulus will become a cue for that behavior.

This process can be studied in the laboratory by reinforcing a hungry mouse with food for pressing a lever when a light is on and by not reinforcing it for pressing the lever when the light is off. The mouse will learn to press the lever only in the presence of the light. In our everyday lives, this process occurs continually. For example, couples who date regularly can "tell" when it is time to leave a party. Each has learned that when one partner gives certain cues—perhaps becoming quieter or acting edgy—the other will be reinforced for preparing to leave. In the absence of that cue, neither is likely to be reinforced for leaving.

Role of Antecedents in Avoidance Behavior and Extinction

In order to avoid an unpleasant outcome, you have to know that such an outcome is about to occur. This means that your avoidance behavior is guided by the antecedents—the cues—you get from your environment. If your avoidance behavior is successful, the unpleasant event does not occur.

Principle 9: An antecedent can be a cue or signal that an unpleasant event may be imminent. This is likely to produce avoidance behavior. Suppose that when you were in your early teens, you weren't adept at social niceties and often made a poor impression on others. This may have led to unpleasant experiences, and you may have gradually learned to avoid certain social situations. You learned to be shy. Now, several years later, you are much more adept at social behaviors. But you continue to avoid particular kinds of social events—parties, for example, or dancing—and other situations that in the past would have been unpleasant. You continue to respond to the antecedent as a cue to avoidance, even though the actual unpleasant event doesn't take place anymore. Why?

Avoidance learning is highly resistant to extinction, because the antecedent stimulus evokes the avoidance behavior and the person who has learned the avoidance response has no opportunity to learn that the old, unpleasant outcome is no longer there.

Children and teenagers are often punished for their sexual behavior, and this punishment is likely to produce various kinds of avoidance behavior. Some will simply learn to avoid being caught, but others may learn to avoid sex. As children grow older and marry, the situation changes. Parents are unlikely to punish their married children's sexual behavior. What was formerly punishable behavior is now permissible. And yet, the person who has learned to avoid making love as a way of avoiding punishment may continue to avoid, even though the situation has changed and the punishment is no longer a threat.

This is how much "neurotic" or maladjusted behavior is learned. Because you were once punished—in childhood, for example—in the presence of a particular stimulus, you continue to engage in old habits of avoidance that to someone else might seem quite "foolish." You may avoid situations that could be pleasant for you, because the signals that control your avoidance behavior continue to operate. One of the techniques of self-modification is to gradually make yourself engage in previously avoided behaviors and situations that now seem to be desirable. Only then can you know whether you will still be punished for the behavior.

Stimulus Control and Automatic Behaviors

Now we are in a position to return to our discussion of the ways in which behavior evolves from regulation by others through self-regulation to automatic stimulus control. How can we reduce maladaptive automatic behavior and bring it back under self-regulation?

When an antecedent has consistently been associated with a behavior that is reinforced, it gains what is called **stimulus control** over the behavior. We respond in a seemingly automatic way. As an experienced automobile driver, you no longer slow down at lights yelling "Stop!" to yourself, or even saying it subvocally. You slow down and brake when the amber light appears even though you are singing, listening to the radio, or thinking about last night's movie. Because of its previous association with a variety of reinforcements, the amber light has stimulus control over your stopping the car. Coming to a halt at the amber light has repeatedly allowed you to avoid collisions, escape fear, earn the praise of your driving instructor, and even elicit your own self-congratulation. In the normal processes of performance, language control is dropped, because immediate recognition and response to specific situations is much more efficient. In most situations, excessive self-speech is undesirable, since it can actually interfere with our performance. Like Hamlet, we become "sicklied o'er with the pale cast of thought." It is better that we run on the automatic pilot of stimulus control.

Better, that is, when we are running well. Unfortunately, those undesirable behaviors that you now wish to change are very likely under stimulus control, and that stimulus control must be broken and rebuilt. For some people, the stimulus control is so strong that it seems almost irresistible, in spite of the fact that it evokes an undesired behavior. One of our students wrote: "I have been losing some weight, but there is one situation I just can't resist. That's when people who work in my office bring in doughnuts from King's Bakery. They are too much. When I get to work, as soon as I see that King's Bakery box, I know I'm in trouble!"

Many overweight people have this same kind of problem. The sight of certain foods automatically stimulates them to eat, whether they are hungry or not. Their task is therefore to reduce the automatic control of certain stimuli.

A most important tactic for rescuing behavior from an undesirable automatic condition is to insert new antecedents at the very time the old antecedents are about to begin their work. Self-speech antecedents are particularly useful, especially when the "automatic" cue is also self-directed language. For example, you might stop saying to yourself "I can't resist eating this" and say instead, "You can do it. Hang in there!"

Stimulus control can be the goal of a self-modification plan even when no automatic sequence exists. An antecedent can be set up, a desirable behavior arranged to occur in its presence, and reinforcement programmed to follow. In this way, a new automatic sequence can be created. One of our students, for example, wanted to be more efficient. She wrote: "I always do my planning as soon as I get off the bus that takes me to school. This puts the planning under the control of that antecedent. I go straight from the bus to an empty classroom and spend a few minutes planning the day, then reinforce myself for the planning." For this student, getting off the bus had gained stimulus control over the act of planning.

RESPONDENT BEHAVIOR AND CONDITIONING

Not all learning is based on the reinforcement of operant behavior. Some behaviors are automatically controlled by antecedent stimuli. These behaviors have built-in, nonlearned triggers. For example, when the knee tendon is struck lightly, leg extension follows automatically. The antecedent stimulus of striking has control over this reaction. A fleck on the eyeball is the controlling stimulus for eye blinking. Milk in the mouth produces salivation automatically from the earliest hours of life. Behaviors for which there are original, controlling antecedent stimuli are sometimes called **reflexes**. Humans have fewer of these automatic behaviors than do organisms with less complicated nervous systems, but we do have reflexes, and they are important.

Here is a small experiment that will illustrate one of your reflexive responses. Have someone agree to surprise you with a sudden loud noise sometime in the next few days. For example, ask a friend to slam a book onto a table when you seem to expect it least. Observe your reactions: you tense, whip around, and blink. This is a reflexive response; the stimulus alone is sufficient to cause it. Only repeated familiarity with the stimulus will allow the behavior to fade. But notice, too, that there is an *emotional* component to your reaction—a feeling of arousal and emotional fullness, a discomfort that is much like a small fear reaction that reaches its peak a second or two after the stimulus and then gradually subsides.

This experiment illustrates the control that the antecedent stimulus has over emotional reactions. Behaviors of this type have certain properties in common: for example, they are largely controlled by the autonomic nervous system, they involve smooth muscles, and they are highly similar among individuals of the same species. These behaviors are sometimes called **respondent** behaviors because they occur originally in response to the antecedent stimulus.

The most important characteristic of all respondent behaviors is that the antecedent stimuli are adequate to produce the behavior. This kind of antecedent control over reactions is important because, through this basic process, many emotional reactions become associated with particular antecedents, so that the antecedent comes to elicit them.

A person who is very shy may experience considerable anxiety when meeting strangers. Some people become very upset if they have to stay in an enclosed place. Others are extremely afraid of heights, or airplanes, or snakes. How do these stimuli come to gain control of the person's reaction, so that an emotion such as anxiety is elicited? One explanation is that antecedent stimuli gain control of a person's reactions through the process of **respondent conditioning**.

Respondent Conditioning

Respondent conditioning involves pairing a stimulus that elicits some response with one that does not, in such a way that the two stimuli occur together. The individual reacts automatically to the original stimulus in the presence of the new (or *conditioned*) stimulus.

After a number of such pairings, the person will react to the new, conditioned stimulus by itself and in nearly the same way that he or she reacted to the original stimulus. In this way, automatic reactions can be transferred to what was originally a neutral antecedent (that is, an antecedent with no stimulus control over a reaction). What was once a neutral stimulus becomes a conditioned stimulus—a stimulus that has control over a reaction—by being associated with an antecedent that already has stimulus control. A new stimulus control is developed.

Schematically, first you have an antecedent—call it A_1—that elicits a response. If A_1 is always preceded by another antecedent—call it A_2—then, after a few such associations, A_2 will develop nearly the same stimulus control over the response that A_1 has. If the response is some emotional reaction, through this process of respondent conditioning the new antecedent (A_2) will develop the capacity to elicit the emotional reaction even if A_1 does not occur.

This conditioned stimulus (A_2) can then be paired with a new neutral stimulus (A_3), and A_3 will then come to elicit that emotional reaction. This pairing of A_2 with A_3 (and A_3 with A_4, A_4 with A_5, and so on) is called **higher-order conditioning.**

The chart below summarizes respondent-conditioning processes and explains how we develop emotional reactions to so many antecedent stimuli.

Reflex	$A_1 \rightarrow$ Response	Automatic, unlearned, triggered response.
Respondent conditioning	$\begin{cases} A_1 \\ A_2 \end{cases} \rightarrow$ Response	Pairing the "trigger" stimulus with some new, neutral stimulus.
Conditioned response	$A_2 \rightarrow$ Response	In the absence of A_1, A_2 produces the response.
Higher-order conditioning	$\begin{cases} A_2 \\ A_3 \end{cases} \rightarrow$ Response	A_2 (conditioned stimulus) is now paired with a new neutral stimulus.
Higher-order conditioned response	$A_3 \rightarrow$ Response	Now, A_1, A_2, and A_3 can all elicit the response, frequently an emotion.

Emotional Conditioning

A number of years ago, John Watson and Rosalie Rayner (1920) demonstrated how an emotional reaction can be conditioned so that it comes to be elicited by an antecedent that was previously neutral. From the earliest days of our lives, a sudden loud noise is an adequate stimulus for a fear reaction. To associate that stimulus with one that was neutral, Watson and Rayner followed this procedure. A baby was presented several times with a white rat, and he showed no signs of fear. Then he was presented with the rat, and a few seconds afterward, a very loud, unexpected noise was made behind him. The baby reacted automatically to the startling noise with fear. After several experiences in which the rat was presented just before the frightening noise—so that fear was experienced while seeing the rat—the rat became a conditioned stimulus. By itself, it became sufficient to elicit the fear, even if the noise did not occur. Thus, what had been a neutral stimulus became a frightening one.

In a similar way, emotional reactions can be transferred to many new stimuli in your life. As you have new experiences, you may undergo new associations between conditioned emotional reactions and new stimuli, so that the new stimuli will come to elicit the original emotional reaction.

Once a conditioned reaction has been established, a new stimulus may be associated with the conditioned stimulus, so that the new antecedent also acquires stimulus control over the emotional response (higher-order conditioning). For example, if the experimenters were to play a certain tune every time the rat were presented, the baby would come to fear the music, through higher-order conditioning.

Principle 10: Through conditioning, antecedents come to elicit automatic reactions that are often emotional. In most everyday situations, conditioning and operant learning are going on at the same time. For example, a student who is trying to study but hates it and is not reinforced for it not only suffers the effects of not being reinforced but may also develop a conditioned boredom reaction to studying (Watson, 1978).

Most chains of events contain both behavioral and emotional components (Miller, 1969; DiCara, 1970; Staats, 1968). For example, think of a person who, having failed a driver's test once, goes back for a second try. The person is, at the same time, walking into the testing station (the observable behavior) and experiencing feelings of anxiety or tension. Many environmental circumstances produce *both a behavioral reaction and an emotional one.* That is, antecedents have an effect on both your behavior and your feelings.

Respondent Conditioning and Language

Many, if not most, conditioned stimuli are words. Parents deliberately try to condition emotional reactions to language as they teach their children that the street is "Dangerous!" or that the burner is "Hot! Hurt you!" As explained earlier, a behavioral as well as an emotional reaction comes to be cued by the same stimulus. The child both withdraws from the dangerous situation and develops an emotional response not only to the stimulus but also to the word for it. For adults, too, emotional reactions are often conditioned to words. If we are told that a spider or snake is "poisonous," we have a different emotional response to it than if we are told that it is "harmless."

This same effect is present when we use language to ourselves. A situation that we tell ourselves is dangerous or depressing can produce fear or depression even before we actually experience it. Some fears are "cognitively learned" (Wolpe, 1981). Therefore, many situations affect us not so much because of their consequences but because of the way we define the situations to ourselves. Staats (1975) has provided an elegant theoretical explanation of the interrelationships among behaviors, language cues, and emotions. Goldfried (1979) has recently developed strategies for restructuring self-statements to produce more adaptive emotional reactions as well as more effective coping with problems.

MODELING

Much human learning occurs by simply observing what others do. This is called learning through **modeling**.

Principle 11: Many behaviors are learned by observing someone else (a model) perform the actions, which are then imitated. Golf, dancing, chess, and bridge; expressions of love and of anger; even fears—all are learned through modeling. By simply observing a model, you learn behaviors. This kind of learning allows you to develop wholly new behaviors and to modify old ones.

You learn both desirable and undesirable acts this way. For example, you may have grown up with hardworking and ambitious parents. Now you realize that you, too, have these characteristics. Your parents may also have been rather irritable and inclined to blow up when frustrated. To your chagrin, you see that this description fits you as well. Of course, in your life there have been hundreds of people setting different kinds of examples for you. Your present behavior is not a carbon copy of any one person. Rather, you have borrowed a bit of this from one, a bit of that from another, and blended them together to make the unique you.

Learning through observation follows the same principles as direct learning. The consequences of your model's behavior will determine whether you will imitate the behavior. Reinforced model behavior is strengthened *in you* and punished model behavior is weakened *in you*. We learn cues and signals from models. We can even gain emotional conditioning from seeing models frightened by stimuli such as snakes or spiders. And there is evidence that we can learn to be calm, at least to a certain degree, by watching models behave calmly before stimuli of which we are afraid.

In your own self-change project, you can deliberately use this ability to learn through modeling to develop new behaviors. For example, a young man who wasn't very sure of himself on dates asked a friend if they could double-date, so he could see how his friend handled himself. A woman who had an unreasonable fear of birds accompanied a friend who didn't have that problem, to see how her friend dealt with birds.

These examples also illustrate that behavior learned through modeling follows the same developmental sequence as all other behavior. In developing their dating behavior and relaxation-around-birds, both people were first having their new behaviors regulated by *others* (the models). Soon they were able to move to the stage of self-regulation through self-modification programs that included practice and self-reinforcement. And eventually both of them developed automatic competence and relaxation.

CHAPTER SUMMARY

Control Theory

Merely setting goals and collecting observations on behavior can often bring about behavior change. This process is explained by control theory. Just as a thermostat regulates temperature, setting a standard and comparing real information to that standard can regulate behavior. To some extent, human beings may be "hard-wired" to self-regulate in this way, like the robots we have created in our own image. Other aspects of self-regulation are not well explained by control theory. Human beings make choices that are not anticipated. Sometimes we cannot "automatically" self-regulate because we do not know how to perform the required behavior. And not all our behavior is self-regulated; much of it is controlled by the external environment. In particular, much of our behavior is under the control of other people.

Regulation by Others and Regulation by Self

All behavior, as it develops, passes through this sequence: (1) control by others, (2) control by self, and (3) automatization. Control by others is

---

BOX 4-2

THE PRINCIPLES OF SELF-REGULATION

Principle 1: From early life to adulthood, regulation by others and the self (particularly verbal instructions) acts as a powerful guide to behavior.

Principle 2: Operant behavior is a function of its consequences.

Principle 3: A positive reinforcer is a consequence that maintains and strengthens behavior by its added presence.

Principle 4: A negative reinforcer is an unpleasant consequence that strengthens behavior by being removed from the situation.

Principle 5: Behavior that is punished will occur less often.

Principle 6: An act that was reinforced but no longer is will begin to weaken.

Principle 7: Intermittent reinforcement increases resistance to extinction.

Principle 8: Most operant behavior is eventually guided by antecedent stimuli or cues.

Principle 9: An antecedent can be a cue or signal that an unpleasant event may be imminent. This is likely to produce avoidance behavior.

Principle 10: Through conditioning, antecedents come to elicit automatic reactions that are often emotional.

Principle 11: Many behaviors are learned by observing someone else (a model) perform the actions, which are then imitated.

exercised by parents, instructors, models, books, bosses, spouses, friends. When a new behavior is being learned, it is regulated by these external sources. As we gradually become more skillful in a behavior, we take over self-regulation—by reminding ourselves, by practicing, by setting goals, by collecting observations. When a behavior is fully learned, it becomes automatic. In this stage, it is under environmental control. That is, it is a smooth response to situations and does not even require any thought. When this smooth flow is interrupted—by a change in the environment or a change in our goals—it is possible to retrieve behavior from this automatic condition and bring it back under self-regulation. The skills we use in retrieving and regulating these automatic behaviors are called learned resourcefulness. Learned resourcefulness includes skills in managing language, consequences, antecedents, respondent conditioning, and modeling.

Language Regulation

The most common method of controlling behavior is through language. Young children gradually incorporate the speech of their parents and teachers and give themselves the same kinds of instructions that they have heard from others. Even as adults, we are controlled by the speech of others. In difficult situations, or when we are retrieving behavior from automaticity, our own self-directed speech is a powerful regulator of our own behavior. Even when behavior is automatic, it may occur in response to subvocal speech. What we say to ourselves controls what we do.

Consequences

Operant behaviors are strengthened or weakened by what follows them. Behavior is said to be "stronger" if it is more likely to occur in a particular situation.

A positive reinforcer is a consequence that strengthens behavior by its added presence. A negative reinforcer is an unpleasant consequence that strengthens behavior by being removed from the situation. You learn to escape or avoid unpleasant consequences. What is a reinforcer—positive or negative—for one person is not necessarily so for another and not necessarily so at all times. Some people dislike pastrami; even those who like it would not find a pastrami sandwich reinforcing immediately after a Thanksgiving feast.

Behavior that is punished will occur less often in the future. Punishment means either taking away a positive event following a behavior or adding a negative event following a behavior. Both kinds of punishment decrease the likelihood of the behavior.

An act that is no longer reinforced, either positively or negatively, will weaken. This is called extinction. In this process, the behavior has no reinforcing consequence and therefore weakens.

Intermittent reinforcement, however, increases the resistance of a behavior to extinction.

Antecedents

Eventually, most behavior is guided by antecedents. These guiding antecedents, called discriminative stimuli or cues, come to control behavior that has been reinforced only when the cues are present. Many cues signal that danger is imminent. Escaping from those cues is reinforced by a reduction in anxiety, and we learn to avoid them. Avoidance behavior is highly resistant to extinction. Thus, many problem behaviors continue even after real danger has disappeared, because the cue causes us to act as though something we used to fear were still a threat. (This is a description of many "neurotic" behaviors.)

It is normal for behavior to develop to the point that it is automatically controlled by antecedent stimuli. When these sequences are undesirable, automatic behavior can be retrieved and brought back under self-regulation. Tactics that can be used include inserting new antecedents, narrowing the behaviors that follow an antecedent, and constructing entirely new sequences of antecedent—behavior—consequence.

Respondent Behavior and Conditioning

Respondent behavior refers to those behaviors that are originally controlled by antecedent stimuli. In respondent conditioning, a neutral antecedent is associated with a stimulus that can elicit an automatic reaction, and, after a series of associations, the once neutral stimulus becomes capable of eliciting the reaction. In higher-order conditioning, another neutral event is paired with this antecedent, and it, too, acquires the capacity to produce some reaction.

This process is important because many emotional reactions may be conditioned to particular antecedents in this way. Various emotional reactions, such as joy or depression, may come under the control of antecedent stimuli, so that just encountering the antecedent elicits that reaction. Normally, both operant learning and respondent conditioning are going on at the same time.

Conditioned stimuli are frequently words. Thus, language produces emotional reactions—even language we address to ourselves. Because operant and respondent processes are both present when language is antecedent to behavior, what we say to ourselves affects both behaviors and emotions. Many self-change programs require a change in our self-speech.

Modeling

Many behaviors are learned simply by observing a model. Learning through observation follows the same principles as direct learning. The consequences of the behavior for the model will determine the strength of the behavior in the observer. Even emotional conditioning can be learned by watching models who are frightened or calm.

YOUR OWN SELF-DIRECTION PROJECT: STEP FOUR

This chapter has presented background material that you need in order to embark on a successful self-modification project. It's important, therefore, that you have a good grasp of the principles that govern your behavior. To make sure, answer the learning-objectives questions on pages 88–89.

If you can answer these questions, you can feel confident that you have a good grasp of the principles that explain your behavior and that you are ready to apply these principles toward self-understanding. If you cannot, reread the chapter. Find the answers, and write them down. Then answer the questions again.

Now think about your behaviors that you have been observing, get out your observation notes, and answer the following questions about your own target behaviors.

First, consider the antecedents of your behavior.

1. What stimuli seem to control the behavior? In what situations does the behavior occur?
2. Do you react automatically to some cue with undesirable behavior?
3. Do you react to some cue with an unwanted emotion? What is the conditioned stimulus for it?
4. What are you saying to yourself before the behavior?

Second, look at the behavior itself.

5. Is it strong and quite frequent, or is it weak and not very frequent? What does this tell you about what you can do to change it?
6. Is any element of your problem due to something you are avoiding, perhaps unnecessarily?
7. Are you aware of models in your past whose behavior (or, perhaps, some aspects of it) you may have copied?
8. Does any part of your goal involve changing behaviors that are resistant to extinction either because they are intermittently reinforced or because they are avoidance behaviors?

Third, examine the consequences of the behavior.

9. Are your desired behaviors positively reinforced?
10. What about actions that make the desired behavior difficult? Are they reinforced?
11. Is it possible that the desired behavior is being punished?
12. Is your own self-speech rewarding or punishing your behavior?

Answer these questions carefully. The next four chapters discuss various ways to move toward self-change by using techniques that solve different problems. Some techniques are for the person who is not being reinforced for a desired act. Others are for the person who needs to develop stimulus control for a desired act. Still others are for the person who already has inappropriate stimulus control over undesired acts. Some are for those who are showing conditioned emotional responses. Your answers to the questions above will tell you which kinds of techniques you should use in your own plan for self-change.

CHAPTER FIVE

Antecedents

OUTLINE

- Identifying Antecedents
- Modifying Old Antecedents
- Arranging New Antecedents
- Chapter Summary
- Your Own Self-Direction Project: Step Five
- Tips for Typical Topics

LEARNING OBJECTIVES

Identifying Antecedents

1. How do you identify antecedents? What are three possible points of difficulty in identifying them?
2. What two kinds of self-statements can be antecedents?
   a. Explain self-instructions.
   b. How do beliefs serve as antecedents, and how can you identify them?
   c. What are two common maladaptive beliefs?

Modifying Old Antecedents

3. In the first steps of a self-change plan, how can you avoid the antecedents of problem behavior?
4. What are some of the situations in which indulging in consummatory behaviors is most likely?
5. Explain the strategy of narrowing antecedent control.
6. Explain reperceiving antecedents. What are "hot" and "cool" cognitions? How does distraction work?
7. Explain the strategy of changing chains.
   a. What is the advantage of building in pauses?
   b. Explain pausing to make a record.
   c. How do you unlink the chain of events?
   d. At what part of the chain is it best to try breaking the chain?

Arranging New Antecedents

8. How can you use self-instructions to promote new, desired behavior?
   a. Are self-instructions best when precise or general?
   b. How can you use self-instructions to remind yourself of beliefs or of long-range goals?

112

c. In using self-instructions, which is more effective—saying them to yourself or thinking about them?
9. What are negative self-instructions? How can they be eliminated?
10. Explain the thought-stopping procedure. Besides stopping the unwanted thought, what else should you do?
11. Explain how you can build stimulus control to cue a desired new behavior—for example, concentrating while studying.
12. What is stimulus generalization? What can you do to develop it for a new, desired behavior?
13. Explain the precommitment strategy. How can you use other people's help in precommitment?

At this point, you have a clear understanding of the principles that govern your behavior, and should have gathered data about your behaviors, the situations in which they occur, and their consequences. Each of the next three chapters discusses one of the A-B-C components. The present chapter discusses the A issues—ways of arranging antecedents so that desired behaviors become more likely. Chapter Six treats the B issues—how behaviors themselves can be changed, replaced, and originated. Chapter Seven is devoted to the C issues—ways of rearranging the consequences of behavior to gain better self-direction. Finally, Chapter Eight discusses ways of organizing and incorporating all these ideas into an effective plan.

The separation of these topics is unfortunate, but unavoidable. It is not possible to present them simultaneously on the same printed page. But remember: you cannot design a full self-direction plan until you have read *all* the material in these four chapters. A, B, and C units are all required for full analysis and planning, although each person may emphasize one or the other somewhat differently. A good self-change plan is based on all three.

Continue to work at your self-direction project as you read these chapters. The material is organized so that each chapter allows some planning and analysis, but a full plan will require all elements.

IDENTIFYING ANTECEDENTS

An effective plan for self-improvement depends on accurate discovery of your current system of cues. Discovering antecedents is the first task.

A married couple had been quarreling. In the past, they had constructive arguments in which they tried to solve their differences. Lately, however, the man had found himself flying off the handle in the middle of an argument, calling his wife names, and swearing. We suggested that he keep a record of what happened just before he lost his temper. He thought about what had happened in the past and made current observations for several days. As a result, he discovered a consistent antecedent of his anger: "It's a particular expression on her face. I think of it as her holier-than-thou expression, and it makes me angry."

In this case, the unwanted behavior was cued by a single stimulus. For other behaviors, there may be a number of antecedents that have stimulus control. When any one of them occurs, so does the problem behavior. "Hurt feelings" was the concern of one young woman, who discovered all these antecedents: "(a) her mother or brother questioning specific decisions or behaviors, (b) her roommate asking her not to be around for a while, (c) her ex-husband questioning her dating or implying that the separation was her fault, and (d) her boyfriend failing to meet her as planned or flaunting the fact that he dated her acquaintances" (Zimmerman, 1975, p. 8).

Do you have a good understanding of the antecedents of your own problem behavior? There are three possible points of difficulty. First, have you been recording fully and accurately? Not doing so is the most common (and most self-defeating) error. Many fine students have told us, "You can't seriously mean that I'm supposed to write all that stuff down. I know what the problem is, and I do notice the situations. Writing them down is just making up exercises for a course." But we are very serious. Only the most experienced self-analyzer can do without written records. Written records force you to keep your attention on problem situations, in which perceptions tend to rush by and become blurred. Cues to problem behavior are often the ones that make you anxious, the ones you don't like to notice and remember.

The second most likely difficulty is not beginning early enough in your chain-of-events analysis. If you begin recording at the moment your problem is clear and overt, you can be nearly certain that you have not begun early enough in the chain. This point is illustrated by one student who became alarmed at his increasing amount of beer drinking. "It happens at night," he reported. "I stay home, cook a little something, turn on the TV. I'm bored, get depressed, start popping the beer cans. The antecedent seems to be that I feel lonely." Recognizing his feelings of loneliness was a giant step forward, but that was clearly not the first link in the chain. We suggested that he work further backward: what chain of events produced the loneliness? "I've had three disastrous love affairs in the past year," he wrote. "Self-confidence—zero. Every time I meet a woman, I tell myself not to bother. I've been staying home. Twice last week I could have gone out, once to an auto show and once on a blind date. I declined. The next time a chance like that comes up, I'll try to notice what I'm saying to myself. It's probably some self-putdown."

Not every antecedent is so far removed from the behavior as this self-criticism made during a telephone conversation. But this student saw the long chain that linked last week's refusal of a date to this week's lonely drunkenness. Discovering this distant antecedent allowed him to design a self-modification plan for a more stimulating social life.

The third most likely difficulty with discovering antecedents is that of identifying self-statements, and it will require a lengthier discussion.

Discovering Self-Statements

Self-directed messages and thoughts are among the most powerful influences on subsequent behavior. There are two types: (1) self-instructions, and (2) beliefs.

Self-instructions. Self-instructions can be obvious: "Get out of here!" "I've got to study tonight!" "I go three blocks and turn left." "Be calm, be relaxed." However, self-instructions are sometimes difficult to identify because they occur in a "still, small voice," so swiftly that only careful attention reveals them. The task is to amplify the words until they are loud and clear. It's like bringing self-directions back from the underground, so that they can be consciously controlled. Once this principle is understood, most self-instructions *can* be detected. All that is needed is careful attention during antecedent conditions. What are you telling yourself?

The first task is to discover whether or not self-instructions are the antecedents of your problem behavior. To make that discovery, turn up the amplifier of your still, small voice. Hear yourself thinking. Then record it as an antecedent.

Beliefs. Beliefs may be more difficult to discover. Belief statements may occur so rarely that they are not often observable. You must infer them through logical analysis of your self-observations. By beliefs, we mean the underlying assumptions on which your self-speech and other behaviors rest.

Recall the example of the young woman with "hurt feelings." All the instances in which she felt hurt—whether by mother, brother, roommate, ex-husband, or boyfriend—presented a common theme. If she had discussed her records with us, we would have asked her, "What is common to all these situations? Why does each of these events hurt you? What belief can you see operating here?" She might have answered, "It seems as though I want approval from everyone all of the time. I suppose I believe that I must be loved by everyone and that each disapproval means that I'm not loved." The conversation might have continued as follows:

"Do you really believe that?"

"I suppose so; it's the way I behave."

"Is it logical?"

"Not really. People can disapprove of some things their loved ones do."

"Must everyone love you, constantly?"

"No. That's absurd."

"What would be a preferable belief?"

"That it is acceptable to be disapproved of sometimes, even by those one loves."

Albert Ellis (1979) has theorized extensively about the role that such self-defeating beliefs play in self-speech and behavior. Marvin Goldfried (1979) and his associates found that changing beliefs often lead to widespread benefits, emotionally and behaviorally. A group of unassertive people believed that standing up for themselves would be followed by disapproval and embarrassment. They came to see that they let themselves be mistreated by waiters, cashiers, and even friends because of these illogical, imagined outcomes. Once they began to anticipate different outcomes—greater respect and comfort—their assertiveness increased (Goldfried, 1977). Two maladaptive beliefs occur most frequently. The first is the belief that constant love and approval from everybody is a necessity. The second is that all our undertakings must be performed with perfection (Goldfried, 1979).

In examining your self-observations for relevant antecedents, don't overlook the possibility that a maladaptive belief may be contributing (Arnkoff & Glass, 1982). Be systematic in searching out these beliefs. Consider each instance of your problem. Search for some common theme, some assumption that underlies all these instances. Write out that theme, as precisely as possible, and examine it. Is it rational? Is it adaptive? Do you really believe it, now that it is explicit? In our experience, many people find that they can then readily accept a quite different belief. One doesn't have to be always perfect. One can do very well with some disapproval. By accepting a more reasonable belief, you can change a controlling antecedent and begin a new pattern of self-direction (Thorpe, Amatu, Blakey, & Burns, 1976).

Examining her journal records allowed a graduate student, Kathy, to see that her frantic social activity was based on a belief that she had to make very frequent contacts with her friends, or lose them. She realized that this belief was highly exaggerated. This allowed her to contact friends only when she wanted to. She reported that she was *less* lonely, because the times she spent with her friends became more satisfying.

The first task of self-modification is to use the power of antecedents to reach goals. The strategies you can employ to accomplish this task will be discussed under two main headings: modifying old antecedents (including avoiding antecedents, narrowing antecedents, reperceiving antecedents, and changing chains) and arranging new antecedents.

MODIFYING OLD ANTECEDENTS

Avoiding Antecedents

If all you have in front of you is two pieces of celery and a bowl of soup, you have already avoided some of the antecedents of overeating—the sight of a heaping plate of spaghetti, for example. Chronic alcoholics who successfully control drunkenness often do so by never confronting the crucial antecedent of overdrinking—the first drink. Most people who stay off cigarettes also follow a policy of not having the first one. If you are a habitual overeater or smoker or drug user, sometimes almost nothing is as reinforcing as your "habit." For such behaviors, perhaps the most promising type of self-modification plan is one in which you *avoid* the antecedents that set the time and place for your **consummatory behavior** (behavior that is consummated, or climaxed, by its own ends—such as eating, drinking, or sexual activity). The smoker avoids cigarettes, the drinker avoids drinks, and the overeater avoids fattening foods. They all know that if they are exposed to those stimuli, they will very likely perform the undesired behavior again. Therefore, people with this kind of problem can work out self-direction plans in which they avoid the antecedent.

A middle-aged, overweight man wanted to diet but reported that progress was always followed by disaster. So he began to record the antecedents of his eating binges and realized that, although he normally stayed on his diet quite regularly, there was one situation in which he always ate too much. This was when he and his wife were invited to someone else's house for dinner, something that occurred fairly often. Their friends were good cooks, and the result was that the man always overate. He solved his problem by setting a simple rule, to which his wife agreed. Until he had lost 20 pounds, they wouldn't accept any dinner invitations. When someone called to invite them for dinner, he would explain that he had to lose weight and that, because his would-be host or hostess was such an excellent cook and he couldn't possibly resist the food, he must regretfully decline.

Self-control becomes most difficult when you are around others who are indulging. Marlatt and Parks (1982) have conducted extensive research on people with addictive behaviors, particularly consumers of drugs, such as alcohol, heroin, marijuana, or tobacco. They report that relapse in persons resisting addictive behaviors is very likely to occur when in the presence of others who are engaging in that behavior.

Social cues may need to be avoided for a variety of behavioral goals. For example, Heffernan and Richards (1981) studied students who had self-initiated attempts to improve poor study behaviors. Those who were successful were more likely to use the simple procedure of studying in an environment where they would *not* have to interact or talk with other people.

In other circumstances, a private environment can be the cue for problem behavior. A young man was concerned with what he felt was "excessive" masturbation, an activity in which he indulged three times a day. The reinforcer was fairly obvious here—the sexual pleasure itself—although, by masturbating, he also gained some temporary relief from social anxieties. The young man avoided the antecedent—the place in which masturbation usually occurred. He began to use a less private campus restroom.

This strategy of avoidance is one that you can begin immediately. Later you will learn how to develop new behaviors for the situations in which you cannot avoid the antecedent. After all, you can't avoid parties all your life. But avoiding the antecedents to unwanted, indulgent behaviors will allow your self-controlling responses to be strengthened before they are again tested in tempting situations. By the time you return to parties, you will know when you must say no and how to do it.

Avoiding antecedents for drinking, drugs, smoking, or overeating is particularly important when you are emotionally upset. Feelings of anger, fear, depression, or disappointment are certain to make indulgence more tempting, and more likely. Even the excitement of unusual happiness tends to make abstainers more likely to violate their resolutions, but negative emotions are the most dangerous conditions for relapsing into indulgence (Marlatt & Parks, 1982; Shiffman, 1982). Therefore, avoiding your problem antecedents is especially wise during periods of emotional arousal.

Narrowing Antecedent Control

Undesired behavior may be deliberately linked to a gradually narrower range of antecedents. The idea is to narrow the range of situations that control the behaviors down to a fine point, or to narrow the behaviors that occur in a situation.

For example, Goldiamond (1965) helped control sulking behavior in a client by a program that allowed him to sulk, but only on a particular "sulking stool." Nolan (1968) reports a case of restricting smoking to a certain chair that was uncomfortably located.

This technique has been best studied in the control of insomnia. The insomniac wants the situation of being in bed to automatically produce sleep, but instead it stimulates tossing, turning, thinking, reading, turning the radio on and off, and everything but sleep. Bootzin (1972) recommends narrowing the stimulus control of the bed. With the exception of sex, nothing else should be done there—no reading, television watching, conversation, or worrying. If still awake after ten minutes, the insomniac should leave the bed and not return until sleepy. This system of narrowing appears to be the best self-modification technique for insomnia, even in severe cases (Lacks, Bertelson, Gans, & Kunkel, 1983).

A similar strategy for making studying more automatic is to leave the study desk when daydreaming, or eating, or chatting (Spurr & Stevens, 1980).

There is one caution regarding the use of narrowing antecedents: the narrow antecedent should not positively attract problem behavior. Jack narrowed his smoking antecedent by having cigarettes only in his tool shed. But this dull and dirty room soon became a refuge from his chaotic family life, and he retreated there more and more "to have a smoke." This actually increased his smoking. A subsequent plan of self-reward for resisting urges to smoke corrected the problem (Peterson, 1983).

Reperceiving Antecedents

Some antecedents cannot be avoided, and cannot be narrowed. There are unexpected situations. Other smokers suddenly appear, or everyone suddenly decides to go for pizza. There are times when tempting situations are an inescapable part of daily routines. A useful strategy is to change the nature of the situation by changing the way you think about it. By attending to certain parts of the situation, and not to others, you can perceive the antecedent in a different way.

For example, it is possible to attend to either the "hot" or the "cool" aspects of any situation. Walter Mischel and his associates have studied the ways that children learn to resist temptations (for example, Mischel, 1981;

Cantor, Mischel, & Schwartz, 1982). By the sixth grade, children are aware that attending to the "cool" rather than the "hot" qualities of tempting things will help them to resist unwise choices. "Hot" perceptions of a stimulus refer to its consummatory qualities, while "cool" perceptions refer to abstract qualities. A "hot" perception of a marshmallow would be "They taste yummy and chewy"; a "cool" marshmallow perception would be "They are puffy like clouds" (Mischel, 1981). A "yummy" marshmallow is more likely to be snatched and eaten than is a "cloudlike" marshmallow.

Adults as well as 12-year-old children know this idea, but in problem indulgent responses, we often err by letting hot perceptions dominate our attention.

A cool perception does not include any attention to the experience of consuming the smoke of a cigarette or joint, its pleasures or effects. Transforming an antecedent condition by concentrating on its cool qualities will reduce arousal, reduce frustration, and ultimately reduce the likelihood of succumbing to temptation.

A dieter who successfully used a reperceiving strategy reported that she was unbearably tempted when others were eating dessert. She would concentrate on the chocolate pie and begin to salivate fiercely while thinking of the rich, sweet flavor and the creamy pudding on her tongue. This hot perception was changed to a cool one. She began to observe the abstract qualities of the situation. She noticed that these people were moving parts of the brown triangles of pie onto forks and carrying the bites to their heads. They put forks and bites into an opening in their heads called a "mouth," and they moved their jaws around before they swallowed. A cool perception of smoking tobacco or marijuana would concentrate on the visual image of the cylinder of paper with leaf bits inside it, the glowing ember of fire on the end of the tube, and the pursed lips of the smoker.

Another strategy—employed even by very young children—is to distract yourself from the temptation by thinking about something else. This is not a suggestion to avoid thinking about the general issue. But at the moment when the temptation is present and inescapable, think about something else. It will make giving in less likely. Not only children use this tactic. Beginning joggers who included distracting thoughts while running were much more likely to still be running three months later (Dubbert, Martin, Raczynski, & Smith, 1982). For more experienced and able runners, this was not true. For experts, careful attention to actual performance was correlated with success (Okwumabua, Meyers, Schleser, & Cooke, 1983). But in early stages of mastery, distracting yourself from the temptations to smoke, eat, drink, dope, or stop running is a good device.

Changing Chains

Another strategy that can be used to control antecedents is to change the chain of events that produces the undesired behavior. Many behaviors are the result of a fairly long chain of events. An antecedent produces some behavior, which leads to a particular consequence, which is itself the antecedent of yet another behavior, and so on. Thus the end behavior, which may be an undesired act, is the result of a long series of antecedent–behavior–new antecedent–new behavior. By the time you reach the end of the chain of events, the impulse to perform the final, undesirable behavior is so strong that it is very difficult to restrain. A good strategy is to interrupt the chain of events *early* (Ferster, Nurnberger, & Levitt, 1962; Bergin, 1969).

In this kind of situation, the final behavior in the chain is usually the one that you recognize as the problem behavior. For example, you may say to yourself "The problem is that I drink too much." But the act of drinking is embedded in a sequence of behaviors, which involves getting the alcohol, making some kind of drink, perhaps sitting down, and then drinking. Sometimes, by analyzing the chain of events that culminates in the final behavior, it is possible to identify an early, weak link in the chain. An interruption there can prevent the occurrence of the final behavior.

Annon (1975) reports the case of a problem drinker who used a complex "scrambling" of previous chain links to stop drinking. This person had consumed up to a pint of vodka before bedtime each night for several years and could no longer sleep without it. He analyzed the components of the usual chain of events that led to drinking—coming home, turning on the TV, going to the refrigerator, putting ice in the glass, pouring and drinking the vodka, going to the bathroom, undressing, showering, going to bed, pouring another drink, and so on. The man reorganized this chain into a different order. For example, he moved showering to immediately after coming home, delayed going to the refrigerator until after undressing, and substituted cola for vodka in the glass. This scrambling had the effect of decreasing the vodka-drinking probabilities, since it broke up much of the antecedent control.

Building in pauses.   When a chain is well established, you may find yourself responding without thinking, whether the antecedent is a rude statement or a plateful of food. A helpful technique for dealing with this automatic quality of chained antecedents is to pause before responding.

The pause technique is particularly useful for indulgent behaviors. For smoking, gradually increasing pauses between the urge and lighting up, or between puffs, is an effective technique for reducing the number of cigarettes smoked (Newman & Bloom, 1981a, 1981b). For excessive drinking, a pause between the urge for another and allowing oneself that next drink is highly recommended. The same is true for eating problems. A "two-minute pause" in the middle of each meal may be the single most effective technique for dieters (Sandifer & Buchanan, 1983). This may be because the pause allows a clearer perception of whether you are really still hungry.

Whether smoking, drinking, or eating is the problem, a two-minute pause is often enough for the urge to pass. During that pause, the body can be read more accurately. Does it really need that cigarette? Are you getting drunk? Are you really hungry? Merely asking these questions during the pause will break up the automatic sequence of consume, consume, consume.

The pause technique is useful for a variety of social problems as well. A man had developed the undesired habit of becoming verbally aggressive when others said something he thought was foolish. He worked out a scheme to reinforce himself for pausing a few seconds before responding aggressively. Often those few seconds were enough for him to think of a more appropriate response than a rude remark.

What you do during the pause makes a difference, of course. A man was upset because he often spanked his children. "I know that I hit them when they disobey me—particularly when they bicker with each other and I tell them to stop and they don't. So I tried just pausing for a second before spanking them. Sometimes that worked, but sometimes it didn't. I just waited a second and then hit the child anyway. So I started saying to myself, 'Now, think. Don't just stand here being angry and then hit. Think. What should I do right now to get the children to behave?'" What that man did during his pause was to give himself instructions.

Pausing to make a record.   Recording an unwanted behavior *before* you do it may reduce its frequency. If you require yourself to make a record early in the chain of events, you gain greater control over later events than if you wait until the last links in the chain (Kazdin, 1974f). For example, as you feel the first signs of panic coming over you, stop and make a rating of the degree of panic you feel. That gives you time to realize that your reaction is (probably) out of proportion to the actual event and that there are ways in which you can cope.

In general, the earlier in the chain of events you make the interruption, the more effective your plan will be. A couple who had developed a destructive pattern of arguing learned to recognize the first signs of such a pattern and arranged to stop immediately to make entries in their structured diaries. Usually this pause was sufficient to break the chain of their destructive arguing.

Unlinking the chain of events.   A young woman had a problem with excessively frequent urination. She reported that she went to the bathroom an average of 13 times a day. She was upset by this personally and sometimes socially embarrassing situation. She had seen a physician, who assured her that there was no medical problem.

In gathering the baseline data, she realized that two separate antecedents led to urination. First, she almost never went into a bathroom (for example, to wash her face or comb her hair) without using the toilet. Second, she went to the toilet at the first hint of bladder pressure. To break up the control of the first antecedent (entering a bathroom), she used this simple plan. She would go into a bathroom, perform some behavior that didn't involve using the toilet, and then walk out. For example, she would enter, wash her hands, and leave. Or she might comb her hair or put on lipstick and then leave. In this way, she broke up the inevitable relationship between going into a bathroom (the antecedent) and using the toilet (the behavior).

To break up the control of the second antecedent (the initial hint of bladder pressure), she used the pause technique. Upon feeling the first hint of pressure, she required herself to pause for five minutes before urinating. This technique was sufficient, because the passage of five minutes usually found her engaged in some other behavior.

Suppose your problem is that you eat too many between-meal snacks. What is the chain that leads to this final step? First, you may feel slightly bored or have nothing to do for a couple of minutes. Second, you start moving toward the kitchen. Third, you open the refrigerator or pantry and search for food. Last, you eat the food. If this is your chain, you may interrupt it by having an intervention plan that calls for performing at step 2 some behavior other than moving toward the kitchen. It can be *any* behavior—for example, making a phone call.

This strategy of unlinking a chain is necessary whenever problem antecedents cannot be avoided. The old antecedent must lead to a new, desired behavior instead of the old, undesired act. The next case illustrates an unusual use of this strategy.

A depressed young woman discovered through her A-B-C analysis that her "down" feelings were preceded by interactions with other people that made her feel uninteresting, ignored, and even rejected. These feelings would quickly turn into almost obsessive thoughts about her worthlessness, and a deep depression would set in. The chain looked like this:

Step 1	*Step 2*	*Step 3*
Disappointing interactions ——→ with others	Thoughts of personal ——→ worthlessness	Feelings of depression

She reasoned that not every interaction with others could turn out perfectly for her. Her plan called for changing the second link of the chain. Whenever she felt an interaction to be disappointing, she would, as quickly as she got home, insert a new and pleasant event—sewing. This was an entirely new activity for her, and she began with no previous interest or skill at dressmaking.

She said, "I never thought of sewing as something good, but I've discovered that those simple things can have a lot of meaning. And now I'm much less dependent on other people." At the end of her program, she felt much more mature, and her depressions were no longer a problem (Tharp, Watson, & Kaya, 1974).

Long chains can be altered most effectively by intervening at both ends. The research and theory supporting this position have been presented by Frankel (1975), who also reports the case study in Box 5-1. As you read this case, notice three features in particular. First, the antecedents were changed both at the beginning and at the end of the chain. Second, the father had to learn a new behavior to be inserted in the chain. Third, the outcome of the new chain had to be reinforced. This illustrates how a well-developed plan will often require a combination of strategies.

BOX 5-1

A FAMILY'S CHAIN

Chains of events are often composed of the behaviors of several people. This case illustrates a chain of family behaviors that produced unhappiness for all three members.

The Chain

1. Mother asks Bobby to do something at home. (When Father asks him, there is usually immediate compliance.)
2. Bobby refuses.
3. Mother gets very irritated, screams, and/or hits Bobby.
4. Bobby screams back and rarely complies.
5. When no compliance, either Mother goes and gets Father, or Father hears incident occurring and barges in. (Or Father is told of the incident on returning home.)
6. Father and Bobby yell at each other. Usually Father hits Bobby or physically forces him to get moving on task. In any case, Bobby eventually complies.

This chain of events lasted from a few minutes to several hours, ending when the father, on coming home, learned of the incident and forced compliance. The incidents didn't always go all the way through the chain above. When Bobby complied with his mother's demands or when she didn't tell her husband about an incident, the incident stopped at those points.

The Plan

It seemed that Bobby had learned to use one of his parents to get to the other one. A simple analysis of the problem behavior might have stopped after step 3, when Mother screams and/or hits Bobby. The time lag between steps 3 and 6 was sometimes hours, and the whole behavior chain didn't always occur, being intermittently completed by Father. To achieve modification of this sequence, Mother was instructed to extinguish her behavior in response to Bobby's noncompliance (step 3). She agreed to either remain calm or leave the room until she could respond to Bobby calmly. In no case was she to call Father or was he to come in. Father also agreed to spend three hours a week with Bobby doing something of Bobby's choosing. At the three-month follow-up, the parents reported that Bobby's incidents of aggression and noncompliance in the home had been reduced to a level not considered a problem. They rated Bobby's aggression at a raw score of 65 (compared to 80 initially). At the one-year follow-up, the parents reported that Bobby's behavior at home continued not to be a problem.

In the old chain, Bobby was receiving a strong reward for his misbehaviors—interaction with Father, even though it was an aggressive kind of interaction. It turned out that Father had never learned to play with his little boy. In the new chain, the three hours a week of play with Dad were strongly rewarding to both Bobby and his father.

Adapted from "Beyond the Simple Functional Analysis—The Chain: A Conceptual Framework for Assessment with a Case Study Example," by A. J. Frankel, 1975, *Behavior Therapy*, 6, 254–260. Copyright 1975 by Academic Press, Inc. Reprinted by permission of the author and Academic Press.

ARRANGING NEW ANTECEDENTS

So far we have spoken of avoiding, narrowing, or rearranging antecedents, but a critical problem is often creating *new* antecedents that will cue desirable outcomes. New antecedents can be inserted at the beginning of a chain or at any point throughout it. We will first treat verbal antecedents (self-instructions) and then other forms of stimulus control.

Initiating Positive Self-Instructions

Self-instructions are powerful. This power can be used to promote self-direction by developing new self-speech in problem situations. As you discover the role of self-speech antecedents in your problem situations, it is very likely that one of two conditions is present. Either you are giving yourself instructions and assigning labels that cue undesired reactions, or your problem behavior is "automated" and you can't identify any self-statements. In either event, the same strategy is called for. *Insert into the chain of events new self-instructions that will guide the desired behavior.* Almost every self-modification plan should include the use of some new self-instructions (Meichenbaum, 1977).

Designing a plan of self-instruction is very simple. The strategy is merely to substitute new instructions for the self-defeating ones you now use. Don't tell yourself anymore "I can't do this!" Say, instead, "I can" (and tell yourself how).

Here are the self-instructions that a shy man used to talk himself through approaching a new acquaintance: "Go up to her and say hello. Don't forget to smile. Look into her eyes. Face her directly. Be open." If you are explicit, giving yourself instructions can guide you through a new and unfamiliar behavior by reminding you of some steps you might forget in the stress or excitement of the situation.

The form for new self-instruction is very simple. Decide what you want to do, and tell yourself to do it. The instruction should be brief, incisive, and clear.

Self-instructions have been reported in the research literature as reducing specific fears (Arrick, Voss, & Rimm, 1981); reducing nail biting (Harris & McReynolds, 1977); increasing exercise and increasing studying behavior (Cohen, De James, Nocera, & Ramberger, 1980); and improving a variety of other problem behaviors. Dush, Hirt, and Schroeder (1983) recently analyzed 69 separate research reports on change through self-statements. They concluded that the evidence is for considerable improvement as compared to control subjects who did not use self-statements.

Even complex interpersonal behavior can be improved with self-instructions. For example, the principal of an elementary school found it extremely difficult to express any negative reaction to her teachers. She could praise them but not give them suggestions for improvement. If she wanted to say "This is not an adequate lesson plan; you must prepare it in more detail," she became embarrassed and often wound up speaking in such generalities that the teacher didn't understand what she was trying to say. She prepared a small "script" of what she wanted to say to the teacher—short, precise, and to the point—such as "Your being late this week has inconvenienced your team members." She rehearsed this sentence in her imagination several times just before the interview. Then she talked herself through the actual situation as follows: "Be pleasant. Be patient. That's right. Now. Here's a pause. Say it." Then she said aloud, "By the way, your being late this week has inconvenienced your team members. Can that be corrected?" Four such interviews were all she needed to gain the necessary confidence to be able to give negative feedback comfortably.

Make your self-instructions precise. For example, if you are attempting to alter belief statements, state your new belief aloud as a reminder before you enter a difficult situation (Kanter & Goldfried, 1979). A young student who had just moved into her own apartment (against her parents' wishes) reminded herself while driving back home on Saturdays, "Remember, I can tolerate their disapproval. They continue to love me. I have made the right decision. I don't need to have approval constantly." Even during a problem situation, statements of belief or judgment can guide your reactions. When the topic of living alone comes up once more, this student can say to herself "I'm overreacting; I don't need to feel upset" and then add a precise self-instruction: "Relax now. Try to change the subject."

Self-instructions can be rehearsed, aloud or in imagination, when you anticipate a problem situation. Other forms of practice may also be used, such as writing out the intended self-instructions and rereading them just before the event.

Belief statements about the self can also be rehearsed immediately before the event—for example, "I can stay calm. I can make interesting conversation. I can handle it." Reminding yourself of your good qualities and competence is useful, because these self-statements can cue behaviors of competence. But making absurd statements will be of little use. One study of women who had attempted to cope with depression discovered that both the successful and the unsuccessful women used encouraging self-instructions. But the successful ones *believed* the positive things they told themselves (Doerfler & Richards, 1981). Telling yourself "I am the most brilliant woman in the state of Illinois!" will not affect your behavior much, unless you believe it's true!

Self-instructions can also remind you of your long-range goals. Before approaching a woman, the shy man described earlier said to himself, "Remember, this is important to me. I've got to learn how to talk to women or I'll die a hermit." This kind of self-statement will bring your long-range goal forward in your mind and increase your incentive to perform the next new behavior.

Couldn't you get all these benefits by just "remembering" what to do, without actually saying the words? Perhaps, but unless you say the words, your "remembering" may be too vague to be useful. Actually saying the words, in your mind or imagination or even aloud, brings up self-speech

BOX 5-2

SELF-INSTRUCTIONS FOR STUDYING: A SELF-EXPERIMENT

A college student's instructors reported the following case:

Betty was 19 years of age, enrolled as an undergraduate student at a large urban university, and currently sharing an apartment with two students. Although Betty always studied (read) at home, she described the process as a "hassle" in that she frequently talked on the telephone, snacked on "junk foods," conversed with her roommates, and/or listened to music while reading. Because she was enrolled in a class that required a great deal of reading, she wanted to decrease these behaviors.

Behavior Observations

Betty made observations of her studying once every five minutes for approximately one hour per evening, five evenings per week (Sulzer-Azaroff & Mayer, 1977). She would note whether or not she had been studying in the previous five minutes. Because the length of time spent studying varied, the number of observed time samples ranged from 6 to 15, with the majority equaling 12 per session. Studying was defined as "sitting in a chair, reading a textbook, underlining important facts and/or taking notes on a separate sheet of paper." All data were transcribed onto 8½- × 11-inch paper that was divided into squares, each representing a five-minute time sample.

Experimental Phases

Baseline.   During this ten-day phase, Betty continued to study in the living room. Although most studying occurred during the early evening hours, on two occasions Betty read during the afternoon. Other than recording data according to the described procedures, Betty was asked not to attempt to alter her studying behaviors.

Experimental demands.   Betty wrote a series of instructions on an index card referring to studying:

> It's important to study to get good grades. I need to study to understand new material. I'm not going to talk to my roommates, because it's important that I learn this material. It's important that I learn this material; therefore, I will not talk on the phone. I will remain studying even though I feel the urge to eat or drink something. Because listening to music distracts me and it is important that I learn this material, I will not play the stereo.

Betty agreed to read the card once immediately prior to reading and was told that the procedure would help to increase her studying. Immediately thereafter, a brief behavioral rehearsal was conducted. She did this for 13 days.

Self-instructions.   Then Betty constructed a second card, listing an additional series of instructions:

> OK. I've got my books out, and I'm turning to the right page. This is what I am supposed to be doing, because it will help me to be a better student and earn good grades. Studying also helps me understand new material, which is important in getting good grades. Because I need to learn this

BOX 5-2

SELF-INSTRUCTIONS FOR STUDYING *(continued)*

material, I will not talk to my roommates or talk on the phone. Even though I feel the urge to get up and get something to eat or drink, I will not, because it is important for me to learn this material. Therefore, I will keep reading the textbook and take good notes.

During the next six days, Betty read the second card once every 15 minutes throughout the studying hour. She continued to read the first card prior to studying. All other procedures were similar to the initial baseline phase.

Withdrawal.   During the next ten days, Betty was asked not to read either card. This was done to test whether the instructions were still needed.

Self-instructions 2.   This six-day phase was similar to the first condition; she read both cards to herself again.

Results

Figure 5-1 represents graphically the percentage of time Betty studied. Studying percentages were computed by dividing the number of times Betty recorded herself as reading by the total number of observations taken that session. In Figure 5-1, baseline average rates for studying equaled about 59%. Under the demand-phase conditions, studying increased to about 73%. After the self-instruction phase was implemented, studying increased to approximately 96%. During the withdrawal phase, the behaviors fluctuated widely, but they leveled out again at about 96% after the treatment was reinstated.

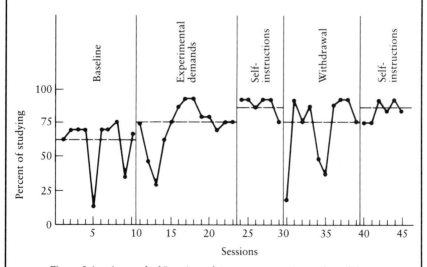

Figure 5-1.   A record of Betty's studying across experimental conditions.

From "Applications of a Simple Self-Instruction Procedure on Adults' Exercise and Studying: Two Case Reports," by Richard Cohen, Patricia De James, Beth Nocera, and Maria Ramberger, 1980, *Psychological Reports, 46,* 443–451. Copyright 1980 by Psychological Reports. Reprinted by permission.

from the underground and allows it to exercise full power. In our experience, beginning students most often fail to harness the power of self-instructions because they don't truly self-instruct. They "figure it out," decide that saying the words is "silly," and skip over the crucial behavior—actually saying the words in the critical situation.

Saying the words makes all the difference. And self-instructing is itself a skill that needs to be acquired through frequent practice.

Eliminating Negative Self-Instructions

As you begin to perform some self-defeating behavior, you may actually instruct yourself to do it. Your self-observations can show this pattern. For example, a young woman who didn't seem to be able to relax when she was with men reported that as soon as a man started talking with her, she would say to herself things like "He's not going to like me" or "I'm going to be shy" or "I'm not going to make a good impression." These "self-instructions" made her tense and made her act in a less attractive manner.

A middle-aged man who wanted to become a jogger but found it difficult reported that even on short, light runs, he would say to himself, "This is probably killing me. I'm going to have a heart attack." Or he would actually visualize a scene in which he had a heart attack, staggered, and fell dead in his jogging clothes. (The fact that his doctor had assured him that it was perfectly all right for him to jog moderately didn't seem to make any difference.) Needless to say, this kind of thinking discouraged his jogging, so he tried to eliminate such thoughts.

A man whose job was less than perfect said that while at work, he would say things to himself such as "This is so boring. How depressing! This is awful!" which made him like his job even less. A dieter confided in us that when she got a bit hungry, she would say to herself "I'm starving" or "I *must* have something to eat" and then rush off to eat as if she were really starving.

In all these kinds of situations, *replace the self-defeating thoughts with incompatible ones, including thoughts that contain positive self-instructions.* For example, when the shy young woman realized that she was thinking "He's not going to like me; I'm going to be shy," she said instead, "No, not this time. Now, remember: smile, make eye contact, stay calm, listen carefully to what he is saying." She was substituting "self-coaching" for the unwanted self-defeating thoughts.

The jogger substituted these thoughts for his negative ones: "If I go slowly, there is no danger. There is no better way to spend my time than getting into good shape." The dieter who said "I'm starving" corrected herself by saying, "No, I'm not. I'm just a bit hungry, and that's good, because it means I'm losing weight." The man who didn't like his job substituted thoughts like "It's not so bad. I need the money, and it's an easy job."

Words guide your actions. They are antecedents you produce for your own behavior. Thus, it is important that you notice them and change them to desirable self-instructions.

Suppose a newly hired salesperson fails to make a sale to her first customer. If she says to herself "I was never cut out to be in sales" or "I'll never learn to do this," her future disaster is already clear. If, on the other hand, she says to herself, "Hmmm, I'm going to learn how to do this," then there is the possibility of future success. Those two ways of speaking to the self will produce very different actions—and two very different levels of success (Rehm, 1982).

Thought Stopping

A specific kind of self-instruction, called **thought stopping**, has been developed to eliminate unpleasant or self-defeating thoughts (Wolpe, 1958). In their extreme form, such intrusive thoughts are called *obsessions*. They may concern almost any subject—sex, aggression, self-criticism—or they may be nonsense phrases. In their milder forms, these self-degrading and self-defeating thoughts—such as "I'm no good" or "I'm a loser"—are rather common. They may be visual as well as verbal, and may take the form of some unpleasant image that, like a persistent tune, will not get out of your mind.

Thought stopping is a simple technique. As soon as the unwanted thought occurs, say to yourself "Stop!" Say it sharply, and if not aloud, say it clearly in your mind. As in the case of other self-instructions, it is vital that you actually verbalize "Stop!" This verbalizing brings back from the underground the directing power of language.

Thought stopping includes a second step: immediately substitute another thought. The substituted thought should be the opposite of the unpleasant one (Cautela, 1983; Turner, Holzman, & Jacob, 1983). If you imagine a scene in which you are humiliated, say "Stop!" and immediately imagine a scene in which you encounter success. One of our students suffered from embarrassing and repeated sexual fantasies. Using thought stopping, she substituted images of being alone, on a beach, in deep relaxation.

If the intrusive thoughts are verbal, replace them with opposite statements. Thought-stop your negative self-appraisal, and substitute something positive about yourself (Hays & Waddell, 1976). Box 5-3 reports a case of obsessive love corrected by thought stopping. Notice that the woman used cue cards to remind her of the opposite, substituted statements. In another case, after saying "Stop!" to unwanted thoughts of being dominated, a woman read, "I'm my own boss. I can do what I want." This was written on the back of a photo of her taken at the airport in a previous year (Martin, 1982). This helped her think about the pleasant prospects of future independent travel.

Building New Stimulus Control:
The Physical and Social Environments

You can also arrange new physical antecedents (or cues) to stimulate the behavior that you want. The simplest instance of this procedure can be illustrated by expanding our discussion of narrowing antecedents of intellectual work—studying or writing. A good way to begin developing this

BOX 5-3

FALLING OUT OF LOVE THROUGH THOUGHT STOPPING
by Gail deBortali-Tregerthan

Mary, a mother of two young children, was "hopelessly" in love with Dan. But Dan had proven to be dishonest, as well as a liar and an exploiter, and had no intention of going back to her. Mary wrote: "I feel desperate. I know he was just using me, but I still love him. I think about him all the time. I spend half my day crying, and I can't sleep at night. Everything reminds me of him—presents he gave me, TV shows he liked. I find myself doing things like driving past his house or cooking the meals he liked to eat. I ring him up all the time, yet I know there is absolutely no hope of our ever being together again. I don't even think I want to be with him really. I just want to be able to forget him."

When Mary was asked to describe the content of her thoughts about Dan, it became obvious that these were always positive. She thought about the good times they had had and about the qualities she admired in him. She almost never thought of his selfishness, arrogance, or meanness.

Mary's first step toward solving her problem was to make a list of all Dan's bad points and of all the unfair things he had done to her: "Those days after his wife came back—waiting all day for the phone to ring and then realizing that he'd just forgotten. The way he was using me as a housekeeper."

She also listed the advantages of not being in love with him. For example:

I will not feel so depressed and worthless.

I will be nicer to my children.

I will not be such a drag on my friends.

I will be able to cope with the nursery school committee and the PTA again.

These lists were written on a card that Mary kept with her at all times. She also made a tape recording of them. She read the lists or played the tape at least a dozen times a day and tried to recreate in her mind the scene that was being described, with all its details and emotions. Whenever she found herself thinking something positive about Dan, she would think "Stop!" and substitute an item from the "bad Dan" list. She also used another form of antecedent control— avoiding things that triggered thoughts of Dan. She threw away his presents and stopped watching his favorite TV programs and cooking his favorite foods. She no longer drove past his house or rang him up. She kept herself very busy doing other things, so her thoughts would be on them rather than on Dan.

In order to tell whether these methods were working, Mary kept a record of her daily moods. She imagined a scale of 0–10, where 0 equaled "as bad as I have ever felt" and 10 equaled "like my old self again." Each evening she looked back at the day and tried to decide what her mood rating had been that day. She also kept a record of the number of positive thoughts she had about Dan.

In the beginning, Mary's mood ratings were around 1 or 2, and her positive thoughts about Dan were almost constant, too many to count. Then things started to improve. Some days were bad, but each week the average mood rating was higher, and the average number of positive thoughts about Dan was lower.

After seven weeks, none of Mary's thoughts of Dan was positive, and her mood ratings averaged 7. She stopped listening to her tape and reading her lists. "I really don't want to be reminded of him at all now."

One month later, as she was going to bed, she reached for her notebook, recorded a 10, and realized she hadn't thought of Dan all day.

habit is to increase the environmental stimulus control over concentrated writing. You can arrange a special "writing" environment so that (1) whenever you are in that situation, you are concentrating, and (2) while you are in that situation, you are not performing any other behavior. So you begin by learning to concentrate while writing at a certain place in which you *never do anything else* but write.

But if you don't have a place that you can reserve for this one behavior, you can make a particular *arrangement* of cues. A man had only one table in his room, which he had to use for a variety of activities, such as writing letters, paying bills, watching TV, and eating. But when he wanted to do concentrated studying or writing, he always pulled his table away from the wall and sat on the other side of it. In that way, sitting on the other side of his table became the cue associated only with concentrated intellectual work.

Arranging the social aspects of the environment can also be helpful in creating new stimulus control. Sometimes the desired behaviors themselves are not fully available to you. We have been discussing concentrated intellectual work. Suppose that no matter how diligent you are in removing yourself from your desk when not concentrating, the concentrated work still does not come. Using the stimulating value of other people can provide the necessary first step. Brigham (1982) suggests that the first environment chosen for studying should be one in which studying is a high-probability response—such as the library. He suggests that "a change in behavior could be accomplished by identifying a friend who regularly studies in the library and asking to study with that person. . . . [You should] reinforce the friend for being a study partner. Such reinforcement will . . . increase the likelihood that the friend will reinforce [your] studying behavior" (p. 55).

One of the most powerful cues to behavior is that same behavior performed by other people in the same environment. We have discussed this principle earlier, in observing that people trying to abstain from alcohol or drugs are most likely to relapse in social situations where others are indulging (Marlatt & Parks, 1982). These same effects can be used to positive advantage when you have difficulty "priming" that first behavioral step; that is placing yourself in an environment where others are performing your desired behavior can provide a powerful antecedent for your own similar performance.

The social environment can cue behavior in other ways. Friends, family, and acquaintances interact with us in habitual ways, and these interactions can build cues that are not always desirable. Frequently, the responses are emotional. People who are depressed often find themselves unable to "break out" of frustrating and unrewarding patterns with their associates. Doerfler and Richards (1981) studied a group of women who had self-initiated efforts to control their depression. Of those who were successful, 67% had made dramatic changes in their social environments, whereas few unsuccessful subjects had done so (14%).

These are all examples of deliberately establishing antecedent stimulus control, so that you can perform a desired behavior reliably in at least one situation. For some goals, only one situation is necessary. For others, however, you will want to perform the behavior in many situations. For example, Fo (1975) found that students are better off if they can study in many situations, so that each opportunity to study can be seized. Thus, in many cases it is desirable to broaden the range of effective antecedents for a desired target behavior.

Stimulus Generalization

Many behaviors—studying, writing, abstaining from drugs, social skills, better eating behaviors—will need to be performed eventually in a variety of environments. **Stimulus generalization** is the process by which a behavior that has been learned in the presence of one antecedent is performed in the presence of other, similar antecedents.

The more similar the new situation is to the original situation, the easier it is to generalize your newly learned behavior. Therefore, you will want to think about the similarity between other situations and the one in which you can already perform the desired behavior. You should begin generalization by performing the target behavior in the situation that is most similar to the original one.

A middle-aged woman suffered from a very strong fear of speaking in front of groups. Through self-modification, she developed the ability to speak to a group of three or four friends. Having accomplished that, she wanted to generalize the newly acquired ability to new groups. She thought that it would be easier if the new group contained at least a couple of friends from the old one, because the new situation would then be very similar to the one in which she first practiced. She arranged things so that such an opportunity would come up. When it did, she performed the target behavior and then reinforced it.

Once you have developed a behavior that you can perform in certain situations, you should gradually move into similar situations. Use self-instructions. A great strength of self-instructions is that they can be used in many situations, creating a bridge from familiar to unfamiliar circumstances. Self-instructions are portable cues. They can be taken with you from party to party, from home to library. Thus, self-instructions enhance the development of a broad skill base, just as stimulus generalization does.

Precommitment and Programming of the Social Environment

Precommitment means to arrange in advance for helpful antecedents to occur. This arrangement can be made when some problem situation is anticipated, especially for those moments of maximum difficulty.

A smoker had been off cigarettes for about two months. He had stopped several times in the past, but each time he had gone back to smoking. He had been successful this time because he had identified those situations in which he had lapsed in the past, and had taken steps to deal with them. One of the problem situations was being at a party. The drinks, the party atmosphere, and the feeling of relaxation represented an irresistible temptation to "smoke just a few," although in the past this had usually led to a return to regular smoking. One night, as the man and his wife were getting ready to go out to a party, he said, "You know, I am really going to be tempted to smoke there. Will you do me a favor? If you see me bumming a cigarette from someone, remind me of the kids and that I really don't want to go back to smoking." (One of the reasons he wanted to quit was because he knew he was setting a bad example for his children.)

This man arranged in advance to be reminded. He precommitted himself to facing the knowledge that he would end up smoking again if he tried to have just a few, and he made this precommitment at a time when he was not strongly tempted—*before* going to the party.

This intelligent strategy was possible because he had profited from previous mistakes. Each time a smoker returns to smoking, it is a lapse, but it is also a source of *information* about what kinds of situations are most tempting (Hunt & Matarazzo, 1973). The man used this information to cope better with the problem situation by enlisting the help of his wife.

Asking other people to cue or remind you can be an effective way of arranging antecedents. You are not asking to be nagged, of course, but simply to be reminded of what you wanted to do back when you were not being so sorely tempted.

You can encourage family and friends to help you achieve your goals by asking them to provide cues and reinforcers for the behaviors you want to develop and by asking them not to support undesired behavior (Stuart, 1967). A student of ours wrote: "With the help and cooperation of my family and friends, an agreement was made not to smoke cigarettes in front of me for one month. If they were going to smoke, they would let me know, so I could leave the room until the smoke cleared. My girlfriend and parents were especially helpful (though occasionally irritating) when they reminded me about my project. During situations that encouraged smoking, such as mealtime, driving, parties, and so on, they would remind me of my goal. This was very encouraging, because it showed that they were concerned and wanted to help. As they continued with their support, I began to feel more determined and obligated to quit."

Precommitment, in the form of reminders, can also be arranged without the help of others. Setting an alarm clock is one obvious way. Preparing a daily or weekly schedule of obligations is another. For example, an overweight student began to plan the day's meals each morning and found that she was better able to diet by not having to make any decisions when mealtime came.

CHAPTER SUMMARY

Identifying Antecedents

The identification of current antecedents requires careful record keeping. Be sure to trace back the chain of antecedents to its logical beginning. The task of discovering self-instructional antecedents involves carefully observing and amplifying the quiet thoughts that instruct you. Self-defeating beliefs can be discovered by writing out all instances of your problem behavior and identifying their common theme. The maladaptive nature of these beliefs can then be observed.

Modifying Old Antecedents

The first strategy for achieving antecedent control is to avoid the antecedent for the problem behavior. This is particularly appropriate for consummatory behaviors—such as overindulgence in food, drugs, or sex—because they automatically strengthen themselves on each performance by producing their own reinforcements.

Particularly avoid situations where other people are engaging in your indulgent habit. This is especially important when you are in an emotional state.

Antecedents can sometimes be avoided by narrowing the problem behavior down to a very restricted antecedent—smoking, sulking, or studying only in a special place reserved for that behavior. Narrowing by allowing only desirable behavior to occur in special places can also be effective. Thus, you should leave the special desk if you are not studying, or leave the bed if you are not able to sleep.

Antecedents can also be "avoided" by reperceiving them—by attending to their "cool," abstract qualities rather than their "hot," pleasurable features. Or temptations can be lessened merely by distracting yourself with thoughts of something else.

Chains of behavior develop as one act becomes the cue for the next, which in turn becomes the cue for the next, and so forth, with the entire chain being reinforced by the final reinforcement. Although it is the final act that is likely to be seen as the problem, the entire chain is implicated. Changing the chain can interrupt the automatic, "uncontrollable" nature of the problem. A chain can be scrambled, interrupted by pauses or record keeping, or changed by substituting one or more links. For long chains, it is advisable to change elements both at the beginning and at the end of the chain.

Arranging New Antecedents

A most effective way to arrange new antecedents is through self-instructions. Prior to the occasion for a wanted behavior, instruct yourself clearly and incisively. These instructions can pertain to actions or to beliefs; that is, you can instruct yourself about the details of the action you plan to take, or you can instruct yourself about your own good qualities and competence.

Self-defeating or unpleasant self-statements can be replaced with more positive ones. Particularly stubborn self-statements can be reduced by using the technique of thought stopping. A key to success in thought stopping is to substitute new, adaptive self-statements. Self-instructions should actually be said, aloud or subvocally, as clearly as possible and as close in time as possible to the moment of the actual behavior.

The physical environment can be rearranged to increase stimulus control over desired behavior. The technique is to restrict the desired behavior to a particular environment. The social environment can be arranged to stimulate desired behavior by being in the presence of others who are performing the behavior you desire. Eventually, most behaviors are desirable in several situations, so that techniques of stimulus generalization are recommended. Desirable behaviors should gradually be extended to similar situations, thus broadening the range of controlling antecedents. Self-instructions should be used to bridge between situations. Self-instructions will then become portable, reliable cues, allowing self-regulated behavior in many situations.

Precommitment—arranging in advance for helpful antecedents to occur—is especially useful when moments of maximum difficulty are anticipated. When you know that cues to your undesired behavior are going to be present in a situation, precommit to having cues present that will assist your new performance—reminders from others, the ring of an alarm clock, or self-reminders of your goals.

YOUR OWN SELF-DIRECTION PROJECT: STEP FIVE

By examining your structured diary and/or your self-recording, identify the antecedents of any problem behavior relevant to your goals. Devise a plan for either increasing or decreasing antecedent stimulus control. As one procedure, use new self-instructions, but use at least one other technique as well.

Write this plan out, just as you have done for the previous two steps. Chapters Six and Seven are likely to contain ideas that you'll want to incorporate in your final plan.

TIPS FOR TYPICAL TOPICS

Anxieties

No doubt you are avoiding the frightening situations when you can. What are the antecedents to which you react? tension or fear? Note the worrisome things you tell yourself. Are they true? For example, "I'm failing this test. This is a catastrophe!" First, are you actually failing? Second, is it a catastrophe? compared to an earthquake? Can you identify maladaptive beliefs such as "Anything less than perfect is failure"?

Assertion

Distinguish between assertion and aggression—one is appropriate, the other is not. Many nonassertive people get very angry before they finally speak up, so that when they do act, they are more likely to be aggressive—verbally—than if they had asserted themselves earlier (Linehan, 1979). Therefore, it is desirable to act assertively early in the chain of events. Early intervention in the chain can be approached through *beliefs* and/or through *self-instructions*. Goldfried (1979) and his associates have shown that timid people often have "beliefs" that they are willing to abandon as soon as the beliefs come under scrutiny—for example, the belief that others will reject or punish them for the slightest bit of standing up for themselves. Search out such beliefs. They may well be irrational, because more respect is usually accorded those who respect themselves. Changing such beliefs can lead to changed behavior. Self-instructions are particularly useful in coaching yourself through unfamiliar behavior: "Remember, be firm. That's right, you needn't be unpleasant. Just state your position firmly. Good."

Depression

When you notice a change in your mood, try to discover what thoughts have led to it. Thoughts such as "I'm a loser" or "I never do anything right" will certainly depress your mood and should be replaced by more positive self-statements (Rehm, 1982). Use thought stopping. Rehearse positive self-statements, so that you can use them immediately as replacements. This is especially important if you are depressed, because you will tend to criticize yourself for criticizing yourself: "I just thought that I'm a loser. What a stupid thing to think" (Hollon & Beck, 1979). Have a replacement thought ready: "I'm a lo—— Stop! I'm a loyal and sensitive friend."

Be especially vigilant about negative self-statements after some disappointment. When depressed, you will be likely to overgeneralize and tell yourself that you are worthless in general (Carver & Ganellen, 1983). Prepare positive self-statements, and expect to use them immediately after disappointments.

The second major tactic for antecedent control of depression is the scheduling of pleasant activities (Hollon & Beck, 1979)—a powerful antecedent of good mood that is not often used by depressed people (Fuchs & Rehm, 1977). The type of activity—entertainment, socializing, exercise, fantasizing, handicrafts—is not crucial, so long as it is pleasant for you. Schedule these activities regularly and frequently, and stick to the schedule.

Family, Friends, Lovers, and Coworkers

Self-instructions are especially useful as antecedent control in strained relationships. If relationships are severely distressed, you may wish to use avoidance, for a time, by limiting interaction to certain situations.

Overeating, Smoking, Drinking, and Drug Use

As an immediate first step, avoid the antecedents. Avoid the situations that are the cues for your indulgence, particularly those where others will be indulging. This avoidance is particularly important when you are emotionally upset (Marlatt & Parks, 1982). If you failed to avoid, then escape the situation (Shiffman, 1984). If you cannot escape, distract yourself with other thoughts or activities. If you cannot be distracted, concentrate on the abstract, cool qualities of indulging.

Analyze the chains that lead to the problem behavior. The chains often lead as far back as shopping. Not buying the marijuana in the first place is the most effective point at which to break the chain. You can interrupt the overeating chain at several early points—for example, by shopping when you are *not* hungry (to prevent overbuying), by not *buying* fattening foods, by not even walking down the cookie-and-cracker aisle, and by not allowing yourself to become so hungry that you will gorge (Stuart & Davis, 1972). Overeating is likely to have multiple antecedents—many chains all leading to excessive eating. You may eat when bored, sad, angry, or happy. You may always eat what is offered to you, even if you are not hungry. You may eat because the food is there or because you want to relax. Learning to eat properly requires careful observation of all those antecedents—emotional, social, and physical (Stuart & Davis, 1972; Leon, 1979).

A plan should address both ends of the chain.

Interfering at the end of the chain—right at the moment of the over-whelming urge to eat—can often be done by a recommitment strategy. Require yourself to write out an answer to these questions before giving in to the urge (Youdin & Hemmes, 1978; L. W. Rosen, 1981):

1. Why do I want to eat this food, when I have started a program to stop overeating?
2. Whom am I fooling by eating this food?
3. Do I want to be overweight?
4. Do I want this food more than I want a normal weight?

The same principles apply to smoking and drug use. Interfere early in the chain by reducing or eliminating the supply of cigarettes, by rationing them if you are cutting down, or by not buying and carrying cigarettes if you are stopping. Interfere late in the chain, right at the moment of the strongest urge, by asking goal questions:

1. Why do I want to smoke this cigarette (or joint), when I have started a program to quit smoking (or using pot)?
2. Whom am I fooling by smoking this cigarette (or joint)?
3. Do I want to keep on being a smoker (or a drug user)?
4. Do I want to indulge more than I want to break my habit?

All diet programs should include a two-minute pause in the middle of every meal. For alcohol, drugs, and tobacco, requiring a two-minute pause between the urge and the indulgence is an effective technique for reducing violations.

Studying and Time Management

Three specific forms of antecedent control have proven effective: (1) Write out a planned schedule, and keep it as a reminder in some obvious place. Plan at least a week at a time. Daily plans don't work as well (Kirschenbaum, Humphrey, & Malett, 1981). (2) Use self-reminders of goals and values. Ask several times a day, "Is this the best use of my time right now? If it's not, what would be?" (Lakein, 1973). (3) Study while not interacting with other people (Heffernan & Richards, 1981). Studying can sometimes be facilitated by studying with an effective partner or in the library where others are also studying, but do not interact with others except before and after your studying time.

The Other Sex

What are the specific situations in which you have problems? Consult the list in Chapter Three. Many students, for example, feel they don't know how to ask for a date, or fear rejection so much that they never ask. Do certain situations cue you to avoid social interactions? What negative self-instructions do you give yourself, such as "He'd probably just laugh if I asked him out"? Can you discover any self-defeating beliefs, such as "If I ask her out and she refuses, it's a disaster" or "If there's a lull in the conversation, it means we are bored, and that's terrible" or "I really need to impress him, so I better show off"?

Use self-instructions to coax yourself through particular situations, such as making conversation: "Remember, talk about what she wants to talk about. Ask her what she is interested in, then talk about that. Express interest in her."

You may feel you don't know what to do in certain social situations, or become fearful in them. These problems can be dealt with after reading the next chapter.

CHAPTER SIX

Behaviors

OUTLINE

- Substituting New Thoughts and Behaviors
- Substitutions for Anxiety and Tension
- Relaxation
- Developing New Behaviors
- Shaping: The Method of Successive Approximations
- Chapter Summary
- Your Own Self-Direction Project: Step Six
- Tips for Typical Topics

LEARNING OBJECTIVES

Substituting New Thoughts and Behaviors

1. What is the best approach to ridding yourself of an unwanted behavior?
2. What is an incompatible response?

Substitutions for Anxiety and Tension

3. What are some activities that are incompatible with anxiety? How would you use them in a self-change program?
4. How do you meditate?

Relaxation

5. Describe the tension-release method for relaxation.
   a. Where do you practice relaxation?
   b. When should you practice?
   c. How is relaxation used as an incompatible response?
   d. How is it combined with self-instructions?

Developing New Behaviors

6. What is the fundamental way of mastering a behavior?
7. Explain imagined rehearsal.
8. How are imagined rehearsal and relaxation combined?
9. How does one use models in developing new behaviors?
10. Explain imagined modeling. What are the recommended procedures?
11. What is the value of practice in the real world?

Shaping: The Method of Successive Approximations

12. Explain the general procedure for shaping.
13. What are the rules for shaping?
14. How can relaxation be combined with shaping?
15. What are some common problems in shaping?

Any plan for self-modification involves developing some new behavior. The principles for developing new behaviors in self-modification programs are the same as those that govern learning in all settings. Self-modification techniques have been devised and refined by psychologists to assist in the self-conscious use of these principles.

This chapter is organized into five main units. The first section discusses procedures for *substituting* a more desirable for a less desirable behavior. Bringing a new behavior into position—in place of an undesired one—can be a ready solution to some problems. The second section discusses substitutions for anxiety and tension. The third section concentrates on a particular new behavior—*relaxation*—because it is such a useful response to substitute for anxiety and worry. Many readers can already relax effectively, but will need to bring this "new" behavior into the chains that now produce worry and anxiety. The fourth section is devoted to techniques for developing new behaviors in general, particularly when the behavior is genuinely new or unknown to you. The principal techniques are *modeling* and *rehearsal*. Finally, we will discuss a fundamental strategy for acquiring new behaviors and bringing them into self-modification programs: *shaping*, or the method of successive approximations.

SUBSTITUTING NEW THOUGHTS AND BEHAVIORS

Substituting positive self-statements for negative ones, substituting "Stop!" for intrusive thoughts, substituting new elements into chains—these are all examples of a general principle of self-modification. *The task is always to develop new behavior, not merely to suppress old behavior.* Simply eliminating some undesired habit has been likened to creating a behavioral "vacuum." If something is not created to take its place, the old behavior will quickly rush back in to fill the void (Davidson, Denney, & Elliott, 1980; Tinling, 1972). Eventually, some new behavioral development is necessary. Beginning immediately with the tactic of substitution is economical, because the effort of developing the new may automatically suppress the undesired thought or behavior.

Andrea, a young woman who was bothered by too-frequent arguments with her father, began to observe her own behavior. She discovered the following chain of events. Her father would make a comment about some aspect of her behavior that seemed to bother him (for example, he disapproved of her career goals). Usually Andrea would respond with a frown and the comment that he should mind his own business. This would enrage him, and they would be off to another bitter argument. Andrea knew that her father basically loved her and that he was simply having a difficult time adjusting to the fact that she was now an adult. She reasoned that if she substituted kind remarks and a smile when he opened up some topic about her behavior, they might be able to discuss it in a friendlier fashion. Instead of setting out to *decrease* frowning and unkind comments, she set out to *increase* smiling and kind comments.

Thereafter, when he made some remark about her behavior or goals, Andrea would smile at him and strive to disagree as pleasantly as possible. (Of course, she kept a record of her responses and also used other techniques to maintain them.) Increasing the desirable behavior had the effect of calming her father, and they progressed through a series of amicable conversations to a new understanding.

The same tactic of substituting new behaviors for undesirable ones was used by Ron, a college junior. Ron's girlfriend had told him very clearly that his long daily telephone calls were getting oppressive. Ron wanted to keep the relationship, and he genuinely wanted to please her. He set out to reduce his telephone calls to no more than one every other day. For the first few days, he did suppress the urge to call, but he found himself brooding and telling himself that her attitude proved that he was a distasteful person. Ron then adopted a plan that used two substitute behaviors. First, he substituted more favorable (and more realistic) self-statements. At 9:00 on noncalling nights, he said to himself "I am able to be thoughtful and generous in adopting her preferences." Second, he systematically substituted another behavior for that time block. Because he was an able student, he substituted an hour of studying for the phone call. Note that merely suppressing the phone calls not only left a vacuum but allowed feelings of worthlessness and anger to slip in. The substitution strategy allowed him a more realistic self-appraisal, increased his study time, and did make him a more desirable friend.

Incompatible Behaviors

When possible, it is a good tactic to select a substitute behavior that is *incompatible* with the undesired one.

What exactly is an "incompatible response"? *An incompatible response is a behavior that prevents the occurrence of some other behavior.* Smiling is incompatible with frowning. Sitting is incompatible with running. Going swimming is incompatible with staying in your room. Being courteous is incompatible with being rude. For many undesired behaviors, there may be several incompatible ones available.

A male student was active in campus politics and had been elected to the Council of the Associated Students. In the meetings, he found that he was talking too much and losing his effectiveness because he was irritating the other members. He felt the impulse to talk, he said, with "the force of a compulsion." He first tried simply not talking so much. He did have some success, but after considering the use of incompatible responses, he reasoned that he could do better by choosing a more active and positive alternative behavior. He chose "listening." This was a genuinely new act, not merely the suppression of an old one. It resulted in less talking, which he wanted, and also in greater listening, which he came to value more and more.

An effective program for reducing nail biting has been developed that substitutes grooming of the nails and cuticles for biting them (Davidson, Denney, & Elliott, 1980). This proved to be more effective than any technique aimed only at reducing biting. It is useful to choose an incompatible behavior, even though it is of no particular value in itself. A man who wanted

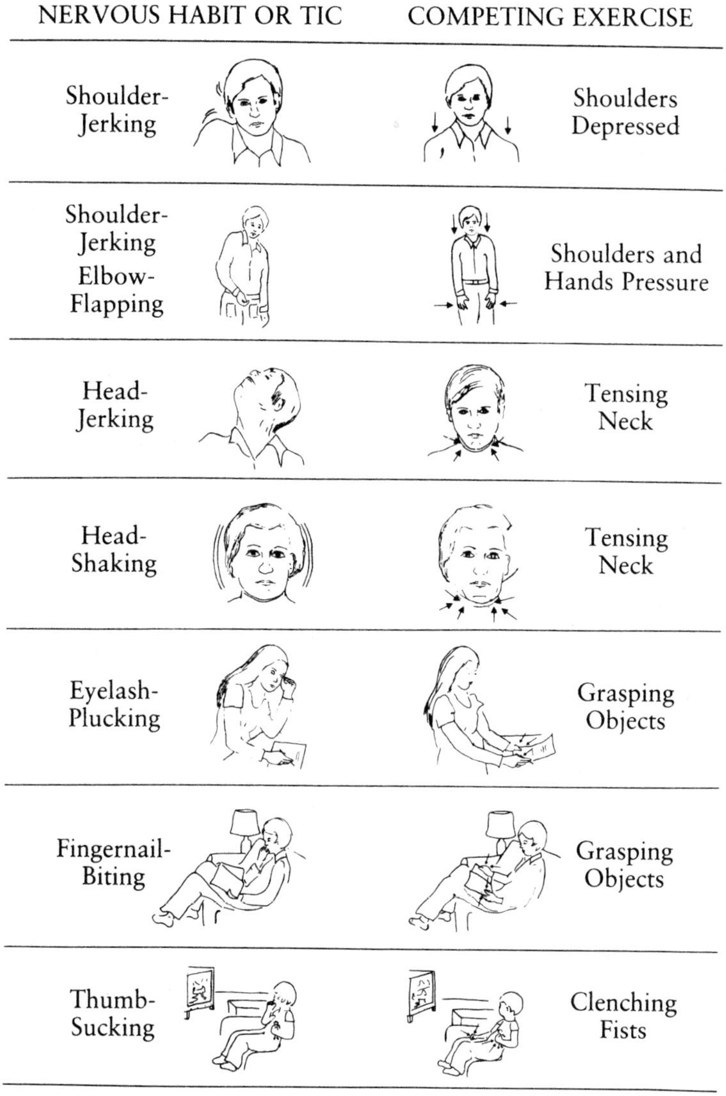

NERVOUS HABIT OR TIC		COMPETING EXERCISE	
Shoulder-Jerking			Shoulders Depressed
Shoulder-Jerking Elbow-Flapping			Shoulders and Hands Pressure
Head-Jerking			Tensing Neck
Head-Shaking			Tensing Neck
Eyelash-Plucking			Grasping Objects
Fingernail-Biting			Grasping Objects
Thumb-Sucking			Clenching Fists

Figure 6-1. A pictorial representation of the various types of nervous tics or habits. The left-hand column illustrates the different tics or habits. The adjacent illustration in the right-hand column illustrates the type of competing exercise used for that nervous tic or habit. The arrows in each of the Competing Exercise illustrations show the direction of isometric muscle contraction being exerted by the client. (*From "Habit Reversal: A Method of Eliminating Nervous Habits and Tics," by N. H. Azrin and R. G. Nunn, 1973,* Behaviour Research and Therapy, *11, 619–628. Copyright 1973 by Pergamon Press, Ltd. Reprinted by permission.*)

to stop cracking his knuckles all the time decided that whenever he felt like cracking his knuckles, he would *instead* make a fist. A young woman who sometimes scratched her skin until it bled substituted patting for scratching. A visual illustration of some incompatible responses for replacing nervous habits can be seen in Figure 6-1. The research evidence for the effectiveness of these techniques is excellent (Azrin, Nunn, & Frantz-Renshaw, 1982; Rosenbaum & Ayllon, 1981).

The substitution of positive self-statements for negative ones is an element in almost all contemporary treatments for depression (Beck, Rush, Shaw, & Emery, 1979; Rehm, 1982; Lewinsohn, Biglan, & Zeiss, 1976). Negative self-evaluations are always a part of being depressed. The following are typical depressed self-statements (Rehm, 1982):

1. After a minor quarrel with a friend: "I'm just that way. I can't get along with anyone."
2. After being praised by the boss: "He's just doing that to make me feel better because he criticized me last week."
3. After making an "A" on the first exam: "It was an easy test. I'll fail a hard exam."

None of these statements tell the whole story. Equally true (but incompatible) self-statements could be substituted. Try to think of substitute statements for each one. The substitutes should emphasize the positive aspects of the events. These statements should then be made in place of the self-critical ones.

When you select an incompatible behavior you want to increase at the expense of some unwanted act, be sure you keep a record of how often you do the one instead of the other. It's a good idea to select an incompatible behavior as soon as possible and begin to count it, even if you are still doing a baseline count on the unwanted target behavior. Keeping a record of the incompatible behavior will encourage you to perform it (Kazdin, 1974f).

BOX 6-1

RELIEVING DEPRESSION WITH INCOMPATIBLE THOUGHTS

"My problem is that I get depressed, and then I think about death and suicide, and this frightens me. Sometimes I just don't care what happens." This young woman tried a plan of listening to music or talking to friends when depression began, thinking that they would produce feelings incompatible with depression. Although she kept this plan for 48 days, no real improvement occurred.

Then, "I thought why not fight fire with fire—use good-feeling thoughts to combat depression thoughts. This would be an incompatible behavior (in the mind)."

She selected a fantasy, which she called "my good dream." Whenever a depressed thought or feeling began, she immediately substituted her "good dream" and held the dream in her mind until her feelings moved "back up at least to neutral."

Here is a typical entry from her journal, which she kept along with her frequency counts and mood ratings.

"The bus driver was in a foul mood and, just as I was going out the first door, shouted 'Go to the back!' This made me feel like a fool and really started my depression. Ten minutes had gone by when I reached my job, and by then I was really starting to sink. So I took 15 minutes to try and counter my depression with my good dream. I went in 15 minutes late, but it worked."

It worked remarkably well, as her graph shows (see Figure 6-2). Her depressions dropped from three hours a day to virtually zero. After day 67, she stopped using any self-modification plan. We never found out what her "good dream" was.

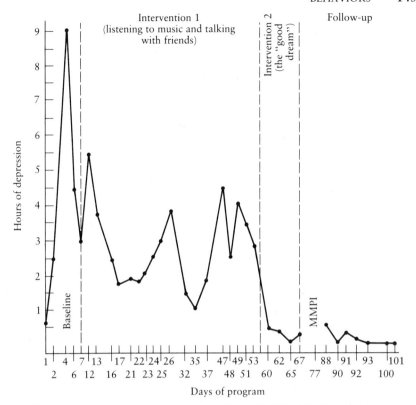

Figure 6-2. Hours of depression per day. (*From "Self-Modification of Depression," by R. G. Tharp, D. L. Watson, and J. Kaya, 1974, Journal of Consulting and Clinical Psychology, 42, 624. Copyright 1974 by the American Psychological Association. Reprinted by permission. [Condensed from the Extended Report, University of Hawaii, 1974.]*)

SUBSTITUTIONS FOR ANXIETY AND TENSION

A young married student complained to us, "I don't see how this system [substituting incompatible responses] will work for me. I really don't need to learn anything new. I just need to get rid of my fears. When my husband wants to make love, I want to make love too, very much, but when the crucial moment comes, I get so nervous that I can't carry on."

In fact, substituting an incompatible response is probably the best strategy for her. A goal common to many plans for self-modification is to achieve mastery over fears, anxiety, nervousness, or tension. In this section, we will discuss a variety of responses that are incompatible with anxiety, and we will discuss how to arrange their substitution.

Phobias, Fears, and Avoidance Behavior

There are people who are so afraid of dogs that they will not enter a house until they are certain that no dogs are there. Others fear open places so much that they will not leave their own homes. An unreasonable fear of heights may prevent a person from using an elevator. Others, like the young married woman above, fear sex so that they are unable to respond with any pleasure. These **phobias**—strong, irrational fears that interfere with normal life—produce avoidance behaviors, and the avoidance is reinforced by reducing the anxiety that would come from dogs, open spaces, heights, or sex.

Many milder, common anxieties also cause people to avoid the cues that produce them. Many students are anxious during tests. The anxiety can grow strong enough to produce extreme avoidance, even to the extent of dropping out of school.

Coping with an unreasonable fear by substituting an incompatible response is the best way to deal with the feared situation (Goldfried, 1977). The basic form of this plan is to develop a new behavior that is incompatible with anxiety and then substitute it for the anxiety as you gradually approach the feared situation.

From Sex to Kung Fu: Substitutions for Anxiety

Many behaviors are incompatible with anxiety. Simple *attention* to a different aspect of the situation can interfere with anxiety. For example, Frederick Kanfer (1975) has suggested that an extremely withdrawn person go to a drugstore for a cup of coffee and specifically record for 15 minutes the number and types of interactions of people sitting at the counter. A shy and insecure woman might feel less anxious at parties if she made a point of making notes about the occupational background of a certain number of guests. In other words, if you are attending to the task of recording and interviewing, you will be less influenced by the anxiety-provoking aspects of the situation. This also allows the natural reinforcement of social gatherings to take effect.

Concentrating the attention has been used to reduce test anxiety. Focusing on the test itself (not on the fears, the grade, the consequences, other people, or the instructor) can reduce anxiety in an examination (Sarason, 1980).

Sexual arousal, too, can be used to combat anxiety, because the two are incompatible. There are limits to the use of this substitute, but, when feasible, it can be helpful. Gary Brown (1978) reported a case in which a client suffered extreme anxiety whenever he had to drive past a cemetery at night. Usually he avoided driving at night, but if he did have to drive past a cemetery, he had "an overwhelming compulsion to stop the car, turn the inside light on, and look at the back seat." The client was instructed to practice driving past a cemetery near his home while imagining scenes of sexual activity with his wife. He began the imagined scenes when he was far enough from the cemetery that anxiety would not interfere and arranged to be maximally aroused just as the tombstones appeared. He did this 30 minutes each day for several days. His anxiety at the cemetery dropped to zero, and after a few days he was able to drive past without sexual arousal *and* without fear.

Gershman and Stedman (1971) have reported cases in which Oriental defense exercises were used as behaviors incompatible with anxiety. Their "Mr. P." feared closed places—elevators, locked rooms, trains, and others—

and had begun to feel anxiety when wearing tight clothes and even his wedding ring. Their plan had Mr. P. go into a closet and, as soon as the door closed, engage in kung fu exercises (at which he was already adept). His anxiety disappeared after no more than 20 seconds. After several such trials, he was able to stay in the closet for up to an hour without doing his exercises or feeling any anxiety. He then began to practice in elevators, and it took him only two sessions to feel comfortable there, too. All his anxieties disappeared, and a six-month follow-up showed no signs of recurrence. These same investigators reported similar results for Mr. R. who used karate exercises to inhibit his anxieties.

Vigorous *exercise* is a behavior incompatible with many forms of anxiety. Marlatt and Parks (1982) recommend exercise as a substitute behavior for drinking, drug use, or smoking. As tension begins, substitute a session of vigorous running, aerobics, or racquetball. This can effectively replace the tension that cues indulgence in drugs. One of our students used jogging to replace the anxiety he experienced during marital difficulties. He found that the reduced anxiety allowed him to do better thinking and problem solving.

Meditation: A Substitution for Anxiety

Meditation produces physical and mental conditions that are incompatible with anxiety. When it is practiced just before contact with a feared situation, it can produce relaxation. Boudreau (1972, pp. 97–98) reported the case of a college student who "expressed fears of enclosed places, elevators, being alone, and examinations. His avoidance behavior to these situations was extreme, having started when he was 13. The physiological sensations he experienced gave him the additional fear of mental illness." The man was instructed to practice meditation for half an hour every day after imagining some fear-inducing scenes and *also at the actual appearance of fear-evoking situations.* "Marked improvement followed," says Boudreau. "Within one month, the avoidance behavior to enclosed places, being alone, and elevators had all disappeared. Once his tension level had decreased, he did not experience abnormal physiological sensations, and this reassured him as to his physical and mental state."

In general, the continued practice of meditation and its use in many situations is associated with a better capacity to cope with a variety of stresses (Shapiro & Walsh, 1980). Marlatt and Marques (1977) found that meditation led to less alcohol drinking, and Throll (1981) found that it produced improvement on a variety of psychological tests measuring general stress.

Current research indicates that meditation is as effective as any other way of producing relaxation for use as a response incompatible with anxiety (Throll, 1981; Woolfolk, Lehrer, McCann, & Rooney, 1982). In the next section of this chapter, we will present specific training instructions for learning another way to relax, called the **tension-release method** or **progressive relaxation.** Select the method that is most pleasant for you. The technique is less important than the amount of practice you devote to it. For that reason, it is important to enjoy it (Throll, 1981).

RELAXATION

Relaxation is a behavior that can be used to cope with a wide variety of problem situations. According to the dictionary, relaxation is "the casting off of nervous tension and anxiety." It is both a mental and a physical response—a feeling of calmness and serenity and a state of muscular release and passivity.

Relaxation is easily learned, if one is willing to devote practice to it. The method used is not important (Barrios & Shigetomi, 1979, 1980; Lewis, Biglan, & Steinbock, 1978; Miller & Bornstein, 1977)—the relaxation is. If you are already adept at some technique for inducing relaxation, there is no reason for not using your own. Any form of relaxation will do, as long as you can produce it quickly, thoroughly, and at your own instructions.

BOX 6-2

HOW TO MEDITATE

There are several ways to meditate. The interested reader is referred to Shapiro (1980) for a full discussion. Here is one method that has proven useful to our students.

Sit in a comfortable chair in a quiet room away from noise and interruptions. Pay no attention to the world outside your body. It is easiest to do this if you have something to focus on in your mind. For example, concentrate on your breathing or use a mantra, a word you say softly over and over to yourself. Here are three different mantras: *mahing, shiam,* and *wen.* Choose one. Don't say the mantra out loud, but think it, silently and gently.

When you first sit down and begin to relax, you will notice thoughts coming into your mind. After a minute or two, begin to say the mantra in your mind. Do this slowly, in a passive way. As you say the mantra to yourself, other thoughts will come. As a matter of fact, after a while you may realize that you've been so busy with these thoughts that you haven't said your mantra in several minutes. When you become aware of this, just return gently to the mantra. Don't fight to keep thoughts out of your mind; instead, let them drift through. This is not a time for working out solutions to problems or thinking things over. Try to keep your mind open, so that as thoughts other than the mantra drift in, they drift out again, smoothly as the flowing of a river. The mantra will return, and you will relax with it.

It is important to make this a gentle process, a relaxing time. Don't fight to keep thoughts out of your mind. Don't get upset if you are distracted. Merely let the mantra return.

It is best to meditate in preparation for activity—for example, before you go to work—rather than after you are already tensed up. If used as soon as you begin to feel tense, it is a good coping reaction.

People often nod off to sleep while meditating. Don't try to use meditation as a substitute for sleep. If you do go to sleep, usually you will find that five minutes of meditation afterwards will make you quite awake. Some people notice that meditating makes them feel very awake—so much so that if they meditate before bedtime, they can't get to sleep.

But don't use alcohol, drugs, tobacco, or any other substance to achieve relaxation. If you do, you won't learn the independent self-direction of relaxation you need to overcome real-life anxieties.

A reliable method for learning to relax is to use deep muscular relaxation. As you read this sentence, try relaxing your hand and arm or your jaw muscles. If you can do so, you will realize how much energy you tie up in excess muscular tension. You can also experience subtle mental changes as your muscles "cast off their tensions" (Evans, 1976).

Once you have learned relaxation, you will use it to replace anxiety responses in situations in which you are now uncomfortable or that you now avoid. The basic idea is to learn to produce relaxation *at the first sign of tension*. That is the reason for the *tension-release method*, which calls for *tensing* muscles and then *releasing* them. You will learn to recognize the signs of tension, so that when you feel them later in real-life situations, you can quickly produce the release that is relaxation. In this way, you can use the first signs of tension (for example, while taking tests or talking to strangers) as the cue to relax and interrupt the tension process early in its sequence. This method of recognizing tension and producing relaxation is a very effective strategy for coping with any form of anxiety (Goldfried, 1971, 1977; Goldfried & Trier, 1974; Snyder & Deffenbacher, 1977).

The mastery and use of relaxation will be discussed in three steps: (1) how to use the instructions; (2) where to practice; and (3) using relaxation as an incompatible response.

How to Use the Relaxation Instructions: Step 1

The tension-release instructions (Box 6-3) are like a set of exercises, one for each group of muscles. The final goal is to relax all groups simultaneously to achieve total body relaxation. Each muscle group can be relaxed separately. Relaxation cannot be achieved all at once, so you should follow a gradual procedure in learning it. First you learn to relax your arms; then your facial area, neck, shoulders, and upper back; then your chest, stomach, and lower back; then your hips, thighs, and calves; and finally your whole body.

The general idea is to first tense a set of muscles and then relax them, so that they will relax more deeply than before they were tensed. You should focus your attention on each muscle system as you work through the various muscle groups. This will give you a good sense of what each set feels like when it is well relaxed and when it is tense. The exercises may require 20 to 30 minutes at first. As you learn, you will need less and less time.

Choose a private place, quiet and free of interruptions and distracting stimuli. Sit comfortably, well supported by the chair, so that you don't have to use your muscles to support yourself. You may want to close your eyes. Some people prefer to lie down while practicing. You may find it especially pleasant to practice before going to sleep.

The basic procedure for each muscle group is the same: *tense* the muscle, *release* the muscle, and *feel* the relaxation. You may want to memorize the

BOX 6-3

RELAXATION INSTRUCTIONS

Muscle groups	*Tension exercises*
1. the dominant hand 2. the other hand	Make a tight fist.
3. the dominant arm 4. the other arm	Curl your arm up; tighten the bicep.
5. upper face and scalp	Raise eyebrows as high as possible.
6. center face	Squint eyes and wrinkle nose.
7. lower face	Smile in a false, exaggerated way; clench teeth.
8. neck	a. Pull head slightly forward, then relax. b. Pull head slightly back, then relax.
9. chest and shoulders	a. Pull shoulders back till the blades almost touch, then relax. b. Pull shoulders forward all the way, then relax.
10. abdomen	Make abdomen tight and hard.
11. buttocks	Tighten together.
12. upper right leg 13. upper left leg	Stretch leg out from you, tensing both upper and lower muscles.
14. lower right leg 15. lower left leg	Pull toes up toward you.
16. right foot 17. left foot	Curl toes down and away from you.

First for each muscle group	*Then for the whole body*
Tense the muscles and hold for five seconds.	Now tense all the muscles together and hold for five seconds.
Feel the tension. Notice it carefully.	Feel the tension, notice it carefully, then release. Let all tension slide away.
Now release. Let the tension slide away, all away.	Notice any remaining tension. Release it.

BOX 6-3

RELAXATION INSTRUCTIONS (*continued*)

Feel the difference

Notice the pleasant warmth of relaxation.	Take a deep breath. Say softly to yourself "relax," as you breathe out slowly.
Now repeat the sequence with the same group.	Remain totally relaxed.
Repeat again. Do the sequence three times for each group of muscles.	Repeat breathing in and then out slowly, saying "relax," staying perfectly relaxed.
Tense. Release. Learn the difference. Feel the warmth of relaxation.	Do this three times.
	The exercise has ended. Enjoy the relaxation.

In your daily life,
in many situations
Notice your body's tension.
Identify the tense muscle groups.
Say softly to yourself "relax."
Relax the tense group.
Feel the relaxation and enjoy it.

Adapted from *Insight vs. Desensitization in Psychotherapy,* by G. L. Paul. Copyright 1966 by Stanford University Press. Reprinted by permission.

specific muscle groups and the exercises for each. For example, the hands are exercised by making a fist and the forehead by raising the eyebrows. You will want to know the instructions by heart, so that you can relax quickly and at any time or place, according to your own self-instructions. This is the reason for the final exercise—saying "relax" slowly and softly as you breathe out while totally relaxed. You can then transfer this self-instruction into your natural environment and produce relaxation instead of anxiety (Cautela, 1966).

Where to Practice Relaxation: Step 2

As soon as you have practiced enough that you can tense and relax some muscle groups, it's time to begin the exercises in other situations. You can practice tension release of some muscle groups while driving, riding the bus, attending lectures or concerts, sunbathing at the beach, sitting at your desk, or washing dishes. Relax whatever muscles are not needed for the activity you are engaged in at the moment. Choose a wide variety of situations. It is best not to begin with a situation that represents a particular problem for you.

It's not necessary to use all muscle groups during this practice. Exercise those groups that you've learned to control in your private sessions. If you detect tension in one group—your face or your throat, for example—practice relaxing those.

This phase of practice has three purposes. First, you learn to detect specific tensions. You will discover that you are prone to tension in particular muscle groups. For some people, it's the shoulders and neck that tense up most often; for others, the arms or the face. Relaxing these specific groups will decrease your overall tension.

Second, you learn to regulate the *depth* of relaxation. While it is crucial to learn total, deep muscle relaxation—even to the point of physical limpness—it is not necessary or desirable to use this full response to combat all tensions. Relaxation is a physical skill, just as weight lifting is. The strong man does not use his full strength to carry eggs, although he has it available for moving pianos. As we will discuss shortly, you can use *deep* relaxation as a response incompatible with anxiety in specific situations that you find difficult. But *graduated* relaxation of muscle groups is a highly valuable skill, and you can begin to learn it by practicing both shallow and deep relaxation. You will be fully skilled when you can totally relax without using the tension technique. Tensing the muscles before relaxing them is only a training method, and it should be dropped as soon as you can relax without it. Then, just saying "relax" to yourself or simply deciding to relax will produce the relaxation at the depth you want.

Practicing relaxation in many situations will prepare you to use it as a general skill for self-direction.

As the next step, it is particularly important to *practice while you are experiencing some tension*. Use tension as a cue for your practice sessions. When you feel the signs of anxiety—whether as mental discomfort or as muscular tension—immediately substitute a relaxation practice session.

If anxiety-producing occasions do not occur during the time you are practicing, you can imagine scenes that have caused tension in the past. While imagining them, go through your complete relaxation practice (Suinn, 1977).

If it is simply not possible to discover the specific moments of heightened anxiety, you can use one of two strategies: Practice relaxation prior to and during a situation that you judge ought to be difficult. Or, if you cannot detect increased tensions from moment to moment, practice relaxation at several predetermined times of day no matter what the situation (Deffenbacher, 1984).

The third purpose of this step is to learn to relax in as many situations as possible. Even if you set out to combat a specific anxiety in a specific situation, the odds are high that you will find additional situations in which relaxation is useful (Goldfried, 1971; Zemore, 1975; Goldfried & Goldfried, 1977). Sherman and Plummer (1973) trained 21 students in relaxation as a general self-direction skill. All but one reported at least one way in which they had benefited from the training; the average was 2.1 per person. The most common situations in which they used relaxation were social situations, sleep problems, test anxiety, handling of interviews, and efforts to increase energy and alertness. Sherman (1975) reported that two years after training, the students still used the strategy. Deffenbacher and Michaels (1981) found that students who learned to use relaxation as a coping skill for test anxiety stayed less anxious in tests even after 15 months. Furthermore, they demonstrated a reduction in their overall experience of anxiety.

Using Relaxation as an Incompatible Response: Step 3

Susan, an 18-year-old freshman, was extremely nervous while taking tests. She studied long and effectively but made only D's and F's on examinations, even though she could answer the questions after the exam was over. She came from a small rural high school, where the teachers overlooked her poor exam performances because she was one of their brightest students and excelled in projects and reports. In the large university, she lost this personal understanding and support.

Susan's counselor first gave her some brief paper-and-pencil tests to measure her anxiety and also three subtests of a well-known IQ measure. She then had four training sessions, one per week, to learn how to relax. The method she followed was the same one you are learning in this book. She first practiced at home and then extended her practice into real-life situations in which she was reasonably comfortable. After her fifth session, she had to take a number of course examinations. Using her cue word "calm" (like our "relax"), she relaxed during the examinations and performed remarkably well. Before her relaxation training, her average test score was 1.0 (on a 4-point system). After relaxing, her scores averaged 3.5. She completed the term with a 2.88 grade point average.

Susan then repeated the anxiety and IQ tests she had taken before relaxation training. When compared to her first scores, the tests indicated that her test anxiety was reduced and that her general level of tension was also lower. She even improved on two of the IQ measures. Obviously, relaxation cannot improve "intelligence," but replacing anxiety with relaxation allowed Susan to perform closer to her real potential (Russell & Sipich, 1974).

The case of Susan is a good example of the use of relaxation as a response incompatible with test anxiety. Susan followed exactly the same procedures we have suggested for you, except that she had some assistance from her counselors in the initial stages of her relaxation training. But, basically, her counselors gave her the advice we are giving you. Susan's success is by no means unique. Research has indicated that her "cue-controlled relaxation" is particularly helpful to test-anxious students (Russell, Miller, & June, 1975; McGlynn, Kinjo, & Doherty, 1978; Denney, 1980; Russell & Lent, 1982; Russell, Wise, & Stratoudakis, 1976). It has also been used to correct many other specific anxieties, such as fears of the dental chair (Beck, Kaul, & Russell, 1978).

The usefulness of relaxation as a substituted response is not limited to anxieties. Other problems have benefited from relaxation also, such as insomnia (Nicassio & Bootzin, 1974; Weil & Goldfried, 1973) and pain (Levendusky & Pankratz, 1975). Ernst (1973) reports a case in which relaxation was used to stop "self-mutilation" by a woman who repeatedly bit the insides of her lips and mouth, causing tissue damage and pain. She learned deep muscle relaxation during a baseline period in which she recorded with a golf counter the frequency of her self-biting. Then she began to relax, using the golf-counter click as the cue. She paid particular attention to relaxing the muscles of the jaw and lower face. As Figure 6-3 indicates, she almost totally stopped her self-mutilating behavior. That happy outcome continued through months of follow-up.

One of our students reported: "I want to reduce spacing out in class; that is, I want to increase the number of times my attention is on what the lecturer is saying. My mind wanders to all sorts of things, such as feelings I've been having about people or escape fantasies—you know, like backpacking or getting 20 acres of land and living on it with my friends. Another way I have of not being there is one I learned in grammar school, where I felt the teachers were powering me around. I'd find something ridiculous in what they said and laugh to myself about it or tell the person next to me. My plan is to use deep muscle relaxation to feel easy, instead of using my old tricks. That way my mind will wander less. I'll come in to the lecture hall five minutes early, relax, and then try to listen to what's going on." This student's plan was very successful; he reduced the frequency of mind wandering by 50%.

You may notice that both the spaced-out student and the mouth-biting woman used two forms of behavior incompatible with their problem behavior—self-recording and relaxation—which may account for their success.

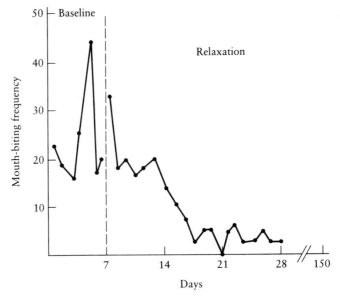

Figure 6-3. Daily self-recorded mouth-biting frequencies. *(From "Self-Recording and Counterconditioning of a Self-Mutilative Compulsion," by F. A. Ernst, 1973,* Behavior Therapy, *4, 144–146. Copyright 1973 by Academic Press, Inc. Reprinted by permission.)*

As a general rule, you should use relaxation just before the time you expect your anxiety to begin—just before the plane takes off; while you are waiting to walk to the front of the room to give your talk; during the earliest stages of sexual foreplay; immediately before you go in for an interview or an exam; or while you sit in the dentist's waiting room.

You may be thinking "But I can't always predict exactly when tension will begin." Right! And this is why you must learn the tension phase of the relaxation program. You will then be able to recognize the beginning stages of tension and use that information as the cue to relax. Typical cues that tension and anxiety are beginning include neck and shoulder tightening, upset stomach, clenched fists or jaws, and teeth grinding (Deffenbacher & Suinn, 1982).

Combining Relaxation with New Self-Instructions

New self-instructions should be combined with relaxation. In an experiment, students using relaxation during examinations were compared with students who combined relaxation with a series of encouraging self-instructions. The combined group performed better on geology multiple-choice and fill-in-the-blank tests (Collins, Dansereau, Garland, Holley, & McDonald, 1981).

An education major used this combined approach while beginning her student teaching. The slightest sign that she was losing control over her pupils caused her to tense, and she responded by scolding. She wanted to be gentler and more positive with the children. Her plan called for the self-cue "relax" at the first sign of muscular tension. She also added self-coaching during the relaxation, saying to herself "You can stay in control" and "Be gentle." The most effective procedure involves combining relaxation with correction of self-defeating thoughts (Deffenbacher & Hahnloser, 1981).

DEVELOPING NEW BEHAVIORS

Simply rehearsing a new behavior, over and over, in the situations in which you want it to occur is the fundamental way of mastering that behavior. All the other methods that this book teaches are merely ways of making that rehearsal more likely to take place. Practice does make perfect. Actually performing the behaviors—that is, rehearsing them—is the final technique for attaining your goal.

Often, however, it is difficult to arrange actual rehearsals. You can't always rehearse relaxation in the presence of some feared object, such as snakes, because (fortunately!) snakes are not always around. You may not be able to get enough rehearsals for relaxing in examinations, because no exams may be scheduled for several weeks. And many avoidance behaviors are so strong that approaching them for rehearsal is more than your current anxiety level will allow.

Imagined rehearsal may solve these problems.

Imagined Rehearsal

Rehearsing behavior in one's imagination is called **imagined** (or **covert**) **rehearsal**. There is convincing evidence that imagined rehearsal can improve many physical skills—for example, shooting free throws in basketball (Richardson, 1967).

Research evidence points to the fact that, in reaching your goals, actual events and actual behaviors are much more effective than imagined ones. Therefore, actual practice and performance are the final strategies. However, since imagined events and behaviors can influence actual behavior, using imagined events has many advantages. Imagined events and behaviors can be practiced quickly and easily. Most important, they can be controlled: imagined snakes are less likely to move suddenly toward you than real ones.

Imagined rehearsal can be used to provide *preliminary* rehearsals, to provide *extra* rehearsals, and to provide rehearsals that *emphasize* certain features of a behavior or situation. Thus, imagined rehearsal can often speed up your journey toward your goal. It is a form of visual self-instruction. For example, in 1976 the U. S. Olympic ski team, before making difficult downhill runs, would rehearse the entire run in their imaginations, thinking of each bump and turn and how they would cope with it. They turned in better runs than they had before, and the United States won some surprising medals (Suinn, 1976). These techniques were also used to train athletes for the Summer Games of 1980 and 1984 (Suinn, 1984).

To use imaginary practice, try to imagine the situation and your behavior in complete, minute detail. For example, if you imagine an introduction to a stranger, you should think about the way the imaginary person looks, the expression on his or her face, what the person says, how you react, and all the other details of the physical situation. You may have to imagine the situation in its component parts in order to concentrate separately on imagined sounds, textures, and other elements.

It is important that you attain a vivid picture (Wisocki, 1973; Paul, 1966). It doesn't have to be as clear as if you were watching a movie, but it should be as clear as a very vivid memory. Sometimes your imaginary scenes become more vivid with practice. A good way to check the vividness of these imagined behaviors-in-situations is to compare it with that of some scene you recreate in your imagination, a scene you know and can visualize very well— for example, what it looks, feels, smells, and sounds like to be lying on your bed in your room. First, visualize the scene of your room. Then compare the visualized behavior-in-a-situation with the scene of your room. The two should be nearly equally vivid. Also, you should be able to start and stop an image at will.

Imagined rehearsal is particularly appropriate when you are preparing to cope with high-risk situations. Earlier, we mentioned that the dangers of relapse into substance abuse are highest when other people around you are drinking, smoking, or taking drugs. As a first stage of self-modification, these situations should be avoided. But eventually, you will encounter this high-risk situation, and you will want to have coping skills ready. Imagining these high-risk situations—a restaurant, bar, party, banquet—and rehearsing in your imagination your coping responses to them can be useful in building skills to prevent relapse (Marlatt & Parks, 1982).

In imagined rehearsal, use the coping skills that you intend to use in real life, whatever they might be. Religious individuals, for example, have profited more in imagined rehearsal of coping skills if they use the religious imagery that is important to them. Nonreligious imagery of coping, such as saying "I see myself coping with that difficult situation" was less effective for religious Christians than imagining "I can see Christ going with me into that difficult situation" (Propst, 1980).

Actively imagining yourself in a coping situation is probably the key element in this kind of rehearsal. One technique for getting a good image of yourself coping is to remember a time when you coped well and then transfer it into the imagined problem situation. Test-anxious students who used this tactic actually raised their grade point averages. The students remembered a previous situation in which their coping skills were high (running a radio broadcast, tending a busy bar, playing in a recital). They then transposed that competent self-image into an imagined test situation (Harris & Johnson, 1980).

Imagined Rehearsal and Relaxation

One of the best uses of imagined rehearsal is in the practice of relaxation. In this technique, called **desensitization**, you imagine yourself remaining calm and relaxed in different situations, and you carry out the imagined rehearsal while being actually in a state of deep muscle relaxation.

You may find it necessary to approach feared situations gradually, maintaining your state of calm relaxation. Suppose that you become tense when you take tests. You know, of course, that there are different kinds of tests, some worse than others, ranging from unimportant simple quizzes to make-you-or-break-you final exams, and some make you more anxious than others. You might write down situations in hierarchical order. For example,

taking a test that doesn't count for very much
taking a test when I am not prepared
taking a surprise test
taking a test when the professor watches me all the time
taking a midterm exam
taking a final exam that determines my grade in the course.

It would be most unusual if these situations happened to come along in exactly that order. In imagination, though, you can rehearse them in any order and as many times as you wish.

Liza, one of our students, used the preceding list with imagined rehearsal plus relaxation. Since her courses had only midterms and finals, she wanted to prepare in advance for those situations and to proceed gradually. After learning deep muscle relaxation, she lay on her couch with a pillow, just as she had done when practicing relaxation. While deeply relaxed, Liza imagined the first item in the list—taking a minor test—while being just as relaxed as she was at that moment. She held that scene for a minute or two, imagining all sorts of details—feeling the hardness of the desk at which she sat, putting the pencil in her mouth while thinking of an answer, going back over each answer—and all the while remaining perfectly calm. Then she cleared her mind, checked herself for any signs of tension, relaxed again, and went on to the next item. She tried to do one of these sessions each day.

Liza spent about 10 to 15 minutes on the exercise, although the length of time varied with her mood and ability to relax deeply. In general, she went down her list in order—from least to most difficult. But she moved around some, too, occasionally trying to begin with a difficult situation. If she couldn't visualize it and stay calm, she relaxed again and moved back to an easier level.

About five weeks into the semester, Liza had to take a quiz, entirely unannounced, in her geology class. She was so surprised that she nearly panicked. She was able to induce relaxation by going through a rather hasty tension-release exercise. She relaxed enough to do well on the quiz, although she barely finished in time.

This incident illustrates the only error that Liza made in her plan. During the same weeks in which she was using imagined rehearsal, she should also have been practicing the relaxation response in many outside situations. Then she would have been better prepared to relax in the geology lecture hall.

The pop quiz motivated her to continue the imagined rehearsals. By the time midterm exams arrived, Liza had been able to imagine being relaxed throughout her entire hierarchy and had used relaxation several times in her actual lecture halls. Both steps were probably important. Imaginary rehearsal with relaxation gave her some practice in situations before they came up. Actual rehearsal of relaxation in various physical surroundings gave her practice in the situations in which she would later face the tension-producing tests.

Simply exposing yourself to a tension-producing situation will slightly reduce your tension in it (Goldfried & Goldfried, 1977; Greist, Marks, Berlin, Gournay, & Noshirvani, 1980). But you will achieve better results if you can practice your relaxation while in the situation. Thus, imagining yourself in tension-producing situations while being relaxed is a good way to get ready to cope with the reality.

Modeling

Learning through observation of models is one of the basic processes by which learning occurs—for adults as well as for infants.

Finding and imitating good models is an extremely important part of self-regulation. That is because models help us to identify effective behaviors. No amount of rehearsal will benefit your learning if the wrong behaviors are being rehearsed. Remember the benefits that Olympic-quality athletes experienced by imagined rehearsal of their skills. These results were achieved because the athletes knew exactly what to do; their imagined rehearsals were of a correct performance. But novice athletes may be made worse by imagined rehearsals, because they do not know what to rehearse. One study found that imagined rehearsals of tennis serves improved accuracy for experienced tennis players but made novices less accurate (Noel, 1980; see also Suinn, 1983). Imagined rehearsal is useless or harmful when the goals are poorly defined. Merely imagining being "a better public speaker" or "trying harder" or "being more assertive" will not lead to improvement. Imagined rehearsals must be precise and correct (Suinn, 1984).

How are these specific and correct behaviors discovered? They are discovered in models—by observing those who already are expert. Whether your goal is better tennis, better social skills, or any other behavior, a fundamental strategy is to identify a model, analyze the model's skills, and use those skills as your standard.

If you find someone who has the very skills you want, don't hesitate to try straight imitation. None of us minds using imitation when we are learning tennis or driving, but you may be embarrassed to think of imitating others' social or personal behaviors. As we counseled the student who watched how his friend dealt with women, "If you decide to smile when you meet someone, as he does, you will be smiling your own smile, not his. You will be answering with your own comments, not his. You will do everything in your own style. You'll be yourself, but yourself smiling and answering."

One of our students set out to improve his social skills, because he felt that others were not friendly toward him. He concentrated on becoming a better listener and chose as his model a woman whom he enjoyed talking to because she *was* such a good listener. He watched her carefully. She did not look around the room as the other person talked. She always turned to face the other person, even when sitting beside the person in a booth. She was patient while the other person collected his or her thoughts. He used these behaviors as his own goals for better listening. Once he noticed at a party that everyone seemed to enjoy talking with her. He asked directly "How do you make people so interested in talking to you?" She said "First I find out what they're interested in, and then I ask about that." The student reported that this technique turned out to be just as effective for him as it was for his model.

If observation doesn't reveal the crucial part, ask your chosen model to explain something. A talented young swimmer asked her heroine, a conference champion, how she managed such sustained and disciplined practice. The answer was clear and provided an excellent model. "*Preschedule* your practice times and your goals for the day," she said. "Never make your decisions on the way to the pool! If we did that, no one would ever practice hard."

Another student used a friend as a model for developing better conversational skills. After asking for advice, she asked the model for even more help. The student wrote: "I had Stephanie coach me. I really felt stupid, but she gave me a few hints after watching me try to improve. She said, 'You did it OK, but you kept laughing, and I thought you were being sarcastic. Stop moving around, and don't talk so fast, because all your words run together. And your face turned red.' This coaching was the most important factor in my project, because a lot of times I tend to blame my behavior on others—'She talked me into it' or 'He made me feel guilty'—and ignore the important defects in my own communication skills."

Imagined Modeling

In using imagined rehearsal, some people have difficulty imagining themselves doing acts they cannot perform in real life. For instance, imagining that you are sending back your overcooked steak may seem so unrealistic that you lose the scene or you end up imagining yourself eating the steak anyway. If this happens, you might use the technique of imagined modeling.

This process is similar to imagined rehearsal, except that you imagine someone else, instead of yourself, performing the behavior, being reinforced for it, and so forth. In general, this technique has been found effective (Cautela, 1976; Kazdin, 1974a, 1974b, 1974c, 1974d, 1982). For example, students using this technique actually demonstrated improved grades as well as reduced anxiety during tests (Harris & Johnson, 1980).

When you use others as imagined models, you don't have to use real persons who are known to you, although you may do so. Here are some recommended procedures for imagined modeling:

1. Imagine a model who is similar to you in age and sex (Kazdin, 1974b).
2. Imagine different models in each situation, rather than one person only (Kazdin, 1974d, 1976b).
3. Imagine a model who begins with the same difficulties you have—one who must cope with the problem rather than one who has already mastered the problem (Meichenbaum, 1971; Kazdin, 1973a). For example, your model should also be afraid of the pigeons, although able to approach them; your model is also tempted by fattening food; your model has to muster up some courage to send the steak back.
4. Imagine your model being reinforced for successful coping, preferably with desired natural outcomes (Kazdin, 1974d, 1975, 1976a, 1976b).
5. Imagine your model self-instructing during the performance. Make those self-instructions the ones that you will use in your eventual real-life performance (Tearnan, Lahey, Thompson, & Hammer, 1982).

Imagined modeling can be used as a first step in preparing yourself for imagined rehearsal. But increase the degree of *your* imagined performance, not that of someone else. If you imagine only others as models, the technique is not likely to be effective (Gallagher & Arkowitz, 1978). There is no need to use imagined modeling if you are able to effectively use rehearsal, either actual or imagined. If you can successfully imagine yourself rehearsing behaviors, it is probably better to use yourself as your own model. And most effective of all is to move from imagined modeling into actual practice. For individuals learning to be more assertive, for example, those who combined covert modeling with actual practice showed the greatest improvement in social situations requiring assertive behavior (Kazdin, 1982).

Mastery in the Real World

We cannot emphasize too much that, no matter how valuable all the imagined techniques are, they are only bridges to performance in the real world. Imagined rehearsal and all its supporting tactics can help you prepare for real-life situations. *But you must rehearse your developing behaviors in the actual situations in which you want them to occur.* Therefore, no plan is complete without tactics for transferring your behavior from imagined rehearsal into real life.

For example, Gershman and Stedman (1971) had one of their clients use karate exercises as the incompatible behavior for anxiety about his flying lessons. He constructed a hierarchy of items such as "gaining altitude," "saying to myself 'How high *am* I?' " "passing over tree tops too low," and so on. He went through the various items while vigorously engaged in his karate exercises, until he was able to consider them without anxiety. Then he began to transfer the plan into real life. He rehearsed before going to the flying field and again in the men's room before reporting to his instructor. He developed confidence and eventually became able to fly without anxiety.

In a long series of studies, Jerry Deffenbacher has demonstrated considerable benefit from programs that include relaxation in real anxiety-producing situations. Specific target anxieties are reduced, such as test anxiety, fear of flying, fear of public speaking, fear of cats, and the like. But in addition, a general reduction in anxiety occurs, so that the person is less tense and uncomfortable in ordinary daily activities. There are even other side benefits: people who use relaxation in real problem situations also become less depressed, less hostile, and more assertive. Relaxation, when well practiced in real situations, becomes a general coping skill (Deffenbacher & Suinn, 1982).

Whether you have used imagined relaxation rehearsal for dieting or being assertive, for test anxiety or fear of birds, the next step is planning to transfer these behaviors into real life. Often we do need to begin in our imagination, but the real-life situation is far more effective as a learning arena than its imagined substitute (Sherman, 1972; Flannery, 1972; Goldstein & Kanfer, 1979). When one learns new responses, even from models, it is the rehearsal in the actual situation that brings about long-lasting change (Bandura, Jeffery, & Gajdos, 1975; Blanchard, 1970; Thase & Moss, 1976).

SHAPING: THE METHOD OF SUCCESSIVE APPROXIMATIONS

Whatever your goal behavior may be, you should anticipate that you will not be able to master it at the first effort. Even if you have a perfect model, the expert behavior may have to be acquired a piece at a time. Even though you have become competent in relaxation, you may have to approach the feared situation by taking small steps toward it. A general procedure for behavioral improvement is this: start from the point in your current store of behaviors that is the closest approximation to your eventual goal. Practice this approximation, and it will become the basis from which the next improved step can be taken. Move toward full mastery in a process of steady, successive approximations. This method is known as **shaping**.

Shaping involves the gradual raising of standards. A steady experience of success reinforces and strengthens gradually improving performance. This method avoids the greatest hazard to learning—failure and discouragement in the early stages. This failure and discouragement very frequently is due to the setting of unrealistically high standards for improvement. This is typical of dieters who violate their standards by going on eating "binges." Excessively strict standards for dieting, in the absence of success experiences in self-control, is the condition most likely to produce binge eating. Those dieters who set careful shaping steps for reducing calories—steps gradual enough that they have the experience of succeeding in them—are more likely to develop self-control (Hawkins & Clement, 1980; Gormally, Black, Daston, & Rardin, 1982).

How Shaping Works in Self-Modification

Your baseline tells you your *current* level of performance. And that—or just beyond it—is where the shaping process should begin.

There are two simple rules for shaping: (1) *you can never begin too low*, and (2) *the steps upward can never be too small*. Whenever you are in doubt, begin at a lower level or reduce the size of the steps. This has the effect of making it simple to perform the desired behavior, because you feel that your movement upward is easy. And this is very important, for it increases your chances of success.

One of the most common reasons for failure in self-directed projects is the lack of shaping. Some students resist using shaping because they believe that they "should" perform at certain levels and don't "deserve" to be reinforced for performance that is below that level. This is a maladaptive belief, because it makes learning impossible. Shaping increases your ability to do what you believe you should do. If you find shaping at a very low level embarrassing, keep it a secret, but do reinforce yourself heavily for starting.

Here is the shaping schedule of a student who wanted to attain the goal of many hours of studying per week:

Baseline: I am now actually studying an average of 40 minutes per day.
Level 1: I will begin my reinforcement for studying 45 minutes per day, five days a week. This should be easy to do, since I have done it several times in the past.
Level 2: I will require myself to study 60 minutes per day to get the reinforcer.
Level 3: One hour, 15 minutes.
Level 4: One hour, 30 minutes.
Level 5: Two hours.

Notice how carefully the student followed the two rules for shaping: start low and keep the steps small. This allowed her to move, slowly but inevitably, toward her goal.

Notice also that the first steps were smaller than later steps. This is generally a good idea, because very small initial steps will ensure that some progress is made, whereas later it may be possible to make progress more quickly.

When you are following a shaping schedule, you must remain flexible. *Be ready to change your schedule.* You may have to do it, for example, if some of the projected steps turn out to be too large. What you plan on paper may not work out in practice, and you may have to reduce the size of the steps. You may have to stay at the same level for several time periods, or you may have to return to an earlier level if some setback occurs. The basic rule for these and all other problems in shaping is: *don't move up a step until you have mastered the previous one.* Notice that the student's plan outlined above is not tied to specific dates for changing levels.

These rules for shaping won't work if you don't follow them. The biggest reason students do not use shaping is that they don't think they deserve to gain some reward for such a low level of performance. "Now listen, I need to cut out smoking *all* the time, and you're telling me I should start out just cutting it out in one particular, easy situation? I ought not to get reinforced for that. It's too easy." The word "ought" there is the operative word. It is what will keep this person from succeeding. A second reason for not using shaping is your impatience to get on to total self-change. It makes taking a small step seem too little. So you try for a big step and stumble. Stop telling yourself what you "ought" to do, and start at a level you *can* do. Stop yearning to start at the top, and start where you can really get started. A journey of a thousand miles begins with a single step.

Box 6-4 illustrates the steps of a long and successful journey made by a woman who had far to travel before she could become a student at all.

BOX 6-4

SHAPING AWAY SCHOOL PHOBIA
by Harriet Kathryn Brown

The most complex "project report" turned in by any student in the many classes in self-modification that I've instructed was this. This shaping program was almost entirely self-invented. The student wrote:

> I was 28 years old, separated from my husband, and wanted to return to the university. But I experienced anxiety attacks when just physically present on the campus—rapid heartbeat, cold sweat, shaking, acid stomach, skin rash, and a mindless urge to flee. A long way to go! I started a plan to shape my way back into school.
>
> Step 1: Drive onto campus through the east gate, around the mall circle, and out the west gate. Do this two or three times a week for three weeks. This meant three to five minutes of anxiety, but it was bearable. I was then ready for the next shaping stage.
>
> Step 2: Park on campus, and walk around for ten minutes. Do this two or three times a week for three weeks. I had to avoid particular buildings where I felt the most uncomfortable, but I made it,

(continues)

BOX 6-4

SHAPING AWAY SCHOOL PHOBIA (*continued*)

and upped the shaping step. I gradually improved, and the next steps lasted one or two weeks each.

Step 3: Walk around 20 to 30 minutes.

Step 4: Walk around, then sit in an empty classroom for ten minutes while reading a book.

Step 5: Sit in the classroom reading for an hour. By then it was January, and I wanted to sign up for a noncredit writing class. I knew that I wrote reasonably well, and there were no grades involved. This was the least threatening class I'd ever find—except that the class was scheduled for a building that I still avoided. There were two weeks till class began.

Step 6: Sign up for the class. For three days in a row, drive on campus, park outside the scary building, and walk around the outside of it.

Step 7: Walk through the building once without stopping—three days in a row.

Step 8: Sit in the actual classroom. Start with ten minutes, increase each day as much as possible until I can do one hour.

Once I was relaxed enough to actually stay in the classroom, the course was really no problem. In fact, I enrolled in another noncredit writing course during the following semester. Now I was ready to attempt my first class for credit. I checked out the room, and felt comfortable enough in it. I was on my way!

The text for that course was [this book]. As a result, my next steps used more techniques. Up to this point, I'd been using food to reward myself for each of these shaping achievements. That was doing my weight no good, so I found a variety of better reinforcers. My favorite is to let myself put on rock music, stand in front of the mirror, and lip-synch while pretending to be a star like Linda Ronstadt. But there are others, too—like picturing myself wandering in a beautiful garden.

I reinforced myself each day for keeping to my study schedule, with a separate reinforcer just for going to class.

Step 9: Go to class each day. Reinforcement daily.
Study each day. Reinforcement daily.
Use relaxation exercises daily. I enjoyed them; no reward needed.
Use relaxation before and during tests.
Use positive self-statements before and during tests.

Got an A.

I won't write down all the rest of the steps. I took another credit class the following semester, and after that two at once. I no longer needed to check out the classrooms in advance. Gradually I dropped the reinforcement for attending class; I was falling in love with school, and am now a full-time student. Success on exams was high enough that my test anxiety got killed. I continued to use reinforcement for a regular study schedule; in fact, I still do. My attendance record is now 100%, compared to only

BOX 6-4

SHAPING AWAY SCHOOL PHOBIA (*continued*)

75% in that first noncredit course. I've gone from school-phobic to school-fanatic!

Occasionally I like to look back to my records of those early "walking around" stages. It's all in my journal, which I have kept since I was 12 years old.

Relaxation and the Method of Approximations

Often relaxation plans require successive approximations. For example, several of our students have been unable to maintain relaxation when going abruptly into a major examination. They have used graduated steps in approaching the dreaded situation, such as going into the examination room two or three days before a test and practicing in the empty hall.

Some of our students have used detailed schedules of steps along a shaping continuum.

Linda, a college senior, wrote: "I am really very afraid of birds, under almost any conditions. This sometimes makes me look like a fool—for example, I won't go to the zoo because there are so many birds around, loose as well as in cages—and often causes me unnecessary fear and trepidation. My life would be more pleasant with fewer fears!"

Here is Linda's hierarchy:

A. When *one or two birds* are 15 yards away:
   1. Turn and face the birds.
   2. Take one step toward the birds.
   3. Take two steps toward the birds.
   4. Continue until I have walked a total of 5 yards toward the birds.
   5. Begin step B.
B. When *more than two birds* are 15 yards away:
   1. Turn and face the birds.
   2. Take two steps toward them.
   3. Take four steps toward them.
   4. Continue until I have walked a total of 5 yards toward the birds.

She then repeated the procedures, beginning at a 10-yard distance, first from a single bird and then from a group of birds. Next, she repeated the procedure beginning at 5 yards. In the last stages, she would begin at 3 yards from the birds and move to within 3 feet of them, then gradually increase the amount of time, in seconds, that she spent close to them.

At first, Linda had difficulty, but she reported that by getting her boyfriend to hold her hand, her anxiety was considerably lessened. This worked well until, perhaps out of boredom, the boyfriend gave her a "playful push" and she found herself frighteningly close to the birds, which set her back about three weeks. (It also set their romance back a bit.)

Using friends, as Linda did, is a good idea (Moss & Arend, 1977). Be sure to tell them not to give you a playful push. Having a friend around when you are coping with nervousness in a social situation is particularly appropriate, so long as the helper has a serious desire to be helpful.

The use of friends to gradually shape advancing steps is a general strategy well worth considering, especially if your goal is behavior in a social situation. For goals such as public speaking, employment interviews, improved conversation, or asking for dates, the conditions of rehearsal can be shaped. The first step might be to rehearse in your imagination. The second step should be to rehearse in actual behavior, but privately. The third step can then be rehearsal in the presence of someone you trust, with the final step rehearsal in the actual goal situation (Goldstein, Sprafkin, & Gershaw, 1979).

Examples of Shaping Schedules

Alan, a young man whose goal was to have more dates, had followed chain-of-events reasoning and decided that the chain he needed to follow was: (1) go where women are, (2) smile at them, (3) talk with them, and so on. Step 3 could be broken down into talking with women about "safe" subjects, such as school or the weather, and then progressing to more adventurous conversational topics. After achieving the first steps in the chain, Alan decided to shape his behavior according to the degree of controversy he would bring into the conversation. He chose this dimension because he was made very uncomfortable by conversational disagreements.

Alan's baseline showed that he did very little talking with women on any subject whatsoever. He reasoned that it would be a mistake to move immediately into conversations on controversial issues. Therefore, for level 1 he chose to increase only talking about school. After he could comfortably perform at level 1, he would raise his sights and try a foray into more exciting but (for him) dangerous topics, such as whether a movie was funny or not. That was level 2. Level 3 was at an even higher level of potential controversy—university politics. Level 4 was interpersonal relationships and sex, and level 5 was the most difficult of all for him—national politics, personal philosophy, and the like.

Shaping in this fashion has two advantages. First, as with all shaping procedures, you can perform at a level that allows you to succeed. Second, it encourages analysis of the component parts of a situation—analysis that can result, for example, in seeing that there are levels of difficulty in handling a conversation or that being attractive is the result of several different behaviors. You can work on one part at a time instead of trying to deal with all levels of difficulty at once.

Here are some other examples of shaping. A young woman who wanted to be a writer remarked that she could write only a few paragraphs at a time. She would then "clutch up," unable to go on. She kept records of how many paragraphs she wrote on the average and started off requiring herself to do *one* more than that. Then she raised it to two more, three more, and so on.

A very withdrawn woman who felt she needed to become assertive "in about seven or eight different kinds of situations" started by requiring herself to practice assertiveness in two of the easiest situations and then added the others one at a time.

Problems in Shaping

You can't expect the course of learning to be smooth all the time; this seems to be everyone's experience. The important thing is to keep trying—staying within a shaping program—even if it is the 39th revision of the original schedule.

Encountering plateaus. When you follow a shaping schedule, you are likely to encounter plateaus. You may make excellent progress week after week and then suddenly stop. Moving up all those previous steps seemed so easy; then, all of a sudden, a new step—the same size as all the others— seems very difficult. The easiest way to continue upward when you reach a plateau is to reduce the size of the steps. If that is not possible, continue the plan for a week or so. The plateau experience is so common that it should be expected and "ridden out." This is particularly true for dieting, where physiological changes in your body may lead to less weight loss for a period of time (LeBow, 1981).

Losing "willpower." You now know enough about the principles that govern behavior/environment relationships to know that there are many reasons why you don't perform a given behavior. In our experience, the loss of self-control in the middle of intervention is most often due to some failure in the shaping program.

For example, a student will say, "To hell with it. I can't do it. I want to get in that library and stay there, but I just can't make it. I haven't got enough willpower. And besides, this whole idea of self-change is ridiculous, because the whole problem is really whether I myself have got the willpower to improve myself. I don't, so I quit."

In our terms, this may be a shaping problem. For example, two hours in the library may be much too severe an increase over current performance. Instead of two hours, this student should have set his first approximation at only 30 minutes. Some students with a near-zero baseline might, as a first approximation, merely walk to the library and go up the steps, then return home to get their reinforcer. But many self-modifiers are simply too embarrassed to perform such elementary steps. Instead, they increase the step to a "respectable" level, which is often outside their performance capacity, and finally quit altogether in a huff of "willpower" failure.

You may experience this failure of self-control in two ways. First, you simply may not get started on a self-modification project. You would like to achieve the final goal but somehow cannot get around to starting toward that goal. This is a shaping problem, and you need to start with a very low step. Remember, if it's embarrassingly low—"Yes, I jog around my living room three times every day"—then just don't tell anyone, but do it. Second, you may have started but find that you are not making progress. This may also be a shaping problem, and you need to use smaller steps.

The whole point of shaping is to make it as easy as possible to start and to continue. Therefore, you require yourself to do so little more than you can presently do that it is easy to perform the target behavior. Then, after practicing a bit, it becomes easy to move up one more short step. With each step, self-confidence will increase.

Not knowing how to begin. By referring to the baseline, you can determine your capability for certain tasks. For others, however, you may not know how to begin. You may not know exactly which acts do come first in a chain-of-events sequence. In this case, you may want to use someone else as a model to get an idea of a starting point.

A young woman chose as her model another woman who was effective in getting acquainted with new people. The model's first behavior was merely to smile responsively. So our young woman used "smiling responsively" as the first step in her shaping plan. Observing models is especially appropriate when you are uncertain about the exact behaviors you should choose to develop.

Mark Twain knew about shaping, although he didn't use that word. In *Pudd'nhead Wilson's Calendar*, he wrote "Habit is habit, and not to be flung out of the window by any man, but coaxed downstairs a step at a time." Coax yourself.

CHAPTER SUMMARY

Substituting New Thoughts and Behaviors

Substituting a desired behavior for an undesired one is preferable to a plan that merely suppresses the bad habit. Substitution of overt behaviors, of self-statements, and of thoughts should be considered; these can often be effectively combined. The selection of an *incompatible* behavior is generally a good tactic. If the incompatible behavior is itself desirable, so much the better. But even when the substituted behavior has no intrinsic merit, it is better to substitute a neutral response than merely to suppress the old. Keeping records of the substitution will help to strengthen the new behavior.

Substitutions for Anxiety and Tension

You can reduce fears and anxieties by (1) identifying carefully the situations in which you are uncomfortable, (2) choosing a behavior that is incompatible with anxiety, and (3) practicing the behavior in the situation that produces anxiety. Several behaviors that are incompatible with anxiety have been discussed, including distraction of attention, sexual arousal, martial arts, exercise, and meditation.

Relaxation

Whenever you want to get rid of an undesired behavior, choose an alternative behavior for that same situation. When emotional reactions are the problem, relaxation is a useful incompatible response.

At the beginning, relaxation should be practiced privately, then quickly employed in many real-life situations. As soon as relaxation is a well-developed skill, it should be practiced in those situations that produce anxiety. Ideally, relaxation should be practiced immediately before the time when anxiety usually begins. You may combine relaxation with positive self-instructions.

Developing New Behaviors

Rehearsing a behavior, over and over, in the actual situation is the best way of mastering that behavior. When rehearsals are difficult to arrange in real life, imagined rehearsal may be used in the initial stages. Imagined rehearsals must be vivid and include both situation and behavior. When imagining behaviors in feared situations, use relaxation. But imagined rehearsal is only a prelude, a bridge to actual rehearsal in real-life situations. Your ultimate plan must include actual performance in actual situations.

Effective behaviors can be identified by observing models who are achieving the goals that you want. Identify a model, analyze the model's skills, and use those skills as your standard. Don't hesitate to ask your model's help in explaining or even coaching those skills. If you have difficulty imagining yourself rehearsing your goal behaviors, imagine your models performing. Imagine more than one model in the situations that are difficult for you. Imagine them coping, self-instructing, and succeeding. This should be only the first step, however. Next, imagine rehearsals with yourself as the performer. The third step is the most important: transfer those behaviors into real life. It is the rehearsal in the actual situation that brings about long-lasting change.

Shaping: The Method of Successive Approximations

Most self-direction plans, particularly those that call for developing some desired behavior, require shaping. Shaping means that, instead of requiring yourself to perform the complete new behavior, you require yourself to perform only a part. Then, in a series of successive approximations to the final goal, you gradually increase the size of your steps. The two main rules of shaping are: (1) you can never begin too low, and (2) the steps can never be too small. You can shape your behavior along any desired continuum.

Common problems in shaping are *plateaus*—progress stops and you find it hard to go on—and *lack of "willpower"*—you are either requiring yourself to start too high or using steps that are too large.

In the next chapter, which discusses self-reinforcement, you will learn methods for rewarding each step along the way.

YOUR OWN SELF-DIRECTION PROJECT: STEP SIX

You should now be able to draw up another version of your plan for self-modification, taking into account the methods for developing new behaviors. Consider your own goals, and write plans for reaching them. At this stage, try to include each of the basic tactics discussed in this chapter: substituting new thought and behaviors (especially relaxation); overt and imagined modeling and rehearsal; and shaping. Specify ways that you might use each of these tactics.

The next chapter discusses methods of self-modification through control of consequences. Your final plan will include elements of antecedent control, new behavior development, and consequence control.

TIPS FOR TYPICAL TOPICS

Anxieties

Expect to use the full range of suggestions offered in this chapter. Develop a plan that includes (1) practicing an incompatible behavior, probably relaxation, and (2) gradually approaching the feared situation, first in (3) imagined rehearsal, then in (4) the actual situation.

For anxiety about public speaking, it is important that the imagined rehearsal also include the material to be spoken. Being well-prepared includes the performance, as well as the relaxation.

For test anxiety, there is evidence that self-instructions should be combined with relaxation, so that during tests self-defeating thoughts are replaced with active, coping self-instructions (Deffenbacher & Hahnloser, 1981). Being well prepared helps, too.

For all specific fears, this chapter contains the most important material. Your plan should rely heavily on the suggestions included in the body of this chapter.

Assertion

You need not wait to practice new assertive skills until real opportunities occur. Research results encourage the use of imagined rehearsal as a first stage in developing assertive behavior. When imagining the scenes, use relaxation as a prelude (Shelton, 1979). Be sure to imagine the full scene, including a favorable outcome (Kazdin, 1976b).

Begin your rehearsals in the most familiar and comfortable surroundings, at home or with good friends. Practice a particular skill there—positive self-statements, eye contact, remarks that begin with "I."

After several days of this practice, you might use this as the next step in the shaping schedule: Pick five different people, in different places, and state your opinion to them. Do this for about five days (Shelton, 1981a, 1981b). Those who engage in overt practice make consistently greater gains in assertion, and the gains are maintained for longer periods (Kazdin & Mascitelli, 1982).

Depression

The new behaviors needed to combat depression are those that lead to pleasant activities. Your plan should be aimed at increasing pleasant activities drastically. Do not overlook small pleasures. Fuchs and Rehm (1977), who have developed an effective self-control program for depression, encourage depressed people to set three subgoal activities for each major goal and to make those activities personally pleasant, no matter how modest they are—calling a friend for a chat or going to the library to get a book. Our students

---

BOX 6-5

THE BEST POSSIBLE WEIGHT LOSS PROGRAM

The American College of Sports Medicine (1983) has released a position stand on "Proper and Improper Weight Loss Programs." Here is a summary of that position:

1. Prolonged fasting and diet programs that severely restrict caloric intake are scientifically undesirable and can be medically dangerous.
2. Fasting and diet programs that severely restrict caloric intake result in the loss of large amounts of water, electrolytes, minerals, glycogen stores, and other fat-free tissue (including proteins within fat-free tissues), with minimal amounts of fat loss.
3. Mild calorie restriction (500–1000 kcal less than the usual daily intake) results in a smaller loss of water, electrolytes, minerals, and other fat-free tissue, and is less likely to cause malnutrition.
4. Dynamic exercise of large muscles helps to maintain fat-free tissue, including muscle mass and bone density, and results in losses of body weight. Weight loss resulting from an increase in energy expenditure is primarily in the form of fat weight.
5. A nutritionally sound diet resulting in mild calorie restriction coupled with an endurance exercise program along with behavioral modification of existing eating habits is recommended for weight reduction. The rate of sustained weight loss should not exceed 1 kg (2 lb) per week.
6. To maintain proper weight control and optimal body fat levels, a lifetime commitment to proper eating habits and regular physical activity is required.

From American College of Sports Medicine Position Stand, "*Proper and Improper Weight Loss Programs,*" (1983). In *Medicine and Science in Sports and Exercise,* Vol. 15, No. 1, 1983. Copyright American College of Sports Medicine 1983. Reprinted by permission.

have used an enormous range of activities: engaging in the "good dream," embroidering or sewing, reading travel folders, cactus gardening, or browsing in the gourmet section of the market.

Two acts you should increase are: (1) notice the good things that happen to you, and (2) exercise. Both raise one's mood. In an experiment, a group of depressed women were asked either to engage in vigorous exercise at least three times a week or to engage in other activities. Those who did the aerobic exercise showed a marked lowering of their depression, while the others did not (McCann & Holmes, 1984).

Family, Friends, Lovers, and Coworkers

The crucial task in improving strained relationships is selecting the specific behavior that will produce the long-range goal. Gottman and his coworkers (Gottman, Notarius, Gonso, & Markman, 1976) found that married people are ruder to each other than they are to complete strangers. Gottman's group set up rules for people involved in quarrelsome relationships: be polite; really listen to the other, without assuming that you know what she or he is going to say; be willing to compromise; express your feelings, and expect the other person to do the same.

Any or all of these rules would make excellent goals for improving strained relationships.

Overeating, Smoking, Drinking, and Drug Use

There has been a great deal of controversy on the best way to stop smoking, especially on whether it is better to quit cold turkey or to cut down gradually (Bernard & Efran, 1972; Flaxman, 1978). A review of the research literature (Pechacek & Danaher, 1979), however, concludes that the best way is a fairly rapid cessation. Abrupt quitting should be delayed for two weeks or so (Flaxman, 1978), until self-directional skills have been organized and practiced. You can, for example, set a date two weeks away, and use this period for conducting self-observation, designing the plan, thinking how you will cope with urges to smoke, and practicing your plan.

Using a preliminary "practice" period is a good principle to follow with dieting as well. Choose a moderate reduction of calories as your first shaping goal, and for two weeks or so practice the general skills of self-control. Then steadily cut the calorie level to your actual shaping-step goals. Learn to substitute less caloric foods; for example, eat fruit instead of dessert, or drink water instead of soft drinks or beer.

A regular program of exercise is vital to weight control. The evidence is overwhelming: dieting should be combined with exercise (Leon, 1979; Cohen, Gelfand, Dodd, Jensen, & Turner, 1980; Dahlkoetter, Callahan, & Linton, 1979; Stalonas, Johnson, & Christ, 1978; Katahn, Pleas, Thackrey, & Wallston, 1982). Regular exercise is also a potent antidote to the use of drugs, alcohol, and tobacco—particularly if you substitute exercise for the usual end-of-the-day snack, cocktail, or drug (Marlatt & Parks, 1982).

For all consummatory behaviors, the development of alternative responses is crucial. Choose one or more alternatives, and perform them at high-risk moments or in response to urges to indulge. Distraction from the urge will result. Distraction and substitute behaviors are among the most effective methods for resisting temptations to smoke (Shiffman, 1984).

Relaxation is an extremely valuable alternative behavior. Tension or anxiety often leads to overconsumption—of food, alcohol, tobacco, or dope. Include relaxation in your plan. Learn to relax, and apply relaxation at the first cue that you are tense. Apply it at the first sign of your craving.

Try shaping, eliminating overeating in a few situations at a time. For example, if you regularly overeat in eight different situations, start by trying to eat correctly in one or two of them. Once those are under control, move on to the others.

Studying and Time Management

Three specific new behaviors should be developed for studying more effectively: (1) Make *written outlines* or summaries to organize the material; (2) *rehearse* these outlines or summaries by repeating them aloud (without looking at your notes); (3) *practice for tests* by asking yourself questions and answering them (Robinson, 1970). What you do within a scheduled block of study time does make a difference.

For other scheduled blocks (housecleaning, cooking, writing letters, or doing volunteer work), you may know well enough how to perform the behavior. For your self-change goal, the issue is actually sticking to the schedule. Thus, motivation is crucial; the next chapter will address that problem.

The Other Sex

If social anxiety prevents you from making friends, develop a full plan as discussed for specific anxieties. Relaxation is the incompatible behavior to choose. There are two stages in developing new behaviors that are smooth and pleasing to others: selecting the behaviors, and rehearsing them. If you don't know what to do, ask someone who is successful, or watch carefully. Modeling is especially important in improving social skills (Lipton & Nelson, 1980). If your problem is initiating conversations, for example, observe someone who does it better than you do. If these behaviors seem alien or difficult, use imagined rehearsal with relaxation as a preliminary stage.

Some students feel that their problem is not so much feeling anxiety with others as simply not knowing what to do. Here are behaviors that psychologists teach people to help them improve their social skills: (1) Listen to the other person. This includes not interrupting; indicating that you are listening by saying things like "uh-huh" or nodding; not changing the subject; and not sitting silently for long periods. If you don't know what to talk about, talk about whatever the other person was just talking about. (2) Use appropriate body language. Here we suggest you use the acronym SOLER to remind yourself of what to do (Egan, 1977):

S   Sit facing the person,
O   with an Open posture (no crossed arms, for example),
L   Lean slightly forward,
E   make Eye contact,
R   and Relax.

Practice these behaviors as much as you can. You can use them in shaping, building one step at a time into your present behavior patterns.

CHAPTER SEVEN

Consequences

OUTLINE

- Discovering and Selecting Reinforcers
- Using Others to Dispense Reinforcers
- Self-Administered Consequences
- Techniques of Self-Reinforcement
- Self-Punishment and Extinction
- Reinforcement in Plans for Self-Modification
- Chapter Summary
- Your Own Self-Direction Project: Step Seven
- Tips for Typical Topics

LEARNING OBJECTIVES

Discovering and Selecting Reinforcers

1. What is a contingent reinforcer?
2. What is the simple formula for self-modification using reinforcers?
3. How can intermittent reinforcement schedules and avoidance behaviors make it difficult for you to discover your reinforcers?
4. How do you use activities, things, or people as reinforcers?
   a. What is the Premack principle?
   b. How do you pick reinforcers to use?

Using Others to Dispense Reinforcers

5. How do you use mediators to reinforce self-change behaviors? What does the mediator do?
   a. Should you ask for praise?
   b. How can you reinforce the mediators?
   c. What should you do if you share reinforcers with the mediator?

Self-Administered Consequences

6. Can people self-administer rewards contingently? What affects whether they do it or not?
   a. When people administer their own consequences, do behaviors actually change?
   b. Does the change occur according to the principles of reinforcement?
   c. If a self-administered reward is not a reinforcement, what is it?
   d. Is self-reinforcement really reinforcement, or is it feedback? Describe the experiments on the question.

Techniques of Self-Reinforcement

7. How soon after the desired behavior should reinforcement come?
8. Explain how to use token reinforcers. What is their main purpose?

9. How do you use imagined reinforcement?
10. Explain how to use verbal self-reinforcement.
    a. Why do people sometimes not use self-praise?
    b. What is the relationship of self-reinforcement to depression?
11. Should you ever get noncontingent positive events? When?

Self-Punishment and Extinction

12. Can you count on using extinction to change your own behavior? What is a better procedure?
13. Why is self-punishment usually insufficient?
    a. Is losing a positive event punishment enough? Or should you try to arrange to add on some negative event?
    b. Explain precommitted punishment. Is it properly a punishment or a deterrent?

Reinforcement in Plans for Self-Modification

14. How is reinforcement used in conjunction with antecedent control of behavior?
15. How is it combined with developing new behaviors? For example, how is it combined with imagined rehearsal or shaping?
16. What kinds of self-modification plans should include self-reinforcement?

One of the basic formulas for self-regulation is to arrange rewards for desired behaviors.

How is positive reinforcement used in self-modification? *The basic principle is that a positive event is made contingent on the desired behavior.* The idea of **contingency** is very important. A reinforcer is one that is delivered after, and only after, a certain response. If you gain a reward whether or not you perform some behavior, that reinforcer will not affect the behavior. If, instead, you can gain the reinforcer only by performing the behavior, that behavior will be strengthened—that is, it will be more likely to occur again. It is the contingent relationship that is important, not the positive reinforcer alone.

The use of reinforcement was one of the first techniques studied in the field of self-directed behavior. Fifteen years ago, when we wrote the first edition of this book, reinforcement was the cornerstone of all self-change plans, because it was the best understood of techniques. As psychology's understanding of self-control processes has deepened, many new procedures have emerged, and these often seem more sophisticated than simple reinforcement. Five years ago, many writers seemed ready to put old reinforcement out to pasture. More recently, however, there is a new consensus: reinforcement is still the most reliable horse in the stable. Contingent rewards, when delivered by the social environment, will strengthen the behaviors they follow. Very little in psychology is more certain than that.

DISCOVERING AND SELECTING REINFORCERS

The simple formula for self-modification is to rearrange the contingencies so that reinforcement follows desirable behavior. To do so, you need to know what reinforcers you have available for rearrangement. This section discusses ways of discovering and cataloging reinforcers, so that you'll be able to select reinforcers you can use.

Direct Observation of Reinforcing Consequences: Possibilities and Problems

Ramon kept careful baseline records of his studying behavior. He recorded the situations and opportunities for studying (for example, "at library, 42 min."). He also recorded his actual study time ("4 min.," "15 min.," and so on). The baseline rate of actual study time was very low—less than 20% of the time he was in an appropriate study situation. What was the reinforcer for all this inattention-while-in-study-situation? Ramon was able to report it instantly: instead of reading, he spent his time talking with the friends who sat near his usual table.

This reinforcer, incidentally, was not only clear but very available for rearrangement. Ramon designed an intervention plan that required him to spend at least 60 minutes studying in his room, a behavior he would then reinforce with a trip to the library, where he could converse with single-minded devotion. He reported that his plan increased both his study time and his socializing.

It is likely that, in this kind of situation, you will have discovered the reinforcer for your undesirable behavior while observing yourself. The easiest kind of intervention plan is simply to rearrange the reinforcers that you are already getting so that they are used to reinforce some desirable behavior rather than some undesirable behavior.

Of course, situations are not always so simple. There are cases in which the reinforcers, although evident, cannot be so easily detached from the problem behavior and rearranged in an intervention plan. This is the case with *consummatory responses*, such as eating or drinking. Problems can also arise when the reinforcing consequences of behavior are not so obvious. Sometimes the most careful observer can't discover what they are. Two conditions that commonly obscure reinforcers are *intermittent reinforcement schedules* and *avoidance behaviors*.

Intermittent reinforcement schedules.   If each instance of your problem behavior were followed by reinforcement, careful observation could reveal the reinforcer in question. But some of your more persistent actions are followed by reinforcement only some of the time. Remember that intermittent reinforcement leads to greater resistance to extinction. Thus you might expect to find that an intermittent reinforcement schedule is responsible for maintaining especially persistent problem behaviors.

Suppose, for example, that some problem behavior receives reinforcement on an average of only once every 25 times. If this behavior occurred five times per week, it might take five weeks of observation to detect the *first* instance of reinforcement. Before you could establish that a 1-to-25 ratio was the intermittent schedule, you would need hundreds of observations, and the baseline period would necessarily extend for a year or two. This kind of observation might be interesting scientifically, but it wouldn't be appealing at all if you wanted to change your behavior.

Avoidance behaviors. Avoidance behavior creates even worse problems for the person trying to discover reinforcers, because the aversive consequence may not occur at all. When you have been punished for a behavior in the presence of a cue, that cue will come to elicit avoidance of the behavior. Thus, you will not be punished again and will not be able to observe the negative reinforcer, because it will not occur. Although avoidance learning probably accounts for many problems, you might keep observing forever and not detect the specific unpleasantness you are avoiding.

Bill, a sophomore, wanted to go out for his dormitory's intramural basketball team. He had not played competitively in high school and had not even played many pickup games since he was about 14, although he enjoyed shooting baskets alone. Bill told us that he really had a baseline. During three semesters of college in which he had wanted to go out for a team, he just couldn't make himself do it. He wanted to know how he could discover the reinforcer for not-going-out. Of course, he couldn't discover such a reinforcer, and neither could a professional. In a case like this, we can suspect a pattern of avoidance learning. During high school, some unpleasant consequence probably followed Bill's efforts to participate in organized basketball. That consequence might well be lost in his history of learning. Even if Bill had been able to remember the punishment he once received, he would have needed new positive reinforcers to strengthen the behavior he now wanted—joining the dormitory team.

In summary, if you can discover the reinforcers that are supporting some undesirable behavior, you may be able to rearrange them so that they will reinforce some desirable behavior. Three conditions can interfere with this process: (1) The behavior may be unalterably attached to the reinforcer. (2) The problem behavior may be on an impossible-to-detect intermittent reinforcement schedule. (3) You may be engaging in avoidance behavior. In these three conditions, the reinforcers may not be discoverable or controllable. Your strategy, then, must be to discover reinforcers that *are* controllable. The reinforcers don't need to be those that are actually maintaining your problem behavior. You can use *any* pleasant event, as long as it increases the frequency of your desired behavior.

Positive Reinforcers

If you cannot rearrange or even discover the reinforcers for a particular behavior, you can still modify your behavior by selecting some reinforcer and making it contingent.

A positive reinforcer is anything that will increase the occurrence of the behavior it follows. Reinforcers can be things, people, or activities. A "thing" reinforcer might be a doughnut, a $5 bill, a new dress, a fancy shirt, a stereo record—anything you want or would like to have. A "people" reinforcer might be praise or approval, going on a date with your girlfriend, or talking with your boyfriend on the phone—spending time with someone you enjoy. An "activity" reinforcer is any event that you enjoy—playing a game, going to a movie, or having dinner out. Even "doing nothing"—talking with friends or loafing—can be a reinforcer. Usually these kinds of potential reinforcers are not limited to any one behavior or situation. You may just feel like going out for a beer or a pizza. Any kind of special occasion like that can be used as a reinforcer. *The task is simply to connect contingently the occurrence of the reinforcer with the target behavior.*

The most important reinforcers are those that will eventually maintain your new behavior, once it is solidly in place. Those reinforcers can be used to support the steps along your way. For example, one of our students aspired toward membership in the scholarly society Phi Beta Kappa. That meant harder work, with the reward of higher grades. She used the reinforcer of "grades awarded" to increase her studying time, except that she awarded the grades herself on a daily basis. She entered an A for excellent, a B for good, and so forth, beside each day's entry in her study record. If she had studied very well, she gave herself an A; if fairly well, a B, and so on. Another student wanted to increase her range of friends. She reinforced making friendly overtures to new people with the reward of phone chats with her best friend.

Using these logical reinforcers—ones similar to the rewards you are striving toward—is highly desirable. But if you cannot arrange logical reinforcers, any pleasant event can reinforce behavior. The range of reinforcers is potentially as wide as the range of objects in the world—as wide as the range of human activities. As an example of this variety, here is a partial list of the reinforcers used by our students:

praising oneself	putting on makeup
taking bubble baths	not going to work
making love	"doing anything I want to do"
going to a movie or a play	going to parties
going to the beach	being alone
mountain climbing	"doing only the things I want to do,
spending time at a favorite hobby	all day"
spending money	"not doing my duty sometimes"
playing records	goofing off
listening to the radio	watching TV
eating favorite foods	gardening
going out "on the town"	making long-distance calls
playing sports	playing with a pet
getting to "be the boss" with a	buying a present for someone
boyfriend	spending extra time with a friend
"pampering" oneself	reading pornography

taking long breaks from work
taking a "fantasy break"
window shopping

reading mystery stories
lip-synching (pretending to be a rock
star in front of a mirror)

Activities are excellent reinforcers. Actually, *any activity that you are more likely to perform can be used to reinforce any behavior that you are less likely to perform (when you have a free choice)*. This is known as the **Premack principle**, after the psychologist who studied the phenomenon most systematically.

Suppose that you have defined your goal in terms of a behavior-in-a-situation that you would like to increase. You try to think of some pleasurable reinforcer you can connect to the target behavior, but nothing seems available. The Premack principle tells you that you can use any one of certain behaviors that you engage in every day—such as taking a bath, going to work or school, eating, watching TV, or talking to friends on the phone—to reinforce the target behavior by connecting its occurrence to the goal behavior. The design of the plan is to require yourself to perform the goal behavior *before* you perform the behavior that occurs frequently.

Shirley wanted to increase her exercise time to 15 minutes each day. Taking a shower was one of her preferred behaviors. Following the Premack principle, she simply arranged not to take a shower until she had done her exercises.

Select for a Premack-type reinforcer some behavior that is not aversive. The behavior can be simply neutral. For example, although not many people find brushing their teeth wildly pleasurable, very few probably find it really unpleasant. The point is to select a behavior that is (or can be) frequent in free-choice conditions. Thus, you might also select an activity that is not as frequent as you would like it to be. For example, one student chose "dreaming about my trip to Europe" as a reinforcer, in spite of the fact that this daydreaming generally occurred less than once a day. She liked to lie quietly and picture the different routes she might take on her trip, the hotels in which she might stay, and the different museums she might visit. This activity required quiet, a relaxed atmosphere, and time enough to get thoroughly into the fantasy. She reasoned that this was a good Premack-type reinforcer, because given the opportunity, it would be very frequent.

A good strategy is to employ the behavior that you usually perform *instead* of the target behavior as the *reinforcer* for that target behavior. For example, a man who wanted to spend some time in the evening reading serious literature instead spent all of his time reading whodunits. This was a very frequent behavior, and it interfered with his reading the cultural material. So he used the whodunit reading as a Premack-type reinforcer. If he spent a certain amount of time reading serious material, then he would reinforce that behavior by allowing himself the more frequent activity—reading mystery stories.

Examples of Premack-type activities used in published cases of self-directed behavior change include eating, urinating (Johnson, 1971), sitting on a particular chair (Horan & Johnson, 1971), smoking, making telephone calls

(Todd, 1972), and opening daily mail at the office (Spinelli & Packard, 1975).

Given the tremendous scope of any list of possible reinforcers for any one individual, how can you decide which are the potentially effective reinforcers for yourself? Answering the following questions may help you.

1. What will be the rewards of achieving your goal?
2. What kind of praise do you like to receive, from yourself and others?
3. What kinds of things do you like to have?
4. What are your major interests?
5. What are your hobbies?
6. What people do you like to be with?
7. What do you like to do with those people?
8. What do you do for fun?
9. What do you do to relax?
10. What do you do to get away from it all?
11. What makes you feel good?
12. What would be a nice present to receive?
13. What kinds of things are important to you?
14. What would you buy if you had an extra $20? $50? $100?
15. On what do you spend your money each week?
16. What behaviors do you perform every day? (Don't overlook the obvious or the commonplace.)
17. Are there any behaviors that you usually perform instead of the target behavior?
18. What would you hate to lose?
19. Of the things you do every day, which would you hate to give up?
20. What are your favorite daydreams and fantasies?
21. What are the most relaxing scenes you can imagine?

Wherever you are in your own self-direction project, stop at this point and take a few minutes to think about the questions above. You should be able to give specific answers to each question. If you can, you will have a good-sized catalog of possible reinforcers. Eventually you will choose one or more reinforcers from this list.

Consider each reinforcer in these terms. Can I stand withholding it from myself, one or more times, if I don't earn it? Putting a reinforcer on contingency means that you may have to withhold it. Don't choose a reinforcer that you simply will not give up. Consider also, how potent is this reinforcer? Choosing a trivial reward will bring trivial results. The trick is to strike a balance between too important and trivial. The ideal reinforcer should be something you could stand losing (temporarily) if you had to, but you would be very disappointed.

USING OTHERS TO DISPENSE REINFORCERS

Using important other people to dispense reinforcement has been beneficial in a wide variety of problem behaviors, such as reducing delinquent acts (Tharp & Wetzel, 1969), complying with health-care practices (Becker & Green, 1975; Blackwell, 1979; Brownlee, 1978), and dieting (Weisz & Bucher,

1980; Brownell, Heckerman, Westlake, Hayes, & Monti, 1978). When your family, friends, or associates become involved in reinforcing your self-change behavior, long-term maintenance of the behavior is much more likely (Hall, 1980; Stokes & Baer, 1977; Shelton & Levy, 1981).

For example, using money to reinforce eating habits increases weight loss, but when the money is dispensed by the dieter's spouse, the long-range effectiveness of the program is even greater (Saccone & Israel, 1978; Israel & Saccone, 1979). The praise given by the husband in the case in Box 7-1 dramatizes this point.

One of the most effective weight-control studies ever reported used spouses as mediators. Spouses modeled good behavior: they paused while eating, did not eat snacks in the partner's presence, avoided buying high-calorie foods, rewarded habit change, and assisted in record keeping (Brownell, Heckerman, Westlake, Hayes, & Monti, 1978). Help this elaborate may not be necessary, but spouses must not sabotage a dieter's efforts (Pearce, LeBow, & Orchard, 1981). When spouses do successfully mediate a program of weight loss, excellent side benefits are likely. Women whose husbands cooperated showed significant improvement in marital happiness and a drop in depression (Weisz & Bucher, 1980).

A study of people who had tried to quit smoking found that those who had spouses and other companions who provided positive reinforcement were more likely to have successfully stopped (Wood, Hardin, & Wong, 1984; see also Mermelstein, Lichtenstein, & McIntyre, 1983).

If your reinforcer is something tangible, such as money, you can give it to another person and explain what you must do in order to get it back. If the reinforcer is some activity, you can arrange to get permission from those who are present, stipulating that permission should be granted only if you perform the target behavior. Carmen, a college freshman, wanted to increase her studying time. She arranged with her daily aerobics classmates that they wouldn't let her join in unless she reported at least an hour's studying already that day. A most interesting case has been reported in which a granddaughter delivered point-system reinforcement to her grandfather, thereby increasing his exercise, juice drinking, and medicine taking (Dapcich-Miura & Hovell, 1979).

Friends and roommates can be useful as mediators. One of our students wrote: "I have to be wearing my contact lenses by the time I go home this summer. If I don't, my mother will say I'm wasting money. Besides, I don't like the way I look." The reinforcer she chose was an unusual one. "If I meet my goal for each day, my roommate [the mediator] will let me use her fountain pen to doodle and write with for 15 minutes. I like that fountain pen because it writes without smudging and because of the sound it makes on the paper. I will ask my roommate to dispense the reinforcer and to check with me each day how many hours I've worn my contacts. And when I'm up to 10 hours a day, I'll buy my own pen!" By the end of 42 days, she was wearing the lenses 12 hours a day, with perfect comfort.

Carmen—who apparently liked the system of using mediators—felt guilty about her infrequent letters and phone calls to her parents, who were thousands of miles away from her campus. She arranged with them that they would send her monthly allowance only after she wrote or called in the last week of the month. Everyone was delighted. More letters got written, and her parents raised her allowance $10!

BOX 7-1

SOCIAL REINFORCEMENT BY THE SPOUSE IN WEIGHT CONTROL: A CASE STUDY

The subject, Mrs. L., was a 44-yr-old female, 5 ft 6 in. tall and weighing 174 lb. She had made numerous unsuccessful attempts to lose weight over the past ten years employing treatments ranging from "do it yourself remedies" to an assortment of fad diets and then drug therapy administered under a physician's care. Her husband had also tried a treatment of verbal abuse during which he routinely made statements such as "You are so fat I am ashamed to be seen with you." He also offered to buy Mrs. L. a new wardrobe if she would lose 30 lb. The most weight ever lost was 12 lb in six weeks with drugs. She remained at the new weight for 12 weeks of treatment, and gained the weight back within one month when medication was discontinued. With all treatments the consistent pattern was weight loss for a few weeks followed by a return to old eating habits and weight gain again. Mrs. L. frequently snacked while cooking or shopping, remarking that she did not have the necessary willpower to lose weight.

During an initial phase of self-observation and the arrangement of new antecedents, she lost less than one-half pound per week. Then a plan involving social reinforcement was added. The subject stated that Mr. L.'s verbal abuse of her weight was highly aversive. Therefore, the frequency of these comments was made contingent on weight loss. If Mrs. L. lost 2 lb a week, Mr. L. was to compliment his wife two or more times each evening for progress being made on her diet. No derogatory comments about her figure were allowed. If the weekly criterion was not reached, Mr. L. was to use verbal abuse of Mrs. L.'s figure as frequently as desired. A contract was signed by both persons with each spouse serving as a reliability check for the other. Mr. L. was to assure accurate weighins, and Mrs. L. made sure no verbal abuse of her weight was used inappropriately. When the contract was violated, the offended spouse used a verbal reminder such as "You just called me a fat hog; this violates the contract we made."

Greatest weight losses were reported during the social-reinforcement phase (39 lb). Mrs. L. attributed her success to self-confidence created primarily by praise she received from her husband. She indicated that maintaining weight at or below the goal (135 lb) during follow-up was due to praise and gradual weight loss resulting in altered eating habits (i.e., eating only at the dining table and consuming smaller portions).

Mr. and Mrs. L. stated that social reinforcement resulted in better social interactions at home. Both were pleased with the weight loss and increased affection shown toward each other. They indicated that this positive behavior would continue in other aspects of their relationship.

From "Social Reinforcement by the Spouse in Weight Control: A Case Study," by J. L. Matson, 1977, *Journal of Behavior Therapy and Experimental Psychiatry, 8,* 327–328. Copyright 1977 by Pergamon Press, Ltd. Reprinted by permission.

Mediators can also provide praise. The power of praise coming from those we care about cannot be overestimated. In all likelihood, praise—for increasing studying, losing weight, staying on a good-health regimen, stopping smoking—is much more effective than material reinforcers. And the more important the mediator is to you, the more powerful that praise will be. A good self-modification plan should almost certainly contain this element. Arrange with your important others to praise your reaching each shaping step.

The importance of social praise as reinforcement is nicely illustrated by a smoking "clinic" experiment. The clinic provided recent ex-smokers with a special telephone number. They could call to hear a tape-recorded message praising them for continuing not to smoke. Among these ex-smokers, a significantly higher proportion remained abstinent than among those who were not given the number. Arranging to have the praise of others is effective, even when it comes from the recorded voices of strangers (Dubren, 1977).

Praise and encouragement delivered by others is no doubt one of the most effective elements of Alcoholics Anonymous, whose members are all committed to helping one another remain abstinent. Similar support groups are forming around the country for a variety of behavioral goals, from weight loss to divorce recovery to reducing child abuse. An instructor of a course that uses this book as the text organized her students into special self-supporting groups. For example, those students whose goal was weight loss met together regularly and worked out mutual-reinforcement plans for improved eating habits. Such support groups can be extremely helpful, especially when mediators in natural relationships are difficult to find. For long-term benefits, though, whenever possible the reinforcement plans should involve those other people who will be close to you in your regular and continuing life. This becomes even more important after the novelty and early enthusiasm of your self-modification plan diminish (Fisher, Lowe, Levenkron, & Newman, 1982). Exercisers who stick with their programs long enough to experience real health benefits are more likely to have a regular aerobics partner (Lawson & Rhodes, 1981) or a supportive spouse (Heinzelmann & Bagley, 1970).

Whenever you use a mediator, it is important that the person understand exactly what he or she is supposed to do—namely, that he or she is supposed to reinforce contingently and is not supposed to punish you. If you fail to perform the target behavior and the mediator withholds the reinforcer, that is unpleasant enough. You don't need further punishment such as scolding, which may even cause you to discontinue your plan altogether. Nagging by people in a smokers' network leads to failure (Wood, Hardin, & Wong, 1984).

The effectiveness of mediated reinforcement depends on the mediator's actually delivering the reward, of course. Only failure can be expected if the reinforcement is not produced—as in the case of a husband who repeatedly failed to reward his wife's improvements by the dinner dates he had agreed to; or a mediator who could not find the promised dress in the shops of a small town; or a careless instructor who gave a grade of "D" despite greatly improved study habits (Peterson, 1983). These failures caution us to choose mediators wisely. Make sure the mediator can and will cooperate, or it may harm the relationship.

If your behavior change will affect others, consider the issue fully with them, and decide together how they might serve as mediators for you. Ellen's husband and children warmly applauded her decision to finish her college degree. But when she began a program to increase study time, her family began to punish her by comments that housework was being neglected (Peterson, 1983). An excellent plan here would be for Ellen's husband and children to reinforce her studying by doing some extra housework.

The "good" mediator's tasks are really very simple: give you your reinforcement when you are meeting your standard, and don't give it when you're not. But you must appreciate that this can put them in a different relationship to you, and it can sometimes be awkward—especially when they have to withhold your reinforcer. So reinforce *their* good mediating. Simple praise and expressions of thanks—especially at awkward moments— can help to keep their help.

Arranging mediators' help often requires sensitivity to their situation. This is especially true when your reinforcers are theirs, too.

Sharing Reinforcers

Sometimes the reinforcers that you select are shared with other people or affect them as much as they affect you. Even in such a case, it is *your* behavior that establishes the contingency. For example, a young woman chose going to the movies with her boyfriend as a reinforcer. She needed his cooperation in her intervention plan because if she failed to perform the target behavior, she would have to miss seeing the movie with him. But if she did miss the movie, *so would he.* The pleasurable experiences we have with other people— being together, doing favorite things, loving—are often very powerful reinforcers and thus are ideal choices for an intervention plan. But if you want to use them, you must have the cooperation of the other person.

Many times one person will decide to modify a particular aspect of his or her behavior because a friend or lover is concerned about it. A man might smoke, for example, and his friend might disapprove. It is often possible to use the other person who is not changing his or her behavior as a partner in the process of change. This is particularly true when your goals are valued by the partner. The change in your behavior becomes the reinforcer for the partner's behavior of cooperation. Or the partner may simply care enough to be willing to share a reinforcer. We know of a wife who agreed with her student husband not to talk with him until he had spent so many minutes on a paper he was writing.

Using activities with others as reinforcers is effective not only because the reinforcer is a powerful one but also because it brings another force to bear in your intervention plan. The other person, who may stand to lose if you fail to perform the target behavior, will put pressure on you to do it. If your determination begins to lag, your friend may say to you, "You better do it! I want to see that movie!"

A special situation arises when a couple undertakes the same plan together. Before deciding on such a course, both partners should make sure that they are equally committed to the plan and goals. When two partners both try to lose weight, for example, and one or both subtly sabotage the other's efforts, they may be less successful than if only one were trying (Zitter & Fremouw, 1978).

SELF-ADMINISTERED CONSEQUENCES

Reinforcement dispensed by mediators is a powerful technique for increasing behavior strength, frequency, and probability. But can contingent reward administered by the *self* have the same effect? After all, the idea of contingency is that rewards are *not* freely available. They appear only when a standard is met, and otherwise are not available. If the self administers rewards, they *are* presumably available to the self whether or not the standard is met. If you know that the reward is there for the taking, whether or not you meet your standard, will self-reward actually reinforce the behavior? This is one of the liveliest questions in contemporary psychology. Because it is so important to self-regulation, it is important that you understand something of the issues.

Actually, there are two interrelated problems. The first is: can people actually self-administer rewards contingently? Or, in self-control terms, can people abstain from taking immediate rewards in favor of gaining long-term rewards? The second issue is: if people do administer consequences contingently, do these consequences really reinforce and punish behavior?

We will discuss these two issues in turn.

Learning Self-Reward and Self-Control

The answer to the first question is actually quite clear: yes, people can and do self-administer rewards contingently. People can and do abstain from taking immediate rewards in favor of gaining long-term, more desirable ones. Self-reinforcing can be learned by imitating others (Bandura, 1971), by following instructions (Kanfer, 1970), by receiving rewards for self-reinforcing (Speidel & Tharp, 1980), or through classlike lectures (Heiby, Ozaki, & Campos, in press). Bandura and his associates have taught even pigeons, monkeys, and dogs to "self-reinforce"—that is, to not take freely available rewards until after they have performed the desired behavior. These animals were taught by an experimenter who removed the food trays if the animals tried to take the reward before performing. Once learned, self-reinforcing persisted for some time (Bandura & Mahoney, 1974; Mahoney & Bandura, 1972; Mahoney, Bandura, Dirks, & Wright, 1974). Catania (1975) argues that this isn't really self-control, any more than refraining from shoplifting is self-control. If there were no external punishment for shoplifting (or taking the food), everyone would eventually walk out with whatever reinforcers they wanted.

Theoreticians who make this kind of argument point out that there has to be some external reason to self-reinforce and to stick to the planned contingencies. Rachlin (1974) correctly points out that a student would not make moviegoing contingent on studying unless the external reasons for studying—grades and career success—were meaningful.

This argument is clearly correct. Our own research (Speidel & Tharp, 1980) indicates that children can be taught to *accurately* self-reward, but if the contingencies for accuracy are removed, the children will begin to take an inaccurately large amount of reward. For contingent self-rewarding to occur, there must be some external or longer-range reason present. When this meaningful reason is present, people will not "cheat" or take quick rewards.

Children develop this capacity as they mature. Recall the research by Walter Mischel (1981) reviewed in Chapter Five. Children resist taking quick, small rewards in order to earn larger, later rewards. They even use strategies to help themselves resist, such as distracting themselves and using "cool" instead of "hot" thoughts. They self-regulate in order to gain rewards that they really want. Would these children "resist" taking the immediate reward if there were no larger later reward involved? Of course not. In order for self-reinforcement—or any kind of self-regulation—to occur, there must be some longer-term contingency present, some reason for self-regulation.

In self-modification, the external contingencies are provided by your goals. You choose your goals because achieving them will improve your life. When you are working for goals that you genuinely value, self-rewarding and self-punishing can certainly be carried out. Competent self-directors do so all the time. Thousands of students who have used this textbook have done so. Not every student does, of course; and some do better than others in holding to accurate contingent self-rewarding. But *can* people self-control and self-reinforce? Of course they can.

Do Self-Administered Consequences Actually Reinforce and Punish?

After 20 years of puzzling over this issue, psychologists are beginning to phrase the questions more precisely. In contemporary terms, there are now two separate issues: (1) When people administer their own consequences, does behavior actually improve? (2) Does this improvement occur according to the conditioning principles of reinforcement and punishment as outlined in Chapter Four?

The first question has been addressed by a multitude of studies (see review articles by Bandura, 1971; Kanfer, 1970; Ainslee, 1975; Catania, 1975; Rachlin, 1974; Morgan & Bass, 1973; Sohn & Lamal, 1982), and the answer here, too, is: yes, when people self-administer contingent consequences, their behavior is indeed likely to improve. Though not every study reports this for every behavior, the vast majority of research supports this conclusion for a wide range of behaviors, including manual work by children, arithmetic problems by college students, schoolwork by elementary school pupils, accuracy of judgment by adults, and specific programs for weight loss, smoking, assertiveness, and the like. Yes, self-administered consequence programs do improve behavior.

This by no means ends the debate, because self-administered contingency always occurs in the context of many other events. Sohn and Lamal (1982), for example, seem to despair of the entire field, because in virtually every study, something other than the self-reward was present. These other factors included experimenter influence, longer-range goals or rewards, standards for performance, or some other form of external contingency. Therefore, Sohn and Lamal argue, it is impossible to tell whether or not self-administered contingent consequences would bring improvement if there were no external or overriding contingencies.

But we have already established that self-reinforcement will *not* occur at all unless there are overriding, larger-issue influences. Therefore, self-reinforcement can only be found embedded in a context of external reinforcement. Trying to study self-reinforcement anywhere but in a larger, external context is like insisting on studying flamingos at the South Pole. They don't live there, and they can't live there.

Even that does not end the debate. Given the larger context—of long-range goals, of the eventual positive outcomes of your self-modification program—does self-reward operate like *reinforcement?* Do the principles of conditioning described in Chapter Four explain the positive effects of self-reward?

Skinner (1953) himself, the father of the operant-conditioning movement, expressed doubt. Radical behaviorists (such as Brigham, 1982) continue that skepticism. Bandura (1981) argues that self-reinforcing plans create incentives along the way to the eventual goal. Ainslee (1975), Catania (1975), and Rachlin (1974) point out that self-reward is a very complicated process that contains many effective elements. For example, when you reinforce your behavior, you are calling your own attention to it. You are giving yourself clear information, clear feedback (Castro & Rachlin, 1980). You are making the behavior more vivid, even more vivid than in self-recording alone. You are teaching yourself to discriminate between correct and incorrect performances. You are reminding yourself of your long-term goals and of your rules for getting there (Nelson, Sprong, Hayes, & Graham, 1979). You are learning *self-awareness* (Catania, 1975).

The usefulness of self-reward in self-modification programs is accepted by virtually every psychologist. There are problems to be avoided, and some kinds of systems are preferable to others. These issues will be discussed in the next section. But as a general conclusion, research evidence continues to support its use. Successful self-controllers, regardless of the problem area— overeating, studying, dating, or smoking—are three times more likely to use self-reward procedures than are unsuccessful self-controllers (Perri & Richards, 1977; Perri, Richards, & Schultheis, 1977; Heffernan & Richards, 1981).

There appears to be only one condition in a self-modification program in which reinforcement should not be used. When you already have enough motivation to perform the behavior, it is unnecessary (or even harmful) to add self-reinforcement. For example, students who were already competent and motivated to do mathematics problems and homework showed *lower* performance in self-reinforcement programs (Heatherington & Kirsch, 1984). But for behaviors that need strengthening, self-reinforcement remains a strong and reliable technique.

BOX 7-2

SELF-REWARD AND PUNISHMENT: IS IT REINFORCEMENT OR FEEDBACK?

Here is an important and amusing example of research strategies and logic in this field. Rachlin (1974) has argued that self-rewarding works *not* by reinforcing, but by clearly *marking* behavior, making people more *attentive*, and so increasing accurate *self-observation* and self-monitoring. To test this, Castro and Rachlin (1980) had people who attended a weight-reduction clinic pay the clinic *more* money if they *lost* more weight. These dieters lost as much weight as another group that took money as a "reward" for losing weight. Castro and Rachlin concluded that if these contingencies worked like reinforcement and punishment, then those who paid for losing weight should have lost less because they were punished, and those who took money should have lost more because they were reinforced. Therefore, contingencies work as *feedback*, and not according to conditioning principles.

Bandura (1981) attacked this study by pointing out that of course consequences are evaluated according to usual social standards. It is not "punishing" to pay a professional for effective services; we happily pay accountants who save us money, dentists who save our teeth, or clinics that help us lose weight. Therefore, no "punishment" had been studied at all.

The debate heated up and moved to Bogotá, Colombia, where Castro and his colleagues (Castro, de Pérez, de Albanchez, & de Léon, 1983) resolved to "punish" their weight losers in a way that had no correspondence to ordinary professional life. One group of clients that came to their weight-reduction clinic agreed to a bizarre plan. For each pound lost, each person mailed one dollar (equivalent) to their most hated political party, or they cut the money up with scissors into tiny pieces in the presence of the clinic staff. This group lost *more* weight than another one that took the same amount of money per pound lost to spend on a special treat! The Castro group concludes that contingencies do not operate as reinforcement and punishment. They do not argue that self-reward is ineffective. The self-reward group also lost weight. But they do insist that self-reward and self-punishment operate primarily by providing information, making people pay more attention to their own behavior.

Bandura has not yet had time to reply in print. We suspect that he may mention the rewarding effects of playing this bizarre game with the clinic staff. Would you find it "punishing" to be told to cut up money in little pieces, especially if you were led to believe that it would help you lose weight? Doing something outrageous can be a lot of fun.

Whatever the conclusion, the Rachlin/Castro/Bandura debate illustrates the complexity involved in self-administered contingencies. All agree on one point: contingent consequences work. But how?

TECHNIQUES OF SELF-REINFORCEMENT

Prompt Reinforcement

How often should you get reinforcement? The ideal situation is one in which the reinforcement occurs immediately after you perform the desired behavior. The longer a reinforcement is delayed, the less effective it is. And if it has to compete with some other strong reinforcer that is occurring immediately after the problem behavior, it will not be effective at all.

This is a very important thing to keep in mind when you plan for behavior changes. Remember, whatever your current behavior, it is now being reinforced in some way. Whatever your goal, it will be reinforced at some *later* time, when it is achieved. The dieter is reinforced immediately for overeating. Only weeks from now, when a new, thinner image is reflected in the mirror, will this person be reinforced for *not* eating. At nine o'clock in the morning, shortly after a nice breakfast, a dieter will choose to diet. At noon, walking through the cafeteria line, our same dieter may choose to ignore the diet.

This kind of choice, which depends on how far away in time the reinforcers are, has been studied carefully by psychologists (Ainslee, 1975). Their conclusion is that there are points in time when an immediate reinforcement will be chosen by anyone, and that the closer you draw to immediate reinforcement, the more likely it is that you will choose it. For this reason, self-reinforcement systems are a vital part of self-directed strategies. By providing yourself with extra immediate reinforcement, you can tip the balance and cause yourself to choose long-term-goal behaviors. If the dieter arranges the reinforcement of, say, watching an enjoyable TV program immediately after (or even during) self-restraint, dieting is more likely to be observed than if he or she depends entirely on the long-range rewards of being slim someday. In other words, it is the TV program that competes right now with an extra bowl of spaghetti, not the dim dream of slimness in what, at the moment, may appear as a faraway future (Bandura, 1981).

A student who was wild about women chose exercise as his goal. So he enrolled in an aerobics class that contained almost all women. He reported that just being in that atmosphere provided all the reinforcement he needed to keep to his goals. A year later, he was a strong and enthusiastic aerobicizer. His new feelings of health and attractiveness were reinforcement enough, and he exercised regularly without women present (though he still liked doing it better when they were around).

A married student had developed the habit of swearing excessively. His baseline average was more than 150 swearwords per eight hours. He worked out a plan in which he got strong reinforcers from his wife if he reduced his daily average by 10% for one week. Unfortunately, he never made it to the end of the week. After one or two days of good language, he would revert to his old habits. We advised him to reduce the delay of reinforcement. His new contract, agreed to by his wife, called for *daily* reinforcement if he reduced his undesired language by 10%.

The general principle is that the reinforcer should be delivered as quickly as reasonable after the desired behavior is performed. In some cases, *it is vital that the delay be extremely short*. This is especially true when the undesired behavior consists of consummatory or fear responses. For example, a cigarette in the mouth *right now* is more reinforcing than the thought of cleaner lungs six months from now. A piece of pie in the mouth *right now* feels a lot better than that remote picture of the scales, weeks or even months from now, showing a drop of several pounds. Biting your nails *right now* is more rewarding than the thought of the movie you will go to as a reinforcer Saturday night.

The same kind of problem exists for people who are afraid of some situation, such as talking in front of an audience or going into the water to swim. It feels much better to avoid the feared situation *right now* than to think about how nice it will feel when you get a reinforcer at the end of the week.

Whenever the target behavior has to do with very strong habits or feared objects, provide yourself with positive reinforcement immediately after performing the desired behavior. For example, a smoker asked his wife to praise him immediately each time he resisted the impulse to light a cigarette.

Tokens

When you cannot arrange to have the reinforcer follow quickly after the behavior, **token reinforcers** are appropriate. A token is a symbolic reinforcer—symbolic because it can be converted into real reinforcement. Money, for example, is a token reinforcer, for it is the things that money can buy that make money attractive and therefore represent the real reinforcement. Such devices as poker chips, gold stars, checkmarks, ticket punches, and dollar bills have all been used as tokens.

Many people choose a **point system** of token reinforcement to modify their behaviors. The performance of a desired behavior earns a specified number of "points," which can be "spent" for reinforcement. The cost of reinforcement—so many points per reinforcer—is specified in the point-system contract.

The main function of tokens and points is to bridge the delay between the time when you perform the desired behavior and the time when you can take the reinforcer. For many people, the chosen reinforcer is something they are going to do at the day's end. They may use a particularly nice supper, the opportunity to watch TV, or a talk with friends in the evening as a reinforcer contingent on their having performed the target behavior earlier in the day. For all of these delayed reinforcers, tokens can be used during the day to provide immediacy.

A man who wanted to substitute being-nice-to-friends for being-rude-to-friends selected watching TV in the evening as his reinforcer. Since he couldn't be sure when the opportunity to be nice to his friends would arise during the day and couldn't rush off to watch TV as soon as he had performed his target behavior, he decided to use a token system. He carried a 3 x 5 card in his pocket and made a check on it when he performed the target behavior. Then, later in the evening, he would allow himself to watch TV if he had earned the number of points his shaping schedule required for that day. He used his tokens cumulatively. The more points he earned during the day, the more TV he could watch at night. His "menu" looked like this:

1 token	30 minutes of TV watching
2 tokens	60 minutes
3 tokens	90 minutes
4 tokens	as much as I want

This is a simple point system. By adding behaviors and rewards, point systems can be expanded into a complex token "economy." A group of five students who lived together had difficulty in arranging their household duties fairly and reliably. The three men and two women devised a *group* self-modification plan, using the point system reprinted below. It specified each important household task, with the points to be awarded for doing each one. And it specified the reinforcers that the household had to offer, with the number of points that each would cost. Each member was free to choose both tasks and reinforcers.

Tasks	*Points*	*Tasks*	*Points*
Prepare evening meal	150	Do laundry	200
Prepare sandwiches	60	Plan meals	40
Prepare extra snacks	80	Plan shopping	60
Wash up dishes (major)	30	Weekly shopping	200
Wash up dishes (minor)	10	Minor shopping	30
Dry up dishes (major)	30	Record prices (major)	60
Dry up dishes (minor)	10	Record prices (minor)	10
Clean living room	30	Write down recipe	25
Clean kitchen	30	Write diary	20
Clean bathroom	30	Empty fireplace	10
Tidy living room	10	*Reinforcers*	
Put out milk bottle	5	Evening meal	50
Take in milk	30	Lunch	20
Pay milk bill	30	Film	50
Tie refuse sack	5	Drink	50
Put refuse out	30	Meeting etc.	50
Empty-tidy sink	10		

From "The Use of a Token Economy to Regulate Household Behaviours," by J. F. Masterson and A. C. Vaux, 1982, *Behavioural Psychotherapy, 10,* 65–78. Copyright 1982 by Academic Press, Ltd. Reprinted by permission.

The living group kept careful data and were convinced that the point system made their household run more smoothly. More tasks were actually performed on time, and the members all felt that the amount of work and benefits were fairly distributed. In fact it was typical that more points were earned than were ever spent. They concluded that their mutual encouragement and verbal reinforcement provided rewards in addition to the points (Masterson & Vaux, 1982).

Notice also that the group's list of reinforcers included several items, from food to watching films. This illustrates another advantage of point systems: you can use a variety of reinforcers for the same behaviors, which will help to keep reinforcement fresh and desirable. If you can exchange your earned points for watching TV, having a snack, or playing with the dog, you can choose the reinforcer that is most attractive to you at the moment. One of our students included as the last item on his reinforcement menu: "Every Saturday morning, *anything* I want to do!"

A point system can be adjusted to surgical precision. One of our students wrote: "This was my first point system:

Eating a light, balanced breakfast	1 point
Eating a light, balanced lunch	1 point
Eating a light, balanced supper	1 point
Eating no more than two light snacks per day	1 point
Daily exercise	1 point

When I got 35 points, I could buy an art poster.

"Then I noticed where I was failing most often—too much snacking on weekends. So I added an item:

On Saturday and Sunday, no more than two light snacks	3 points

"My second big insight was that I would earn 3 or 4 points each day, and then pig out on a snack or supper and blow the calorie count for the rest of the day. So I added another item:

Bonus for a perfect day	3 points

That did it!"

Box 7-3 presents an excellent self-modification plan that incorporates three of the principles discussed so far in this chapter. To increase exercising, this woman used self-reinforcement (a small amount of money), a husband/mediator to dispense larger rewards, and a point system to bridge the gap between performance and the delayed larger rewards. Good self-modification plans integrate several techniques.

BOX 7-3

SELF-MODIFICATION OF EXERCISE BEHAVIOR

While regular physical exercise itself can be reinforcing to some persons, for [this woman] it was not. In order to establish and maintain an exercise habit, an attempt at self-directed behavior change seemed appropriate.

Method

A prior attempt to establish an exercise routine using the Premack principle (tooth brushing at night contingent upon the completion of a series of calisthenics) had not been successful, for the contingency was ignored. Therefore, the present plan placed control of the reinforcers in the hands of another person. The husband was the logical choice, and the intervention plan was put into a written contract that he and she signed. The plan had the following features:

BOX 7-3

SELF-MODIFICATION OF EXERCISE BEHAVIOR (*continued*)

1. The form of exercise was jogging.
2. Money and social activities of the woman's choice (for example, going to a movie or eating at a restaurant) were the reinforcers. She received 25¢ immediately after jogging. At the end of each week, if she had jogged every day (and earned $1.75), she could select and engage in one of several possible social activities with her husband. Otherwise, none of the social activities was permitted.
3. The husband dispensed the reinforcers and tabulated points.
4. In addition, points were earned for jogging. The long-term goal was set at 40 points per week . . . where four points could be earned by jogging 1 mile within 9.59 min. and . . . more earned by increasing the distance . . . and reducing the time. This was approached through a series of intermediate steps. The plan was to begin with the jogging of 1 mile, with gradual increments of 0.25 miles.

Results

The results of the intervention plan can be seen in Figure 7-1. At the end of the first week of intervention, 20 points were earned, representing a sharp increase in exercise activity from a baseline of zero. After this initial spurt, progress slowed but increased to 23 points in the second week. Jogging had occurred on only 4 days, but, because of the increased distance run, more points were earned. The third week showed a drop in total number of points to 20. Jogging had occurred on 4 days, and again during the fourth week of intervention occurred on only 4 days of the week. Up to this point, the social-activity reinforcer had not been given, because jogging had not occurred daily during any of the 4 weeks. A change

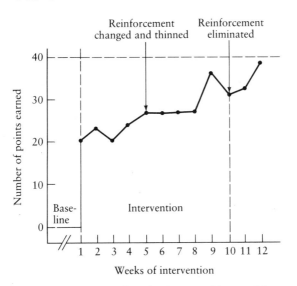

Figure 7-1.   Number of points earned by exercising.

(*continued*)

BOX 7-3

SELF-MODIFICATION OF EXERCISE BEHAVIOR *(continued)*

in the program was adopted at the start of the fifth week. The activity reinforcer was made available after earning 25 or more points per week (rather than running every day), and the 25¢ payment was eliminated. This was followed by an increase in total points to 27 for the fifth week. The 12th week showed the highest level of activity, with 38½ points earned—only 1½ points short of the long-term goal, even though the activity reinforcer had been eliminated at the beginning of the 10th week.

Formal reinforcement was terminated before the long-term goal (40 points per week) was reached, for two reasons. First, the subject had become satiated with the activity reinforcer. For 2 weeks prior to its elimination, she had earned enough points to gain the reinforcer but had not bothered to "collect" it. Second, the natural positive results of regular physical exercise were being noticed. She felt better and more energetic than when she began the program. She had lost several pounds without any change in eating habits. With these natural reinforcements, the long-term goal was soon reached. As the natural environment had taken over and begun to maintain the desired behavior, the program was judged to have been successful.

The key to the success may have been the placement of control of the program with another person. The mediator, the husband, was firm in his commitment to the plan and the rules agreed upon. The contingency between the behavior and the reinforcers was maintained rigorously.

From "Self-Modification of Exercise Behavior," by M. L. Kau and J. Fischer, 1974, *Journal of Behavior Therapy and Experimental Psychiatry, 5,* 213–214. Copyright 1974 by Pergamon Press, Ltd. Reprinted by permission.

Imagined (Covert) Reinforcement

If things, people, or activities act as reinforcers, imagining them may also be reinforcing (Epstein & Peterson, 1973a, 1973b; Ascher, 1973; Wisocki, 1973; Krop, Calhoon, & Verrier, 1971; Blanchard & Draper, 1973; Cautela, 1970, 1971, 1972; Marshall, Boutilier, & Minnes, 1974). **Imagined reinforcers** have been traditionally called **covert reinforcers** by behavior analysts.

Imagined reinforcers are probably not as powerful as their actual counterparts. But imagined reinforcers have the advantage of being completely portable and easily accessible. Although you may be unable to travel or go skin diving during the winter, you can imagine doing so. Imagining pleasant and relaxing scenes, such as a lazy swim on a hot day, can be used to reward yourself for performing a desired behavior (Cautela, 1973). Imagined reinforcement is used the same way as any other kind of reinforcement: it is arranged to follow a desirable behavior.

To discover potential imagined reinforcers, you can record the frequencies of your thoughts and fantasies and select imagined reinforcers in the same way you would other reinforcers. Or you can consider imagining any of the reinforcers you discovered when you answered the 21 questions in the section on positive reinforcers.

The very best imagined reinforcement is an anticipation of rewarding, realistic outcomes. Dieters can use images of themselves after losing weight— slim, attractive, athletic, fashionably dressed, or whatever image of themselves reflects the wish they want to fulfill by losing weight (Horan, Baker, Hoffman, & Shute, 1975)—to reinforce their dieting (Cautela, 1972). This kind of reinforcer has the advantage of being realistic and logical and of representing a bridge to the world of actual contingencies. Not only will reinforcement benefits be present, but long-range goals will be brought to mind, and thus commitment will be strengthened again. The depressed person can use anticipation of feeling good to reinforce efforts to overcome low moods; the smoker can imagine better health and breath to reinforce efforts to stop smoking; the test-anxious person can imagine being able to take tests calmly and getting back an "A."

It is also possible to imagine unrelated reinforcers, such as some favorite scenes of extreme pleasantness. Particularly in anxiety-producing situations, such as test taking, this kind of unrelated reinforcer may have some advantage if the imagined scene helps to produce relaxation. Such relaxation can produce a respondent conditioning effect, increasing relaxation in the test-taking situation (Bajtelsmit & Gershman, 1976).

Although there are many advantages to using imagined reinforcement, a few words of caution are in order. To be effective, the images must be vivid (Wisocki, 1973). Since not everyone can produce vivid, lifelike images, it is necessary that you practice the imagined reinforcement until you can almost feel the water, almost touch the clothes, or hear the music almost as clearly as if you were at the concert. To practice, begin by calling up scenes from memory, which may produce more vivid images than purely imagined scenes. If you cannot produce images as vivid as memories, you should not rely on imagined reinforcement.

Verbal Self-Reinforcement

Praise is one of the fundamental methods of control in all human society. Parents, teachers, coaches, politicians, and lovers all encourage behavior by praising. *Verbal reinforcement* is only a technical term for praise and an acknowledgment that praise is a most powerful reinforcer. We discussed techniques for arranging the praise of others so that it will reinforce your behavior. Here we discuss verbal *self*-reinforcement—that is, self-encouragement following desired behavior. Recall the discussion of the power of bringing self-directions up from the underground. That same technique can be used to increase the reinforcing power of self-speech as well. Every individual experiences pleasure at meeting a goal and at behaving according to his or her own standards. But if that pleasure can be made verbal, brought up from the underground, it can take on stronger reinforcing properties.

The technique is merely to tell yourself, "Good! You did it." Say it either covertly or aloud, but say it clearly. Say it after each instance of your desired behavior.

The importance of this form of self-reinforcement should not be overlooked. It will ensure that you focus on your improved performance (Shelton

& Levy, 1981; Meichenbaum, 1977). In our experience, self-praise is omitted from self-modification plans for two reasons. First, you may think it sounds silly or absurd. It is not. Don't underestimate the power of language. Second, you may think that self-reinforcement is conceited or "bragging." That is also incorrect, because bragging is an effort to get reinforcement from others. Self-reinforcement is a realistic recognition of accomplishment. It does not involve puffing yourself up without reason. It is not an attempt to get others to praise you. Verbal self-reinforcement is a way of marking off your successes justly and privately (Rehm, 1982).

The use of verbal or covert self-reinforcement has been researched most intensely in studies of depression by Elaine Heiby. There appears to be a generalized "skill" of self-reinforcement (Heiby, 1982). Some individuals reinforce themselves less than others do regardless of their situations or activities. Individuals who are depressed have a lower frequency of self-reinforcement than do nondepressed people (Heiby, 1981), and depressed people use verbal self-*punishment* frequently (Rehm, 1982). Does low self-reinforcement "cause" depression? Not necessarily, but those who are low self-reinforcers may be at higher risk for depression. When external reinforcement is lost, low self-reinforcers are more likely than others to become depressed (Heiby, 1983a, 1983b).

These research reports are consistent with the major theories of depression. It appears that the loss of external reinforcement and support—a run of bad grades, the loss of a friend or loved one, the loss of a job—can make anyone depressed. But those who have the skill to reinforce, encourage, and support themselves are less likely to be pitched into a severe depression. Self-reinforcers are better able to ride out periods when external reinforcement is taken away.

Therefore, there is every reason to include self-reinforcement in your life as often as it is earned. There is even more reason to include self-reinforcement in self-modification plans, especially if a component of the problem is depression. Praising yourself, silently or aloud, is a reinforcer that is always accessible, is easy to use, and is likely to have generalized good effects. We recommend that it be included in every plan.

If you have difficulty in praising yourself contingently, make that goal a part of your plan. Positive self-statements can themselves be increased by reinforcement (Krop, Calhoon, & Verrier, 1971; Krop, Perez, & Beaudoin, 1973). Giving yourself reminders (cues) to make positive self-statements and then following the statements with some form of reward is an effective procedure (Epstein & Hersen, 1974).

Noncontingent Positive Events

Are there ever any conditions when positive events should be added to your life, freely, richly, and noncontingently? Indeed there are, and the discussion of depression leads naturally into this topic. A life that is empty of pleasant events is almost certain to be a depressed life. Psychologists, as well as depressed people, have puzzled for years as to whether or not simply increasing pleasant events will cause depression to lift. There is now evidence that increasing pleasant events increases positive aspects of well-being in general (Reich & Zautra, 1981). Peter Lewinsohn's influential theory suggests that depression is brought about by the loss of external reinforcement, and his suggested treatment includes the increasing of pleasant activities (for example, Lewinsohn, Sullivan, & Grosscup, 1980).

Most psychologists recommend that pleasant events be arranged to follow some behavior that will contribute to decreasing depression. Pleasant events can be used to reward making new social contacts, to reward assertive responses, to reward better study habits, and the like. But *in addition* to these tactics, merely increasing pleasant activities in general is a wise course for those suffering depression.

In fact, a general change in the balance of pleasant to unpleasant events is advisable for people wrestling with a variety of problems. Marlatt and Parks (1982) discuss this in terms of getting the "wants" in balance with the "shoulds." A life that is too filled with duties that are felt as "shoulds," with little time for enjoying the things that are "wants," is a life set up for problems. Problems are likely to erupt in destructive binges of consumption: food, drink, drugs, or escapism. For such situations, Marlatt and Parks (1982) suggest a change in lifestyle, including time for relaxation each day: time for meditation, for exercise, or especially "free time"—the opportunity to do whatever is pleasant and available at the moment.

So the answer to the opening question of this section is: yes, there are people whose plans should be to increase pleasant activities that can occur freely, richly, and noncontingently.

The irony is that those people who most need to increase pleasant events are the ones least likely to do so. In fact, increasing free pleasant events may have to be taken as a goal for self-modification, and that plan will require reinforcement for increasing pleasant events!

Marsha, one of our 19-year-old students, was struggling to stay in school. She had registered for morning classes starting at 7:30, because at 2:00 each weekday she reported to the bakery where she was a salesclerk. She worked until 10:00 each night. Then she had papers to write, exams to prepare for, and all the tasks of personal life. She lived with her partially disabled mother, so housework, laundry, and shopping occupied most of her time on the weekends. She dated very rarely, and Sundays she slept, exhausted and dull.

Marsha's first step toward self-modification was to create her catalog of reinforcers. It included such things as new clothes and a new stereo, but it became clear to her that she had no time to wear new dresses and no time to listen to new tapes. Each reinforcer she listed required time for its enjoyment, and what Marsha did *not* have was time.

Where was it to come from? Where could any pleasant events fit into that life crowded with "shoulds"? On analysis, she realized that the weekend might be rearranged: Saturdays were stuffed with all the duties, and Sundays were a dead loss of sluggish sleep and dullness. There were three things that

Marsha wanted to do, but had never managed to arrange: visit a favorite aunt, practice yoga, and attend a discussion group. How could she motivate herself to rearrange her weekends to allow for these pleasant events? For several weeks, she never "got around" to it. Her final plan involved the use of the Premack principle. Of all her duties, the one she enjoyed most was housekeeping, which she performed vigorously and with pleasure. So she selected one behavior, cleaning the bathroom, and did not allow herself to perform it until after she had done at least one of her desired pleasant activities. The outcome of this plan was an increase in the three desired activities, less sleeping and moping on Sunday—and the bathroom stayed as clean as ever.

The point of Marsha's case is this: while it is often desirable to make changes in your lifestyle so that free, noncontingent pleasant activities are increased, it may be necessary to use reinforcement plans to bring that about.

BOX 7-4

INCREASING HONEST THOUGHTS BY REINFORCEMENT

A student suffered from persistent depression. She believed that she would be far less depressed if she could be honest with herself and others. Thus her target behavior was to increase the number of "honest, authentic statements made to myself and other people."

Examples of "honest, authentic statements" included:

"That made me angry!"
"Even if she is my sister, I don't like what she is doing."
"I just put on an act—a good act, but totally phony."
"I don't agree. Pro football is brutal."

Figure 7-2 shows the frequencies of this student's honest statements. After 20 days of baseline self-observation, she began her first intervention plan. She called it "autosuggestion" and required herself each morning to "*will* myself to feel better, psych myself up, just not indulge my black morning moods." For about three weeks, the plan worked. Her number of honest statements climbed, and so did her mood. Then both quickly tumbled. At that point she began the following full program of tokenized reinforcement.

"For each verbal expression of feeling or opinion (talking to myself included), I will award myself 1 point, to be redeemed on the following schedule: For each 5 points, I'll have 15 minutes of free time to do anything I choose; *or* each point will be paid in money at the rate of 1¢ per point, and this money can be spent on 'luxury' things I usually wouldn't buy. Bonus for attaining a new high will be rewarded by a special event of equal value. Also, for each time my morning autosuggestion works, I will get 5 points. My morning coffee will also be contingent on getting myself into a better mood." Her honest statements quickly jumped to more than 30 a day. There were ups and downs, but the average stabilized at more than 20. She terminated the plan after about a month and a half. Psychological tests, and her own report, showed that her depression was remarkably improved (Tharp, Watson, & Kaya, 1974).

BOX 7-4

INCREASING HONEST THOUGHTS BY REINFORCEMENT
(*continued*)

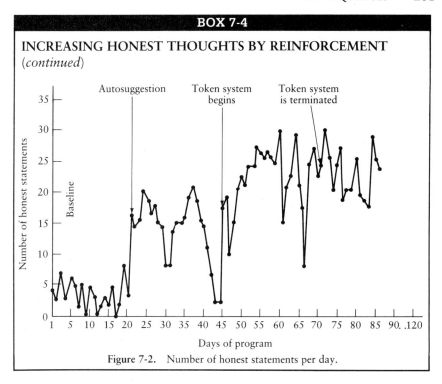

Figure 7-2. Number of honest statements per day.

SELF-PUNISHMENT AND EXTINCTION

Extinction

Extinction is the weakening of a behavior by withdrawing reinforcement from it. This is a simple strategy when used in the laboratory. If an experimental animal is no longer given food pellets, it will eventually quit pressing the bar. In self-direction, however, extinction is more complicated. When real-life reinforcers are withdrawn and behaviors reduced, other behaviors may rush in to fill the vacuum. When used alone, extinction is very rarely an effective self-directing strategy.

The following case illustrates the point. A student wanted to reduce the frequency of cutting his trigonometry class. His midterm grade was "D," and it was obvious that poor attendance was the reason. His A-B-C analysis clearly showed that class cutting was being reinforced by shooting pool and playing pinball, because he was going to the Billiard Palace instead of the classroom. His plan called for withdrawing this reinforcer: when he cut class, he would go home immediately. But this plan didn't result in less class cutting, since he found himself listening to the stereo in his room instead. The correct procedure here would have been to reinforce class attendance, perhaps by making the Billiard Palace contingent on it. *When you withdraw reinforcement from an undesired behavior, you should simultaneously increase reinforcement for the alternative, desired behavior.*

Why Punishment Alone Is Insufficient

Punishment alone is usually an undesirable strategy. This is true for either kind of punishment—adding an aversive stimulus to a situation or removing a positive event. Most plans that rely solely on punishment don't work. In fact, they can make things worse. One way that behaviors become resistant to punishment is by being first mildly punished and then positively reinforced. You might actually increase the behavior's resistance to punishment by supplying a small punishment followed by the usual reinforcement.

A second reason for avoiding punishment is that punishment alone doesn't teach new behaviors. Punishment suppresses the behavior it follows, but what happens *instead* is determined by the reinforcement that follows the behavior that is substituted. Your plan should provide for designating and reinforcing desired alternatives to your problem behaviors. Otherwise, the plan is incomplete.

One of our students had three part-time jobs plus a full load at college. Her first plan consisted of punishing herself for *not* performing a desired behavior by depriving herself of one of the few things in her life that she enjoyed. She had somehow managed to keep two hours free every Friday afternoon, and she always used them to go to the beach with a close friend. Her plan proposed to punish excessive eating by giving up this weekly pleasure. We strongly disagreed with this idea. Her life needed enrichment, not a further impoverishment of positive reinforcers. We suggested that she reward dieting by adding another social activity—if necessary, at the expense of her quite adequate study time. To lose her one weekly contact with a friend would have made her even more dependent on her only other real pleasure—food. Besides, her overall happiness required a broader spectrum of pleasant events. Punishment would have restricted her life and would have also made dieting less likely.

The third reason for not including punishment in your plan is that you will be less likely to carry out your plan. In a course in behavioral self-control, Worthington (1979) found that only one-third of the students actually inflicted self-punishment when their plans called for it.

When you are performing some undesired behavior, you should be able to positively reinforce an incompatible behavior instead of punishing the undesired behavior. Reinforce nail grooming instead of punishing nail biting. Before you decide to use punishment, search for an incompatible behavior that you can positively reinforce instead.

The Loss of Positive Events as Punishment

If you insist on using punishment, it should involve giving up something pleasant that you usually receive. This is better than using an aversive stimulus as punishment (Kazdin, 1973b). In other words, don't whip yourself and don't pinch yourself.

Here are some examples of punishment in the form of giving up usual pleasures. One person might not allow herself to take a customary bath if she has not studied enough. Another might not allow himself to eat certain preferred foods if he has performed some undesired behavior. If you are accustomed to going to a movie on Saturday night, you could punish yourself for your nonperformance of a target behavior by staying home. Many people use the general category of "things I do for fun" to require themselves to perform some target behavior before they allow themselves to engage in the "fun" activities. Another student, who was in love with a man in another state, used the daily letters she received from him. Each day she handed the unopened letter to a friend. If she performed her target behavior, she got the letter back, unopened. If she did not perform the target behavior, her friend was instructed to open and read the love letter.

A few of our students have had success with such plans, but a better strategy is to combine positive reinforcement with punishment, so that you lose *additional* rewards, not customary ones. A plan to increase studying could call for an extra movie per week if your goal is met, but only if your goal is met.

A token system can be used for a combination program. Lutzker and Lutzker (1974) report a program used by a dieter with the help of her husband. She could earn several reinforcers for losing a half-pound or more each week, but the most effective part of the plan involved a "household duties" punishment. Before beginning the plan, she and her husband divided the household chores into "his" and "hers," with the husband taking on more chores than he had before. Each week, after her weigh-in, if she had lost weight or stayed even, he continued doing the chores on his list for the next week. If she had gained weight, she had to do his chores in addition to her own. She lost weight.

Precommitted Punishment

Precommitment refers to making some arrangement in advance, so that you will be more likely to make choices of behaviors that are in your long-term best interest. *Precommitted punishment,* therefore, means arranging in advance that some particular punishing event will take place if you perform a certain undesired act. Precommitted punishment may be appropriate when the undesired behavior is so rewarding that no new reinforcers can be found to counter it.

You can arrange advance control of yourself by giving over some kind of forfeit to a helper. For example, you can require yourself to study for two hours before going to a movie. To enforce this behavior, you can give a friend $10 and instruct the friend to call you every half hour from 7 to 9 o'clock. If you don't answer the telephone, the friend is to mail the money to your worst enemy (Rachlin, 1974). One of our students wanted to completely eliminate using sugar, no longer adding it to coffee, cereal, or other foods. So she selected a cup from her treasured collection of handmade coffee cups, marked it with a piece of tape on the bottom, and instructed her husband to break it if she used any sugar.

In these precommitment strategies, the trick is to make the penalty so heavy that in fact you never apply it. Precommitment should work as a *deterrent*, not as a *punishment*. In this way, precommitment is consistent with our general recommendation that you should not in fact punish yourself. In precommitting, you must arrange for penalties that would be so unpleasant that you simply won't incur them.

A heavy forfeit, however, presents problems of its own. The specter of a great loss may create new anxieties, and the helper who holds the forfeit may begin to seem a menace. A middle-aged man was determined to stop smoking. His wife, who had recently stopped, was willing to cooperate to almost any extent. The husband was an avid collector of cacti and other small succulent plants. Over the years, his garden had grown down the wall and into the lawn, and even the kitchen counter often held young plants as a kind of incubator. His precommitment plan arranged that for *every* cigarette he smoked, his wife was to destroy one young cactus. The precommitment worked, in the sense that he smoked no cigarettes for seven days. But the threat was intolerable. He prowled the house and garden wondering which plant would be sacrificed if he smoked. And how would they die— drowned in the toilet or crushed under his wife's heel? After one week, he canceled the agreement and felt at ease with his wife once again.

Any form of self-punishment, even when used as a deterrent, brings about problems and should be approached carefully. Precommitted punishment should be used only temporarily and only when you can quickly bring desirable behavior under the control of positive reinforcement or natural rewards (Rachlin, 1974).

Punishment as a Temporary Solution

Punishment can be a temporary and partial tactic for achieving some goals. But, remember, it is only temporary and only partial. There is no point in using self-punishment except when it leads to positive reinforcers.

There is one form of self-punishment that can perhaps be recommended in the early stages, and that is the "punishment" of facing up to the negative consequences of a problem behavior. Imagining the real consequences of shoplifting, for example, can be a powerful deterrent: prison, publicity, and the loss of contact with family and friends (Gauthier & Pellerin, 1982). Imagining the continued loneliness and frustration of social withdrawal can provide strong motivation to persevere in building social skills. A systematic plan for reminding yourself of these long-range punishments can keep you from drifting from your goals. Youdin and Hemmes (1978) recommend to dieters that they stare at their naked bodies in the mirror for 60 seconds a day while thinking about overeating. L. W. Rosen (1981) reports a successful program for weight loss in which dieters agreed that if they decided to overeat, they would do so while watching themselves in a mirror, with as few clothes on as possible. The dieters found the vision "disgusting," and commonly stopped the eating session. Force yourself to read the latest figures on cancer and smoking. Reminding yourself of the negative consequences of some problem behavior can be considered not only as punishment, but also as another way of building and maintaining commitment.

REINFORCEMENT IN PLANS FOR SELF-MODIFICATION

Now we must consider the place of reinforcement in the A-B-C sequence. Powerful as reinforcement may be, it must be organized into a total intervention plan that involves antecedents, behaviors, and consequences. As you read this section, bear in mind the preliminary plans you have developed in Step Five (antecedents) and Step Six (developing new behaviors) of your own self-direction project. By adding reinforcing contingencies to these plans, you will bring them to full potential.

Reinforcement and Antecedent Control

In Chapter Five, we described several methods for achieving antecedent control: avoiding antecedents, narrowing them, and building new ones by performing the desired behavior in new situations. *Each of these tactics involves a behavior change that should also be reinforced.*

For example, avoiding old antecedents was recommended as a first tactic for reducing undesirable consummatory responses. Thus, avoiding the morning cup of coffee can reduce the temptation to smoke; avoiding parties, at least for a while, can help bring overeating, pot smoking, or drinking under control. But this tactic involves a sharp decrease in reinforcement, since old reinforcers are lost. Therefore, new reinforcement is needed—reinforcement gained for avoiding the old antecedents.

The dieter who refused dinner invitations for a month arranged with his wife that they would go to a movie on the nights when the parties were held. A student who was smoking too much reinforced her avoidance of pot parties with a long telephone chat with a friend the next morning. The young man who avoided excessive masturbation by choosing a busier restroom carried a paperback mystery with him and read it only while using the new facility. Each of these plans replaced the lost reinforcement with a new one, made contingent on avoiding an antecedent.

The same principle applies to behaviors performed in the presence of new antecedents: reinforcement should follow. Stimulus control of behavior is built by reinforcing behavior in the presence of the cue. Since your eventual goal is to have your new, desired behaviors become habitual and automatic, you must build this stimulus control through reinforcement in the presence of the new antecedent.

Reinforcement and the Development of New Behaviors

Every new behavior will require some reinforcement. If the behavior itself doesn't carry enough immediate reinforcement automatically, you will need to add additional contingent rewards. The necessity of reinforcing most new behaviors is a general principle, which we will illustrate with a discussion of two topics: imagined rehearsal and shaping.

Imagined rehearsal.   Imagined (covert) rehearsals influence real performances. In rehearsing a desired behavior in your imagination, it is useful to follow it with an imagined reinforcement (Kazdin, 1974d).

Cautela (1972, 1973) gives several examples of imagined reinforcers, such as swimming on a hot day and hearing good music. Suppose you are a dieter who wants to practice control of overeating. You imagine, sometime during the day and wherever you happen to be, that you are "sitting at home watching TV.... You say to yourself 'I think I'll have a piece of pie.' You get up to go to the pantry. Then you say, 'This is stupid. I don't want to be a fat pig.'" You should follow this imagined scene with the imagined rein-forcement—the swim or the music. Here is another scene you can rehearse in imagination: "You are at home eating steak. You are just about to reach for your second piece, and you stop and say to yourself 'Who needs it, anyway?'" and then imagine the reinforcer (Cautela, 1972, p. 213).

Imagined rehearsal can be a way of practicing when your own behaviors are not yet firm enough to earn reinforcement in the real world. A young man who had almost no experience or skills in approaching young women was taught to imagine the following scene and to self-reinforce it with imag-ined swimming in a warm river.

> Say to yourself "I think I'll call Jane for a date." As soon as you have this scene clearly, switch quickly to the reinforcement. As soon as you have the reinforcement vividly, hold it for two seconds. Then imagine that you walk to the phone and start to dial (reinforcement). You finish dialing. She answers. You say hello and ask her if she is free Saturday night. You tell her that you would like to go out with her.... Now do the whole sequence again. Make sure that the image is vivid. You can see the kitchen, feel the telephone. This time try to imagine that you are comfortable and confident as you call [Cautela, 1973, p. 30].

A similar example, adapted from Kazdin (1974d), is for the person who wants to become more assertive.

1. Imagine that you are eating in a restaurant with friends. You order a steak and tell the waiter you would like it rare. When the food arrives, you begin to eat and notice that it is overcooked.
2. Imagine that you immediately signal the waiter. When he arrives, you say, "I ordered this steak rare, and this one is medium. Please take it back and bring me one that is rare."
3. Imagine that in a few minutes the waiter brings another steak, rare, and says he is very sorry this has happened.*

When imagining assertiveness—saying no when a person asks for a favor you really don't want to do, protesting against being shortchanged, objecting when someone cuts in front of you in a line, sending an undercooked steak back—let the positive reinforcement grow naturally out of the rehearsed behavior: you get the steak you want! If you are rehearsing in your imagi-nation how to deal with a persistent door-to-door salesperson, you can follow your imagined firmness by imagining the person leaving quickly and your own feelings of competence and self-assurance. Whenever possible, use

---

*From "Effects of Covert Modeling and Model Reinforcement on Assertive Behavior," by A. E. Kazdin, 1974, *Journal of Abnormal Psychology, 83,* 240–252. Copyright 1974 by the American Psychological Association. Reprinted by permission.

a desirable "natural outcome" as your reinforcer. The advantage of using brief, independent scenes is that you can reinforce the various stages along the way.

Shaping.   The technique of shaping also illustrates the necessity of reinforcing all new behaviors. There is one remaining rule for correct shaping: each step must be reinforced.

The definition of each shaping step is actually a standard or criterion. For example:

Step 1:   2000 calories per day
Step 2:   1800 calories per day
Reinforcer: one hour of television per evening

For step 1, the reinforcer is taken when the standard for that step is met (2000 calories). For step 2, the standard becomes 1800 calories daily, and only then will television be watched.

Shaping steps are no different from any other behavior. If their natural consequences are not yet strong enough, they require arranged reinforcement. The case of Linda (Chapter Six), who feared birds, is a good illustration. As she built a schedule of steps closer and closer to the birds she feared, she didn't use any extra reinforcement at first, since she received strong rewards from her pride in mastering the fear. But when her schedule brought her quite close to the birds, she got stuck. At this point, Linda introduced a token system. For each step up in her shaping schedule, she earned so many points, which she could turn in at the end of the day to "buy" certain privileges, such as allowing herself extra dates, doing "idiot" reading, and so on. Her goal was to increase her total positive reinforcements so that she would gain something for getting really close to the birds. In Linda's case, two separate forms of reinforcement were employed. One was the formal token system. The earlier, less obvious reinforcement was the presence of her boyfriend. She originally elected to include him because his presence made her feel more relaxed. But his walking beside her also had reinforcing value for the approach behavior.

Cheating.   Taking the reinforcer without having performed the target behavior is a fairly common occurrence in self-modification. Almost everyone does it sometimes. You should watch yourself very carefully, however, because cheating more than occasionally—say, more than 10% of the time—indicates a shaping problem. Therefore, you should redesign your shaping schedule so that you will be reinforced for performing at some level that you find realistic. As long as you are able to provide a contingent reinforcement, you are building toward the final goal, no matter how small the steps are or how low you begin. If you cheat, don't abandon the project—redesign it.

A young man whose final goal was to save $7 each week began by requiring himself to save 50¢ each day (he put it in a piggy bank), even though he had almost never saved any money before. He used the reinforcer of eating supper only after he had put the money in his piggy bank. After three days, he skipped his saving for one day but went ahead and ate supper anyway. This was the beginning of a two-week period during which he skipped more often than he saved but ate his supper anyway. He realized that this kind of cheating was due to a problem in his shaping program. So he wrote a new contract, in which he required himself to save only 25¢ each day—a more realistic place to begin, in his case—in order to gain the reinforcer.

When to Include Self-Reinforcement in Your Intervention Plan

Now that we have discussed methods for adding reinforcement to self-change projects, both for antecedent control and for developing new behaviors, the questions to be answered are: When should self-reinforcement be included in the project? When can it be omitted?

We suggest the following rule of thumb: during the process of learning, make sure that any *new* behavior is followed promptly by some reinforcement. Some behaviors will be reinforced naturally and immediately, merely by being performed, and require no contrived reinforcement. For example, a tennis player who coaches herself with self-instructions will be reinforced by the swift consequences of her improved play. In social interactions, the game is also swift, and improved behaviors are likely to produce their own rewards. In such situations, inserting self-reinforcement after each performance of the behavior can be distracting. Indeed, inserting self-reinforcement into a situation that is intrinsically or immediately rewarding can even detract from performance (Kirsch, Heatherington, & Colapietro, 1979; Lepper, Greene, & Nisbett, 1973; Barrera & Rosen, 1977).

But many new behaviors, particularly in their early stages, are not followed by natural reinforcement. Natural reinforcement can be a long time coming for the dieter, the beginning exerciser, the fearful, the shy, or the academically disadvantaged student who is just beginning to learn study skills (Green, 1982). Self-conscious, contrived reinforcement is designed to strengthen behavior until the behavior becomes self-sustaining by producing its own rewards. Therefore, our rule of thumb—that new behavior should be followed by some reinforcement—most often means that you should include some form of contrived reinforcement in the early stages of your plan. This may not always be necessary. But don't exclude reinforcement unless you are confident that the environment itself will provide the necessary immediate reinforcement.

Objections to Self-Reinforcement

If you are encountering the idea of control through consequences for the first time, you probably find it peculiar. Some students object. They don't believe that a desired behavior *should* be deliberately self-rewarded. Virtue should be its own reward. We agree. The goal is to make your desired behavior so smooth and successful that the natural consequences of daily life will sustain it. When you reach that stage, self-reinforcement (and all the rest of you plan) can go underground; only your skill will be left showing. Self-reinforcement is a temporary strategy, like verbal self-control, to be used only until behaviors have become automated in their settings. But, like talking to yourself, reinforcing your behaviors will continue to be a useful, temporary device whenever virtue again fails to reward itself enough.

Some of our students have continued to object. "Even if we grant that point," they say, "you can't learn—really learn—under these conditions of self-bribery. It's all an act, not real behavior." Well, we reply, what is real, and what is an act? If you could put on an act of playing tennis well enough to win real matches, would you feel embarrassed because "it's just an act"? Skill is a real thing, however you learn it. But if you mean that "self-bribed" behavior cannot sustain itself, you have a point. If you are motivated to perform your new behavior only by the artificial rewards in your plan, you probably won't continue, once you tire of playing the game. Remember that we cautioned you to select a behavior-change project that you really value. If your changed behavior will bring greater self-respect and a happier life, then these rewarding consequences will sustain you over the long haul. Self-reinforcement is to be used only now, and at those times in the future when a stronger push is needed to get you off center and rolling again.

CHAPTER SUMMARY

The most basic formula in self-modification is to arrange that reward follows desired behaviors.

Discovering and Selecting Reinforcers

Your A-B-C records may reveal the reinforcers that are maintaining undesirable behavior. The simplest plan is to arrange for these same rewards to follow your new goal behavior. This is not possible with indulgent behaviors, because the act consumes the reinforcer. Therefore, some other reward must be used to reinforce nonindulgence. Intermittent reinforcement and avoidance behaviors make discovery of reinforcement difficult. Here, too, you must identify reinforcers that are available and controllable.

A wide variety of possible rewards can be used, including preferred things and preferred activities. The nature of the reward is not important, so long as your plan makes the reward contingent on the desired behavior.

Using Others to Dispense Reinforcers

The use of mediators as dispensers of contingent rewards is a highly desirable feature of self-modification. Research evidence overwhelmingly supports the power of this strategy in changing behavior. The use of mediators is advisable in every case in which it can be arranged, particularly in maintaining gains. Praise by mediators is probably even more important than material reinforcement. Attention should be paid to the mediators; their cooperative behavior will also need reinforcement. Sharing reinforcers with the mediator, or other partner, can help provide motivation, but care should be taken to make sure your partner shares your goals.

Self-Administered Consequences

Vigorous debate surrounds the question of whether self-reward acts as a reinforcer, or serves only to call attention to the behavior. Various evidence has been presented and critiqued, but the debate goes on. Virtually every psychologist agrees, however, that self-administered consequences do affect behavior.

Techniques of Self-Reinforcement

Contingent rewards should follow desired behavior as rapidly as possible. This can often be achieved by using a point system or other form of token reinforcement. Points are gained as soon as the behavior is performed, and then are exchanged later for real reinforcers.

Imagined reinforcers can also be used to provide rapid rewards. In this technique, a reinforcer from your list is imagined immediately after the behavior occurs. Especially useful is imagining the long-range eventual outcome of your self-modification program.

Verbal self-reinforcement—praising yourself—following desired behavior is an effective technique that should be included in every self-change program.

Increasing the amount of rewards in your life is part of the goal of self-modification. Good plans will add to the total of pleasant events in your daily schedule.

Self-Punishment and Extinction

Neither extinction nor self-punishment teaches any new behaviors. Most intervention plans that rely *solely* on self-punishment don't succeed. There are some situations in which self-punishment may be necessary—if, for example, there are no positive reinforcers available, or if the undesired behavior is so strongly reinforcing in itself that a direct, counteracting consequence is required for not performing it. Indulgent behaviors are typical examples of this situation.

If you do decide to use punishment, you should follow these rules:

1. Remove something positive instead of adding something negative. (Always try to figure out a way to increase behavior by adding something positive.)
2. Use punishment only if it leads to more positive reinforcement.
3. Devise a plan that combines punishment with positive reinforcement.
4. You may use precommitted punishment as a deterrent strategy, but only temporarily until the desired behavior can be supported by positive consequences.

The only recommended form of "punishment" is the systematic facing of the negative long-term consequences of a problem behavior. This helps build commitment.

Reinforcement in Plans for Self-Modification

Rewards need to be integrated into plans for controlling antecedents (Chapter Five) and developing new behaviors (Chapter Six). For example, rewards can be added to *imagined rehearsal* and to *shaping*. The general point is that reinforcement should follow all new behaviors in a self-modification plan. If the natural environment does not provide it, arrange specific rewards to be delivered by yourself or your mediators.

YOUR OWN SELF-DIRECTION PROJECT: STEP SEVEN

Review the previous versions of your plan, which included elements of antecedent control and development of new behavior, in light of what you have just learned about rearrangement of consequences. Plan to follow new behaviors with reinforcement. Be sure to include verbal self-reinforcement, plus at least one other technique.

The result may well be your final plan. After reading the next chapter, you will be better able to combine A, B, and C elements into a comprehensive and sound package.

TIPS FOR TYPICAL TOPICS

Anxieties

As you get closer and closer to the feared situation, you may need reinforcement. Add it to your plan at that time. For all plans, include verbal reinforcement. Use it at each stage and for each behavior.

Assertion

Most nonassertive people suffer from the unreasonable expectation that some awful consequence will necessarily follow from their attempts to assert themselves: "If I do, he won't be my friend anymore." Instead, use imagined positive reinforcement, and anticipate favorable outcomes. If you assert yourself early, moderately, and politely, the actual consequences are likely to be pleasant. However, if you realistically expect to be punished by someone for asserting yourself (for example, by a hostile waiter who doesn't want to take your steak back), you can take steps to minimize the effects of that punishment by practicing being assertive in your imagination, by relaxing, and by concentrating on the positive consequences of your behavior (Shelton, 1979).

Use shaping and reinforcement, beginning with assertive behaviors that are likely to produce success. As you risk more, you may feel guilty or hurt after having been assertive. If these feelings persist, they will decrease your chances of maintaining the gains you have made. So try to eliminate those feelings by using thought stopping and by concentrating on the positive consequences of your newly learned assertiveness.

Some of our students have abandoned improving assertion as their goal because they were punished by others for being too "aggressive." Women in particular often meet disapproval for behavior that is interpreted as "aggressive" (Leviton, 1979). Iris Goldstein-Fodor and Renée Epstein (1983) have discussed this problem thoughtfully and urge that these realities of women's lives be considered in their efforts to become reasonably and fairly assertive. The line between assertiveness and abrasiveness is different for every person, depending on her (or his) own values and the values of friends and associates.

Our own advice is to use your A-B-C journal analysis. Think over the A-B-C elements of the situations in which you felt too passive. Then reconstruct those situations as you wish you had behaved. Anticipate the consequences as they are likely to occur in your real social world. Take those into account in establishing goals. For whatever goals you choose, reinforce those gradually practiced behaviors in the ways this chapter suggests. Anticipate that others will respond to you differently. If their response is unfavorable, think again. Have you gone too far? Or is it *their* responsibility to change?

Depression

Use self-reinforcement to increase the frequency of your desired behaviors. Your plan should have this general form: (1) *Schedule* pleasant activities frequently. (2) *Reinforce* yourself for engaging in the activities. Be very liberal. Reinforce only on contingency, but begin with shaping steps that you can meet (Fuchs & Rehm, 1977). (3) *Replace* denigrating self-speech with realistic self-praise. Be sure to include verbal self-reinforcement for each desired behavior.

An effective technique for increasing the number of pleasant events in your life is to make sure you notice the ones that do occur. Keeping daily records of pleasant events is a reliable way to bring them to your attention. These may include such things as seeing a rainbow, talking with friends, a smile from the other sex, the taste of an excellent olive.

It is almost certain that you are getting less reinforcement than you need from other people. In order to increase those rewards, you will probably have to build new habits—making yourself more available to others, or being more skillful in your interactions. Therefore, some problem solving and social-skill building should be a part of your overall plan (Lewinsohn, Sullivan, & Grosscup, 1980).

Family, Friends, Lovers, and Coworkers

Reinforce yourself for doing what is needed to improve the relationships, and be sure to reinforce the others: "Hey, that was really nice. We sat and talked about our problem without anyone blowing up. I really appreciate the effort you are making."

Very often, interpersonal problems develop because one person begins to punish the other. Being punished often incites people to revenge, and a vicious circle is established. One punishment leads to the next. This, in turn, leads to more punishment, and so on until the relationship is destroyed. One way of breaking this vicious circle is to realize that you can reinforce someone else by paying attention or making some statement that is rewarding.

Ask yourself "How can I reinforce desired behavior?" Your intervention plan might involve paying attention to the "good" things the other person does and reinforcing the person for them. You then reinforce yourself for reinforcing the other. In a book on how to achieve a good marriage, Knox (1971) suggests keeping records like this:*

The husband records:		
Wife's desirable behavior	Wife's undesirable behavior	Husband's response to wife's behavior
The wife records:		
Husband's desirable behavior	Husband's undesirable behavior	Wife's response to husband's behavior

Comparing the two records allows you to see if you are in fact trying to punish your spouse's undesired behavior instead of trying to reward his or her desirable acts. This record can also show how your spouse's behavior represents an antecedent for your behavior, and vice versa. It tells what changes you should ask of your spouse and what changes you should try to make in yourself.

Two people working together to improve their relationship can develop specific agreements: you give up this, and I'll give up that; you do this, and I'll do that. Since certain changes in another person to whom you are close can be a powerful incentive for you to change, this kind of mutual agreement is a powerful technique.

Overeating, Smoking, Drinking, and Drug Use

Reinforcement is a vital element in your plan. Reinforce yourself for avoiding the situations that cue excessive consumption.

Use reinforcement to strengthen all the behaviors your self-control requires, such as recording all the food you eat, resisting urges, exercising, making graphs, and avoiding temptation. Reward these *behaviors*. Do not make reward contingent on weight. Daily fluctuations in weight can be very deceiving. If you perform the dieting behaviors, weight loss will follow.

As often as possible, use the natural reinforcement that your long-range self-control will bring. Consider the benefits of your diet: do you feel better, happier, more alive? Consider the benefits of giving up tobacco, three of which you will enjoy as soon as you quit: immediate clearance of smoke from your lungs, clearance of carbon monoxide from your blood, and reduced risk of sudden death (Pechacek & Danaher, 1979). Remind yourself of these three rewards. Remind yourself of the immediate and long-term benefits of giving up alcohol or drugs. These, too, are quite numerous. One of the benefits of weight loss is lowered depression (Wing, Marcus, Epstein, & Kupfer, 1983), and better mood and feelings of pride are reinforcers that you should notice even in the earliest stages of dieting, abstaining from drugs,

*From *Marriage Happiness: A Behavioral Approach to Counseling,* by D. Knox. Copyright 1971 by Research Press. Reprinted by permission.

or giving up tobacco. Attend to these feelings, and use them as self-reinforcement. When dieting, look at your body in the mirror. Enjoy your improved appearance (Owusu-Bempah & Howitt, 1983).

Odds are that you will continue to need other forms of reinforcement to replace the consummatory behaviors. Reinforce alternatives, and arrange for reinforcement from others. Successful weight losers received positive feedback from several external sources, such as parents and peers (Perri & Richards, 1977).

The evidence is completely convincing that the use of significant others as mediators will help your plan. Read the text material on pages 182–187 carefully, and include mediators in some way.

Studying and Time Management

Reinforcement is highly important in studying and time scheduling—much more important than unsuccessful students believe. In fact, successful students tend to develop self-reinforcement techniques on their own, without a course or a book like this one (Heffernan & Richards, 1981; Perri & Richards, 1977). Often reinforcement can be obtained by a simple rearrangement. For example, use pleasant occupations (leisure or hobbies) to reinforce the more difficult ones such as studying, so that one is directly tied to the other and reinforces it. In drawing up your time-management plan, make sure that a pleasant block of time follows any particularly difficult one, and follow the rule that you must complete the difficult activity before you move to the pleasant one.

Whenever you can't arrange your activities as described above, use other reinforcers, however arbitrary—movies, candy, cash, tokens. Your basic plan should (1) be based on a firm schedule, (2) include enough pleasant activities, and (3) provide for reinforcement for following the schedule.

The use of reinforcement for studying is especially important if your study habits have not yet been well developed in high school or early college courses (Green, 1982). One of the advantages that competent students have over "disadvantaged" students is that the advantaged already reinforce themselves for studying.

But there are times of "blocking" and distraction when studying and writing will not come even for competent students—in fact, even for professors. Programs of reinforcement have proven effective in increasing productivity even for seasoned academic writers who were temporarily "blocked" (Boice, 1982).

The Other Sex

Imagined rehearsal and reinforcement are particularly appropriate for practicing the early stages of approach—making conversation and asking for dates. Use the logical imagined reinforcement of friendliness and acceptance by the other person. The natural reinforcements offered by the other sex are strong enough to maintain behavior, once confidence and skill have been achieved.

CHAPTER EIGHT

Planning
for Change

OUTLINE

- Combining A, B, and C Elements
- The Features of a Good Plan
- Chapter Summary
- Your Own Self-Direction Project: Step Eight
- Tips for Typical Topics

LEARNING OBJECTIVES

Combining A, B, and C Elements

1. How are A, B, and C elements combined in a single plan?
2. Describe in detail the two-step process for dealing with consummatory behaviors.
   a. How can unwanted stimulus control by various situations be gradually eliminated?
   b. How can the two-stage process be used in projects other than those dealing with consummatory behaviors?

The Features of a Good Plan

3. What are the five features of a good plan?
   a. How are rules used in self-modification?
   b. How are goals and subgoals used?
   c. Why is it important to gather feedback?
   d. How is feedback compared to goals and subgoals?
   e. When do you make adjustments in your plan?
4. What are the major techniques in the checklist that you should use for your project?
5. How can you use brainstorming to generate more ideas on how to carry out self-change?

An effective plan combines antecedent, behavior, and consequence (A-B-C) elements. The goal of this chapter is to help you design such a plan. We will illustrate ways of integrating A, B, and C elements, and then discuss the principles that characterize a sound plan. So far we have treated each technique and principle in isolation, independently of one another. An effective plan for change integrates all these techniques and principles.

216

COMBINING A, B, AND C ELEMENTS

Two Sample Projects

Two sample projects, described in some detail, will illustrate how A, B, and C elements are combined in an effective plan for self-modification.

The student.   Paul wrote: "There are several reasons why I would like to study more. I think I will develop a sense of achievement if I get all A's this semester, and it will improve my chances of getting into seminary. I will also learn discipline and build my self-esteem."

For three weeks, Paul kept a record of how much he studied. And then he began to formulate a systematic self-modification plan. "In the first week I studied quite a bit just because I was keeping records, but by the second and third weeks my average had dropped way off, and I ended up averaging under ten hours per week. Then I began a full-blown self-modification plan.

"I wrote a self-contract. I specified several things to do to change: I scheduled study hours, I gradually built up the amount of time I studied at one sitting, I planned where I would study, I gave myself instructions, and I worked out rewards for studying. When problems came up, I changed my plan to cope with them."

Paul listed all these elements of the plan in his self-contract, along with three escape clauses: He would keep 4:30 to 6:30 as a time to relax; he would devote all day Sunday to church work; and he would not study more than 20 hours a week. Then Paul signed the contract and posted it in his room.

Let's analyze the different parts of Paul's plan from the point of view of antecedents, behaviors, and consequences.

Antecedents: Paul scheduled specific hours that he would study—for example, Tuesday night, 6:30 to 8:30—and the exact places where he would do it—"my desk at home," "college library," or "the local public library." He set certain rules: "I will study at the times designated on my schedule. I will study at least one hour before I take a break." After typing out the entire set of rules, he put this contract with himself into his record-keeping notebook. Just before each study session, he gave himself instructions: "Here's another opportunity to get those A's. I must study now—I scheduled it. Sit down, look over the assignment. Then concentrate on the reading and the note taking. If my attention begins to wander, take up another assignment. Read for one hour, and then reward myself."

Behaviors: Paul used shaping to gradually increase how many hours per day he scheduled for studying. First he set one-and-a-half hours, then two, then two-and-a-half, then increased the time by quarter hours up to three-and-a-half hours. He started by requiring himself to study for one hour without a break, then increased this by ten-minute segments until his study periods were up to two continuous hours.

Consequences: Paul worked out a token system, earning 1 token for every hour of studying. Each token was worth a half-hour of TV watching. Seven tokens were enough to earn his three favorite programs. If he earned 10 tokens, he earned a bonus. He would take off from studying all day Saturday. At a later stage, he raised the cost of the bonus to 15 tokens.

Problems: Paul ran into three sets of problems in trying to change his habits.

"First, I'd get a strong urge not to study, even though it was a scheduled study time. Then, while I was studying, my mind would wander. And sometimes I would think, 'This is pointless. I'll never make all A's anyway.' These thoughts were obviously going to keep me from reaching my goal, so I used thought stopping to block them out and told myself, 'You can do this. You are an able student, and you have good self-discipline.'

"A second problem was that I always got hungry while I was studying, and I would take a break to eat. So I started having a snack just before my study time, and then I'd give myself reminders not to eat any more once I started studying."

Toward the end of the semester, Paul nearly reached his goal of 20 hours of studying per week, but after taking one particularly difficult exam he felt he needed a break, so he didn't study for two days. After that it was hard to get back to his schedule. By this time, the end of the first term had arrived, and Paul found that the biggest reinforcer of all was a gigantic improvement in his grades. "Frankly, I was stunned. I actually made all A's! I really *can* sit down and study for two hours straight, and doing it regularly has a terrific effect on my GPA."

The putdown artist.   We met Edgar in Chapter Three. His problem was that he put down his friends. "When I had the chance, I would put people down without even thinking about it." He began his self-change program by counting the number of putdowns per week and kept records for several weeks. (Some of his records are sampled in Chapter Three.) Edgar then worked out a plan for changing and continued to make observations about his putdowns of his friends.

Antecedents: "I put down my friends as a joke. When we're horsing around, everyone is joking about something or other, and I use these putdowns as my kind of joke. *I* know I am only joking, but my friends don't like it. So I need to be careful in that kind of situation. I also asked my friends to tell me if I was putting them down. Sometimes I didn't even realize I was doing it."

Behaviors: "Each week I tried to reduce the number of putdowns I did— shaping. I also did relaxation exercises, so I could relax more in those horsing-around times. I tried modeling other people who had good interpersonal manners. I did mental practice for about three minutes each day, imagining myself saying nice things to people. I also tried to pause before saying something, so I could ask myself if what I was going to say was a putdown. Instead of putting people down, I tried to compliment them."

Note the large number of different things Edgar is doing: relaxing, pausing, modeling, practicing, and substituting positive remarks for negative ones.

Consequences: "My primary reward for not putting people down was allowing myself to talk on the phone with my friends for a certain number of minutes. I worked out a table to relate the number of putdowns to how long I could talk on the phone:

Number of putdowns	Number of minutes allowed on the phone
20	10
17	15
15	30
10	45
5	indefinite

"As the weeks went by, I changed the ratio of putdowns to time on the telephone: I had to use fewer putdowns in order to talk on the phone for the same amount of time.

"After about three months, I stopped keeping records, but I still perform the mental rehearsals. Even though I still put people down sometimes, it is not to the extent it was before."

Two-Stage Process for Consummatory Behaviors

How can elements of A, B, and C be combined to cope with problems of consummatory behavior? In Chapter Five, we suggested that undesired consummatory behaviors can be reduced by a *two-stage process. In stage 1, avoid the antecedent.* For example, don't go to parties where you will be strongly tempted to smoke, and don't confront yourself with high-calorie food. Your plan should include reinforcement for this avoidance and a way of substituting other pleasant activities. But few antecedents can be avoided permanently. Eventually you want to be able to return to parties, walk into a bakery, or go back to your morning cup of coffee without having a cigarette. *In stage 2, build new behaviors,* so that you can be in tempting situations but not perform the self-indulging or addictive behavior.

Reinforcement is integrated into the two-stage process. In stage 1, you reward yourself for simply avoiding the tempting antecedent situation. In stage 2, you reward yourself for performing a new, desirable behavior in the presence of the tempting antecedent situation.

Larry, a man who had tried unsuccessfully several times to quit smoking, did an analysis of the situations in which he returned to smoking after having quit for a few days. Taking a coffee break or eating lunch with his colleagues (several of whom smoked) was the most likely time for backsliding. Smoking seemed such a pleasure under those circumstances that he just didn't resist. In stage 1 of his plan, Larry avoided these antecedent situations for two weeks, explaining to his friends what he was doing and reinforcing himself for successful avoidance. He was not tempted so much on the weekends, because he spent them with his wife, who didn't smoke. After he had been off cigarettes for several weeks, he entered stage 2, in which he rewarded himself specifically for not smoking with his friends at lunch. After this had worked for a week, he returned to coffee breaks in his daily schedule and reinforced himself specifically for not smoking at coffee breaks. Now Larry's task was to remain vigilant for tempting antecedents and to reinforce himself for not smoking when they occurred. He was able to tell when such an antecedent was present, because he would suddenly realize how much he wanted a cigarette. The morning cup of coffee, a meal, a tense period, another smoker, a party—these were the kinds of tempting antecedents that he had to learn to deal with.

Rehearsal in imagination is a good technique for this kind of situation. Several times a day, Larry would imagine himself in a situation in which he was tempted to smoke—concentrating on imagining all the details, including his own strong craving for a cigarette—and he would imagine himself *not* giving in.

You may also gradually eliminate a situation's stimulus control. If there are a dozen different antecedents to smoking or overeating, try gaining control over them one at a time. This gives you a feeling of progress—a welcome reinforcer. The procedure is a form of shaping, in which you eliminate the easier antecedents, one at a time, and then move on to the more difficult ones.

Drugs, alcohol, tobacco, and food are taken in response to several particular antecedents—watching TV; reading; being with a person who causes tension, feeling bored, depressed, angry, or excited. After discovering your problem antecedents, divide them into *physical* and *emotional* events. First eliminate the stimulus control of the physical events—for example, eating while watching TV—and later eliminate the control of the emotional events—for example, drinking when depressed (Brown, 1984). Physical events are usually easier to control than emotional ones, because they are more obvious. Start with the easier situations, and gradually work up to the harder ones. This will allow you to gradually gain skills and confidence.

One of our students was overweight by more than 100 pounds. She reported: "When I first began my project, I was unable to sit through a movie without eating popcorn. I used shaping to deal with it. First, I took snacks with me. Next, I brought only a soda. Then I chewed gum. Now I'm quite comfortable eating nothing at all at the movies, and I don't even feel tempted by the smell of the popcorn." This success was also an important step in skill building that allowed her to achieve normal weight.

The idea of eliminating stimulus control over unwanted behaviors is not part of commonsense psychology. People tend not to examine their environment to see where it may be controlling their behaviors. They need to learn to spot those situations and to gain control over the situational antecedents that govern their unwanted behaviors. For example, people may overeat in response to the sight of food, to being in Mom's kitchen, to driving past a particular fast-food store—all situational antecedents that control their overeating.

The Two-Stage Process Applied to Other Problems

The two-stage process is not limited to consummatory behaviors. Many projects can follow a two-stage process.

Leslie and Helen worked together, and over the years their relationship deteriorated. Having to deal with each other in their jobs was extremely unpleasant. When they did talk, the inevitable result was anger and hurt feelings. The obvious solution—that of avoiding each other—was impossible, since they had to work in the same room day after day. Leslie decided to try a two-stage intervention program. The first stage was an effort to control the antecedents for both of them.

Stage 1. Leslie instituted a cooling-off period, in which she didn't talk with Helen except when it was absolutely necessary. When she did talk, she confined her remarks to business topics and tried to be either neutral or mildly pleasant. This was reasonably effective. After a couple of weeks, they settled down to occasional brief and relatively calm interactions. Most important, anger seemed to disappear from the picture.

This first stage of Leslie's program is an example of avoiding the controlling antecedent—in this case, talking with the other person—long enough to begin developing other more desirable reactions. It is very important to develop those new and more desirable behaviors. In the case of these two women, for example, if no new behavior had been developed, the cooling-off period would have ended in failure. Eventually their work would have required them to have more substantial conversations, and they would gradually have returned to their old behavior of stimulating each other to anger.

Stage 2. Leslie then went into a second stage, which included three elements: (1) She did not respond to annoying remarks from Helen. Thus, if Helen said "I'm not sure you're doing a good job," Leslie would ignore her. (2) She positively reinforced Helen for pleasant remarks. Thus if Helen said "That seemed to work out very well," Leslie would say, "Why, thanks very much. It's kind of you to say that." (3) She praised Helen for her good work and refrained from criticizing her.

THE FEATURES OF A GOOD PLAN

There is no such thing as one perfect plan for a problem. You could adopt several different plans for the same goal, any one of which might be successful. Not everyone will develop the same kind of plan for similar goals. There are, however, certain characteristics that all good plans share. For example, a successful plan cannot be vague. If only vague intentions were needed to change problem behavior, you wouldn't need the full range of techniques you have been reading about. Sometimes you can change your behavior by simply alerting yourself to the need to do so. But for many problem situations, you need more deliberate plans for self-change.

A Theoretical View of a Good Plan

A successful plan includes these features: (1) rules that state the kinds of behaviors and techniques for change to use in specific situations; (2) goals and subgoals; (3) feedback on your behavior, derived from your self-observations; (4) a comparison of feedback to your subgoals and goals in order to measure progress; and (5) adjustments in the plan as conditions change.

Rules.   Self-modification involves setting rules for oneself in order to reach one's goals. If some behavior is *not* a problem for you, you follow your own rules without paying much attention to them. If you have little difficulty asserting yourself, for example, you don't have to state an explicit rule such as "I must be sure to speak up for my rights when someone is taking advantage of me." But when you are *not* meeting a particular goal, you need to set clear, explicit rules to guide your behavior until that behavior becomes habitual. That's the whole purpose of rules—to make desired behaviors more likely.

In your plan for self-change, the rules are statements of the behaviors and techniques for change you will use in specific situations. Here are several examples of rules that people have included in their self-change plans:

> Every night, between 7 and 9 o'clock, I will practice relaxation exercises for 20 minutes.
> Whenever I feel the first signs of muscular tension, I will immediately say "relax" to myself.
> I will not keep snack foods in the house.
> I will exercise for 20 minutes on Monday, Wednesday, and Friday while watching *MASH*.
> After I have studied for one hour, I will award myself 2 token points.

A typical plan will have more than one rule. For example:

> Each day in my art history class, I will make at least one comment.
> Each time I make a comment, I will make a checkmark on my record card.
> After I have accumulated 5 checkmarks, I will allow myself one glass of wine or beer in the evening.

These three separate rules describe, respectively, the first shaping step for the student, the record-keeping system used, and the token system used for contingent reinforcement.

Goals and subgoals.   Making goals and subgoals explicit is vital to the success of any plan (Spates & Kanfer, 1977). Each subgoal has to be formulated precisely enough for you to be able to compare it with your performance and know whether or not you have achieved your subgoal. Each subgoal has its own rules.

> *Rules for subgoal 1:* Each day I will practice the relaxation exercises (at first I'll do this 20 minutes per day), until I can relax without going through all the muscle tension-release steps.

After this subgoal is reached, a new one is substituted.

Rules for subgoal 2: Each day I will spend at least 10 minutes rehearsing in my imagination applying for a job, until I can think about it with a tension rating no greater than mild.

As each step is achieved, the next step begins with new rules and new subgoals. The goal at each step is the level of performance needed to advance to the next step.

The long-range goal here is relaxation in certain situations, but it is reached by carefully stating a series of subgoals and reaching them one at a time.

Feedback.   Any effective plan must incorporate a system for gathering information about your progress. If you are learning to serve a tennis ball, you don't strike the ball and then close your eyes. You follow the trajectory of the ball, noting its speed, twist, and whether it lands in the proper court or not. Your standard for success is *ball in the court.* If your feedback tells you that it is *out,* you can perform some operation to correct your behavior. Without feedback, you aren't likely to improve—and if you did, you wouldn't know it.

All goal-oriented behavior is governed by this principle. Without some information about your performance (feedback), you cannot correct yourself, whether your goal is to be a better student, a better lover, or a better tennis player. For this reason, your plan must include a system for collecting data. Of course you are already doing that for baseline purposes, as outlined in Chapter Three. But you must continue to self-record for the duration of your plan, so that self-correction can occur.

Comparison of feedback to goals and subgoals.   The next step in your plan is to compare feedback to your subgoal. How are you doing? The answer may be "Terrific!" The ball landed in the court, you studied 15 hours, your mate loves your lovemaking.

But some of the time the answer may not be "Terrific!" Things are not satisfactory, and we see that we are off our ideal standard. Then we make adjustments, and some improvement occurs. Whether these adjustments are major or minor, you won't be sure that they are the right ones—or even that they are needed—unless you record your self-observations and compare them to your goal.

When your feedback tells you that you have achieved your subgoal, move up to the next step. Continue the same plan if it is working; change it if it is not.

This comparison process characterizes successful people in every kind of activity. The writing of novels, for example, might seem dependent on the rush of inspiration and the caprice of the muse. Not so. Firm, daily work goals—in terms of number of pages (or even words) written—have been used by novelists as diverse as Anthony Trollope, Arnold Bennett, Ernest Hemingway, and Irving Wallace. Each of these writers counted his output daily and compared it to his daily goal (Wallace & Pear, 1977). Even author George Sand—the "Notorious Woman" portrayed as impulsive and passionate—observed a nightly work schedule of 30 written pages no matter what her condition, and Jack London required himself to write 1000 words a day before he visited his local saloon (Bandura, 1981).

This process of comparing feedback to goals and subgoals may require a short, deliberate period of taking stock. For example, a woman who has been very successful at losing weight using this book told us that she made an appointment with herself for 30 minutes to an hour each week, on weigh-in day, to review the week's eating and exercise records, judge progress, make necessary adjustments, collect her weekly reward, praise herself for successes, give herself some self-instructions, and make a weekly summary record in a journal.

Adjustments in the plan.   She also made adjustments in her plans from week to week. As you progress, you advance to goals that require new tactics. For example, after a few weeks she decided that eating a good breakfast was no longer a problem, so she stopped rewarding herself for that, but eating too much on the weekends continued to be a problem, so she started a new token system to deal with that. Although your new plan will include different techniques, it will have the same elements that characterize all successful plans: explicit rules, precise goals, gathering of feedback, comparison of feedback to goals, and adjustments as the plan continues.

Formulating the Plan: A Checklist

Let's review the most important issues presented in the preceding chapters. These issues can be formulated as a series of questions. When you can answer all of them positively, you are ready to combine what you have learned into an effective personal plan. Let's begin with goal-setting, commitment, and record keeping.

_____ Have you specified the goal clearly?
_____ Have you made changes in the way you specified the goal as your self-understanding increased?
_____ Have you taken steps to build commitment to do the work of changing?
_____ Have you worked out a self-observation system you can use when the problem behavior occurs?
_____ Do you keep written records?

Here's a checklist of the steps involved in controlling antecedents. You should be able to answer yes to most of these questions.

_____ If your goal is to decrease some unwanted behavior, have you taken steps to discover and eliminate the antecedents of that behavior?
_____ Have you developed a plan to change thoughts that represent the antecedents of the behavior?
_____ Have you examined your beliefs to see whether they are contributing to your problem behavior?

____ Have you developed a plan to cope with the physical antecedents of the behavior?

____ Have you worked out a plan to deal with the social and emotional antecedents of the behavior?

____ Have you taken steps to provide antecedents that will encourage your new, desired behavior?

____ Have you developed some thoughts you can use as antecedents of the new behavior?

____ Does your plan include specific self-instructions?

____ Have you planned for physical antecedents to become cues?

____ Have you asked others to encourage you or structured your social environment to provide helpful antecedents?

Next, consider the issues involved in developing new behaviors. Here, too, you should be able to answer yes to most of these questions.

____ As you try to develop new behaviors, do you use some form of shaping?

____ If your goal is to decrease an unwanted behavior, are you planning to use some incompatible behavior as a substitute?

____ If your problem involves anxiety or tension, are you going to practice relaxation?

____ Have you made provision to rehearse any new behavior you want to develop?

____ Does your plan call for imagined rehearsal?

____ Have you made provision to rehearse in the real world?

Finally, here is a checklist of issues relating to reinforcement. Once again, you should be able to answer most of these questions positively.

____ Have you discovered through self-observation what may be reinforcing your unwanted behaviors? If so, have you developed a plan for using that same reinforcement, or an alternate reward, to strengthen a desired behavior instead?

____ Have you developed a reinforcement plan in which you are rewarded if you take appropriate steps in your plan for self-change?

____ Does your plan include a token system?

____ Does your plan include Premack-type reinforcers?

____ Does your plan include verbal self-reinforcement? Does it include reminders of the reinforcement you will receive if you stick to each step of your plan?

____ Does your plan include any form of precommitted punishment?

____ Does your plan include an arrangement ensuring that you will be reinforced in the real world for any changes you make in your behavior?

Your chances of success increase if you use a variety of techniques. A solid plan involves *antecedents*, the *behavior* itself, and *consequences*. If you have not yet worked out a plan that includes elements of all three, now is the time to do so.

Brainstorming

Once you have reviewed procedures for each of the A, B, and C elements, you are ready to design your final plan. Before settling on a final plan, however, be creative. Use the technique of *brainstorming* (see "Tactic Seven" in Chapter Two and Box 2-1). Remember that the goal of brainstorming is to generate as many ideas as possible, quickly and uncritically. The four rules are:

1. Try for *quantity* of ideas.
2. Don't criticize your ideas; don't even evaluate them. You will do that later.
3. Try to think of unusual ideas.
4. Try to combine ideas to create new ones.

Jim had had a bad case of acne in high school, and had developed the habit of picking at his face. He wanted to stop this habit, because it tended to inflame his sensitive skin, produced infections, and made his face look terrible. But it was an automatic habit, and he was having trouble thinking of ways to stop it. After going through the checklist above, Jim brainstormed solutions:

I have to stop. Let's see. I could . . . slap my face every time I do it. No, that's dumb. [Long pause, no ideas.] Oh, yeah, I was criticizing the idea. Don't do that now. Just produce a lot of ideas, evaluate them later. OK. So, I could slap my face every time I do it. I could ask Lois to tell me to stop whenever I do it. I could ask my parents to tell me, too. I could rub my face instead of picking it. I could pull out my hair instead. Ha! I could suck my thumb, or—I could pick my nose. Ha! No criticism now! I could say to myself "I want to stop picking my face, so I won't do it now." I could do that and rub my face instead of picking. I could remind myself that it might get red or infected. Since I do it when I'm watching TV, I could put a sign on the TV reminding me not to do it. Ditto for studying. Put a sign on my desk. I could report to Lois every day about how much I did it the previous day, and show her that I was cutting down. Ditto my parents. Every day I could cut down a little more over the day before. If I didn't, then I wouldn't get to watch TV that day; but if I did, I'd put aside some money for something—for some clothes or a record. I could force myself to do it for hours at a time until I got so sick of it I'd never do it again. I could . . . .

That's how the brainstorming process works. Having written down these ideas, Jim selected the best ones, designed a tentative plan, and examined it to make sure that it was in accord with the principles he had learned.

A Sample Plan

This is the plan of a young woman who wanted to reduce her anxiety about speaking to her professors. The plan eventually worked fairly well, after several adjustments.

In her report, Laurel wrote: "I almost never talk with my professors. They scare me. Sometimes I have questions. At other times I would just like to talk with them. But I have spoken only to one, Prof. A., all year, and it was only a few sentences at a time. My goal: increase talking with my professors.

"I will develop my behavior gradually, on a shaping schedule. I have to start really low, because my baseline is nearly zero. This is my shaping schedule:

Step 1: Say hello to a professor.
Step 2: Talk with a professor for 15 seconds.

Step 3: Talk with a professor for 30 seconds.
Step 4: Talk for 1 minute.
Step 5: Talk for 2 minutes.

Our analysis: So far, Laurel's plan is generally satisfactory. She should specify how many times she will rehearse each step before moving to the next.

Collecting feedback: "My wristwatch has a sweep-second hand. If I turn the band, the watch will be on my wrist facing up. I can sort of look down to check the time without being too obvious. As soon as the conversation is over, I'll write down notes—how many seconds, the professor's name, where we were, and so forth.

Comparing feedback with standards: "On the inside front cover of my notebook, I'll write my shaping schedule. Then I can check whether or not I have met my goals.

Techniques: "I've decided to use a combination of Premack and food reinforcers. Since I eat lunch every day at school, I'll set a rule that I won't eat lunch until I have performed whatever step is required by my schedule."

Our analysis: Selecting eating lunch as the reinforcer may seem drastic, but since her schedule is reasonable and develops slowly, she probably won't ever need to go without food. At the same time, she gains the reinforcing effect of eating lunch. But there are a few problems with the plan. Other techniques should be included, principally self-instructions before the conversation and self-praise after it. It would also help if Laurel would learn relaxation and then relax herself before approaching the professor. The plan sounds a bit too simple.

Results: "This plan didn't work. I could do steps 1 and 2 okay. But at step 3 I got into trouble because the professor wouldn't quit talking to me, and suddenly I was involved in a complex conversation and became quite nervous. So I worked out a second plan."

Our analysis: Good! Plans should be changed if they don't work.

Plan 2: "The reason the first plan failed was that the professor carried me too far up the schedule. Looking back, it seems inevitable that this would happen. I might have gotten up to 3 minutes, or something like that, but at some point some professor would have just continued talking to me, and I'd be in trouble. I decided to enlist the aid of one particular teacher.

"I wrote my self-change project paper early in the semester and handed it in to Prof. A, who was teaching the course. In the paper, I explained why my first plan failed and asked for his help. I included my new schedule:

Step 1: Talk with Prof. A. in the hall for 15 seconds.
Step 2: Talk with him for 30 seconds.
Step 3: Talk for 1 minute.
Step 4: Talk for 90 seconds.
Step 5: Increase 30 seconds at a time, up to 5 minutes.

"I was going to do each step three times before going on to the next one. There were two parts to this plan. First, I was going to do the talking in the hall. Then, after I got pretty far up the schedule, I was going to repeat the entire sequence in his office, because it was more scary to talk with him in his office than in the hall. After I got to step 4 for talking in the hall, I started step 1 for talking in the office. Even that was too hard, so I put in some new steps. Step 1a was just sticking my head in and saying hello. Step 1b was talking for 5 seconds in the office. Step 1c was talking for 10 seconds in the office. Then I went back to the old schedule. Prof. A. agreed not to force me to talk longer than I was supposed to. Same reinforcer as before, same feedback and comparison."

Our analysis: The rules are clear, albeit somewhat complicated. Goals are present, and feedback and record keeping seem adequate. The double shaping plan is complex but sensible. Still no self-instruction, self-praise, or relaxation in the plan.

Plan 3: "Plan 2 works better. Prof. A. and I are now talking up to 3 minutes in the hall and 2 minutes in his office. But I need to be able to generalize from Prof. A. to other professors. I have decided to use Prof. A. again. Here is my new schedule.

> Step 1: Go up to Prof. A. while he is talking with another professor and say hello to both of them.
> Step 2: Go up and talk to Prof. A. while he is talking with another professor. Say at least a sentence to the other one.
> Step 3: Talk with the other one for 5 seconds.
> Step 4: Talk with the other one for 10 seconds.
> Step 5: Talk with the other one for 15 seconds.
> Step 6: Talk with the other one for 30 seconds, then on up from there by 15-second jumps.

Prof. A. has agreed to cooperate. He'll know where I am in the schedule and will bail me out whenever I complete my time for that particular step. Also, some professors seem unfriendly to me and others are pretty good, so I will go up to Prof. A. only when he is talking with one of the friendly ones."

Our analysis: This is a critical step, for Laurel is building the new behavior so she can use it in a variety of situations. Also, she has realized that an unfriendly professor is a different antecedent than a friendly one, and she has decided to deal with the easier antecedent (the friendly professor).

Plan 3 was apparently successful. By semester's end Laurel was able to talk with several friendly professors, which she considered a significant improvement.

All in all, Laurel did very well. She was wise to change plans when the first plan didn't work. Her plans were generally explicit. Her rules were clear. Her goals were divided into subgoals, and the standards for advancing were made explicit in plans 2 and 3. Her data collection was careful.

We spoke with her several months after the course ended and asked her why she hadn't included relaxation in her plan. She said she really didn't know, and pointed out she could always have backed up and used it if all else had failed. "I just didn't want to wait. Besides, I was right, wasn't I? Must have been—I'm talking to you."

Once you have chosen your plan and decided on each of its elements, write it out and sign it (Kanfer, Cox, Greiner, & Karoly, 1974). This becomes your contract with yourself. The contract should list your rules as well as your goals and subgoals, and it should specify how you will collect feedback. A formal contract increases your chances of success (Griffin & Watson, 1978; Seidner, 1973). Prepare it with all the seriousness of a formal document.

Display your contract. Keep it in your notebook or on your mirror. Make it clear and explicit. When it becomes necessary to change the plan, rewrite the contract and sign the new one.

CHAPTER SUMMARY

Combining A, B, and C Elements

If you are addicted to overeating, smoking, or other consummatory acts, use the two-stage process. *First*, avoid the controlling antecedents, one at a time if necessary. *Second*, develop a new behavior to be performed in response to the old cue. Then, when you are once again confronted with the antecedent, you won't slip back into performing the consummatory act. Like any new behaviors, these will have to be shaped, rehearsed, and reinforced.

Good plans for change must include elements of antecedent control, the development of new behaviors, and control of consequences. You should expect that problems will arise, and you need to be prepared to use more than one approach. For example, you may need to approach the problem in two stages or more.

The Features of a Good Plan

Good plans have: (1) rules that state the techniques to use in specific situations; (2) goals and subgoals; (3) feedback about your behavior based on your self-observations; (4) a comparison of the feedback to your goals and subgoals to see if you are progressing; and (5) adjustments in the plan as conditions change.

Before designing your final plan, review the checklist of important elements to consider and be sure that you can answer yes to most of the questions. Be creative in designing your plan; use the brainstorming technique to generate more ideas. For additional guidance, refer to the full-blown sample plan provided.

YOUR OWN SELF-DIRECTION PROJECT: STEP EIGHT

1. State your goal. If it is a complex goal or one that will take a long time to achieve, state the first short-term goal. State your current level of performance. Your baseline records provide you with information to use in setting your subgoals.

2. State specific rules for each subgoal. What behaviors will you have to perform in each situation to achieve the subgoal? Examine the three preliminary plans you prepared in Chapters Five, Six, and Seven, and consider various alternatives. You may select features from only one of your preliminary plans or combine elements from all of them. Consider each technique. Which ones will you use?

3. Be sure to get accurate self-observations and feedback all along the way, and compare your performance to your goals.

4. Fill out the checklist on pages 224–225 about the plan you are considering. Incorporate as many different techniques as you can. Write out your plan in detail, following the steps described above. Sign your contract, and begin implementing it.

TIPS FOR TYPICAL TOPICS

Look up your particular goal in the Topic Index at the back of the book, and read each section of the book in which that kind of goal or problem is discussed. This will give you ideas for your plan or remind you of anything you have forgotten.

CHAPTER NINE

Is It Working?
Analyzing the Data

OUTLINE

- Graphs
- Analyzing Your Data
- Chapter Summary
- Your Own Self-Direction Project: Step Nine

LEARNING OBJECTIVES

Graphs

1. How do you make a graph of your personal records during your self-change project?
   a. What goes on the horizontal axis?
   b. What goes on the vertical axis?
   c. What is the advantage of drawing a goal line on your graph?

Analyzing Your Data

2. How do you use your graphed data to analyze your progress?
3. Do you ever change your target behavior? When?
   a. Should you have a baseline for any new target behavior?
   b. What about new, incompatible responses?

This chapter discusses the processes of gathering feedback information (self-observations) and comparing it with your goals. Only with feedback can you decide whether you should continue with your plan or modify it. Only with feedback can you know whether it is time to advance. Are you achieving your goals?

This seems like a simple question, and sometimes you can answer it with a clear yes or no. The person who never smokes again, the man who has a woman friend for the first time in his life, the overweight person who drops 10 pounds and keeps them off—all these self-modifiers know they are succeeding. They don't need elaborate techniques for assessing their progress.

More often, though, progress is gradual rather than dramatic. As you shape your responses, as you reach plateaus and go beyond them, as you go through unusual periods in your life, your behaviors gradually change. Often you don't remember clearly from one week to the next exactly how you felt or how often you actually did the things you wanted to do. In fact, many people misjudge their progress, perhaps because they adapt to new performance levels.

People often underrate the progress they are making. Those who don't rely on their data may be tempted to stop a plan even though it is succeeding, simply because they *believe* that it is failing. The reverse, of course, can also happen, and an ineffective plan may be continued because data are not properly collected and examined.

It is crucial that you continue to record your behavior throughout the operation of your plan, because recording provides the evidence you need in order to know whether the plan is having the desired effect.

The best way to organize your data for easy examination is to put them on a graph. Each day you gather your observations, and by the end of a few weeks you have so many pieces of information that interpreting them becomes difficult. By putting them all together on a graph, you can readily see your progress or lack of it. Graphing your data makes it easy to compare your actual performance with your goals and standards.

GRAPHS

Making a Graph

Marlene wants to increase her studying. For one semester, she has kept a record of how many hours she studied each week. Here is her record for the semester: 8, 9¼, 9¾, 9½, 9½, 10¼, 10¾, 10¾, 8, 9½, 10¼, 11, 8½, 12¼, 10¼. With that long string of numbers, it's hard to see whether or not there is an upward progression. Perhaps there is: the last number is higher than the first. With the help of a graph, Marlene could see quite easily whether there is any upward movement over the semester.

On graph paper, Marlene draws the **abscissa**, or **horizontal axis**, near the bottom of the page, and divides it into 16 marks, one for each week of the semester. Then, beginning at the zero point on the abscissa, she draws a vertical line up and marks off 14 equally spaced points on it, one for each hour per week she might have studied. (Her maximum goal was 14.) This is called the **ordinate**, or **vertical axis**.

Always put the passage of time—minutes, days, weeks—on the horizontal axis, and the goal—behavior—on the vertical axis. The point where the two lines meet should be the zero point for both lines. Figure 9-1 illustrates Marlene's graph.

Marlene has a record of the total number of hours she studied each week for 15 of the 16 weeks of the semester. For week 1, the total number of hours was 8. She goes up in a straight line from the spot for week 1 on the horizontal axis, until that line is opposite "8 hours studied." Where the two lines on the graph paper intersect, Marlene makes a dot. She repeats this process for each of the 15 weeks for which she has data, each time connecting the week—for example, week 8—with the total number of hours studied that week—for example, 10¾. Figure 9-2 shows her graph with all the dots in place.

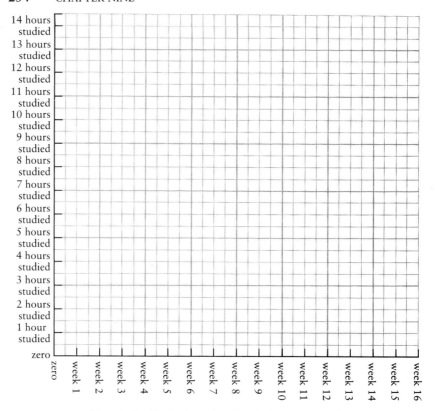

Figure 9-1.   The horizontal and vertical axes of a graph.

To make her progress (or lack of it) even clearer, Marlene connects each point on the graph to the next one, moving from left to right. That gives her a finished graph, illustrated in Figure 9-3. On this graph, each point on the horizontal and vertical lines is numbered, and the whole line is labeled "weeks of the semester" or "hours studied." It is tedious to write "Week 1," "Week 2," "Week 3," and so on, and to write "1 hour studied," "2 hours studied," "3 hours studied." The custom is to write only the numbers along each axis and to use labels underneath and at the side to describe what the numbers stand for.

Sometimes it is unnecessary to include all the numbers on the vertical line. Suppose you are working on losing weight, and your weekly weight varies between 148 and 135 pounds over a semester. It would be silly to start the vertical line at 0 pounds and mark off 135 pounds on it before you got to one you would use in making the graph. Instead, break the line to indicate that you are not starting at 0 (see Figure 9-4).

Using the Graph

By inspecting her graph, Marlene was able to see her data quite clearly. Her pattern was one of general progress, slow and steady, with minor fluctua-

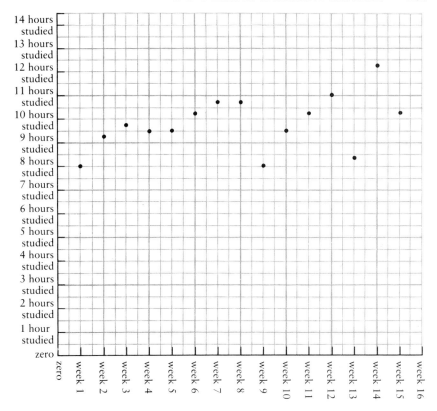

Figure 9-2. The graph with a dot placed at each point representing the total number of hours studied for that week.

tions, except for weeks 9 and 13. She reviewed her daily logs for those weeks and found that during both she had been ill for several days. Marlene concluded that her time-management (plus reinforcement) plan was working rather well. She resolved to continue it for the following semester, and raised her goal to 18 hours of studying per week.

Over the course of your self-modification project, you might make more than one graph as the purpose of your data gathering changes. At first, for example, you might use a structured diary, recording the As, Bs, and Cs of your behavior. Later you might hit upon some particular behavior you want to increase, and at that point start recording how often you do it. You could then make a graph of those data.

You can graph more than one thing at a time. A student who wanted to increase his exercising and cut down on the junk food he ate made up one graph on which he recorded both. Be creative with the graphs: the whole point is to give you an easy-to-read display of your problems and progress.

If you are trying to maintain a certain level of performance—for example, studying so many hours per week, weighing a certain amount, exercising so many times per week, or making a certain number of honest, assertive state-

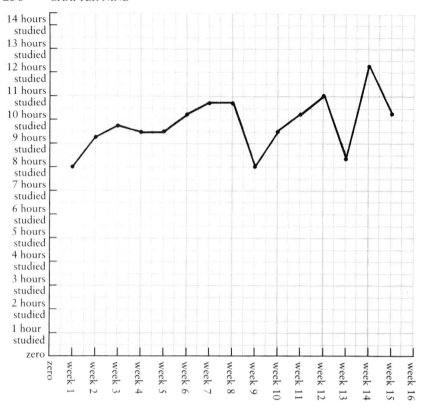

Figure 9-3. The finished graph, with dots connected to show pattern over time.

ments—draw a heavy line on your graph to indicate your goal level. This will enable you to immediately see when your behavior is or is not satisfactory. Figure 9-5 shows the chart of a student whose first plan was to record and briefly think about five pleasant events each day. By checking her graph, she could see that she was making satisfactory progress toward her goal. When she dipped below the goal line, she could notice it right away and take steps to get above the minimal level.

If you use this heavy-line system and for any reason fall so far behind that it's discouraging looking at your graph, then draw a new one with a new heavy line, starting from wherever you are right now. And be sure to adjust the goal line at each point that your shaping schedule calls for a change in the level of your behavior.

ANALYZING YOUR DATA

Tom wanted to increase the number of comments he made in his classes. In his report, he wrote that he found it difficult to speak in public because he was afraid others would think that his comments were silly or trivial. This fear was particularly acute in large classes, in which he felt that whatever

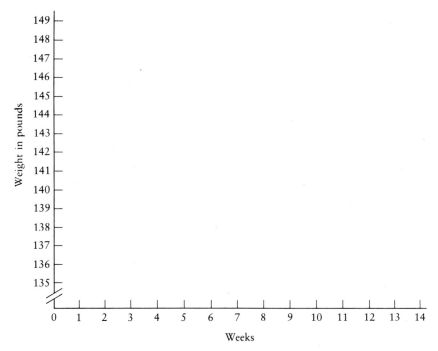

Figure 9-4. Simplified form of graph for weight.

he wanted to say had to be good enough to justify taking the time of so many people. His baseline was zero.

Tom decided to begin by practicing in small classes and then, if that worked, to try it in larger classes. His goal was to speak at least once per day in a class. "My reinforcer was playing in my rock group. This is a very

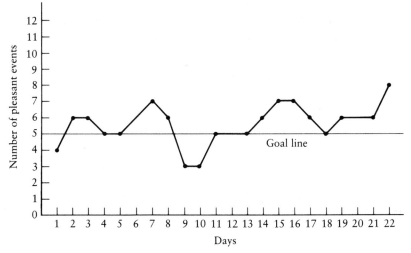

Figure 9-5. Number of pleasant events recorded and thought about each day. Minimum goal = 5 per day.

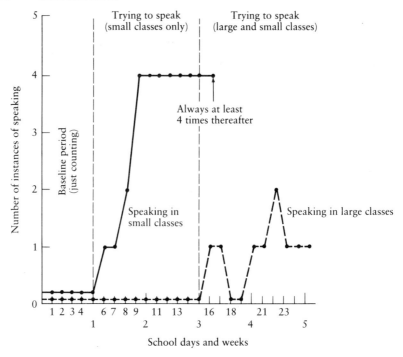

Figure 9-6. Speaking in class.

powerful reinforcer for me in two ways: I really enjoy playing guitar; and if I didn't show up for a gig, five other guys would wring my neck."

Figure 9-6 is a graph of Tom's data. Notice that in making his graph he counted only school days, so each week has only five days. This is sensible, because Tom had opportunities to practice his new behavior only during the school week. He always had his notebook with him when he went to class, so it was easy for him to make a simple check on a sheet of paper every time he spoke up in a class.

Tom's graph shows a rapid improvement in his speaking behavior in small classes. Beginning on the first day of his plan, he began to speak up in class, and within four days he was engaging in what he called "constant participation." Most people progress at a slower rate, as Tom himself did when he went into the second stage of his plan—speaking in large classes. You can see from the graph that he did make some progress, but that his improvements were interspersed with setbacks—days on which he didn't talk at all. This is the kind of situation in which a graph is particularly helpful, for it shows that you are making *some* progress.

Here is another example—the case of a person who didn't make progress for a long time. Vicky, a young woman with a smoking problem, wrote: "For every cigarette I smoked, I marked a piece of paper that I kept tucked into the cellophane of the cigarette pack.

"After examining my baseline, I decided to cut down to no more than 15

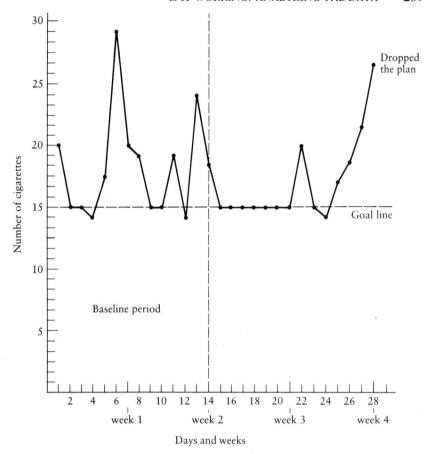

Figure 9-7.   Number of cigarettes smoked (first plan).

cigarettes per day. I used a token-system reinforcer, earning money for whatever I wanted to buy."

Figure 9-7 shows Vicky's graph. Note that she marked a dot on the vertical line for each cigarette she smoked but wrote in only numbers 5, 10, 15, and so on, to get a neater graph. Also note the goal line, drawn at "15 cigarettes."

At the end of the fourth week, Vicky's graph clearly showed that her plan, although briefly effective, was collapsing. She abandoned recording and also the rule for reinforcement she had set for herself. Cutting down was too hard, she said. "Maybe I don't really want to quit." She talked about the clubs where she and Greg often danced, and said everyone there smoked and drank a lot.

After a period of time, she wrote the following: "One night when we were out, Greg laughed at me for not being able to quit smoking. He said I had no willpower. He could quit, he said, but wasn't ready yet. This made me angry. He had been chain-smoking the whole night! 'OK,' I said, 'we should both cut down and stick to it.' He smoked a lot more than I did, so we cut

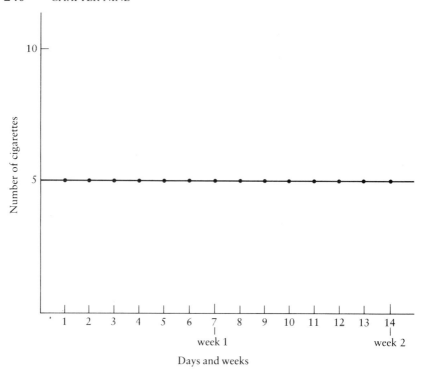

Figure 9-8. Number of cigarettes smoked (second plan).

down proportionately—Greg to one pack a day and me to 5 cigarettes a day. To encourage ourselves not to smoke, we switched brands. (We hate each other's brands.)"

Her second plan, as you can see in Figure 9-8, shows an improvement. It also shows that, under certain circumstances, Vicky could cut down smoking. The plan of cutting down with her boyfriend was a good first step, because they could offer support to each other for *not* smoking. Vicky was encouraged to continue her "competition" with Greg.

Changes in the Target Behavior

During the course of a plan, the actual target behavior may change. If the changed goal represents a new level of self-understanding, this shift can be natural and desirable. A new target behavior is necessary to describe the new goals.

Sally was very shy and withdrawn, especially in groups. She thought about her problem and came to the conclusion that if she smiled more, she would appear less withdrawn and would also gain reinforcement from others. Her original goal (plan 1) was to increase smiling behavior by simply making a note on a card each time she smiled at someone she didn't know well. After she established a baseline, she worked out a plan in which she earned tokens (to be applied later to the purchase of elegant clothes) by smiling at people.

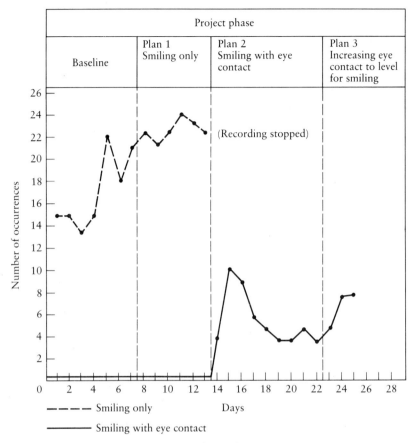

Project phase			
Baseline	Plan 1 Smiling only	Plan 2 Smiling with eye contact	Plan 3 Increasing eye contact to level for smiling

Figure 9-9.   Smiling and eye contact.

She gave herself instructions to smile, and she enlisted the help of her room-mates to administer the token system.

Figure 9-9 presents part of her data. Notice that first Sally improved just because she was keeping records: her smiles increased even during the base-line period. Of course, she was quite pleased.

The increased frequency didn't really change much after she moved into the intervention period of plan 1. Around day 11 or 12, she began to rethink the definition of her problem. "I started to realize," she later wrote in her report, "that although I was smiling more at people, I still appeared with-drawn. This was because I was not looking at them. I was smiling but looking down at the ground. Most people feel that looking into someone's eyes is a sign of interest, so I decided that just smiling at others wasn't enough. I had to smile, *and* I had to make eye contact." So Sally changed her definition of the target, broadening it. In plan 2, she counted not only smiling but also eye contacts that lasted several seconds. She began plan 2 on day 14. In this revised plan, she earned her tokens for smiling *and* maintaining about 3 seconds of eye contact, and she gave herself instructions to do both. These revisions reflected her new understanding of the behaviors that are necessary in order to appear interested rather than withdrawn when talking with people.

Plan 3 represents the last phase of Sally's program. In this phase, she began shaping eye contact so that it would occur as often as smiling alone had occurred in plan 1.

Sally could have avoided this shift in her plan by starting out with a definition of her target behavior that included both smiling and eye contact. But at the beginning of her plan, she didn't realize how important eye contact was. She realized that she needed to add eye contact to her goal only after she had increased her smiling and found that tactic insufficient.

As you continue with your plan, the definition of some category of your target behavior may change. This indicates that you are learning more about your behavior and can make more subtle discriminations among various kinds of behavior. Don't stick rigidly to your original target behavior.

Changing Targets and Establishing a New Baseline

When the changes in target behaviors are substantial and abrupt, it's best to establish a new baseline. It is like beginning a new plan. For example, you might change your behavior from "smiling at people" to "going to public places." This major shift in the behavior to be observed calls for a new baseline.

Sometimes you will *add* something to an ongoing plan, as Sally did when she added eye contact to smiling. If she hadn't been sure that her baseline for eye contact was zero, she would have needed to gather baseline data so that she could judge her progress during her plan for change. You can get a baseline by simply continuing the first target behavior for a few days and, at the same time, counting how often you perform the new target behavior that is to be added to the plan. For example, you might start out with "dieting" as your target and, after a few weeks, decide to add "exercising" to your plan. In that case, you continue to reinforce dieting for a few days while you get a baseline on exercising.

Even if you decide to skip the baseline period for a new target, *do not skip making self-observations*. Continue to keep records of your new target behavior just as you kept records of your old one. Learn how your new target behavior is related to its antecedents and consequences, just as you learned these essential data for the old target behavior. For example, Sally found certain kinds of people easier to make eye contact with than others, and this knowledge helped her develop her new target behavior.

Lack of Baseline for Incompatible Behaviors

If your initial problem was an undesired behavior, you probably began by getting baseline data on that behavior. Later, you may have decided to increase an incompatible response at the expense of the undesired behavior. If you have done that, you are likely to find that while you may have a very good baseline for the undesired target behavior, you don't have a good baseline for the incompatible one. Furthermore, as your plan develops, the incompatible response may change as you develop new understanding and skill. Should new baseline data be recorded?

If the new, incompatible behavior is one that you intend to continue permanently, then you will want to get a separate baseline for it—for example, deciding to increase "reading good books" as a behavior incompatible with "wasting time." Use the same strategies that you would employ for any shift in categories.

If you don't intend to continue the incompatible behavior—for example, slapping your hand instead of cracking your knuckles—then it is not necessary to get a separate count of the incompatible behavior as long as you are keeping a good record of the undesired target. Any number of shifts can be made in the incompatible behavior without affecting the category to be recorded. However, be sure to indicate on the graph each shift in your strategy, because you need to see what works and what does not.

CHAPTER SUMMARY

The data you collect through your observations will lead you to certain decisions about your plan. Your record (often in the form of a graph) may show such clear improvement as to warrant continuing the plan unchanged, as in Figure 9-3 or 9-6. Figure 9-7 illustrates the opposite extreme, indicating that the plan needs careful reworking. This involves rethinking each aspect of the plan for possible change: specifying a behavioral target, making observations, learning how the behavior is related to its antecedents and consequences, and making a plan for change.

If, in the course of your plan, you decide to change the target behavior, you may need to establish a new baseline.

YOUR OWN SELF-DIRECTION PROJECT: STEP NINE

Make a graph of your data, recording *time* on the horizontal axis and the number of *occurrences* of the target behavior on the vertical axis. An accurately made graph will show you whether or not you are effecting changes in your target behavior.

CHAPTER TEN

Problem Solving
and Relapse Prevention

OUTLINE

- Problem Solving
- Common Reasons for Failure at Self-Modification
- Relapse Prevention
- Chapter Summary
- Your Own Self-Direction Project: Step Ten
- Tips for Typical Topics

LEARNING OBJECTIVES

Problem Solving

1. What is the tinkering strategy for dealing with self-change projects?
2. What are the four steps in problem solving?
   a. How can they be applied to your project?
   b. Describe the research on the value of problem solving.

Common Reasons for Failure at Self-Modification

3. How do failures in self-observation contribute to failure in self-modification?
4. What are the reasons why people stop recording?
5. What are six reasons why people might not use the techniques? What can be done to cope with each?

Relapse Prevention

6. Outline fully the relapse process.
   a. What is the difference between a lapse and relapse?
   b. What are the three common kinds of high-risk situations?
   c. Explain the abstinence violation effect.
7. How can you prepare for high-risk situations?
   a. How can you identify your personal high-risk situations?
   b. Describe how to have and use a relapse fantasy.
8. How can you cope with a high-risk situation?
   a. How can you use problem solving for high-risk situations?
   b. List the kinds of self-instructions you should prepare for coping with high-risk situations.
   c. How should you practice using these instructions?
9. How can you stop lapses from becoming a relapse?
   a. What should you do as soon as you lapse?

    b. What kind of self-contract and reminder card should you prepare
       in advance?

It is realistic to expect some problems in self-modification. Anticipating
problems allows you to deal with them as soon as they appear, and before
your newly developed behavior has disappeared. It's like keeping a fire extin-
guisher around. You can put out the small blazes before you need to call
the fire department.

Problems can come up while you are engaged in self-modification, and
they can come up after you are finished. For example, you might go along
well with your exercise project for a few weeks, but then not be able to
make any more progress. Or you might finish a self-change project, such as
stopping drinking too much, only to find to your dismay that the problem
behavior has come back. In this chapter, we deal with both kinds of problems: those that come up while you are actively engaged in self-modification,
and threats of relapse that come up afterwards.

PROBLEM SOLVING

Tinkering with Your Plan

It often happens that your first plan is not enough by itself to change the
target behavior. After you begin, you discover something that makes it more
difficult to manage than you anticipated. Expect that there will be problems.

Start with the best plan you can devise. See what difficulties occur, and
then tinker with the plan, making it more effective in dealing with the unexpected problems.

Rebecca wrote: "There was this person I worked with, Jean, whom I really
didn't like at all. As a Christian, I know that loving one another is an
important command. But I couldn't bring myself to love Jean—not with
agape [God's love]. She felt the same way, which made it worse." Rebecca
decided to work out a self-change plan with the goal of increasing *agape* for
Jean.

Her plan was sound. She wrote a detailed contract that included six shaping steps for talking to Jean in a friendly way.

Step 1: Smile at Jean at least once a day at work.
Step 2: Smile and say "Hi."
Step 3: Go up and ask her "How's everything?"
Step 4: Compliment her on something.
Step 5: Talk about upcoming events at work.
Step 6: Talk about anything else.

Rebecca gathered records carefully on a steno tablet. Her reinforcement
system used candy as an immediate reward for being nice to Jean and tokens
to be used to buy favorite things as longer-term reinforcers.

Results: "The first two steps worked fine, but when I asked Jean 'How's everything?' I caught her off guard, and she began talking so much that I became uncomfortable and wanted to withdraw. While I felt ready to approach her, I wasn't ready for her response. So I revised my plan."

In Rebecca's second plan, she dealt with a problem that she had not foreseen when she devised her first plan. She tinkered with her old plan, changing elements here and there in an effort to make the plan work better.

"I shared this new plan with one of my closest friends. He works with me and knows my problem. I told him that I would let him know when I was planning to talk with Jean and asked him to give me about two minutes and then call me to his office. That way I had enough time to exchange friendly greetings with Jean, without feeling uncomfortable." The reinforcers were the same, and the record keeping continued.

Results: "The two-minute limit worked really well. If I felt like talking to Jean longer, I'd just ask my friend to please wait until I was finished. Also, I dropped the idea of complimenting Jean so deliberately. I felt this wouldn't be sincere. I decided that if she did something I felt I could honestly compliment, I would do so."

After seven weeks, Rebecca wrote: "I can honestly say that things are now fine between Jean and me. The plan really helped, but in my case all the credit goes to God, who worked in Jean's heart as well as in mine to bring us closer together." Tinkering helped a bit, too.

Here's a second example of tinkering with a plan to make it more effective. A 55-year-old man in our class submitted this final report:

"*My goal:* I wanted to build up to running a mile or so every other day. At the time I began, I had never run at all, so my baseline was zero.

"*Antecedents:* What I needed was an antecedent that would get me started! I really don't think I refrained from running because I would get painfully winded or anything. It's just that there always seemed to be something else to do, so I didn't start. Going for a run requires all sorts of behaviors— putting on the shoes and shorts, stretching, then starting to run.

"*Intervention plan:* My first plan was to require myself to run a quarter of a mile every day. I intended to gradually increase my running up to a mile or so. My self-contract was that I would get a dollar to spend on anything I wanted for every time I ran.

"If you look at my graph [Figure 10-1], you'll see that this plan worked for the first three days, but after that I just sort of quit. I drifted for two weeks and then faced up to the fact that I wasn't running.

"After several days of doing nothing, it became painfully obvious that plan 1 was not working. So I listed all the reasons why it was not working:

I've never run a mile, and it seems like a long way to run.
I'm afraid I might give myself a heart attack.
I tell myself "It's too far, and it could be dangerous."
It seems like a lot of trouble.
I find all sorts of excuses for not going running.

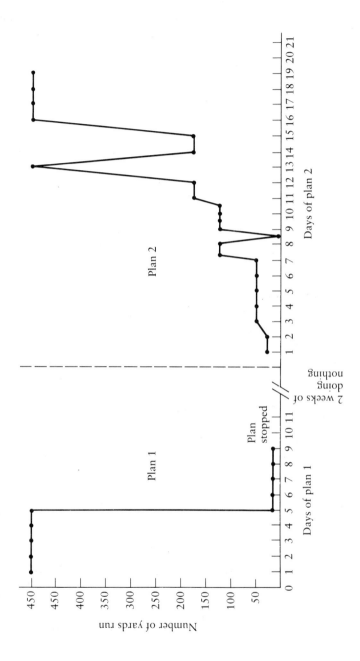

Figure 10-1.   Daily running.

"I decided that I probably wouldn't get a heart attack if I ran really slowly. I made a mental note to ask my doctor about it next time I have a checkup. I also decided that the main reason I didn't go out was that it just seemed like a long way for a duffer like me to go. I guess the main reason I quit was that I was starting too high. Then I remembered the shaping rule about not starting too high. 'Why should I expect to be able to start that high?' I asked myself. And I redesigned my plan as follows:

Stage 1: Put on footwear and clothes, and walk around the house (30 yards).
Stage 2: Walk around the house twice (60 yards).
Stage 3: Walk around the house four times (120 yards).
Stage 4: Walk around the house six times (180 yards).
Stage 5: Once I get to this point, I will run a quarter of a mile. When I can do that, I will try to increase to half a mile, then three-quarters of a mile, and then finally one mile.

"I did several things to make sure that I stuck to this ridiculously easy shaping schedule. *First*, I established the rule that I have to do my 'run' before I can have a beer or eat supper. *Second*, I explained the whole thing to my wife and told her that I really wanted to build up exercising this way. I precommitted myself to do it by asking her (1) to remind me to do it, (2) to call me on it if she saw me eating or drinking a beer before I had done my exercise, and (3) to check on my progress by examining the chart I keep posted on the kitchen cupboard on which I record my daily progress. *Third*, I set aside five minutes each morning to imagine resisting the temptation to have a beer or eat when I come home. I imagine coming home and saying to myself 'Wow, it's time to relax after another hard day!' I see myself getting a can of beer, and, just as I'm about to pop the top, I practice resisting this urge and saying to myself 'But first, I'll go for a short run.'

"At the time of this writing, I am able to run a quarter of a mile regularly and hope to be able to increase." The right-hand part of Figure 10-1 shows the man's progress.

Notice that several things had been interfering with the man's progress: old reinforcers (having a beer as soon as he got home), thoughts (thinking he might have a heart attack), doubts (thinking a mile is too far), and shaping errors (starting too high).

When you are tinkering with a plan that is not working, ask yourself some questions: What makes it difficult or impossible to perform the target behavior? Is it some thought I am having? Is it something I have no control over? (Remember the example of Rebecca finding that Jean talked to her too much.) Am I getting reinforced for a behavior that makes my desired behavior difficult (such as having a beer and sitting down instead of going for a run)?

Analyze the obstacles to performing your target behavior. What antecedents make it difficult to perform the target behavior, or what antecedents are lacking that would make it easier to perform? Have the correct incompatible or alternate behaviors been chosen? Are there still consequences that maintain the old, undesired behavior? Use the A-B-C system to make a systematic check for obstacles to carrying out your plan.

The Technique for Solving Problems

Problem solving means thinking about the obstacles to your progress and figuring out how to overcome them. In a study in which overweight subjects were taught principles of self-modification for weight control, part of the group also learned how to problem-solve using those principles. This second group lost about twice as much weight as the first (Black & Scherba, 1983). In the course of trying to lose weight, the subjects inevitably ran into problems. The problem-solving training helped in applying the principles.

When you encounter a problem, follow this four-step process (D'Zurilla & Goldfried, 1971; D'Zurilla & Nezu, 1982):

1. List all the details of the problem as concretely as possible.
2. Brainstorm as many solutions as you can without at first criticizing any of them. (See "Tactic Seven" in Chapter Two.)
3. Choose one or more of the solutions and think about implementing them.
4. Think of ways to put the solutions into operation, and then check to be sure you are actually carrying out the solution.

The following examples illustrate how each of these four steps can be used to overcome obstacles in your self-change program.

Listing the details.   Kalani wrote: "I've known for years that I overeat. Finally, I began to keep records of when I overeat—what particular times I go off my diet. I listed these as the details of my problem. They were surprisingly regular. I often ate two or three bowls of popcorn while watching TV. I always overate after exercising on Mondays. I usually ate three or four snacks on Saturdays. So it wasn't that I overate all the time—just in specific situations. I set out to deal with those particular situations."

A woman who wanted to give up drinking coffee wrote: "I made up a plan to stop drinking coffee, but after a few days it ground to a halt. Then I made a new plan, but it also fizzled. So I listed the details of what was happening when I went off my plan. I noticed that I'd be thinking 'I need this coffee for energy.' So I started a new plan to give myself some energy when I needed it, using meditation, and after that it was a lot easier to give up coffee."

Listing many alternatives.   One of our colleagues who stopped smoking noted that stopping was easy, but staying off was the problem. So she made a long list of things to do when she wanted a cigarette: chew gum, eat mints, do calisthenics, walk, brush teeth, drink coffee, work with plants, cook, pay bills, make a phone call, mend clothing, iron, shop, groom, shower, take a hot bath, clean closets, drink water, fiddle with hands, smell something pleasant, and so on. When she found herself craving a cigarette, she would take out her list and try to do one or more of the things on it.

Choosing an alternative.   Ruby's goal was to engage in race walking three times a week. "After two weeks, however, I had to acknowledge that I was not keeping records because there was nothing to record. I felt I was already too busy, and the plan to race-walk three times a week was just one more thing I had to do. I needed to have some fun, so I made a list of all the things I could do for fun that would also give me some exercise. I selected ice skating, and set a goal to go once or twice weekly."

Putting the new plan into operation and checking to be sure it's working.   Ruby continued: "I had to force myself to make skating a priority, but I succeeded in going once a week for eight weeks. Although I often didn't want to go, I enjoyed it once I got there. I kept a record, making a checkmark each week when I did go. After eight weeks, I started going twice a week. Now I have to say, I absolutely love skating!"

In taking these four steps, you won't just go through the process in 1-2-3-4 order. Expect to go back and forth from listing details to listing possible solutions.

Larry reported that his target behavior was to stop drinking so many colas at work. He drank several cans every day. He succeeded in reducing his habit, but then he changed jobs and became a night taxi driver. Within a few weeks, he was back to drinking several cans each night to keep himself awake.

Larry listed all the relevant details of the problem:

It keeps me high.
There are convenient machine outlets on practically every corner.
I tell myself that it helps me stay awake.

Then he listed possible solutions:

Tell myself "Don't do it, Larry" whenever I approach a vending machine.
Keep a record in the cab and a total record at home.
Get another job.
Substitute some less harmful drink.
Buy the drink, then throw it in the rubbish.
Get fully adjusted to working at night, so I don't have to use the drinks to stay awake.
Keep track of all the money I'm spending on Cokes.

Larry finally decided to do three things: (1) tell himself "Don't do it"; (2) keep a record of the money he spent and the number of colas he drank each day; and (3) go to small stores where he could buy fruit juice instead of Cokes.

"*Results:* It worked very well. I haven't touched a Coke since I started this project. I have become an orange juice freak instead."

The Value of Problem Solving

Combining problem solving with self-modification techniques is a potent approach to self-change. Richards and Perri (1978) trained students who were concerned about academic underachievement and who wanted better study skills. The researchers trained *some* of these students to use simple problem-solving strategies when they ran into problems. There was a rapid deterioration in the maintenance of study skills among the students who tried *no* problem-solving strategies. By contrast, the students who used problem-solving techniques were able to maintain their improved study skills up to one year after completion of their training. In another study (Perri, Richards, & Schultheis, 1977), ex-smokers who stayed off cigarettes were more likely to have used problem-solving techniques than were those who went back to smoking. Recent reviews of the research have shown that problem solving is helpful for a variety of problems, including various addictions, depression, stress, poor college performance, marital problems, and prevention of unwanted pregnancy (D'Zurilla & Nezu, 1982; Durlak, 1983).

If your plan involves giving up something you enjoy—such as overeating, being lazy, drinking, smoking, or biting your nails—expect problems. When your first plan falters, notice what parts were successful and for how long. Keep the successful features in your later plans. *Notice your successes as well as your failures.* People who focus solely on their failures are more likely to become discouraged and quit (Kirschenbaum & Tomarken, 1982). If, for example, you stop smoking for six days and then have a cigarette, don't think of it as a total failure. After all, you succeeded for six days. Can you repeat those six successful days? What went wrong on the seventh? Use problem solving to cope with that obstacle.

Whenever you get stuck in your self-modification project, review your earlier attempts, and see which parts worked then that you might use again (H. K. Brown, 1984). A man who had successfully completed a project to stop procrastinating reported: "A year or so later, I started a new project— to increase social skills. It didn't work well. I knew my earlier project had been a real success, so I checked back to see what techniques I had used to stop procrastinating. In all, I had used six different techniques, and I could see that four of them could easily be modified for use in my new project. So I branched out, adding these techniques to my current plan, and now my social-skills plan is working."

COMMON REASONS FOR FAILURE AT SELF-MODIFICATION

Efforts to change are not always successful. Understanding the reasons why some people fail at self-modification can help you be on guard. What blocks success for some? What can be done to increase success? In recent years, several theorists have written about this topic (Kirschenbaum & Tomarken, 1982; Peterson, 1983; Stuart, 1980). What follows is a distillation of their ideas and ours.

Failures in Self-Observation

A middle-aged woman wrote: "After I finished your course, I continued exercising four times a week. It was the first time in my life that I'd ever been able to stick to an exercise schedule, and I kept records for several months to be sure I wouldn't quit. Then my husband and I went on a month's vacation to another state. My daily schedule was completely different than it had been at home, and I quit keeping records. Perhaps that's why I stopped thinking about exercising. By the time the month was over, I had hardly exercised at all. When we returned home, I put my record sheet back up on the refrigerator door, and within two weeks I was back to my old aerobic self."

Without good self-observations you may not hold yourself to the goals you want to achieve. It's often too easy to give in to the short-term urge instead of thinking of the longer-term goal. Continued self-observation helps deal with this problem.

Self-observations force us to think more clearly about the causes of our behavior. Kalani, the overweight man, wrote: "I started a project to cut down overeating, but it wasn't getting anywhere. For more than a year, I messed around with one diet after another, but usually went off after a day or two. Then I started keeping careful records of what I ate every day. That's all. No diet, just record keeping. I was amazed. I found out I never overeat at breakfast or at a mid-morning snack. Sometimes I have a bit too much at lunch. But it's supper where I often eat twice as much as I should. And even here, it's not the same for suppers on every night. I almost never overeat on Tuesday, Wednesday, or Thursday. Friday night I go out with my family and eat too much from the buffet at our favorite restaurant. On weekends I often cook a big meal for the family and really stuff it in. Monday nights I work late, and I often eat too much when I get home. So I've learned that it is particular times of the week that stimulate my overeating."

Kalani can now start a plan for self-change that is much more specifically focused than just a vague diet. For example, he can concentrate on one particular day and meal when he overeats and learn new behaviors for that time. Then he can move on to the next day and meal, and so on, until he has the whole week's eating under control. Without such careful self-observations, he would not have known enough about his eating habits.

Keeping records even when you are not being successful at self-change increases your chances of later success. Good self-observations bring greater understanding of the antecedents and consequences of your behavior. Without these observations, you may mislabel the As and Cs, or not be aware of their influence. Vera complained of strong feelings of loneliness. "I thought I was lonely because there was no one I was close to. I kept looking over the available men in my life, thinking one of them could be my boyfriend and then I'd never be lonely anymore. But none of them measured up. So I kept on being lonely. I thought the cause was a general lack of interesting men. I wasn't paying any attention to my own thoughts. When I recorded the thoughts I was having when I dealt with men, it became clear that the thoughts were very negative. I'd meet one of the men I knew and think, 'Here goes another dull conversation. God, why are people so dull?'

"After keeping records on my thoughts for a few days, I could see that this was a pattern. I want to get right into important, meaningful conversations. So I have these negative thoughts when I get into situations that involve small talk. The trouble is, all social situations involve small talk. You don't just meet somebody and start right off talking about the meaning of life.

"So it finally dawned on me that my thoughts were creating the problem. I had to quit being so negative about chatting, because that is how you start to get to know people. That's the project I'm working on now. I think of those conversations as 'openers,' not 'small talk.'"

Note where Vera's self-observation has led. Originally her complaint was loneliness. But after several days of self-observation she realized that to some degree she was the cause of her loneliness because of her attitude toward casual social exchanges. Her new project—to be more positive in her thoughts about casual conversations—will in the long run help her to deal with her loneliness problem.

Why doesn't everyone keep good self-observation records? The experience of "failure" is a major reason. When we are recording a series of failures, we are likely to stop self-observation (Kirschenbaum & Tomarken, 1982). It is important to note whatever successes you have. *Don't record just negative information.* Don't keep a record only of the cigarettes you smoked. Keep a record of the urges to smoke that you resisted, too. Don't just record the days you didn't exercise. Make note of the days on which you *did* exercise. Don't just record the times you were depressed. Note the times you felt good, too.

Your successes may be small at first, but this is all the more reason to record them. "Well, it's true that I only studied for the scheduled amount of time one day last week, but I *did* do well on Tuesday. Now I've got to build on that. I'll make better grades if I do."

Another reason people fail to keep good records is that they are ambivalent about changing. Kalani, the overweight man, told us: "When I was keeping records of my eating, some days I wouldn't record. After this had happened several times, I had to admit to myself that I wasn't keeping the records because I wanted to pig out. So I had to face my true feelings. Did I want to stop overeating or not? I decided I did, so I forced myself to record the reasons why I wasn't keeping a record. That worked well, and pretty soon I went back to keeping records all the time."

Not Using the Techniques

You might read this text, learn the ideas in it, and still not use the techniques for change in your own self-modification project. Why does this happen? Listed below are a series of reasons why people might not use the techniques. Do any of these points apply to you? If so, stop to think: (1) Do I want to cope with that point? (2) How can I cope with it?

You don't believe the techniques will help you.   Some people believe that the best way to gain self-control is through self-punishment. Since we don't recommend this, they don't try the techniques we do recommend. Some people believe that keeping records about one's problem is silly, or it makes them feel uncomfortable. Since this is a keystone of the approach, they don't follow the recommended steps. A few people believe that techniques such as self-reward are self-indulgent or pointless, so they don't use them. Are your beliefs adaptive? Are they preventing you from testing self-modification, and thus preventing you from the opportunity to make a judgment based on your own real experience?

You don't believe you can attain the goal you want.   Your belief that you can cope with the problem affects how hard you try to overcome it, and that in turn affects your success (Bandura, 1977). The exercises in Chapter Two for increasing self-efficacy can help establish feelings of confidence.

You may have lost confidence in your ability to change because you have been observing only your failures (Candiotte & Lichtenstein, 1981). Keeping track of your successes can increase self-confidence.

Some people take credit for their failures but not for their successes (Dweck, 1975). "When I fail, it's my fault. When I succeed, it's luck." Monitor your thinking. Focus on your successes, and realize that you are responsible for the positive things that have happened so far. "When I fail, it's because I didn't try hard enough. When I succeed, it's because I *did* try hard enough."

You really don't want to change.   There are times in all our lives when we are on an even keel, when nothing needs correcting. If you are sincerely satisfied with your present adjustment, work out with your instructor some way to learn the techniques without doing a self-change project. We suggest doing a project, because in our experience it is the best way to learn the techniques. The purpose of this text is not to force you to change something now, but to teach you techniques for change that you can use when you need them.

But if you still feel ambivalent about changing—"Do I *really* want to study more each day?"—then recheck the list of advantages and disadvantages of changing that you filled out (see Chapter Two). Fill it out again. Perhaps you have changed your mind.

Sometimes we don't see the disadvantages of changing until we begin to change. An overweight woman who had lost a lot of weight told us: "After I began to approach normal weight, I saw some disadvantages to it that I hadn't realized before. For one thing, my friends expected me to participate in sports, but I was still as clumsy as ever. I no longer had a ready-made excuse. I don't ever get special consideration from people anymore, like I used to when I was fat. I guess I sort of liked that special treatment."

You can't put in the time and effort required.   A sincere self-modification effort does require the work of using the techniques. Try to pick a topic that is worth that effort.

Sometimes people are already involved in such a stressful life that adding a self-change project seems too much (Peterson, 1983). One of our students who had a full-time job, was involved in divorce proceedings, and was also graduating from college said "I know I should quit smoking, but now is just not the time to work on it." We agreed, and suggested that he might work on stress reduction as his present task.

You started off with some success but then became discouraged.   Dana's project was to make more friends. At first, he only kept records of how often he talked with others. He showed some success almost immediately, probably because just keeping the records encouraged him to talk more. But he didn't use any other techniques. After a few days, the novelty of record keeping wore off, and he slipped back into his old, reclusive ways. He gave up his self-change project, saying that it wasn't working.

Don't expect instant success. Be prepared to use a variety of techniques, and give them a chance to work. Expect to encounter obstacles, and use problem-solving techniques to overcome them.

Other people are discouraging your use of the techniques.   Others may hold beliefs such as those described above—it won't work, it's silly, you just need willpower—and may encourage you not to bother (Shelton & Levy, 1981). Tell them you're going to try the techniques and then decide whether or not they work.

People may also place temptation in your way. "Go ahead, have a cigarette. One won't hurt." Some people may be inconvenienced or made uncomfortable by your efforts to change, and may unthinkingly sabotage your plan. They may do it out of politeness, as when a host at a party urges food on someone who is dieting.

Sometimes people actually punish your attempts to change. This is often true for people—especially women—who are trying to be assertive. A student told us that all her life she had done whatever her older sister suggested. When she began to practice asserting herself, her sister complained that she was becoming "pushy." Your behavior may make people uncomfortable; a new, assertive you rocks the boat.

Not every change you want to make will please those around you. This student eventually gained her sister's cooperation by explaining her goals and the reasons for them. But this is not always possible. You may have to choose: are your new goals worth the opposition of friends or family?

RELAPSE PREVENTION

Jeb took up smoking when he was 15. When he turned 25, he decided it was time to quit. He gave himself a date: "On August 1, I will quit smoking." As the date drew near, he worried about his ability to just quit, but he wanted to try. He woke up that fateful morning, fixed his coffee, reached for a cigarette, said "No," and threw all his cigarettes, matches, and ashtrays into the garbage. During the next ten days, he did not smoke at all.

Other things were changing for Jeb during this time. He and his girlfriend were having increasing difficulties. She wanted to break up, but Jeb didn't. Finally, she told Jeb she wouldn't see him anymore. This depressed him considerably, as he had thought she was *the one*. His depression lingered, made worse by the fact that his grades on his most recent tests were unexpectedly low.

That weekend, to cheer himself up, Jeb went to a local singles bar. He wasn't cheered, however. The sight of all those strangers trying to make a good impression on each other just depressed him more. It also seemed as though everyone was smoking. "God, I feel rotten," he thought. "A cigarette would sure cheer me up right now." When a man at the bar offered him a cigarette, Jeb accepted. A few minutes later, he went to the vending machine and bought a pack of his favorite brand. He ordered another drink, felt his spirits lift, and lit up.

The next day Jeb woke up, poured his coffee, and had a cigarette. A year later, he is still smoking. "I was never sure that I could quit, anyway. When I went back that night, it just proved it. I'm addicted. I can't quit."

Jeb's story contains several elements that may help you prevent a relapse—whether your problem is overeating, smoking, drinking, abuse of substances, or any other kind of situation in which relapse is a distinct possibility.

First, let's define *relapse*. Jeb's first cigarette after quitting need not have signaled a relapse: it was a lapse, but not a relapse. It would be defined as a relapse only if you defined *any* transgression of the rule "total abstinence forever" as a relapse. Jeb made this mistake. Overeaters shouldn't overeat, gamblers shouldn't ever gamble, and smokers should quit forever: these are the final goals. But the fact is that on the way to recovery, many people with these kinds of problems make slips. But a slip is not necessarily a fall. Expect that you will have lapses. The trick is to keep them from becoming relapses.

When a **lapse** occurs, you perform a behavior you are trying to avoid: you take a few tokes, smoke a few smokes. A **relapse** means going back to your full-blown pattern of misuse or other unwanted behavior.

A Model of the Relapse Process

What was going on when Jeb went back to smoking? He was emotionally upset: his girlfriend had left him, his grades were low. He went into a risky situation—a singles bar where many people were smoking. Jeb doubted his ability to quit. He believed that a cigarette would make him feel better, and in fact it seemed to do so. Jeb was unprepared when the man offered him a cigarette, and he accepted it. Afterwards, he felt that he had relapsed and that the relapse was due to conditions within himself—his addiction, his inability to quit, his lack of willpower. The implication was that there was no point in trying to quit again.

G. Alan Marlatt and his coworkers have offered a model of the relapse process (Marlatt, 1982; Marlatt & Gordon, in press). This model is diagramed in Figure 10-2.

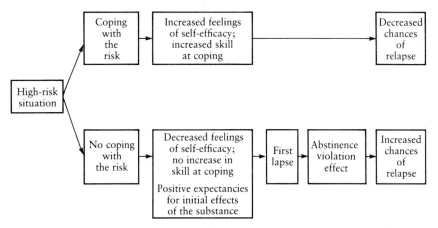

Figure 10-2. The relapse process. (*Adapted from "Relapse Prevention: A Self-Control Program for the Treatment of Addictive Behaviors," by G. A. Marlatt, 1982. In R. B. Stuart (Ed.),* Adherence, Compliance, and Generalization in Behavioral Medicine, *New York: Brunner/Mazel.*)

We can use Jeb's experience to follow through the model. Jeb was in a high-risk situation when he became depressed, went to the singles bar, and was offered a cigarette. A high-risk situation is one that presents a more than usual temptation to lapse into the unwanted behavior. What makes a situation high-risk depends to some degree on your individual learning history; your Aunt Jenny's rhubarb pie may be an irresistible temptation to you, but not to everyone. There are, however, common patterns to high-risk situations. A survey of alcoholics, smokers, heroin addicts, gamblers, and overeaters found that the three antecedents of lapses were negative emotional states, interpersonal conflicts, and social pressures (Cummings, Gordon, & Marlatt, 1980).

Negative emotional state: Jeb was depressed.
Interpersonal conflict: Jeb's girlfriend had left him.
Social pressures: Jeb felt as though everyone in the bar was smoking; someone offered him a cigarette.

At this point Jeb might have coped with the risk. He could have noted that he was very upset, realized that a lapse was likely, and done something about it. That would take him through the top part of the model, where coping in the face of a high-risk situation leads to increased self-efficacy—and, we would add, to increased skill through practice of the coping behavior. This, in turn, would lessen the chances of a relapse.

Unfortunately for Jeb, his behavior followed the bottom part of the model. He did not recognize that he was in a high-risk situation and did nothing to cope with it. He expected that the cigarette would be good, and he was not confident that he could stay off cigarettes. He used his old way of coping with depression—smoking—and had his first lapse. This combination of not coping effectively with a high-risk situation, the belief that the indulgent behavior will make one feel better, and the belief that one probably can't give up the stuff anyway greatly increases the chances of an initial lapse (Marlatt, 1982). Jeb lapsed, and smoked.

Jeb could have gotten up the next morning and gone right back to non-smoking. But Jeb experienced what is called the **abstinence violation effect**. In this situation, the person is committed to *total abstinence*. The gambler takes the pledge never to gamble again; the smoker takes the pledge to never have another cigarette. When they do backslide, they feel guilty and conflicted and blame themselves for the lapse.

Once he had smoked in the bar, Jeb felt his behavior demonstrated what he had always believed—that he could *not* quit smoking, and that it was his personal failing. He ignored the transient nature of the situation that had caused his behavior—his low mood, being in the bar, being offered a cigarette—and focused instead on his own personal characteristics. Ignoring the effects of the situation in causing our behavior is a common pattern in human thinking (Ross, Amabile, & Steinmetz, 1977). In Jeb's case, it led to real problems. Jeb's bad feelings about smoking piled on top of his depression made him feel worse, and he turned to his old way of feeling better—smoking—to lighten his mood. Later he told himself that the lapse was due to his personal failings and that there was no point in trying to quit again. Thus, the initial lapse became a full-blown relapse.

What can you do to lessen the chances that this will happen to you? (1) Prepare for high-risk situations. (2) Cope with them when you meet them. (3) Prevent any lapse that occurs from becoming a relapse.

Preparing for High-Risk Situations

Learn to recognize your own high-risk situations. Being emotionally upset—depressed, angry, frustrated, bored, or anxious—is a major high-risk situation. In the past, you may have used your unwanted behavior—smoking, drinking, overeating, or whatever—as a way of lightening your mood. Thus, you have been reinforced for the very behavior that is now unwanted. A father said to us, "I've tried three times in the past two weeks to stop smoking. Each time, an argument with my teenage son got me back to smoking. He's in a rebellious period, and his actions upset me a lot. I take a walk to cool off—and invariably end up down at the corner store buying a pack of cigarettes."

A second highly risky situation occurs when you are involved in any kind of conflict with another person, as this man was with his son. A student of ours found that every time he got into an argument with a man at work whom he heartily disliked, he would take a break to smoke marijuana, which he was trying to stop doing.

A third risky situation involves social pressure from others to engage in your unwanted behavior. You want to quit overeating, but your Aunt Jenny bakes her special rhubarb pie and brings it over to your house. Your old drinking buddy encourages you to drop your project; he doesn't want to lose *his* drinking buddy. Your friends offer you the foods they know you like, because they want to be hospitable and friendly.

These situations are high-risk for everyone. Your personal high-risk situations can be learned from your own self-observation. This is why it is critically important to continue to keep records even if your plan for self-modification seems to be failing. After the father who argued with his teenage son made accurate self-observations, he was in a position to do something effective: he gave himself instructions not to react so strongly to what his son did, and he practiced relaxation when he got upset.

Keep records of your thoughts when you are upset and have a lapse. "I'm upset. I'd feel better if I ate." "A cigarette would sure relax me now." "A few tokes and I'd feel better." "I need to lighten up. Have a little drink." Or "I've been under a lot of stress. I owe myself a drunk." If you believe that nice things will happen as a result of lapsing, you'll probably tell yourself "Go ahead, it would feel good." Through self-statements, you are tempting yourself.

Your self-observations may tell you about the situations that are high-risk for you—being in a singles bar, social situations, being at a dinner party, or your own thoughts. Use the three general types of high-risk situation—being upset, being in conflict with another, social pressure—to help you find the specific situations that are high-risk for you.

Another technique for discovering your own personal high-risk situations is to have a relapse fantasy (Marlatt & Parks, 1982). Sit down, close your eyes, and pretend you are relapsing. What kinds of situations would it take to get you back to your old behavior? Imagine the scene as clearly as you can so you will know the details of the situation. Here are samples of relapse fantasies our students have told us about. A student who wanted to be more assertive: "I eat at a restaurant. When the bill comes, it seems too high. I start to call the waiter over, but he gives me a superior sneer, and I end up not saying anything." A student who wanted to get up early and go jogging: "The alarm clock goes off, but I'm sleepy because I got to bed late the night before. I groan and think to myself 'Sleep is more important.' Then I turn off the alarm and go back to sleep." A student who wanted to increase her study time: "I've planned to study all Thursday evening, but when I check the TV listings I see there is a fantastic special on, so I watch that instead."

The first step in preventing relapse, then, is to know your own high-risk situations.

Coping with High-Risk Situations

The second step is to develop skills to cope with high-risk situations. You can learn such skills and increase your chances of successfully dealing with high-risk situations when they arise (Chaney, O'Leary, & Marlatt, 1978; Hall, Rugg, Tunstall, & Jones, 1984).

Use problem-solving skills to deal with high-risk situations (Marlatt, 1982;

Marlatt & Gordon, 1980, in press). List the details of the problems, think of as many solutions to the problems as you can, select solutions to use, and check to be sure you are actually implementing the solutions.

Sherwin had given up excessive drinking, but was tempted now and then. "I listed the details of situations in which I drank. One was when I wanted to relax. Another was when I was with a bunch of people. Sometimes I had liquor in the house that was left there after a party. I worked out alternative ways of dealing with those situations. To get myself to relax, I tried meditating and exercising. I made lists of self-instructions to use when I was with other people. I decided to pour out all liquor that was left after a party."

Listing the details of situations in which you are tempted to lapse will suggest specific problems. Instead of thinking "I drink too much," substitute "I drink when I am really upset and alcohol is readily available." Your problem is more specific, and your attack on the problem can focus more closely on the real issues. You might decide that you need to spend less time being upset, for example, and set out to solve some of the problems that commonly upset you.

Many people who overindulge in some substance or activity—drinking, smoking, overeating, gambling, and so on—do so because they feel that they aren't getting enough out of life (Marlatt, 1982). The "shoulds" outweigh the "wants." Listing the details of a problem may reveal this kind of thinking. "I thought to myself, 'Hell, go ahead and have a drink. You've done nothing but work all week, and life is short!'" If this kind of thinking pops up in your list of the details of the problem, then direct your attack toward getting a few more "wants" gratified.

In any case, your detailed list may suggest certain paths you should follow. If you give in to social pressure, then rehearse not giving in. If you overindulge to reduce stress, then you need to develop other ways of reducing stress. If you overindulge to celebrate, work on other ways of celebrating.

Besides general problem solving, there are specific skills you may want to practice. As soon as you realize that you are in a high-risk situation, *give yourself instructions on how to deal with it.* First, you say to yourself, "Danger. This is risky. I could have a lapse here." Then tell yourself specific things to do. These may be instructions on behaviors you want to perform: leave the situation, be assertive in turning down the tempting substance, relax. Tell yourself not to perform the old, unwanted behavior, and what specific things you should do to avoid performing it.

Sherwin wrote: "One Friday after work, the whole office decided to go out for a beer. I wanted to go, to be with them and have some fun, but I knew it was risky. I told myself, 'Be careful. This is a high-risk situation. Order ginger ale. If someone says "Come on, have a beer," I will say "No thanks, I prefer ginger ale." ' " He was warning himself, and also telling himself what to do and how to cope with social pressure to lapse.

Recognize that you may want to give in to the temptation, and give yourself instructions to cope with the rationalizations you make to yourself. Sherwin says to himself, "When I get there, I may say to myself 'I'll just have one beer.' But I won't have one, I'll have several, and I really don't want to do that. So don't have the first one."

Remind yourself of the advantages of changing your old, unwanted behavior. Sherwin thinks, "I'm tempted to drink now, but I really want to stop drinking, because it will make me feel better and be healthier, make me look better, be better for my work, and improve my social life. The advantages outweigh the disadvantages, so I won't drink."

Self-instructions can also help you cope with your feelings that you want to indulge right now. Distract yourself, or switch from hot to cool thoughts about the object of your desire. Instead of thinking "Man, a beer would sure taste good now," Sherwin switches to thinking "The beer looks like a urine specimen." It's important not to continue having hot thoughts about the tempting substance, for you are more likely to give in and lapse if you have those thoughts (Mischel, 1981).

Take a detached view of your craving for a tempting substance (Marlatt, 1982). Instead of thinking "Oh, I really gotta have a beer right now," Sherwin tells himself "I am experiencing an urge to drink now." It is also true that these cravings do pass fairly quickly (Marlatt, 1982), so Sherwin reminds himself of this. "I am experiencing an urge to drink now, but the feeling will pass in a minute. Meanwhile, I should distract myself. Let's see. I think I will pay a lot of attention to this woman sitting next to me. That will keep my mind off the craving. Meanwhile, enjoy my ginger ale."

To sum up, there are several kinds of self-instructions and other coping skills that you should prepare in advance, so that you will have them available when you meet a high-risk situation.

Warn yourself. "Danger!"

Give yourself instructions on what behaviors to perform: relax, be mildly assertive, leave, or whatever.

Remind yourself of rationalizations you may make, and remind yourself you don't want to indulge.

Remind yourself of the advantages of changing.

Cope with feelings that you want to indulge: distract yourself, switch from hot to cool thoughts about the substance.

Take a detached view of any craving you feel, remind yourself that it will pass, and tell yourself what to do until it does pass.

Practice these in your imagination before you get into high-risk situations. Return to the relapse fantasies that you used to predict your high-risk situations. Now replay those situations, imagining yourself using the coping skills. Use the principles for imagined rehearsal discussed in Chapter Six.

Putting on the Brakes: Stopping Lapses from Becoming Relapses

Suppose you make a mistake, and lapse. You smoke, you drink, you overeat, you gamble, or whatever. What now? A plan for coping with lapses—for putting on the brakes before you totally relapse—is essential. Jeb, after a night of lapses, got up the next morning and went right back to smoking, as though he'd never stopped. One of his mistakes was having no plan to cope with lapses. A study compared people who lapsed but eventually stopped smoking with those who lapsed and stayed relapsed. Of the eventual successes, 100% said they had some plan for coping following a lapse. Only half of those who failed had any plan (Candiotte & Lichtenstein, 1981).

The first step in your plan for coping with lapses is to make self-observations. Reinstate counting your cigarettes, and/or keep a structured diary of the situations that lead to smoking. Often when people lapse, they become upset by the lapse and stop self-observation. But it is important to continue self-monitoring. If you have not been self-monitoring, reinstate it. If you do so, you are much more likely to reinstate a full-blown plan for self-modification.

The second step is to make out a self-contract for what you will do if you lapse. What should you put into your contract? Make plans to get back into a self-modification program. If you have not been using a full plan—for example, you are no longer counting, you aren't self-reinforcing, you aren't thinking about antecedents, and so on—you should go back to a full plan: antecedent control for wanted behavior, shaping, reinforcement, imaginary rehearsal, relaxation, and so on. Write out a self-contract: "I promise myself that if I lapse, I will immediately begin counting my lapses. I will continue to count as long as I am lapsing. Also, I will reinstate a full self-modification project to cope with my problem behavior." Sign this, and keep it in your wallet.

Also, make out a reminder card to carry with you. Here is the reminder card used in a study with smokers who wanted to quit:

> A slip is not all that unusual. It does not mean that you have failed or that you have lost control over your behavior. You will probably feel guilty about what you have done, and will blame yourself for having slipped. This feeling is to be expected; it is part of what we call the Abstinence Violation Effect. There is no reason why you have to give in to this feeling and continue to smoke. The feeling will pass in time. Look upon the slip as a learning experience. What were the elements of the high-risk situation which led to the slip? What coping response could you have used to get around the situation? Remember the old saying: One swallow doesn't make a summer. Well, one slip doesn't make a relapse, either. Just because you slipped once does not mean that you are a failure, that you have no willpower, or that you are a hopeless addict. Look upon the slip as a single, independent event, something which can be avoided in the future with an alternative coping response [Marlatt & Gordon, 1980; in Marlatt, 1982, pp. 359–360].

The reminder card points out that you must be wary of the *abstinence violation effect*. Your persistence following a lapse can have a profound effect upon your long-term success. If you think "Well, that lapse was due to the particular circumstances I was in," rather than "I lapsed because I just don't have enough willpower," then you are more likely to persist in your efforts to change (Kernis, Zuckerman, Cohen, & Spadafora, 1982). Blame the situation (including your own lack of preparedness in not expecting the situation) instead of your personality.

If you believe that total abstinence is necessary in order for you to have personal control over the problem behavior, then any violation of abstinence will be thought of as loss of control (Marlatt, 1982). But total abstinence is not likely at first. You may have spent years practicing the behavior you now want to stop, and it's overly optimistic to expect that the first time you quit, you will quit forever. Expect slips, but don't let them snowball. If you are disgusted with yourself, think you don't have any willpower, and can't control this behavior, remember: that's the *abstinence violation effect.* Then go into your plans to keep the lapse from becoming a relapse; put on the brakes.

Lapses and problems are part of the learning process. Perfection will never be attained. The goal is steady improvement—more and more consistent behavior.

CHAPTER SUMMARY

Problem Solving

When your plan for change proves inadequate, tinker with it. Start off with your best plan, and observe what interferes with it. Then revise the plan, taking into consideration the sources of interference. Analyze your mistakes, and learn from them. If you are failing at self-modification, one likely cause is lack of self-observation. Good records help you stick to your goals. Self-observations help you think more clearly about the causes of your behavior, and this in turn allows you to attack the real problems with greater specificity.

Using formal problem solving increases your chances of success, particularly if you run into difficulties. The four steps in problem solving are: (1) list the concrete details of the problem; (2) try to think of as many solutions as possible; (3) choose one or more to implement; and (4) check to be sure you are carrying out the solution.

Common Reasons for Failure at Self-Modification

Common reasons for failure at self-modification include inadequate self-observation and failure to use the techniques. Self-observation is essential to understanding the antecedents and consequences of your behavior and measuring your progress. Encourage self-observation and self-confidence by recording positive as well as negative information. Failure to use the techniques may reflect a lack of confidence in the techniques or in yourself, discouragement by others or yourself, a lack of personal commitment, or your own ambivalence about changing. Learning to recognize these problems will help you to cope with them appropriately.

Relapse Prevention

Encountering high-risk situations can be followed by successful coping with the risk. This leads to increased feelings of self-efficacy and an increase in one's skill level, which in turn leads to decreased chances of a relapse. Alternately, encountering a high-risk situation can lead to *no* coping with the risk, which leads to decreased feelings of self-efficacy and no increase in skill level. These, in turn, lead to the first lapse and the *abstinence violation effect*, which leads to increased chances of relapse.

Common high-risk situations are negative emotional states, interpersonal conflict, and social pressures. Through self-observation and relapse fantasies, you can learn about your own personal high-risk situations.

To lessen the chances of relapse: (1) prepare for high-risk situations; (2) develop skills for coping during high-risk situations; and (3) develop plans to keep lapses from becoming relapses.

YOUR OWN SELF-DIRECTION PROJECT: STEP TEN

Solving Problems

Be prepared to tinker with your self-change plans. What makes it difficult to perform the target behavior? How can the plan be made more effective?

Practice problem solving. Use the four steps to solve problems in your project.

Here is a checklist of the most common reasons for failure. Check if any apply to you, and take steps to cope with the issue. Reread the appropriate section of the chapter, think how it applies to your project, and then act on the implications.

Failures in self-observation:

_____ lack of records
_____ noticing failures only

Misuse of techniques:

_____ infrequent or no reinforcement
_____ use of punishment
_____ attempts to suppress a behavior instead of developing another in its place
_____ use of too few techniques

Not using the techniques:

_____ your belief that they won't help
_____ low self-efficacy
_____ ambivalence about changing
_____ lack of time to do a self-change project
_____ discouragement from others
_____ giving up at the first failure

Preventing Relapse

Keep records of your lapses. Look for negative emotional states, interpersonal conflict, or social pressures as causes of lapses, and for events specific to your behavior. Have a relapse fantasy to see what might cause a lapse. Find out what your personal high-risk situations are.

Use problem-solving techniques to cope with high-risk situations. Do this work now, before you are involved in the situation. List the details of your personal high-risk situations, think of as many solutions to these problems as you can, select solutions to use, and be sure you are using the solutions.

Take time now to prepare the self-statements you will use when you meet a high-risk situation: (1) Use a warning statement. (2) Prepare self-instructions on what behaviors to perform. (3) Remind yourself of any rationalizations you may make. (4) Make a list of the advantages of not giving in to the urge to lapse. (5) Make plans on how to distract yourself and how to switch from hot to cool thoughts. (6) Practice taking a detached view.

Make a written list of these self-instructions, and read it when you find yourself in a high-risk situation.

Once you have made up the self-instructions, use imaginary rehearsal to practice them. Set aside periods in which you imagine suddenly being in a high-risk situation, give yourself a warning, tell yourself what behaviors to perform, and give yourself the self-instructions. Imagine yourself being reinforced by feelings of pride and self-efficacy.

Make out a relapse-prevention contract now. This will include plans on immediately resuming self-observation after the first lapse. The second step will be to resume a full self-change project. Sign this contract, and keep it with you. Also, make out a reminder card to carry with you. (For a sample, see page 264.)

Do all these steps now, *before* you run into a high-risk situation. If you meet one unprepared, you are more likely to lapse—and relapse.

TIPS FOR TYPICAL TOPICS

If your project deals with one of the indulgent behaviors—overeating, smoking, drinking, drug use, gambling—then clearly the material on relapse prevention is for you. Follow all the steps to prevent relapse. But even if you are dealing with some other problem, such as developing your dating skills, you may find that in certain situations you lapse. Under stress, for example, you may note that you are no longer performing as skillfully as you were, and that you show a tendency to slip back into your old ways. In this case, your procedure should be the same as for any lapse. Take steps right away to prevent the lapse from becoming a relapse by instigating record keeping and reinstituting a full-scale self-modification program.

No matter what your topic, you can benefit from using problem solving. Remember, people who use it cope better with the problems they inevitably meet.

CHAPTER ELEVEN

Termination and Beyond

OUTLINE

- Formal Termination: Planning to Maintain Gains
- Beyond the Ending
- Chapter Summary
- Your Own Self-Direction Project: Step Eleven

LEARNING OBJECTIVES

Formal Termination: Planning to Maintain Goals

1. What are the issues of maintenance and transfer of a newly learned behavior?
2. How can you evolve natural reinforcements for a new behavior?
3. Explain how to use thinning.
4. How should you deal with lack of reinforcement from others?
5. How can you get social support for new behaviors?
6. How confident are you that you can maintain the new behaviors? How is this measured?
7. How do you program for transfer to new settings?
8. How important is practice in developing new behaviors? What does it mean to say "Practice *of* perfect—not practice *makes* perfect"?

Beyond the Ending

9. Do people ever carry out lifelong self-modification projects? When might this be necessary?
10. When should you seek professional help?
11. What happens in psychotherapy?
12. How should you choose a therapist?
13. How can you increase the chances that you will use self-change techniques when needed in the future?

Some self-modification plans die a natural and almost unnoticed death, because their useful life spans have ended. The goal is reached, and it is no longer necessary to use self-reinforcement, or shaping, or self-instructions. The new, desirable behavior has become a habit. The old, undesirable behavior no longer seems a problem. This can happen when you reach the goal you originally set for yourself—"I wanted to quit biting my nails, and I have"—

or when you reach a goal you weren't even aware of at the beginning—"I learned that I had to smile at people and not interrupt them but listen carefully, and when I had learned that, my new behaviors just started happening." When a depression has lifted, or loneliness ended, the plan for change receives less attention, and is finally ignored.

Formal self-change plans are a temporary expedient, a device to use when you are trapped in a problem that requires particular planning to solve. When self-modification planning becomes no longer necessary, you have really succeeded in achieving an adjustment whereby you (and your environment) are supporting a pattern that you endorse.

Other people slack off in their efforts to change after they have made some progress toward their goal, even though they haven't reached it. Kalani, who started out to lose 40 pounds, found that after losing 20 he was no longer sticking to his self-change plan. "I think what happened was that I felt better and looked better. But I still enjoy overeating, and I'm not really sure I want to give it up entirely. It's a pleasure, and what is life for? Maybe I'll stay 20 pounds overweight. It's not so bad." This reflects a change in Kalani's goals.

If you find that your plan has petered out before reaching your original goal, list the advantages and disadvantages of changing (see Chapter Two), this time starting from your new level. You may find that you are now content. Or perhaps the listing will show you that you still want to change. The danger here is drifting—halfway to some original goal, pleased with your progress, but disappointed because you haven't gotten all the way to your goal. The listing will help you clarify your values, so that you can be either completely pleased with your progress or prepared to redouble your efforts to change.

There is a real risk that Kalani, or any other dieter, will regain the 20 pounds he lost. Suppose he wants to be sure this doesn't happen? It's *not* unusual for people to revert to their old, unwanted behavior. You can guard against this danger by **formal termination**, in which you take deliberate steps to keep the problem from arising.

FORMAL TERMINATION: PLANNING TO MAINTAIN GAINS

When you develop new behaviors to reach your goal, remember that they *are* new behaviors. Not being well practiced, they can be lost, and the old, unwanted habits may reappear. At this point, you have two goals: (1) to *maintain gains* and (2) to *make sure that any newly learned behavior transfers to new situations* (Marholin & Touchette, 1979). Suppose you have increased your studying to a new, satisfying level, but after a few months notice that it is dropping back toward the old level. That is a **maintenance** problem. Or suppose you have developed good study habits for certain courses, but still don't seem to be studying well for other courses. That is a **transfer** problem. Either way, you are not performing the desired behavior at the level you want.

There are several things you can do to be sure you maintain your gains and to help them transfer to new situations.

Evolving Natural Reinforcements

Suppose you have successfully increased your study time and improved your study habits after a lifetime of being a poor student. Now you should *plan natural situations that will reinforce your new competence without punishing you for skills you still lack.* Where will your studying be reinforced? If you take an advanced course that has several prerequisites—courses that you did very poorly in—you place yourself at a disadvantage. Choose instead courses in which you are getting a fresh start. This way you are much more likely to be reinforced for the new, good study habits that you have learned.

Elizabeth, who had learned through her self-change project to talk comfortably with men, wrote: "I'm still careful in striking up conversations. I look for guys who seem easy to get to know and stay away from the stuck-up ones." She is very sensibly putting herself into situations where she can reasonably expect to be rewarded.

Jack felt awkward in small peer groups, alternating between strained silence and sarcastic remarks. When he was assigned to a six-person team project in one of his courses, he decided to take the opportunity of being a member of the team to change his behavior. Jack reinforced the friendly and task-related statements that he made to other group members, using as a reinforcement the amount of time he allowed himself to spend surfing each week. Jack improved his performance and his comfort, but because he was still not satisfied with his level of improvement when the course was over, he looked for another situation in which to practice. From among several possibilities, he chose to attend evening meetings of the Writers' Club. This was a good choice, because he was interested in writing and had much to say on the subject. Furthermore, lapses into his more aggressive behavior wouldn't be punished too severely, since criticism of the members' work was part of the club's functions. In short, this group was one into which he could bring his newly acquired abilities and from which he could expect enjoyment and relative lack of punishment. The situation reinforced and increased the kind of participation he valued.

When behaviors reflect good adjustment, it is likely they will find natural support and reinforcements. In the early stages of termination, though, it's a good idea to remind yourself of the chain of events that bolster your behavior. A woman who succeeded in losing many pounds through self-reinforcement for reduced eating was delighted to discover that other people found her more attractive. She had many more dates. When she stopped the reinforcement, she posted a sign on the refrigerator door: "Dieting keeps the telephone ringing!"

When your new target behavior has become well established through your self-intervention plan, search for opportunities to practice it in which other people will reinforce you for that behavior. *Make a list of the situations in which you can perform the behavior and are likely to be reinforced for it.*

Thinning: Building Resistance to Extinction

In your self-modification plan, you may get reinforced every time you perform some behavior. That's the way you produce the fastest change. But out in the world, reinforcement isn't so predictable. Once you start thinking about transferring to naturally occurring reinforcers, you should take steps to ensure that your newly gained behaviors are not lost because of extinction. This is necessary because a behavior that has been reinforced *continuously* is most likely to extinguish when reinforcements do not continue to occur.

Don't stop your self-modification plan abruptly. *The best way to ensure that extinction does not occur is to place your target behavior on an intermittent reinforcement schedule.* Once you have established an acceptable level for your target behavior, you can cut down the ratio of its reinforcement.

Odette had been working to be more assertive in certain situations—such as when other people made unreasonable requests. Every time she performed a desirable act of assertion, she gave herself one token. Later she used these tokens to select from a menu of favorite foods. A pizza, for example, cost three tokens; a beer cost one. After several weeks, she felt she had reached a desirable upper limit. She was being assertive when it was called for.

At this point, instead of stopping her reinforcement system, she started preparing for the fact that the world out there couldn't be counted on to reinforce her behavior. So she prepared by thinning her reinforcement schedule—moving to an intermittent schedule of reinforcement. She began to thin in the simplest way—by not getting a token every time. She cut down so that she got tokens only 75% of the time. She then reduced further, to one every other time (50%) and then later to only 25%. She did this over several days, slowly, to guard against extinction of her newly learned behavior.

In thinning, you continue to count the frequency of the target behavior, because there is some danger that it will decline. Some drop from your upper goal might be acceptable, but you'll want to know *if* there has been a drop and, if so, *how much* of a drop. If the natural contingencies are slow to evolve, alternating between periods of thinning and 100% reinforcement can keep your frequency at an acceptably high level.

Dealing with Lack of Reinforcement from Others

Rick took a short course in how to increase open communication in marriage. He had always wanted to be more open, and he carried out a self-change project toward this goal. But his wife, Roberta, was irritated and put off by Rick's efforts to change their mode of communication. Obviously, he was not going to be reinforced by her for his new behavior. Rick then started a plan in which he would invite Roberta to cooperate and try to get her to discuss why she was opposed to his attempts to improve their communication. He praised her for her participation in this kind of discussion and also reminded himself to be patient and not to expect her to change too quickly. He realized that, in the long run, he might be reinforced for his changes—when Roberta, too, had changed—but, meanwhile, he continued to reinforce himself and to keep records of his new behavior, because he felt that it would drop away from lack of reinforcement if he did not.

As the example of Rick and Roberta illustrates, when you change yourself, you may affect others, and they may not reinforce you for your new behavior. Anyone who learns to become assertive, for example, will find that others do not always like those who stand up for their rights. In these kinds of situations, you must notice your own gains and benefits and remind yourself of your goals. See that you are being reinforced for your new acts, even though others may be slow in reinforcing you.

Finding Social Support for New Behaviors

Take deliberate steps to get others to support you. Ask your friends to reinforce you, to prompt you, or to monitor your self-recording. Say "Hey, let me brag a minute: I've been off cigarettes for two months now. For me, that's great!" Or "I've lost five pounds. Do I look any different?" Working with a buddy who is also doing a self-change project is helpful, because you can support each other's efforts to maintain changes. In Karol and Richards' (1978) study, smokers with a buddy who was also trying to stop and who could telephone encouragement to the other showed greater reduction of smoking at an eight-month follow-up than did smokers who had no buddy. Even if you don't have someone who is also trying to change, you can ask a friend to listen to you a bit, to reinforce you when you've been doing well, and to prompt you to continue.

The people you live with are the most obvious source of social support. They can also be a hindrance to your project. If they are, try to get them to support you. One of our students who wanted to stop drinking asked his housemates to keep their alcoholic beverages stored out of his sight so he wouldn't be tempted to drink. This is excellent support, and if people are willing to do this sort of thing for you, be sure to reinforce *them*.

Are You Confident You Can Maintain the New Behaviors?

One of our pessimistic students said, "You know, I've been using all these techniques you teach, and I have been successful in changing. But I bet when I finish this course—which is really like a crutch—I'll flop right back to my old behaviors."

"Yeah, you're right," we agreed.

"What?" he said, surprised. "I thought you said these techniques work."

"They do. But it's you who have done the work, not the course. You're giving it all the credit. As long as you think that, you don't really think you personally have control over the behavior. So you probably won't try to control it, and lo, you won't control it."

You have to understand that the new behavior is under your personal control if you are to have a good chance of maintaining it (Katz & Vinci-guerra, 1982). As your behavior changes, you should deliberately notice that it is coming more and more under your own control. If you do so, you increase the chances that you will maintain the behavior (Sonne & Janoff, 1982).

Before you stop your formal self-modification plan, rate your ability to maintain the new behavior without the plan:

My estimation of my ability to control my behaviors without my self-modification plan is . . .

1	2	3	4	5
no chance at all				total certainty

If your rating is low—below 4—then it's not yet time to stop formal self-modification.

Your ability to maintain the new behavior without your plan need not be an all-or-nothing issue. You might need to continue part of the plan—and the part you are most likely to need to continue is self-observation (Hall, 1980). If you are not sure yet about stopping, try a trial period while continuing careful self-observation.

Programming for Transfer to New Situations

When a behavior is first developing into a habit, it is tied to particular situations. When new situations occur, the behavior may not transfer to them. For example, a man who had learned to control his depression during the fall was surprised to see his mood collapse with the arrival of the holidays—and the loss of pleasant, school-related activities. A woman who exercised regularly in one town found to her chagrin that when she moved away, she stopped jogging. To avoid losing a new behavior through lack of transfer to new situations, *program for transfer*.

A group of clients who had "shy bladder" problems—inability to urinate in public restrooms when anyone was around—were taught to relax in public restrooms, with the result that the time required for them to urinate decreased markedly. Half these clients were also trained to practice using other restrooms, under varying conditions. This provided them experience in transferring the newly learned ability to relax. The other half received no such treatment. Then all were tested under severe conditions, using a crowded public restroom at a sports event. The clients who had been trained to transfer their relaxation were able to relax and use the facilities, but the clients who had not been trained for transfer were unable to relax in the press of a crowded arena restroom (Shelton, 1981b). The behavior they had learned under one condition had not transferred to the new, because they had not practiced transfer.

Another technique to help you guard against losing a newly developed behavior is continued record keeping. It will keep you alert for new situations. When you realize you are entering a new situation, use self-instructions: "This is a new situation. I'd better be careful or [the new behavior] won't transfer to it. Remember to [give yourself instructions to perform the desired behavior], and keep up the self-observations!"

You should also test for transfer before stopping your self-change plan. Melanie, whose study habits in algebra and French had improved following self-modification, also wanted to improve her studying in other subjects. Before stopping the plan, she tested to see if she could perform at the same level in the new subjects.

Practice

At some point, a behavior will "take hold." It becomes easy to do, automatic, a habit. This take-hold point is the result of a complicated system of schedules of reinforcement and antecedents, but it is also related to the number of times the behavior is practiced. John Shelton (1979) writes: "Regardless of the particular methods chosen to promote transfer, practice is crucial. Recall that individuals lose 50% of what they learn during the day following the learning trial. . . . Practice is the one way to overcome this" (p. 238). The more available a response is to a person, the more likely the transfer is, and the availability of the response is directly affected by practice (Goldstein, Lopez, & Greenleaf, 1979).

Think about learning to drive a car. When you begin, you have to concentrate fully on every aspect of your driving behavior. You dare not take your mind off it for a second. But after several years of driving experience, you can drive long distances without this concentrated attention.

The need for practice implies that you should not terminate your program as soon as you reach your goal. Mandler (1954) trained people at a task until they were able to perform it without error 0, 10, 30, 50, or 100 times. The more practice his subjects had, the more easily they transferred their training to new situations. Plan to "overlearn." Goldstein and his colleagues write: "The guiding rule should not be practice *makes* perfect (implying simply practice until one gets it right, and then move on), but practice *of* perfect (implying numerous overlearning trials of correct responses *after* the initial success)" (Goldstein, Lopez, & Greenleaf, 1979, p. 14).

How many overlearning trials should you use? The more, the better. A trial at thinning reinforcement will tell you whether you have adequately overlearned. Continue to keep records. If the target behavior drops alarmingly as soon as you begin to thin the reinforcement, you know that you haven't practiced enough. A second kind of test is to try the target behavior in a new situation. If difficulties arise, go back to practicing with a formal self-change plan. In general, the target behavior is more likely to remain strong and transfer to other situations if you have had a lot of practice and if you have practiced in a number of different situations (Goldstein, Lopez, & Greenleaf, 1979).

In developing a new behavior, you may have used techniques such as imagined rehearsals. Be sure to transfer this practice to real-life situations and practice it there long enough for the new behavior to take hold. The ultimate path for all self-change techniques is practice in real-life situations.

The Risks Involved in Stopping Too Soon

There isn't much of a risk that you will continue the plan too long. On the other hand, there is a risk in stopping too soon: you may lose your gains.

If you have been gradually increasing some desired behavior and stop too soon, you will find out easily enough: you will fall below the termination level. A significant decrease means that you should reinstitute a systematic change program. Be sure to continue self-observation until you know that the desired behavior has taken hold.

BEYOND THE ENDING

Long-Term Projects

Some goals can be achieved only through a long-term effort. Once you have been a heavy smoker, for example, you may have to maintain vigilance for years to stay off cigarettes and reactivate self-change plans if you slip back into smoking.

There are several reasons why you can expect old habits such as smoking, overeating, or nonexercising to reappear. You may deceive yourself a bit and say "Now that I have this under control, I can do it just a little bit." So you try smoking just at parties or overeating just on special occasions. But because such acts have been heavily developed as habits in the past, they return easily. You may soon find yourself smoking or overeating in many situations.

In the past, such acts have beeen associated with certain situations. You were withdrawn socially or were argumentative with friends. As life again brings on depression or tension, you may respond in your old manner. And there may be physiological reasons—addictions—that encourage your return to some indulgent behavior.

The rule for all these problems is the same: expect the habit to return, and reinstate a plan for changing as soon as it does. Follow the steps for relapse prevention. Learn from your mistakes. Suppose you quit smoking but after three months say to yourself "Well, I can smoke just a couple at this party." Two weeks later, you're back to a pack a day. *Learn from that.* The next time you quit, be prepared to deal with parties. It would be a mistake to conclude that you have no willpower. Instead, conclude that you must attend carefully to the particular situations that tempt you.

Once you have learned techniques for self-change, you can continue to be a personal scientist. Continue to informally observe your behavior, its antecedents, and its consequences. Occasionally you decide that some new goal needs a systematic self-direction plan. Whenever you have a goal that you are not reaching, use formal self-modification to help achieve it. Whenever you lapse back into an old, unwanted behavior, use relapse prevention and systematic self-modification to change yourself again.

Seeking Professional Help

There are at least three conditions that limit the usefulness of a self-modification project: (1) Your personal goals may not be clear enough to permit the choice of goal behaviors. (2) The technical problems of designing a plan may be greater than the skills that can be acquired by reading this book. (3) The natural environment itself may be too chaotic or unyielding to allow a plan to succeed. Under any of these circumstances, professional advice may be helpful.

What do professionals do? Although they may take different approaches, they all employ one general strategy: they help establish situations that encourage the development of new behaviors and emotions (Kanfer & Goldstein, 1975; Ullmann & Krasner, 1975; Kanfer & Phillips, 1970).

The principles governing professional help are the same as those by which self-change operates. Helping professionals don't force behaviors and experiences on people against their will. Unless the self-guiding, self-directing functions of the client are engaged in the process, behavioral and emotional changes simply do not occur during psychological treatment. Counselors and psychotherapists point out that their help is effective only when the client is motivated to change.

So if you choose professional help, you will still find yourself engaged in building personal skills of self-direction. Professionals don't solve the problems. They help *you* solve them. They do this by helping you create an environment that fosters your own efforts to change. Psychological helpers use a variety of techniques to create these new environmental supports. Some procedures have been developed into schools of treatment, and there is dispute among practitioners over preferred methods. Ideally, different methods should be selected for different clients with different problems.

Ralph Nader's group has published a booklet on being a consumer of professional help (Adams & Orgel, 1975). It emphasizes several points. You should shop around for someone with whom you think you can work. Use the initial interview with a therapist to make your decision. Should you stick with this person? You need to feel confident and comfortable with your counselor and free to talk about your problems, but whether or not you like the person is not especially important. Do some comparison shopping. Search for a good price. More expensive doesn't mean better help.

Many groups suggest that therapist and client have a written contract specifying the goals and techniques of the process. The contract should detail goals, costs, and time involved. For example, you may feel you want someone with whom you can discuss your uncertainty about career goals or your fears about your upcoming marriage. Make clear to the prospective therapist that these are your goals. If you and the therapist don't come to an understanding about this vital point, you may end up spending a lot of time dealing with things that the therapist thinks are important but in which you have little interest. The contract should be flexible, allowing you to change goals during the course of therapy. Those who suggest a contract stress the fact that it strengthens your commitment to change. The contract system is far from typical among counselors and therapists, but its principles are highly desirable. Its goals may also be achieved by verbal agreement.

As you shop for a professional helper, you may wonder "What am I in for?" or "What will be done with me?" A better question to ask yourself is "What will this professional do to help *me* help *myself*?" A variety of techniques can be used. Some therapists change their approach according to the needs of the client. But most stick fairly close to one or another theory. As an intelligent consumer, you will want to know something about the kind of therapy being offered.

The ideal helper possesses a full range of techniques and varies them according to your needs. Unfortunately, the ideal helper is a rare product. Maximize your chances of finding a good therapist by being a thoughtful consumer and by carefully evaluating the product being offered.

How do you go about choosing a professional helper? Have a clear idea of what you are looking for and what you hope to gain from professional help. Then try to match your needs with what is offered. Shop around. See if there is going to be a contract between you and the professional. Ask the many important questions we have mentioned: "What techniques do you use? What effects can I expect? What are the risks?" Use the first session to evaluate the professional. Change if you are not satisfied.

Self-Modification as a Lifelong Practice

As you terminate your self-change project, what lies ahead? Blue skies and cloudless days, with no problems to darken the horizon? We wish you well, but we predict that sooner or later something in your life will benefit from a systematic application of self-change techniques.

You have learned these techniques by using them on one personal problem, and you have been tested on them. Will you think to use them two years from now, when a new problem comes into your life? You can increase the chances that you will continue to use the techniques if you make a plan *now* for another self-change project (Barone, 1982).

You should practice the techniques in more than one kind of project. If you practice record keeping or positive self-instructions in several different projects, you will be more likely to keep records and to self-instruct when these techniques are needed in the future.

Anticipating problems and thinking of ways of using self-change techniques in dealing with them may also increase your chances of remembering them when the time comes. For example, "I know I spend my money unwisely. So far it hasn't made much difference, but it's just a matter of time till I am on my own, and then it's going to matter a lot. When that happens, I could keep records, set rules, and state those rules as self-instructions." Or "Everybody says that the job interviews for graduates are very difficult and competitive. Well, I could practice relaxation beforehand." Stop for a minute now and think about problems you will probably encounter in the next couple of years. How will you cope with them?

For all of us, self-direction is a daily habit. As you were working on your project, you had to proceed step by step to achieve the kind of performance you wanted. But for many of the areas of your life, self-regulation is already something you do without the formal statements of a self-modification plan. You begin to feel a bit blue, so you tell yourself "Cheer up!" You notice the good things in your life, and you schedule some fun activities. Without thinking about it, you have been doing the things we recommend for someone who is depressed. You used self-instructions, and you noticed and scheduled rewards. Or when you realize that you are growing uncomfortably tense in some situations, you can tell yourself "Relax," release tension from your muscles, and begin to cope.

In sum, you always use self-management to deal with life's problems. When you run into problems that require more formal self-direction, remember the techniques you have learned.

CHAPTER SUMMARY

Formal Termination: Planning to Maintain Gains

Your newly developed behaviors will require special attention if they are to be *maintained* over time and *transferred* to additional situations. Maintenance and transfer can be strengthened by planning for natural reinforcements to occur—that is, by seeking out situations in which the new behavior will be valued or successful. Simultaneously, resistance to extinction can be increased by thinning self-administered reinforcement to an intermittent schedule. Find social support for new, desirable behaviors, and honestly rate your estimation of your ability to control the new behaviors without a formal self-modification plan.

Program for transfer of new behaviors to new, unexpected situations by practicing the behavior in a variety of situations, practicing the behavior well past the first point of learning it, continuing to keep records of your behavior, and using problem-solving techniques.

Beyond the Ending

Even after formal termination, your life conditions may change in ways that cause your new habits to lapse. This is not unusual, and can be countered by the quick application of relapse prevention. Learn from those conditions that bring about lapses.

Professional help for changing may be needed if your goals are confused, if the technical problems of designing a plan are too great for you, or if your natural environment is too chaotic or unyielding to support your change efforts. Professionals can assist you to change, but they do not do it for you. Select a professional carefully. Shop around. Inquire carefully about the techniques and goals that the professional offers. Make sure that there is clear agreement over the goals, techniques, and costs.

Self-direction is a lifelong practice. Use the techniques you have learned in a variety of situations. Have them ready when needed.

YOUR OWN SELF-DIRECTION PROJECT: STEP ELEVEN

As you consider termination, follow these procedures:

1. Make a list of opportunities for practicing your newly learned behavior. Rate these opportunities in terms of how likely you are to be naturally reinforced for the new behavior.
2. If you suspect that your new behavior will not be naturally reinforced, continue to reinforce yourself or arrange for reinforcement from others.
3. Program for resistance to extinction by thinning your self-reinforcement.
4. Find social support for the new behavior.
5. Rate your ability to control the new behavior without a self-modification plan.
6. Program and test for transfer. Practice the behavior in a variety of situations. Continue to keep records. Practice using the problem-solving steps to deal with new difficulties.
7. Practice the new behavior until it is perfect, then practice doing it perfectly. The more you practice after you have reached your goal level, the more likely it is that your behavior will persist.
8. For long-term projects, be ready to reinstate a plan as soon as an unwanted behavior begins to reappear.

REFERENCES

Abrams, D. B., & Wilson, G. T. (1979). Self-monitoring and reactivity in the modification of cigarette smoking. *Journal of Consulting and Clinical Psychology, 47*, 243–251.

Adams, S., & Orgel, M. (1975). *Through the mental health maze*. Washington, DC: Health Research Group.

Ainslee, G. (1975). Specious reward: A behavioral theory of impulsiveness and impulse control. *Psychological Bulletin, 82*, 463–496.

American College of Sports Medicine. (1983). Position stand on proper and improper weight loss programs. *Medicine and Science in Sports and Exercise, 15*, ix–xiii.

Annon, J. S. (1975). *The behavioral treatment of sexual problems: Vol. 2. Intensive therapy*. Honolulu: Enabling Systems.

Arnkoff, D. B., & Glass, C. R. (1982). Clinical cognitive constructs: Examination, evaluation, and elaboration. In P. C. Kendall (Ed.), *Advances in cognitive-behavioral research and therapy* (Vol. 1, pp. 1–34). New York: Academic Press.

Arrick, C. M., Voss, J., & Rimm, D. C. (1981). The relative efficacy of thought-stopping and covert assertion. *Behaviour Research and Therapy, 19*, 17–24.

Ascher, L. M. (1973). An experimental analog study of covert positive reinforcement. In R. D. Rubin, J. P. Brady, & J. D. Henderson (Eds.), *Advances in behavior therapy* (Vol. 4, pp. 127–138). New York: Academic Press.

Azrin, N. H., & Nunn, R. G. (1973). Habit reversal: A method of eliminating nervous habits and tics. *Behaviour Research and Therapy, 11*, 619–628.

Azrin, N. H., Nunn, R. G., & Frantz-Renshaw, S. E. (1982). Habit reversal vs. negative practice treatment of self-destructive oral habits (biting, chewing or licking of the lips, cheeks, tongue or palate). *Journal of Behavior Therapy and Experimental Psychiatry, 13*, 49–54.

Bajtelsmit, J. W., & Gershman, L. (1976). Covert positive reinforcement: Efficacy and conceptualization. *Journal of Behavior Therapy and Experimental Psychiatry, 7*, 207–212.

Bandura, A. (1971). Vicarious and self-reinforcement processes. In R. Glaser (Ed.), *The nature of reinforcement*. New York: Academic Press.

Bandura, A. (1977). Self-efficacy: Toward a unifying theory of behavioral change. *Psychological Review, 84*, 191–215.

Bandura, A. (1981). In search of pure unidirectional determinants. *Behavior Therapy, 12*, 30–40.

Bandura, A. (1982). Self-efficacy mechanism in human agency. *American Psychologist, 37*, 122–147.

Bandura, A., Jeffery, R. W., & Gajdos, E. (1975). Generalizing change through participant modeling with self-directed mastery. *Behaviour Research and Therapy, 13,* 141–152.

Bandura, A., & Mahoney, M. J. (1974). Maintenance and transfer of self-reinforcement functions. *Behaviour Research and Therapy, 12,* 89–97.

Bandura, A., Reese, L., & Adams, N. E. (1982). Microanalysis of action and fear arousal as a function of differential levels of perceived self-efficacy. *Journal of Personality and Social Psychology, 43,* 5–21.

Barling, J., & Abel, M. (1983). Self-efficacy beliefs and tennis performance. *Cognitive Therapy and Research, 7,* 265–272.

Barone, D. F. (1982). Instigating additional self-modification projects after a personal adjustment course. *Teaching of Psychology, 9,* 111.

Barrera, M., & Glasgow, R. (1976). Design and evaluation of a personalized instruction course in behavioral self-control. *Teaching of Psychology, 3,* 81–83.

Barrera, M., & Rosen, G. M. (1977). Detrimental effects of a self-reward contracting program on subjects' involvement in a self-administered desensitization. *Journal of Consulting and Clinical Psychology, 45,* 1180–1181.

Barrios, B. A., & Shigetomi, C. C. (1979). Coping skills training for the management of anxiety: A critical review. *Behavior Therapy, 10,* 491–522.

Barrios, B. A., & Shigetomi, C. C. (1980). Coping skills training: Potential for prevention of fears and anxieties. *Behavior Therapy, 11,* 431–439.

Beck, A. T., Rush, A. G., Shaw, B. F., & Emery, G. (1979). *Cognitive therapy of depression.* New York: Guilford Press.

Beck, F. M., Kaul, T. J., & Russell, R. K. (1978). Treatment of dental anxiety by cue-controlled relaxation. *Journal of Counseling Psychology, 25,* 591–594.

Becker, M. H., & Green, L. W. (1975). A family approach to compliance with medical treatment. *International Journal of Health Education, 18,* 175–182.

Bellack, A. S., Rozensky, R., & Schwartz, J. (1974). A comparison of two forms of self-monitoring in a behavioral weight reduction program. *Behavior Therapy, 5,* 523–530.

Bergin, A. E. (1969). A self-regulation technique for impulse control disorders. *Psychotherapy: Theory, Research, and Practice, 6,* 113–118.

Bernard, H. S., & Efran, J. S. (1972). Eliminating versus reducing smoking using pocket tokens. *Behaviour Research and Therapy, 10,* 399–401.

Bernard, M. E., Kratochwill, T. R., & Keefauver, L. W. (1983). The effects of rational-emotive therapy and self-instructional training on chronic hair pulling. *Cognitive Therapy and Research, 7,* 273–280.

Biglan, A., & Campbell, D. R. (1981). Depression. In J. L. Shelton, R. L. Levy, & contributors, *Behavioral assignments and treatment compliance: A handbook of clinical strategies* (pp. 111–146). Champaign, IL: Research Press.

Billings, A. (1978). Self-monitoring in the treatment of tics: A single-subject analysis. *Journal of Behavior Therapy and Experimental Psychiatry, 9,* 339–342.

Black, D. R., & Scherba, D. S. (1983). Contracting to problem solve versus contracting to practice behavioral weight loss skills. *Behavior Therapy, 14,* 100–109.

Blackwell, B. (1979). Treatment adherence: A contemporary overview. *Psychosomatics, 20,* 27–35.

Blanchard, E. B. (1970). Relative contributions of modeling, informational influences, and physical contact in extinction of phobic behavior. *Journal of Abnormal Psychology, 76,* 55–61.

Blanchard, E. B., & Draper, D. O. (1973). Treatment of a rodent phobia by covert reinforcement: A single subject experiment. *Behavior Therapy, 4,* 559–564.

Boice, R. (1982). Increasing the writing productivity of 'blocked' academicians. *Behaviour Research and Therapy, 20,* 197–207.

Bootzin, R. R. (1972). Stimulus control treatment for insomnia. *Proceedings of the 80th Annual Convention of the American Psychological Association, 7,* 395–396.

Bornstein, P. H., & Hamilton, S. B. (1978). Positive parental praise: Increasing reactivity and accuracy of self-observation. *Journal of Abnormal Child Psychology, 6,* 503–509.

Bornstein, P. H., Hamilton, S. B., & Bornstein, M. T. (in press). Self-monitoring procedures. In A. R. Ciminero, K. S. Calhoun, & H. E. Adams (Eds.), *Handbook of behavioral assessment* (2nd ed.). New York: Wiley.

Boudreau, L. (1972). Transcendental meditation and yoga as reciprocal inhibitors. *Journal of Behavior Therapy and Experimental Psychiatry, 3,* 97–98.

Brehm, S. S. (1976). *The application of social psychology to clinical practice.* New York: Wiley.

Brehm, S. S., & Smith, T. W. (1982). The application of social psychology to clinical practice: A range of possibilities. In G. Weary & H. L. Mirels (Eds.), *Integrations of clinical and social psychology* (pp. 9–24). New York: Oxford University Press.

Brigham, T. A. (1982). Self-management: A radical behavioral perspective. In P. Karoly & F. H. Kanfer (Eds.), *Self-management and behavior change: From theory to practice* (pp. 32–59). New York: Pergamon Press.

Brigham, T. A., Contreras, J. A., Handel, G. S., & Castillo, A. O. (1983). A comparison of two approaches for improving social and job placement skills. *Behavioral Engineering, 8,* 104–114.

Brown, G. (1978). Self-administered desensitization of a cemetery phobia using sexual arousal to inhibit anxiety. *Journal of Behavior Therapy and Experimental Psychiatry, 9,* 73–74.

Brown, H. K. (1984). Personal communication.

Brownell, K. D., Heckerman, C. L., Westlake, R. J., Hayes, S. C., & Monti, P. M. (1978). The effect of couples training and partner cooperativeness in the behavioral treatment of obesity. *Behaviour Research and Therapy, 16,* 323–333.

Brownlee, A. (1978). The family and health care: Explorations in cross-cultural settings. *Social Work in Health Care, 4,* 179–198.

Campbell, D. R., Bender, C., Bennett, N., & Donnelly, J. (1981). Obesity. In J. L. Shelton, R. L. Levy, & contributors, *Behavioral assignments and treatment compliance: A handbook of clinical strategies* (pp. 187–221). Champaign, IL: Research Press.

Candiotte, M. M., & Lichtenstein, E. (1981). Self-efficacy and relapse in smoking cessation programs. *Journal of Consulting and Clinical Psychology, 49,* 648–658.

Cantor, N., Mischel, W., & Schwartz, J. (1982). Social knowledge: Structure, content, use, and abuse. In A. H. Hastorf & A. M. Isen (Eds.), *Cognitive social psychology* (pp. 33–72). New York: Elsevier/North Holland.

Carver, C. S., & Ganellen, R. J. (1983). Depression and components of self-punitiveness: High standards, self-criticism, and overgeneralization. *Journal of Abnormal Psychology, 92,* 330–337.

Carver, C. S., & Scheier, M. F. (1982). Control theory: A useful conceptual framework for personality-social, clinical, and health psychology. *Psychological Bulletin, 92,* 111–135.

Castro, L., de Pérez, G. C., de Albanchez, D. B., & de Léon, E. P. (1983). Feedback properties of "self-reinforcement": Further evidence. *Behavior Therapy, 14,* 672–681.

Castro, L., & Rachlin, H. (1980). Self-reward, self-monitoring, and self-punishment as feedback in weight control. *Behavior Therapy, 11,* 38–48.

Catania, A. C. (1975). The myth of self-reinforcement. *Behaviorism, 3,* 192–199.

Cautela, J. R. (1966). A behavior therapy treatment of pervasive anxiety. *Behaviour Research and Therapy, 4,* 99–109.

Cautela, J. R. (1970). Covert reinforcement. *Behavior Therapy, 1,* 33–50.

Cautela, J. R. (1971). Covert conditioning. In A. Jacobs & L. B. Sachs (Eds.), *The psychology of private events: Perspectives on covert response systems* (pp. 109–130). New York: Academic Press.

Cautela, J. R. (1972). The treatment of overeating by covert conditioning. *Psychotherapy: Theory, Research and Practice, 9,* 211–216.

Cautela, J. R. (1973). Covert processes and behavior modification. *Journal of Nervous and Mental Disease, 157,* 27–36.

Cautela, J. R. (1976). The present status of covert modeling. *Journal of Behavior Therapy and Experimental Psychiatry, 7,* 323–326.

Cautela, J. R. (1983). The self-control triad: Description and clinical applications. *Behavior Modification, 7,* 299–315.

Chambliss, A., & Murray, E. J. (1979a). Cognitive procedures for smoking reduction: Symptom attribution versus efficacy attribution. *Cognitive Therapy and Research, 3,* 91–95.

Chambliss, A., & Murray, E. J. (1979b). Efficacy attribution, locus of control and weight loss. *Cognitive Therapy and Research, 3,* 349–353.

Chaney, E. F., O'Leary, M. R., & Marlatt, G. A. (1978). Skill training with alcoholics. *Journal of Consulting and Clinical Psychology, 46,* 1092–1104.

Ciminero, A. R. (1974). *The effects of self-monitoring cigarettes as a function of the motivation to quit smoking.* Paper presented at the meeting of the Southeastern Psychological Association, Hollywood, FL.

Clements, C. B., & Beidleman, W. B. (1981). Undergraduate self-management projects: A technique for teaching behavioral principles. *Academic Psychology Bulletin, 3,* 451–461.

Coates, T. J., & Thoresen, C. E. (1977). *How to sleep better.* Englewood Cliffs, NJ: Prentice-Hall.

Cohen, E., Gelfand, D., Dodd, D., Jensen, J., & Turner, C. (1980). Self-control practices associated with weight loss maintenance in children and adolescents. *Behavior Therapy, 11,* 26–37.

Cohen, R., De James, P., Nocera, B., & Ramberger, M. (1980). Application of a simple self-instruction procedure on adults' exercise and studying: Two case reports. *Psychological Reports, 46,* 443–451.

Collins, K. W., Dansereau, D. F., Garland, J. C., Holley, C. D., & McDonald, B. A. (1981). Control of concentration during academic tasks. *Journal of Educational Psychology, 73,* 122–128.

Cooper, J., & Axsom, D. (1982). Effort justification in psychotherapy. In G. Weary & H. L. Mirels (Eds.), *Integrations of clinical and social psychology* (pp. 214–230). New York: Oxford University Press.

Cummings, C., Gordon, J. R., & Marlatt, G. A. (1980). Relapse: Prevention and prediction. In W. R. Miller (Ed.), *The addictive behaviors* (pp. 291–321). Oxford: Pergamon Press.

Dahlkoetter, J., Callahan, E. J., & Linton, J. (1979). Obesity and the unbalanced energy equation: Exercise versus eating habit change. *Journal of Consulting and Clinical Psychology, 47,* 898–905.

Dapcich-Miura, E., & Hovell, M. F. (1979). Contingency management of adherence to a complex medical regimen in an elderly heart patient. *Behavior Therapy, 10,* 193–210.

Davidson, A., Denney, D. R., & Elliott, C. H. (1980). Suppression and substitution in the treatment of nailbiting. *Behaviour Research and Therapy, 18,* 1–9.

deBortali-Tregerthan, G. (1984). *Self-change and attribution-change training: Implications for primary prevention.* Unpublished doctoral dissertation, University of Hawaii, Honolulu.

Deffenbacher, J. L. (1981). Anxiety. In J. L. Shelton, R. L. Levy, & contributors, *Behavioral assignments and treatment compliance: A handbook of clinical strategies* (pp. 93–109). Champaign, IL: Research Press.

Deffenbacher, J. L. (1984). Personal communication.

Deffenbacher, J. L., & Hahnloser, R. M. (1981). Cognitive and relaxation coping skills in stress inoculation. *Cognitive Therapy and Research, 5,* 211–215.

Deffenbacher, J. L., & Michaels, A. C. (1981). Anxiety management training and self-control desensitization—fifteen months later. *Journal of Counseling Psychology, 28,* 459–462.

Deffenbacher, J. L., & Suinn, R. M. (1982). The self-control of anxiety. In P. Karoly & F. H. Kanfer (Eds.), *Self-management and behavior change: From theory to practice* (pp. 393–442). New York: Pergamon Press.

Denney, D. R. (1980). Self-control approaches to the treatment of test anxiety. In I. G. Sarason (Ed.), *Test anxiety: Theory, research, and applications* (pp. 209–243). Hillsdale, NJ: Erlbaum.

DiCara, L. (1970, January). Learning in the autonomic nervous system. *Scientific American,* pp. 30–39.

DiClemente, C. C. (1981). Self-efficacy and smoking cessation maintenance: A preliminary report. *Cognitive Therapy and Research, 5,* 175–187.

Doerfler, L. A., & Richards, C. S. (1981). Self-initiated attempts to cope with depression. *Cognitive Therapy and Research, 5,* 367–371.

Dubbert, P. M., Martin, J. E., Raczynski, J., & Smith, P. O. (1982, March). *The effects of cognitive-behavioral strategies in the maintenance of exercise.* Paper presented at the third annual meeting of the Society of Behavioral Medicine, Chicago.

Dubren, R. (1977). Self reinforcement by recorded telephone messages to maintain non smoking behavior. *Journal of Consulting and Clinical Psychology, 45,* 358–360.

Durlak, J. A. (1983). Social problem-solving as a primary prevention strategy. In R. D. Felner, L. A. Jason, J. N. Moritsugu, & S. S. Farber (Eds.), *Preventive psychology: Theory, research and practice* (pp. 31–48). New York: Pergamon Press.

Dush, D. M., Hirt, M. L., & Schroeder, H. (1983). Self-statement modification with adults: A meta-analysis. *Psychological Bulletin, 94,* 408–422.

Dweck, C. S. (1975). The role of expectations and attributions in the alleviation of learned helplessness. *Journal of Personality and Social Psychology, 31,* 674–685.

D'Zurilla, T. J., & Goldfried, M. R. (1971). Problem solving and behavior modification. *Journal of Abnormal Psychology, 78,* 107–126.

D'Zurilla, T. J., & Nezu, A. (1982). Social problem solving in adults. In P. C. Kendall (Ed.), *Advances in cognitive-behavioral research and therapy* (Vol. 1, pp. 201–274). New York: Academic Press.

Egan, G. (1977). *You and me: The skills of communicating and relating to others.* Monterey, CA: Brooks/Cole.

Ellis, A. (1979). The theory of rational-emotive therapy. In A. Ellis & J. M. Whiteley (Eds.), *Theoretical and empirical foundations of rational-emotive therapy* (pp. 33–60). Monterey, CA: Brooks/Cole.

Emmelkamp, P. M. G. (1974). Self-observation versus flooding in the treatment of agoraphobia. *Behaviour Research and Therapy, 12,* 229–237.

Epstein, L. H., & Hersen, M. (1974). A multiple baseline analysis of coverant control. *Journal of Behavior Therapy and Experimental Psychiatry, 5,* 7–12.

Epstein, L. H., Miller, P. M., & Webster, J. S. (1976). The effects of reinforcing concurrent behavior on self-monitoring. *Behavior Therapy, 7,* 89–95.

Epstein, L. H., & Peterson, G. L. (1973a). The control of undesired behavior by self-imposed contingencies. *Behavior Therapy, 4,* 91–95.

Epstein, L. H., & Peterson, G. L. (1973b). Differential conditioning using covert stimuli. *Behavior Therapy, 4,* 96–99.

Epstein, L. H., Webster, J. S., & Miller, P. M. (1975). Accuracy and controlling effects of self-monitoring as a function of concurrent responding and reinforcement. *Behavior Therapy, 6,* 654–666.

Ernst, F. A. (1973). Self-recording and counterconditioning of a self-mutilative compulsion. *Behavior Therapy, 4,* 144–146.

Evans, I. (1976). Personal communication.

Ferguson, J. M. (1975). *Learning to eat.* Palo Alto, CA: Bell.

Ferster, C. B., Nurnberger, J. I., & Levitt, E. G. (1962). The control of eating. *Journal of Mathetics, 1,* 87–109.

Fischer, K. W. (1980). A theory of cognitive development: The control and construction of hierarchies of skills. *Psychological Review, 87,* 477–531.

Fisher, E. B., Jr., Levenkron, J. C., Lowe, M. R., Loro, A. D., & Green, L. (1982). Self-initiated self-control in risk reduction. In R. B. Stuart (Ed.), *Adherence, compliance and generalization in behavioral medicine* (pp. 169–191). New York: Brunner/Mazel.

Fisher, E. B., Jr., Lowe, M. R., Levenkron, J. C., & Newman, A. (1982). Reinforcement and structural support of maintained risk reduction. In R. B. Stuart (Ed.), *Adherence, compliance and generalization in behavioral medicine* (pp. 145–168). New York: Brunner/Mazel.

Fixen, D. L., Phillips, E. L., & Wolf, M. M. (1972). Achievement place: The reliability of self-reporting and peer-reporting and their effects on behavior. *Journal of Applied Behavior Analysis, 5,* 19–30.

Flannery, R. F., Jr. (1972). A laboratory analogue of two covert reinforcement procedures. *Journal of Behavior Therapy and Experimental Psychiatry, 3,* 171–177.

Flaxman, J. (1978). Quitting smoking now or later: Gradual, abrupt, immediate, and delayed quitting. *Behavior Therapy, 9,* 260–270.

Fo, W. (1975). *Behavioral self-control: Training students in the self-improvement of studying.* Unpublished doctoral dissertation, University of Hawaii.

Frankel, A. J. (1975). Beyond the simple functional analysis—The chain: A conceptual framework for assessment with a case study example. *Behavior Therapy, 6,* 254–260.

Frankel, M. J., & Merbaum, M. (1982). Effects of therapist contact and a self-control manual on nailbiting reduction. *Behavior Therapy, 13,* 125–129.

Frederiksen, L. W. (1975). Treatment of ruminative thinking by self-monitoring. *Journal of Behavior Therapy and Experimental Psychiatry, 6,* 258–259.

Fuchs, C. Z., & Rehm, L. P. (1977). A self-control behavior therapy program for depression. *Journal of Consulting and Clinical Psychology, 45,* 206–215.

Gallagher, J. W., & Arkowitz, H. (1978). Weak effects of covert modeling treatment of test anxiety. *Journal of Behavior Therapy and Experimental Psychiatry, 9,* 23–26.

Gauthier, J., & Pellerin, D. (1982). Management of compulsive shoplifting through covert sensitization. *Journal of Behavior Therapy and Experimental Psychiatry, 13,* 73–75.

Gauthier, J., Pellerin, D., & Renaud, P. (1983). The enhancement of self-esteem: A comparison of two cognitive strategies. *Cognitive Therapy and Research, 7,* 389–398.

Gershman, L., & Stedman, J. M. (1971). Oriental defense exercises as reciprocal inhibitors of anxiety. *Journal of Behavior Therapy and Experimental Psychiatry, 2,* 117–119.

Goldfried, M. R. (1971). Systematic desensitization as training in self-control. *Journal of Consulting and Clinical Psychology, 37,* 228–234.

Goldfried, M. R. (1977). The use of relaxation and cognitive relabelling as coping skills. In R. B. Stuart (Ed.), *Behavioral self-management: Strategies, techniques and outcomes* (pp. 82–116). New York: Brunner/Mazel.

Goldfried, M. R. (1979). Anxiety reduction through cognitive-behavioral intervention. In P. C. Kendall & S. D. Hollon (Eds.), *Cognitive-behavioral interventions: Theory, research, and procedures* (pp. 117–152). New York: Academic Press.

Goldfried, M. R., & Goldfried, A. P. (1977). Importance of hierarchy content in the self-control of anxiety. *Journal of Consulting and Clinical Psychology, 45,* 124–131.

Goldfried, M. R., & Robins, C. (1982). On the facilitation of self-efficacy. *Cognitive Therapy and Research, 6,* 361–380.

Goldfried, M. R., & Trier, C. S. (1974). Effectiveness of relaxation as an active coping skill. *Journal of Abnormal Psychology, 83,* 348–355.

Goldiamond, I. (1965). Self-control procedures in personal behavior problems. *Psychological Reports, 17,* 851–868.

Goldstein, A. P., & Kanfer, F. H. (Eds.). (1979). *Maximizing treatment gains: Transfer enhancement in psychotherapy.* New York: Academic Press.

Goldstein, A. P., Lopez, M., & Greenleaf, D. O. (1979). Introduction. In A. P. Goldstein & F. H. Kanfer, *Maximizing treatment gains: Transfer enhancement in psychotherapy* (pp. 1–22). New York: Academic Press.

Goldstein, A. P., Sprafkin, R. P., & Gershaw, N. J. (1979). *I know what's wrong, but I don't know what to do about it.* Englewood Cliffs, NJ: Prentice-Hall.

Goldstein-Fodor, I., & Epstein, R. C. (1983). Assertiveness training for women: Where are we failing? In E. B. Foa & P. M. G. Emmelkamp (Eds.), *Failures in behavior therapy* (pp. 137–158). New York: Wiley.

Gordon, J. R., & Marlatt, G. A. (1981). Addictive behaviors. In J. L. Shelton, R. L. Levy, & contributors, *Behavioral assignments and treatment compliance: A handbook of clinical strategies* (pp. 167–186). Champaign, IL: Research Press.

Gormally, J., Black, S., Daston, S., & Rardin, D. (1982). The assessment of binge eating severity among obese persons. *Addictive Behaviors, 7,* 47–55.

Gottman, J., Notarius, C., Gonso, J., & Markman, H. (1976). *A couple's guide to communication.* Champaign, IL: Research Press.

Graziano, A. M. (1975). Futurants, coverants, and operants. *Behavior Therapy, 6,* 421–422.

Green, L. (1982). Minority students' self-control of procrastination. *Journal of Counseling Psychology, 29,* 636–644.

Greist, J. H., Marks, I. M., Berlin, F., Gournay, K., & Noshirvani, H. (1980). Avoidance versus confrontation of fear. *Behavior Therapy, 11,* 1–14.

Griffin, D. E., & Watson, D. L. (1978). A written, personal commitment from the student encourages better course work. *Teaching of Psychology, 5,* 155.

Gross, A. M., & Drabman, R. S. (1982). Teaching self-recording, self-evaluation, and self-reward to nonclinic children and adolescents. In P. Karoly & F. H. Kanfer (Eds.), *Self-management and behavior change: From theory to practice* (pp. 285–315). New York: Pergamon Press.

Hall, S. M. (1980). Self-management and therapeutic maintenance: Theory and research. In P. Karoly & J. Steffen, *Improving the long term effects of psychotherapy* (pp. 263–300). New York: Gardner Press.

Hall, S. M., Rugg, D., Tunstall, C., & Jones, R. T. (1984). Preventing relapse to cigarette smoking by behavioral skill training. *Journal of Consulting and Clinical Psychology, 52,* 372–382.

Hamilton, S. B. (1980). Instructionally-based training in self-control: Behavior-specific and generalized outcomes resulting from student-implemented self-modification projects. *Teaching of Psychology, 7,* 140–145.

Hamilton, S. B., & Waldman, D. A. (1983). Self-modification of depression via cognitive-behavioral intervention strategies: A time series analysis. *Cognitive Therapy and Research, 7,* 99–106.

Harris, C. S., & McReynolds, W. T. (1977). Semantic cues and response contingencies in self-instructional control. *Journal of Behavior Therapy and Experimental Psychiatry, 8,* 15–17.

Harris, G., & Johnson, S. B. (1980). Comparison of individualized covert modeling, self-control desensitization, and study-skills training for alleviation of test anxiety. *Journal of Consulting and Clinical Psychology, 48,* 186–194.

Hawkins, R. C., & Clement, P. (1980). Development and construct validation of a self-report measure of binge eating tendencies. *Addictive Behaviors, 5,* 219–226.

Hay, L., & Hay, W. (1975). *Self-recording forms.* Developed at Duke University Medical School, Durham, NC.

Hays, V., & Waddell, K. (1976). A self-reinforcing procedure for thought stopping. *Behavior Therapy, 7, 559.*

Heatherington, L., & Kirsch, I. (1984). The generality of negative self-reinforcement effects: Implications for the use of extrinsic rewards. *Cognitive Therapy and Research, 8,* 67–76.

Heffernan, T., & Richards, C. S. (1981). Self-control of study behavior: Identification and evaluation of natural methods. *Journal of Counseling Psychology, 28,* 361–364.

Heiby, E. M. (1981). Depression and frequency of self-reinforcement. *Behavior Therapy, 12,* 549–555.

Heiby, E. M. (1982). A self-reinforcement questionnaire. *Behaviour Research and Therapy, 20,* 397–401.

Heiby, E. M. (1983a). Depression as a function of the interaction of self- and environmentally controlled reinforcement. *Behavior Therapy, 14,* 430–433.

Heiby, E. M. (1983b). Toward the prediction of mood change. *Behavior Therapy, 14,* 110–115.

Heiby, E. M., Ozaki, M., & Campos, P. E. (in press). The effects of training in self-reinforcement and reward: Implications for depression. *Behavior Therapy.*

Heinzelmann, F., & Bagley, R. W. (1970). Response to physical activity programs and their effects on health behavior. *Public Health Reports, 85,* 905–911.

Hiebert, B., & Fox, E. E. (1981). Reactive effects of self-monitoring anxiety. *Journal of Counseling Psychology, 28,* 187–193.

Holden, A. E., O'Brien, G. T., Barlow, D. H., Stetson, D., & Infantino, A. (1983). Self-help manual for agoraphobia: A preliminary report of effectiveness. *Behavior Therapy, 14,* 545–556.

Hollon, S. D., & Beck, A. T. (1979). Cognitive therapy of depression. In P. C. Kendall & S. D. Hollon, *Cognitive-behavioral interventions: Theory, research, and procedures* (pp. 153–203). New York: Academic Press.

Holman, J., & Baer, D. M. (1979). Facilitating generalization of on-task behavior through self-monitoring of academic tasks. *Journal of Autism and Developmental Disorders, 9,* 429–446.

Horan, J. J., Baker, S. B., Hoffman, A. M., & Shute, R. E. (1975). Weight loss through variations in the coverant control paradigm. *Journal of Consulting and Clinical Psychology, 43,* 68–72.

Horan, J. J., & Johnson, R. G. (1971). Coverant conditioning through a self-management application of the Premack Principle: Its effect on weight reduction. *Journal of Behavior Therapy and Experimental Psychiatry, 2,* 243–249.

Horn, D. (1972). Determinants of change. In R. G. Richardson (Ed.), *The second world conference on smoking and health* (pp. 58–74). London: Pitman Medical.

Hunt, W. A., & Matarazzo, J. D. (1973). Three years later: Recent developments in the experimental modification of smoking behavior. *Journal of Abnormal Psychology, 81*(2), 107–114.

Israel, A. C., & Saccone, A. J. (1979). Follow-up of effects of choice of mediator and target of reinforcement on weight loss. *Behavior Therapy, 10,* 260–265.

Janis, I. L. (Ed.). (1982). *Counseling on personal decisions: Theory and research on short-term helping relationships.* New Haven, CT: Yale University Press.

Jannoun, L., Oppenheimer, C., & Gelder, M. (1982). A self-help treatment program for anxiety state patients. *Behavior Therapy, 13,* 103–111.

Jeffery, R. W., & Wing, R. R. (1983). Recidivism and self-cure of smoking and obesity: Data from population studies. *American Psychologist, 38, 852.*

Johnson, W. G. (1971). Some applications of Homme's coverant control therapy: Two case reports. *Behavior Therapy, 2,* 240–248.

Kanfer, F. H. (1970). Self-regulation: Research, issues, and speculations. In C. Neuringer & J. L. Michael (Eds.), *Behavior modification in clinical psychology.* New York: Appleton-Century-Crofts.

Kanfer, F. H. (1975). Self-management methods. In F. H. Kanfer & A. P. Goldstein (Eds.), *Helping people change: A textbook of methods* (pp. 334–389). New York: Pergamon Press.

Kanfer, F. H. (1977). The many faces of self-control, or behavior modification changes its focus. In R. B. Stuart (Ed.), *Behavioral self-management: Strategies, techniques and outcomes* (pp. 1–48). New York: Brunner/Mazel.

Kanfer, F. H., Cox, L. E., Greiner, J. M., & Karoly, P. (1974). Contracts, demand characteristics, and self-control. *Journal of Personality and Social Psychology, 30,* 605–619.

Kanfer, F. H., & Goldstein, A. P. (Eds.) (1975). *Helping people change.* New York: Pergamon Press.

Kanfer, F. H., & Karoly, P. (1972). Self-control: A behavioristic excursion into the lion's den. *Behavior Therapy, 3,* 398–416.

Kanfer, F. H., & Phillips, J. S. (1970). *Learning foundations of behavior therapy.* New York: Wiley.

Kanter, N. J., & Goldfried, M. R. (1979). Relative effectiveness of rational restructuring and self-control desensitization in the reduction of interpersonal anxiety. *Behavior Therapy, 10,* 472–490.

Karol, R. L., & Richards, C. S. (1978, November). *Making treatment effects last: An investigation of maintenance strategies for smoking reduction.* Paper presented at the meeting of the Association for the Advancement of Behavior Therapy, Chicago.

Karoly, P., & Kanfer, F. H. (Eds.). (1982). *Self-management and behavior change: From theory to practice.* New York: Pergamon Press.

Katahn, M., Pleas, J., Thackrey, M., & Wallston, K. A. (1982). Relationship of eating and activity self-reports to follow-up weight maintenance in the massively obese. *Behavior Therapy, 13,* 521–528.

Katz, R. C., & Vinciguerra, P. (1982). On the neglected art of "thinning" reinforcers. *Behavior Therapist, 5,* 21–22.

Kau, M. L., & Fischer, J. (1974). Self-modification of exercise behavior. *Journal of Behavior Therapy and Experimental Psychiatry, 5,* 213–214.

Kazdin, A. E. (1973a). Covert modeling and the reduction of avoidance behavior. *Journal of Abnormal Psychology, 81,* 87–95.

Kazdin, A. E. (1973b). The effect of response cost and aversive stimulation in suppressing punished and non-punished speech disfluencies. *Behavior Therapy, 4,* 73–82.

Kazdin, A. E. (1974a). Comparative effects of some variations of covert modeling. *Journal of Behavior Therapy and Experimental Psychiatry, 5,* 225–231.

Kazdin, A. E. (1974b). Covert modeling, model similarity, and reduction of avoidance behavior. *Behavior Therapy, 5,* 325–340.

Kazdin, A. E. (1974c). The effect of model identity and fear-relevant similarity on covert modeling. *Behavior Therapy, 5,* 624–635.

Kazdin, A. E. (1974d). Effects of covert modeling and model reinforcement on assertive behavior. *Journal of Abnormal Psychology, 83,* 240–252.

Kazdin, A. E. (1974e). Reactive self-monitoring: The effects of response desirability, goal setting and feedback. *Journal of Consulting and Clinical Psychology, 42,* 704–716.

Kazdin, A. E. (1974f). Self-monitoring and behavior change. In M. J. Mahoney & C. E. Thoresen (Eds.), *Self-control: Power to the person* (pp. 218–246). Monterey, CA: Brooks/Cole.

Kazdin, A. E. (1975). Covert modeling, imagery assessment, and assertive behavior. *Journal of Consulting and Clinical Psychology, 43,* 716–724.

Kazdin, A. E. (1976a). Assessment of imagery during covert modeling of assertive behavior. *Journal of Behavior Therapy and Experimental Psychiatry, 7,* 213–219.

Kazdin, A. E. (1976b). Effects of covert modeling, multiple models and model reinforcement on assertive behavior. *Behavior Therapy, 7,* 211–222.

Kazdin, A. E. (1982). The separate and combined effects of covert and overt rehearsal in developing assertive behavior. *Behaviour Research and Therapy, 20,* 17–25.

Kazdin, A. E., & Mascitelli, S. (1982). Covert and overt rehearsal and homework practice in developing assertiveness. *Journal of Consulting and Clinical Psychology, 50,* 250–258.

Kelley, H. H. (1983). Love and commitment. In H. H. Kelley, E. Berscheid, A. Christensen, J. H. Harvey, T. L. Huston, G. Levinger, E. McClintock, L. A. Peplau, & D. R. Peterson, *Close relationships* (pp. 265–314). New York: W. H. Freeman.

Kernis, M. H., Zuckerman, M., Cohen, A., & Spadafora, S. (1982). Persistence following failure: The interactive role of self-awareness and the attributional basis for negative expectancies. *Journal of Personality and Social Psychology, 43,* 1184–1191.

Kirsch, I., Heatherington, L., & Colapietro, E. (1979). Negative effects of tangible self-reinforcement. *Cognitive Therapy and Research, 3,* 49–53.

Kirschenbaum, D. S., Humphrey, L. L., & Malett, S. D. (1981). Specificity of planning in adult self-control: An applied investigation. *Journal of Personality and Social Psychology, 40,* 941–950.

Kirschenbaum, D. S., & Tomarken, A. J. (1982). On facing the generalization problem: The study of self-regulatory failure. In P. C. Kendall (Ed.), *Advances in cognitive-behavioral research and therapy* (Vol. 1, pp. 119–200). New York: Academic Press.

Knapp, T., & Shodahl, S. (1974). Ben Franklin as a behavior modifier: A note. *Behavior Therapy, 5,* 656–660.

Knox, D. (1971). *Marriage happiness: A behavioral approach to counseling.* Champaign, IL: Research Press.

Komaki, J., & Dore-Boyce, K. (1978). Self-recording: Its effects on individuals high and low in motivation. *Behavior Therapy, 9,* 65–72.

Krop, H., Calhoon, B., & Verrier, R. (1971). Modification of the "self-concept" of emotionally disturbed children by covert reinforcement. *Behavior Therapy, 2,* 201–204.

Krop, H., Perez, F., & Beaudoin, C. (1973). Modification of "self-concept" of psychiatric patients by covert reinforcement. In R. D. Rubin, J. P. Brady, & J. D. Henderson (Eds.), *Advances in behavior therapy* (Vol. 4, pp. 139–144). New York: Academic Press.

Lacks, P., Bertelson, A. D., Gans, L., & Kunkel, J. (1983). The effectiveness of three behavioral treatments for different degrees of sleep onset insomnia. *Behavior Therapy, 14,* 593–605.

LaCroix, Z. E. (1973). Management of disfluent speech through self-recording procedures. *Journal of Speech and Hearing Disorders, 38,* 272–274.

Ladouceur, R. (1983). Participant modeling with or without cognitive treatment for phobias. *Journal of Consulting and Clinical Psychology, 51,* 942–944.

Lakein, A. (1973). *How to get control of your time and life.* New York: New American Library.

Lawson, D. M., & Rhodes, E. C. (1981, November). *Behavioral self-control and maintenance of aerobic exercise: A retrospective study of self-initiated attempts to improve physical fitness.* Paper presented at the meeting of the Association for the Advancement of Behavior Therapy, Toronto.

Layden, M. A. (1982). Attributional style therapy. In C. Antaki & C. Brewin (Eds.), *Attributions and psychological change*. London: Academic Press.

Lazarus, A. (1971). *Behavior therapy and beyond*. New York: McGraw-Hill.

LeBow, M. D. (1981). *Weight control: The behavioral strategies*. New York: Wiley.

Leitenberg, H., Agras, S. W., Thompson, L. E., & Wright, D. E. (1968). Feedback in behavior modification: An experimental analysis in two phobic cases. *Journal of Applied Behavior Analysis, 1,* 131–137.

Leon, G. R. (1979). Cognitive-behavior therapy for eating disturbances. In P. C. Kendall & S. D. Hollon (Eds.), *Cognitive-behavioral interventions: Theory, research, and procedures* (pp. 357–388). New York: Academic Press.

Lepper, M. R., Greene, D., & Nisbett, R. E. (1973). Undermining children's intrinsic interest with extrinsic reward: A test of the "overjustification" hypothesis. *Journal of Personality and Social Psychology, 28,* 129–137.

Levendusky, P., & Pankratz, L. (1975). Self-control techniques as an alternative to pain medication. *Journal of Abnormal Psychology, 84,* 165–168.

Leviton, L. C. (1979). Observer's reactions to assertive behavior. *Dissertation Abstracts International, 39,* (11-B), 5652.

Lewinsohn, P. M., Biglan, A., & Zeiss, A. M. (1976). Behavioral treatment of depression. In P. O. Davidson (Ed.), *The behavioral management of anxiety, depression and pain* (pp. 91–146). New York: Brunner/Mazel.

Lewinsohn, P. M., Sullivan, J. M., & Grosscup, S. J. (1980). Changing reinforcing events: An approach to the treatment of depression. *Psychotherapy: Theory, Research and Practice, 17,* 322–334.

Lewis, L. E., Biglan, A., & Steinbock, E. (1978). Self-administered relaxation: Training and money deposits in the treatment of recurrent anxiety. *Journal of Consulting and Clinical Psychology, 46,* 1274–1283.

Linehan, M. M. (1979). Structural cognitive-behavioral treatment of assertion problems. In P. C. Kendall & S. D. Hollon (Eds.), *Cognitive-behavioral interventions: Theory, research, and procedures* (pp. 205–240). New York: Academic Press.

Lipton, D. N., & Nelson, R. O. (1980). The contribution of initiation behaviors to dating frequency. *Behavior Therapy, 11,* 59–67.

Luria, A. (1961). *The role of speech in the regulation of normal and abnormal behaviors*. New York: Liveright.

Lutzker, S. Z., & Lutzker, J. R. (1974, April). *A two-dimensional marital contract: Weight loss and household responsibility performance*. Paper presented at the meeting of the Western Psychological Association, San Francisco.

Mahoney, M. J. (1974). *Cognition and behavior modification*. Cambridge, MA: Ballinger.

Mahoney, M. J. (1977). On the continuing resistance to thoughtful therapy. *Behavior Therapy, 8,* 673–677.

Mahoney, M. J., & Bandura, A. (1972). Self-reinforcement in pigeons. *Learning and Motivation, 3,* 293–303.

Mahoney, M. J., Bandura, A., Dirks, S. J., & Wright, C. L. (1974). Relative preference for external and self-controlled reinforcement in monkeys. *Behaviour Research and Therapy, 12,* 157–163.

Mahoney, M. J., Moura, N. G. M., & Wade, T. C. (1973). Relative efficacy of self-reward, self-punishment, and self-monitoring techniques for weight loss. *Journal of Consulting and Clinical Psychology, 40,* 404–407.

Maletzky, B. M. (1974). Behavior recording as treatment: A brief note. *Behavior Therapy, 5,* 107–111.

Mandler, G. (1954). Transfer of training as a function of degree of response overlearning. *Journal of Experimental Psychology, 47,* 411–417.

Marholin, D., & Touchette, P. E. (1979). The role of stimulus control and response consequences. In A. P. Goldstein & F. H. Kanfer (Eds.), *Maximizing treatment gains: Transfer enhancement in psychotherapy*. New York: Academic Press.

Marlatt, G. A. (1982). Relapse prevention: A self-control program for the treatment of addictive behaviors. In R. B. Stuart (Ed.), *Adherence, compliance and generalization in behavioral medicine* (pp. 329–378). New York: Brunner/Mazel.

Marlatt, G. A., & Gordon, J. R. (1980). Determinants of relapse: Implications for the maintenance of behavior change. In P. O. Davidson & S. M. Davidson (Eds.), *Behavioral medicine: Changing health lifestyles* (pp. 410–452). New York: Brunner/Mazel.

Marlatt, G. A., & Gordon, J. R. (in press). *Relapse prevention: Maintenance strategies for addictive behavior change.* New York: Guilford Press.

Marlatt, G. A., & Marques, J. K. (1977). Meditation, self-control and alcohol use. In R. B. Stuart (Ed.), *Behavioral self-management: Strategies, techniques and outcomes* (pp. 117–153). New York: Brunner/Mazel.

Marlatt, G. A., & Parks, G. A. (1982). Self-management of addictive disorders. In P. Karoly & F. H. Kanfer (Eds.), *Self-management and behavior change: From theory to practice* (pp. 443–488). New York: Pergamon Press.

Marshall, W. L., Boutilier, J., & Minnes, P. (1974). The modification of phobic behavior by covert reinforcement. *Behavior Therapy, 5,* 469–480.

Martin, G. L. (1982). Thought-stopping and stimulus control to decrease persistent disturbing thoughts. *Journal of Behavior Therapy and Experimental Psychiatry, 13,* 215–220.

Masterson, J. F., & Vaux, A. C. (1982). The use of a token economy to regulate household behaviours. *Behavioural Psychotherapy, 10,* 65–78.

Matson, J. L. (1977). Social reinforcement by the spouse in weight control: A case study. *Journal of Behavior Therapy and Experimental Psychiatry, 8,* 327–328.

Mayer, J. (1968). *Overweight.* Englewood Cliffs, NJ: Prentice-Hall.

Mayo, L. L., & Norton, G. R. (1980). The use of problem solving to reduce examination and interpersonal anxiety. *Journal of Behavior Therapy and Experimental Psychiatry, 11,* 287–289.

McCann, I. L., & Holmes, D. S. (1984). Influence of aerobic exercise on depression. *Journal of Personality and Social Psychology, 46,* 1142–1147.

McFall, R. M. (1970). Effects of self-monitoring on normal smoking behavior. *Journal of Consulting and Clinical Psychology, 35,* 135–142.

McFall, R. M., & Dodge, K. A. (1982). Self-management and interpersonal skills learning. In P. Karoly & F. H. Kanfer (Eds.), *Self-management and behavior change: From theory to practice* (pp. 353–392). New York: Pergamon Press.

McGlynn, F. D., Kinjo, K., & Doherty, G. (1978). Effects of cue-controlled relaxation, a placebo treatment, and no treatment on changes in self-reported anxiety among college students. *Journal of Clinical Psychology, 34,* 707–714.

McKeachie, W. J. (1978). *Teaching tips: A guidebook for the beginning college teacher* (7th ed.). Lexington, MA: Heath.

McKenzie, T. L., & Rushall, B. S. (1974). Effects of self-recording on attendance and performance in a competitive swimming training environment. *Journal of Applied Behavior Analysis, 7,* 199–206.

McLaughlin, T. F., Burgess, N., & Sackville-West, L. (1981). Effects of self-recording and self-recording and matching on academic performance. *Child Behavior Therapy, 3,* 17–27.

Meichenbaum, D. H. (1971). Examination of model characteristics in reducing avoidance behavior. *Journal of Personality and Social Psychology, 17,* 298–307.

Meichenbaum, D. H. (1977). *Cognitive behavior modification: An integrative approach.* New York: Plenum.

Menges, R. J., & Dobroski, B. J. (1977). Behavioral self-modification in instructional settings: A review. *Teaching of Psychology, 4,* 168–174.

Mermelstein, R., Lichtenstein, E., & McIntyre, K. (1983). Partner support and relapse in smoking-cessation programs. *Journal of Consulting and Clinical Psychology, 51,* 465–466.

Miller, G. A., Galanter, E., & Pribram, K. H. (1960). *Plans and the structure of behavior.* New York: Holt, Rinehart & Winston.

Miller, N. E. (1969, January). Learning of visceral and glandular responses. *Science,* pp. 434–445.

Miller, R. K., & Bornstein, P. H. (1977). Thirty-minute relaxation: A comparison of some methods. *Journal of Behavior Therapy and Experimental Psychiatry, 8,* 291–294.

Miller, W. R. (1982). Treating problem drinkers: What works? *Behavior Therapist, 5,* 15–18.

Miller, W. R., & Muñoz, R. F. (1982). *How to control your drinking* (rev. ed.). Albuquerque: University of New Mexico Press.

Mischel, W. (1981). Metacognition and the rules of delay. In J. H. Flavell & L. Ross (Eds.), *Social cognitive development: Frontiers and possible futures* (pp. 240–271). Cambridge: Cambridge University Press.

Morgan, W. G., & Bass, B. A. (1973). Self-control through self-mediated rewards. In R. D. Rubin, J. P. Brady, & J. D. Henderson (Eds.), *Advances in behavior therapy* (Vol. 4, pp. 117–126). New York: Academic Press.

Moss, M. K., & Arend, R. A. (1977). Self-directed contact desensitization. *Journal of Consulting and Clinical Psychology, 45,* 730–738.

Nelson, R. O. (1977). Methodological issues in assessment via self-monitoring. In J. D. Cone & R. P. Hawkins (Eds.), *Behavioral assessment: New directions in clinical psychology* (pp. 217–240). New York: Brunner/Mazel.

Nelson, R. O., Hay, L., & Hay, W. (1975, December). *Observational procedures in behavioral assessment.* Workshop conducted at the meeting of the Association for the Advancement of Behavior Therapy, San Francisco.

Nelson, R. O., & Hayes, S. C. (1981). Theoretical explanations for reactivity in self-monitering. *Behavior Modification, 5,* 3–14.

Nelson, R. O., Sprong, R. T., Hayes, S. C., & Graham, C. A. (1979, December). *Self-reinforcement: Cues or consequences?* Paper presented at the meeting of the Association for the Advancement of Behavior Therapy, San Francisco.

Newman, A., & Bloom, R. (1981a). Self-control of smoking—I. Effects of experience with imposed, increasing, decreasing, and random delays. *Behaviour Research and Therapy, 19,* 187–192.

Newman, A., & Bloom, R. (1981b). Self-control of smoking—II. Effects of cue salience and source of delay imposition on the effectiveness of training under increasing delay. *Behaviour Research and Therapy, 19,* 193–200.

Nezu, A., & D'Zurilla, T. J. (1981). Effects of problem definition and formulation on the generation of alternatives in the social problem-solving process. *Cognitive Therapy and Research, 5,* 265–271.

Nicassio, P., & Bootzin, R. R. (1974). A comparison of progressive relaxation and autogenic training as treatments for insomnia. *Journal of Abnormal Psychology, 83,* 253–260.

Nisbett, R. E., & Ross, L. (1980). *Human inference: Strategies and shortcomings of social judgment.* Englewood Cliffs, NJ: Prentice-Hall.

Noel, R. (1980). The effect of visuo-motor behavior rehearsal on tennis performance. *Journal of Sport Psychology, 2,* 221–226.

Nolan, J. D. (1968). Self-control procedures in the modification of smoking behavior. *Journal of Consulting and Clinical Psychology, 32,* 92–93.

O'Banion, D., Armstrong, B. K., & Ellis, J. (1980). Conquered urge as a means of self-control. *Addictive Behaviors, 5,* 101–106.

O'Connor, K. P., & Stravynski, A. (1982). Evaluation of a smoking typology by use of a specific behavioural substitution method of self-control. *Behaviour Research and Therapy, 20,* 279–288.

Okwumabua, T. M., Meyers, A. W., Schleser, R., & Cooke, C. J. (1983). Cognitive strategies and running performance: An exploratory study. *Cognitive Therapy and Research, 7,* 363–370.

Owusu-Bempah, J., & Howitt, D. L. (1983). Self-modeling and weight control. *British Journal of Medical Psychology, 56,* 157–165.

Paquin, M. J. R. (1982). Daily monitoring to eliminate a compulsion. In H. L. Millman, J. T. Huber, & D. R. Diggins (Eds.), *Therapies for adults: Depressive, anxiety, and personality disorders* (pp. 266–268). San Francisco: Jossey-Bass.

Passman, R. (1977). The reduction of procrastinative behaviors in a college student despite the "contingency fulfillment problem": The use of external control in self-management techniques. *Behavior Therapy, 8,* 95–96.

Patterson, C. J., & Mischel, W. (1975). Plans to resist distraction. *Developmental Psychology, 11,* 369–378.

Paul, G. L. (1966). *Insight vs. desensitization in psychotherapy.* Stanford, CA: Stanford University Press.

Pawlicki, R., & Galotti, N. (1978). A tic-like behavior case study emanating from a self-directed behavior modification course. *Behavior Therapy, 9,* 671–672.

Payne, P. A., & Woudenberg, R. A. (1978). Helping others and helping yourself: An evaluation of two training modules in a college course. *Teaching of Psychology, 5,* 131–134.

Pearce, J. W., LeBow, M. D., & Orchard, J. (1981). Role of spouse involvement in the behavioral treatment of overweight women. *Journal of Consulting and Clinical Psychology, 49,* 236–244.

Pechacek, T. F., & Danaher, B. G. (1979). How and why people quit smoking: A cognitive-behavioral analysis. In P. C. Kendall & S. D. Hollon (Eds.), *Cognitive-behavioral interventions: Theory, research, and procedures* (pp. 389–422). New York: Academic Press.

Perkins, D., & Perkins, F. (1976). *Nail biting and cuticle biting.* Dallas: Self-Control Press.

Perri, M. G., & Richards, C. S. (1977). An investigation of naturally occurring episodes of self-controlled behaviors. *Journal of Counseling Psychology, 24,* 178–183.

Perri, M. G., Richards, C. S., & Schultheis, K. (1977). Behavioral self-control and smoking reduction: A study of self-initiated attempts to reduce smoking. *Behavior Therapy, 8,* 360–365.

Peterson, L. (1983). Failure in self-control. In E. B. Foa & P. M. G. Emmelkamp (Eds.), *Failures in behavior therapy* (pp. 172–196). New York: Wiley.

Pezzot-Pearce, T. D., LeBow, M. D., & Pearce, J. W. (1982). Increasing cost-effectiveness in obesity treatment through use of self-help behavioral manuals and decreased therapist contact. *Journal of Consulting and Clinical Psychology, 50,* 448–449.

Presbrey, T. (1979). *Social problem solving: Impact and effects of training on a normal adult population.* Unpublished doctoral dissertation, University of Hawaii, Honolulu.

Prochaska, J. O. (1983). Self-changers versus therapy changers versus Schachter. *American Psychologist, 38,* 853–854.

Propst, L. R. (1980). The comparative efficacy of religious and nonreligious imagery for the treatment of mild depression in religious individuals. *Cognitive Therapy and Research, 4,* 167–178.

Rachlin, H. (1974). Self control. *Behaviorism, 2,* 94–107.

Rainwater, N., Ayllon, T., Frederiksen, L. W., Moore, E. J., & Bonar, J. R. (1982). Teaching self-management skills to increase diet compliance in diabetics. In R. B. Stuart (Ed.), *Adherence, compliance and generalization in behavioral medicine* (pp. 304–328). New York: Brunner/Mazel.

Rakos, R. F., & Grodek, M. V. (in press). An empirical evaluation of a behavioral self-management course in a college setting. *Teaching of Psychology.*

Rehm, L. P. (1982). Self management in depression. In P. Karoly & F. H. Kanfer (Eds.), *Self-management and behavior change: From theory to practice* (pp. 522–567). New York: Pergamon Press.

Rehm, L. P., & Marston, A. R. (1968). Reduction of social anxiety through modification of self-reinforcement: An instigation therapy technique. *Journal of Consulting and Clinical Psychology, 32,* 565–574.

Reich, J. W., & Zautra, A. (1981). Life events and personal causation: Some relationships with satisfaction and distress. *Journal of Personality and Social Psychology, 41,* 1002–1012.

Richards, C. S. (1976). Improving study behaviors through self-control techniques. In J. D. Krumboltz & C. E. Thoresen (Eds.), *Counseling methods* (pp. 462–467). New York: Holt, Rinehart & Winston.

Richards, C. S. (in press). Work and study problems. In M. Hersen & A. S. Bellack (Eds.), *Handbook of clinical behavior therapy with adults.* New York: Plenum.

Richards, C. S., & Perri, M. G. (1978). Do self-control treatments last? An evaluation of behavioral problem solving and faded counselor contact as treatment maintenance strategies. *Journal of Counseling Psychology, 25,* 376–383.

Richardson, A. (1967). Mental practice: A review and discussion (Parts 1 and 2). *Research Quarterly, 38,* 95–107, 263–272.

Roberts, R. N. (1979). Private speech in academic problem-solving: A naturalistic perspective. In G. Zevin (Ed.), *The development of self-regulation through private speech* (pp. 295–323). New York: Wiley.

Roberts, R. N., & Mullis, M. (1980, May). *A component analysis of self-instructional training.* Paper presented at the meeting of the Western Psychological Association, Honolulu.

Roberts, R. N., & Tharp, R. G. (1980). A naturalistic study of children's self-directed speech in academic problem-solving. *Cognitive Research and Therapy, 4,* 341–353.

Robinson, F. P. (1970). *Effective study* (4th ed.). New York: Harper & Row.

Rogoff, B. (1982). Integrating context and cognitive development. In M. E. Lamb & A. L. Brown (Eds.), *Advances in developmental psychology* (Vol. 2, pp. 125–170). Hillsdale, NJ: Erlbaum.

Romanczyk, R. G. (1974). Self-monitoring in the treatment of obesity: Parameters of reactivity. *Behavior Therapy, 5,* 531–540.

Rosen, J. C. (1981). Self-monitoring in the treatment of diurnal bruxism. *Journal of Behavior Therapy and Experimental Psychiatry, 12,* 347–350.

Rosen, L. W. (1981). Self-control program in the treatment of obesity. *Journal of Behavior Therapy and Experimental Psychiatry, 12,* 163–166.

Rosenbaum, M. (1983). Learned resourcefulness as a behavioral repertoire for the self-regulation of internal events: Issues and speculations. In M. Rosenbaum, C. M. Franks, & Y. Jaffe (Eds.), *Perspectives on behavior therapy in the eighties* (pp. 54–73). New York: Springer.

Rosenbaum, M. (in press). A model for research on self-regulation: Reducing the schism between behaviorism and general psychology. In I. M. Evans (Ed.), *Paradigmatic behavior therapy: Critical perspectives on applied social behaviorism.* New York: Springer.

Rosenbaum, M., & Rolnick, A. (1983). Self-control behaviors and coping with seasickness. *Cognitive Therapy and Research, 7,* 93–98.

Rosenbaum, M. S., & Ayllon, T. (1981). Treating bruxism with the habit-reversal technique. *Behaviour Research and Therapy, 19,* 87–96.

Roskies, E., & Lazarus, R. S. (1980). Coping theory and the teaching of coping skills. In P. O. Davidson & S. M. Davidson (Eds.), *Behavioral medicine: Changing health lifestyles* (pp. 38–69). New York: Brunner/Mazel.

Ross, L. D., Amabile, T. M., & Steinmetz, J. L. (1977). Social roles, social control and biases in social-perception process. *Journal of Personality and Social Psychology, 35,* 485–494.

Rozensky, R. H. (1974). The effect of timing of self-monitoring behavior on reducing cigarette consumption. *Journal of Behavior Therapy and Experimental Psychiatry, 5,* 301–303.

Russell, R. K., & Lent, R. W. (1982). Cue-controlled relaxation and systematic desensitization versus nonspecific factors in treating test anxiety. *Journal of Counseling Psychology, 29*, 100–103.

Russell, R. K., Miller, D. E., & June, L. N. (1975). A comparison between group systematic desensitization and cue-controlled relaxation in the treatment of test anxiety. *Behavior Therapy, 6*, 172–177.

Russell, R. K., & Sipich, J. F. (1974). Treatment of test anxiety by cue-controlled relaxation. *Behavior Therapy, 5*, 673–676.

Russell, R. K., Wise, F., & Stratoudakis, J. P. (1976). Treatment of test anxiety by cue-controlled relaxation and systematic desensitization. *Journal of Counseling Psychology, 3*, 563–566.

Rutner, I. T. (1973). The effects of feedback and instructions on phobic behavior. *Behavior Therapy, 4*, 338–348.

Saccone, A. J., & Israel, A. C. (1978). Effects of experimenter versus significant other-controlled reinforcement and choice of target behavior on weight loss. *Behavior Therapy, 9*, 271–278.

Sanders, M. R., & Glynn, T. (1981). Training parents in behavioral self-management: An analysis of generalization and maintenance. *Journal of Applied Behavior Analysis, 14*, 223–237.

Sandifer, B. A., & Buchanan, W. L. (1983). Relationship between adherence and weight loss in a behavioral weight reduction program. *Behavior Therapy, 14*, 682–688.

Sarason, I. G. (Ed.). (1980). *Test anxiety: Theory, research and applications.* Hillsdale, NJ: Erlbaum.

Schachter, S. (1982). Recidivism and self-cure of smoking and obesity. *American Psychologist, 37*, 436–444.

Schefft, B. (1982). *Self-management therapy in the treatment of severe social-evaluative anxiety.* Unpublished doctoral dissertation. University of Wisconsin, Milwaukee.

Seidner, M. L. (1973). *Behavior change contract: Prior information about study habits treatment and statements of intention as related to initial effort in treatment.* Unpublished doctoral dissertation, University of Cincinnati.

Shapiro, D. H. (1980). *Meditation.* Hawthorne, NY: Aldine.

Shapiro, D. H., & Walsh, R. (Eds.). (1980). *The science of meditation: Theory, research and experience.* Hawthorne, NY: Aldine.

Shelton, J. L. (1979). Instigation therapy: Using therapeutic homework to promote treatment gains. In A. P. Goldstein & F. H. Kanfer (Eds.), *Maximizing treatment gains: Transfer enhancement in psychotherapy* (pp. 225–245). New York: Academic Press.

Shelton, J. L. (1981a). Nonassertion. In J. L. Shelton, R. L. Levy, & contributors, *Behavioral assignments and treatment compliance: A handbook of clinical strategies* (pp. 305–330). Champaign, IL: Research Press.

Shelton, J. L. (1981b). The use of behavioral assignments in clinical practice. In J. L. Shelton, R. L. Levy, and contributors, *Behavioral assignments and treatment compliance: A handbook of clinical strategies* (pp. 1–19). Champaign, IL: Research Press.

Shelton, J. L., Levy, R. L., and contributors (1981). *Behavioral assignments and treatment compliance: A handbook of clinical strategies.* Champaign, IL: Research Press.

Sherman, A. R. (1972). Real-life exposure as a primary therapeutic factor in the desensitization treatment for fear. *Journal of Abnormal Psychology, 79*, 19–28.

Sherman, A. R. (1975). Two-year follow-up of training in relaxation as a behavioral self-management skill. *Behavior Therapy, 6*, 419–420.

Sherman, A. R., & Plummer, I. L. (1973). Training in relaxation as a behavioral self-management skill: An exploratory investigation. *Behavior Therapy, 4,* 543–550.

Sherman, A. R., Turner, R., Levine, M., & Walk, J. (1975, December). *A behavioral self-management program for increasing or decreasing habit responses.* Paper presented at the meeting of the Association for the Advancement of Behavior Therapy, San Francisco.

Shiffman, S. (1982). Relapse following smoking cessation: A situational analysis. *Journal of Consulting and Clinical Psychology, 50,* 71–86.

Shiffman, S. (1984). Coping with temptations to smoke. *Journal of Consulting and Clinical Psychology, 52,* 261–267.

Skinner, B. F. (1953). *Science and human behavior.* New York: Macmillan.

Snyder, A. L., & Deffenbacher, J. L. (1977). Comparison of relaxation as self-control and systematic desensitization in the treatment of test anxiety. *Journal of Consulting and Clinical Psychology, 45,* 1202–1203.

Sobell, L. C., & Sobell, M. B. (1973). A self-feedback technique to monitor drinking behavior in alcoholics. *Behaviour Research and Therapy, 11,* 237–238.

Sohn, D., & Lamal, P. A. (1982). Self-reinforcement: Its reinforcing capability and its clinical utility. *Psychological Record, 32,* 179–203.

Sonne, J. L., & Janoff, D. S. (1979). The effect of treatment attributions on the maintenance of weight reduction: A replication and extension. *Cognitive Therapy and Research, 3,* 389–397.

Sonne, J. L., & Janoff, D. S. (1982). Attributions and the maintenance of behavior change. In C. Antaki & C. Brewin (Eds.), *Attributions and psychological change* (pp. 83–96). New York: Academic Press.

Spates, C. R., & Kanfer, F. H. (1977). Self-monitoring, self-evaluation, and self-reinforcement in children's learning: A test of a multi-stage self-regulation model. *Behavior Therapy, 8,* 9–16.

Speidel, G. E., & Tharp, R. G. (1980). What does self-reinforcement reinforce: An empirical analysis of the contingencies in self-determined reinforcement. *Child Behavior Therapy, 2,* 1–22.

Spence, S. (1983). The training of heterosexual social skills. In S. Spence & G. Shepherd (Eds.), *Developments in social skills training* (pp. 275–300). New York: Academic Press.

Spinelli, P. R., & Packard, T. (1975, February). *Behavioral self-control delivery systems.* Paper presented at the National Conference on Behavioral Self-Control, Salt Lake City.

Spurr, J., & Stevens, V. J. (1980). Increasing study time and controlling student guilt: A case study in self-management. *Behavior Therapist, 3,* 17–18.

Staats, A. W. (1968). *Learning, language and cognition.* New York: Holt, Rinehart & Winston.

Staats, A. W. (1975). *Social behaviorism.* Homewood, IL: Dorsey Press.

Stalonas, P. M., Jr., Johnson, W. G., & Christ, M. (1978). Behavior modification for obesity: The evaluation of exercise, contingency management, and program adherence. *Journal of Consulting and Clinical Psychology, 46,* 463–469.

Steenman, H., & Watson, D. L. (1984). *Self-modification of loneliness.* Manuscript submitted for publication.

Stokes, T. F., & Baer, D. M. (1977). An implicit technology of generalization. *Journal of Applied Behavior Analysis, 10,* 349–368.

Stuart, R. B. (1967). Behavioral control of overeating. *Behaviour Research and Therapy, 5,* 357–365.

Stuart, R. B. (1977). Self-help group approach to self-management. In R. B. Stuart (Ed.), *Behavioral self-management: Strategies, techniques and outcome* (pp. 278–305). New York: Brunner/Mazel.

Stuart, R. B. (1980). Weight loss and beyond: Are they taking it off and keeping it off? In P. O. Davidson & S. M. Davidson (Eds.), *Behavioral medicine: Changing health lifestyles* (pp. 151–194). New York: Brunner/Mazel.

Stuart, R. B., & Davis, B. (1972). *Slim chance in a fat world: Behavioral control of obesity.* Champaign, IL: Research Press.

Stunkard, A. J. (1958). The management of obesity. *New York State Journal of Medicine, 58,* 79–87.

Suinn, R. M. (1976, July). Body thinking: Psychology for Olympic champs. *Psychology Today,* pp. 38–40.

Suinn, R. M. (1977). *Manual for anxiety management training (AMT).* Fort Collins, CO: Rocky Mountain Behavioral Science Institute.

Suinn, R. M. (1983). Imagery and sports. In A. A. Sheikh (Ed.), *Imagery: Current theory, research, and application* (pp. 507–534). New York: Wiley.

Suinn, R. M. (1984). Personal communication.

Sulzer-Azaroff, B., & Mayer, G. R. (1977). *Applying behavior analysis procedures with children and youth.* New York: Holt, Rinehart & Winston.

Tearnan, B. H., Lahey, B. B., Thompson, J. K., & Hammer, D. (1982). The role of coping self-instructions combined with covert modeling in specific fear reduction. *Cognitive Therapy and Research, 6,* 185–190.

Tharp, R. G., Gallimore, R., & Calkins, R. P. (in press). On the relationship between self-control and control-by-others. *Revista Latinoamericana de Psicologia.*

Tharp, R. G., Jordan, C., Speidel, G. E., Au, K. H.-P., Klein, T. W., Calkins, R. P., Sloat, K. C. M., & Gallimore, R. (in press). Product and process in applied developmental research: Education and the children of a minority. In M. E. Lamb, A. L. Brown, & B. Rogoff (Eds.), *Advances in developmental psychology* (Vol. 3). Hillsdale, NJ: Erlbaum.

Tharp, R. G., Watson, D. L., & Kaya, J. (1974). Self-modification of depression. *Journal of Consulting and Clinical Psychology, 42,* 624. (Extended Report, University of Hawaii)

Tharp, R. G., & Wetzel, R. J. (1969). *Behavior modification in the natural environment.* New York: Academic Press.

Thase, M. E., & Moss, M. K. (1976). The relative efficacy of covert modeling procedures and guided participant modeling on the reduction of avoidance behavior. *Journal of Behavior Therapy and Experimental Psychiatry, 7,* 7–12.

Thomas, E. J., Abrams, K. S., & Johnson, S. B. (1971). Self-monitoring and reciprocal inhibition in the modification of multiple tics of Gilles de la Tourette's syndrome. *Journal of Behavior Therapy and Experimental Psychiatry, 2,* 159–171.

Thoresen, C. E. (1975, October). *Self-control.* Address delivered at the Southern California Conference on Behavior Modification, Los Angeles.

Thorpe, G. L., Amatu, H. I., Blakey, R. S., & Burns, L. E. (1976). Contributions of overt instructional rehearsal and "specific insight" to the effectiveness of self-instructional training: A preliminary study. *Behavior Therapy, 7,* 504–511.

Throll, D. A. (1981). Transcendental meditation and progressive relaxation: Their psychological effects. *Journal of Clinical Psychology, 37,* 776–781.

Tinling, D. C. (1972). Cognitive and behavioral aspects of aversive therapy. In R. D. Rubin, H. Fensterheim, J. D. Henderson, & L. P. Ullmann (Eds.), *Advances in behavior therapy* (pp. 73–80). New York: Academic Press.

Todd, F. J. (1972). Coverant control of self-evaluative responses in the treatment of depression: A new use for an old principle. *Behavior Therapy, 3,* 91–94.

Turner, S. M., Holzman, A., & Jacob, R. G. (1983). Treatment of compulsive looking by imaginal thought-stopping. *Behavior Modification, 7,* 576–582.

Twentyman, C., Boland, T., & McFall, R. M. (1981). Heterosocial avoidance in college males: Four studies. *Behavior Modification, 5,* 523–552.

Ullmann, L. P., & Krasner, L. (1975). *A psychological approach to abnormal behavior* (2nd ed.). Englewood Cliffs, NJ: Prentice-Hall.

Upper, D. (1974). Unsuccessful self-treatment of a case of "writer's block." *Journal of Applied Behavior Analysis, 7*, 497.

Vygotsky, L. S. (1965). *Thought and language* (E. Hantmann & G. Vokar, Eds. and Trans.). Cambridge, MA: MIT Press.

Vygotsky, L. S. (1978). *Mind and society.* Cambridge, MA: Harvard University Press.

Wallace, I., & Pear, J. J. (1977). Self-control techniques of famous novelists. *Journal of Applied Behavior Analysis, 10*, 515–525.

Watson, D. L. (1978). *Psychology: What it is, how to use it.* San Francisco: Harper & Row (Canfield).

Watson, D. L., Tharp, R. G., & Krisberg, J. (1972). Case study of self-modification. Suppression of inflammatory scratching while awake and asleep. *Journal of Behavior Therapy and Experimental Psychiatry, 3*, 213–215.

Watson, J. B., & Rayner, R. (1920). Conditioned emotional reactions. *Journal of Experimental Psychology, 3*, 1–14.

Weil, G., & Goldfried, M. R. (1973). Treatment of insomnia in an eleven-year-old child through self relaxation. *Behavior Therapy, 4*, 282–294.

Weisz, G., & Bucher, B. (1980). Involving husbands in treatment of obesity—effects on weight loss, depression, and marital satisfaction. *Behavior Therapy, 11*, 643–650.

Wertsch, J. V. (1979). From social interaction to higher psychological processes: A clarification and application of Vygotsky's theory. *Human Development, 22*, 1–22.

Wiener, N. (1948). *Cybernetics: Control and communication in the animal and the machine.* Cambridge, MA: MIT Press.

Willis, S. E., & Nelson, R. O. (1982). The effects of valence and nature of target behavior on the accuracy and reactivity of self-monitoring. *Behavioral Assessment, 4*, 401–412.

Wine, J. D. (1980). Cognitive-attentional theory of test anxiety. In I. G. Sarason (Ed.), *Test anxiety: Theory, research, and applications* (pp. 349–385). Hillsdale, NJ: Erlbaum.

Wine, J. D. (1981). From defect to competence models. In J. D. Wine & M. D. Smye (Eds.), *Social competence* (pp. 3–35). New York: Guilford Press.

Wing, R. R., Marcus, M. D., Epstein, L. H., & Kupfer, D. (1983). Mood and weight loss in a behavioral treatment program. *Journal of Consulting and Clinical Psychology, 51*, 153–155.

Wisocki, P. A. (1973). A covert reinforcement program for the treatment of test anxiety: Brief report. *Behavior Therapy, 4*, 264–266.

Wolpe, J. (1958). *Psychotherapy by reciprocal inhibition.* Stanford, CA: Stanford University Press.

Wolpe, J. (1981). The dichotomy between classical conditioned and cognitively learned anxiety. *Journal of Behavior Therapy and Experimental Psychiatry, 12*, 35–42.

Wood, Y. R., Hardin, M., & Wong, E. (1984, January). *Social network influences on smoking cessation.* Paper presented at the meeting of the Western Psychological Association, Los Angeles.

Woolfolk, R. L., Lehrer, P. M., McCann, B. S., & Rooney, A. J. (1982). Effects of progressive relaxation and meditation on cognitive and somatic manifestations of daily stress. *Behaviour Research and Therapy, 20*, 461–467.

Worthington, E. L. (1979). Behavioral self-control and the contract problem. *Teaching of Psychology, 6*, 91–94.

Youdin, R., & Hemmes, N. S. (1978). The urge to overeat: The initial link. *Journal of Behavior Therapy and Experimental Psychiatry, 9*, 339–342.

Zeiss, R. A. (1978). Self-directed treatment for premature ejaculation. *Journal of Consulting and Clinical Psychology, 46*, 1234–1241.

Zemore, R. (1975). Systematic desensitization as a method of teaching a general anxiety-reducing skill. *Journal of Consulting and Clinical Psychology, 43,* 157–161.

Zimmerman, J. (1975). If it's what's inside that counts, why not count it? 1. Self-recording of feelings and treatment by "self-implosion." *Psychological Record, 25,* 3–16.

Zitter, R. E., & Fremouw, W. J. (1978). Individual versus partner consequation for weight loss. *Behavior Therapy, 9,* 808–813.

Zohn, J. C., & Bornstein, P. H. (1980). Self-monitoring of work performance with mentally retarded adults: Effects upon work productivity, work quality, and on-task behavior. *Mental Retardation, 18,* 19–25.

NAME INDEX

Abel, M., 37
Abrams, D. B., 72
Abrams, K. S., 73
Adams, N. E., 37
Adams, S., 278
Agras, S. W., 72
Ainslee, G., 5, 188, 189, 191
Amabile, T. M., 260
Amatu, H. I., 116
American College of Sports Medicine, 171
Annon, J. S., 120
Arend, R. S., 165
Arkowitz, H., 160
Armstrong, B. K., 84
Arnkoff, D. B., 116
Arrick, C. M., 124
Ascher, L. M., 196
Axsom, D., 42
Ayllon, T., 21, 144
Azrin, N. H., 143, 144

Baer, D. M., 73, 183
Bagley, R. W., 185
Bajtelsmit, J. W., 197
Baker, S. B., 197
Bandura, A., 36, 37, 161, 187, 188, 189, 190, 191, 224, 256
Barling, J., 37
Barlow, D. H., 19
Barrera, M., 18, 19, 208
Barrios, B. A., 10, 148
Bass, B. A., 188
Beaudoin, C., 198
Beck, A. T., 136, 144
Beck, F. M., 153
Becker, M. H., 182
Beidleman, W. B., 19

Bellack, A. S., 74
Bender, C., 84
Bennett, N., 84
Bergin, A. E., 120
Berlin, F., 158
Bernard, H. S., 172
Bernard, M. E., 21
Bertelson, A. D., 118
Biglan, A., 83, 144, 148
Billings, A., 73
Black, D. R., 251
Black, S., 162
Blackwell, B., 182
Blakey, R. S., 116
Blanchard, E. B., 161, 196
Bloom, R., 120
Boice, R., 214
Boland, J., 85
Bonar, J. R., 21
Bootzin, R. R., 118, 153
Bornstein, M. T., 72, 73
Bornstein, P. H., 72, 73, 148
Boudreau, L., 147
Boutilier, J., 196
Brehm, S. S., 40
Brigham, T. A., 21, 131, 189
Brown, G., 146
Brown, H. K., 163, 220, 253
Brownell, K. D., 183
Brownlee, A., 182
Buchanan, W. L., 120
Bucher, B., 182, 183
Burgess, N., 73
Burns, L. E., 116

Calhoon, B., 196, 198
Calkins, R. P., 91
Callahan, E. J., 172

303

SUBJECT INDEX

TOPIC INDEX

The topics listed in this index include but are not restricted to those covered in the "Tips" sections of the book.